THE NEW BIBLE

Pro and Con

by

WILLIAM CAREY TAYLOR

VANTAGE PRESS, INC., NEW YORK

CONTENTS

PART ONE

WHAT I LIKE ABOUT THE NEW BIBLE—
THE GOOD OF IT

PART TWO

WHAT I DISLIKE ABOUT THE NEW BIBLE—
THE EVIL OF IT

FOREWORD

COMING HOME ON FURLOUGH IN OCTOBER, 1952, I QUICKLY purchased a copy of the Revised Standard Version, called "the new Bible." I had read the "new" New Testament in 1946. It soon was my lot to cross the state of North Carolina by bus. I bought daily newspapers as I went. All of them in North Carolina, and the Greenville, South Carolina, dailies, were protesting a proposed burning of the "new Bible." The editorials seemed to me excellent. I was repeatedly asked my opinion. I replied: "I am against it." We never burned a Catholic Bible in Brazil, in spite of its Apocryphal additions to the real Scriptures, its wretched translations, its notes, which often deny at the foot of the page what the Word of God says in the text above, its many false teachings, and its abundance of pictures that are just as false. Rather we encourage all Catholics to buy their own Bibles, knowing they will obtain better versions eventually if they get interested. As T. T. Eaton used to say: "Even a Catholic Bible is full of Baptist doctrine." I would not burn even the version of the Jehovah's Witnesses, which banishes the word *cross*. It is the only version that correctly translates into English the Greek of Matt. 16 and 18: "shall have been bound . . . shall have been loosed," though C. B. Williams gives a similar translation and the same meaning.

Friends insisted that I write to the burner. But I did not know him, so I did not take the liberty to write or telegraph, as I was urged to do. Had I done so, I would have pointed out that such an act would encourage every intolerant priest in the world to say: "I told you so. They are as intolerant as they accuse us of being."

It is not that I have any conscience about burning what is false or immoral, provided it is mine to burn and scandalizes no "weak brother." Hundreds of thousands of converted Catholics in Brazil have burned their images, or buried them. An image, as an instrument of worship, is wholly immoral. The severest command of the moral law forbids it. When you burn such images you burn something one hundred per cent wrong. Nor do I have a Chinese superstition about paper. I have read that primitive Chinese, encountering modern civilization, treated all printed paper as something sacred. Some of the chatter about book burning of late seems to go back to that superstitious reverence for printed paper. Paul's greatest revival came to this climax in Ephesus: "Many of them also which used curious arts brought their books together, and burned them before all men: and they counted the price of them, and found it fifty thousand pieces of silver" (Acts 19:19). But those books were dead wrong, one hundred per cent false and hurtful. If you have in your library a book of magic that teaches baptismal regeneration, destroy it. It belongs with those Ephesian ashes. But note. They burned their own books. They were all to the bad. They didn't do it in church. The books burned were neither Scripture nor about Scripture. I looked to see what the minister in North Carolina finally burned. It was just one page, the page on which Isaiah 7:14 was printed. But on the other side is blessed, beautiful "holy, holy, holy," in the sixth chapter of Isaiah. They burned that to destroy one word on another page. If you burn any Bible to get at one per cent of erroneous translation, you burn ninety-nine times as much truth. And that is not good conduct.

Barney B. Atrobus wrote in *The Baptist Standard*:

> *The Bible-burning days have come*
> *From out the ghost of years.*
> *The shades of William Tyndale rise*
> *To grip the heart with fears.*

.   .   .   .

> *We thought the agony he paid*
> *To set men conscience-free*
> *Would be enough in this old world*
> *For centuries to be.*

> *We reckoned not the human heart*
> *Could ere this thing renew*
> *And strike a match and burn God's Word*
> *In Nineteen Fifty-two.*

Freedom of discussion maintains the right to bring any book, or the translation of any book, before the bar of the public conscience. That, rather than Bible burning, is the liberty we use. At the same time, however, we register our conviction that the will to alter the true translation of the Bible, in the interests of modernism or religious prejudice, is a far more grave offense than burning symbolically a page of Scripture. Let us be fair enough to be intelligently against both the lesser and the greater offense.

Most of the discussions I have heard or read about the new Bible are wholly partisan. They praise virtues and deny faults, or they show only faults, denying or ignoring virtues. The RSV has been on my study desk, with about forty other versions of the New Testament, since 1946. It will continue to be. As a study version, with other versions, I shall use it and recommend it to Bible *students*. As the *one* Bible of any reader, for private or public worship or for teaching, I shall not use it or recommend it. What follows is an appraisal of the benefits of the RSV for Bible students, and the faults that mar it for the prospective class of one-Bible users. I feel conscience-driven to show both sides of the issue.

This is a Southern Baptist study. Baptists are a third of the non-Catholics of the nation. The Oxford Press poll shows they read their Bibles more, and take them more seriously, than others in the land. Probably a majority of the serious readers of the Bible, who seek to make it authoritative in their thought and lives, are of Baptist persuasion. How this new Bible, then, may affect Baptist thought and life and what Baptists will think of it when they make their final judgment, which may take years, *are of momentous importance*. I address myself to my people, therefore, having served them for thirty-eight years by grappling with the linguistic problems of a foreign missionary, by teaching at theological seminaries, and, for a decade now, by working under the great Bible societies of the world on a revision of the Portuguese Bible that corresponds to our own King James. Out of that experience and in that spirit I write.

W. C. TAYLOR

Louisville, Kentucky
December 2, 1953

Part I

Things I Like about the New Bible —the Good of It

CHAPTER ONE

ITS MECHANICAL ATTRACTIONS AND ITS EXCELLENT DICTION

I LIKE THE WAY THE NEW BIBLE IS PRINTED. I LIKE QUOtation marks in my Bible. If the revisers do not know whether John 3:16 should be in quotation marks or not, they can say so, and did, in the margin. Most scholars think the words are not quoted from Christ but are comments by John. Archbishop Temple and Professor Tribble, I believe, put them in quotation marks as coming from Jesus. It doesn't matter to me. There is nothing impossible, unfitting, unlikely, or out of place in his having said them. His life said far more.

I like the translations into our current speech, if in a reverent tone, as substitutes for obsolete words. I never feel right when men call the Holy Spirit a *Ghost*. I like the abandonment of archaic grammatical forms. The place of *thou* in our religion is yet to be settled and is discussed elsewhere. But the expulsion of the tongue-twisting *eth* and *est* forms of verbs, and of similar curiosities of a bygone age, is total gain. There are literally tens of thousands of improvements of the kind mentioned, and the translators have placed us in their debt by making them and spreading the knowledge among millions of people. Some men have told me personally that they returned to reading the Bible because of this aid to understanding it. That fruit is to be judged by it duration and ripened richness and flavor. After all, the generation-to-be has a claim upon Bible diction, which can still be vastly improved in our Bible-to-be. I like parentheses, though the RSV does not always rightly use them.

I love the countless passages of poetry that suddenly loom from the pages of the Bible. They bring us much closer to the Hebrew mind of the prophets, and some of these poems are of our own Christian Psalmists, as in Luke 1 and 2. I like paragraphs, though sometimes those in the RSV are split and arbitrary. I like truth set forth in capital letters. Here the new Bible has a vast balance sheet of losses and gains. I like much—not all—of its use of textual criticism to throw the best possible light on what the original really is, so that it may be faithfully transmitted to us by translation into the English equivalent. Some of the decisions both in text and margin, however, remind me of the Bible phrase, "If the light that is in thee be darkness . . ." I like the marginal references to parallel or explanatory passages, in almost every case. They show up many of the gravest faults of the new Bible. Especially is this true in the seemingly contrary spirit of Old Testament and New Testament Committees. They give countless contradictory translations, in citing the Old Testament in the New, where the same words might have been used, in whole or in part. Also marginal notes could have cleared up the cases where the New Testament quotes either partially or in substance from the Septuagint, whether they are in the author's own words or are conclusions as to the meaning in his New Testament writings.

With major emphasis, I like the coming of *love* into its own, in the place of the pallid Catholic virtue, often degenerating into a well-meaning vice, called *charity*. That is total gain and of the purest value. *Charity* is a medieval usurper. I like a lot of truth that at least made the margin and would say to it: "Come up higher," in our next version. I like the helps at the top of the page that record the march of thought, with a few exceptions that are pointed out, but would like them above the paragraphs rather than so far off, and more of them. They break the monotony of the page and are aids to reading as well as to understanding. But it is imperative that they be kept denominationally impartial, and not the servants of the New Catholicism.

Only a commentary on the whole Bible could show how often, and in how many ways, the Revised Standard Version has made clear, or clearer, a Scripture that was partly or wholly obscure, and whose obscurity we hardly realized till it became evident by contrast with newer, simpler, and more faithful speech.

CHAPTER TWO

ITS ELIMINATION OF THE KING JAMES CATHOLICISM

"SAINT" MATTHEW. WHO INVENTED THAT? YOU NEVER FIND it in the *text* of your Bible. The New Testament writers do not call each other or anyone else by that title. The older Greek texts do not have it in the names of our New Testament books. It reflects a dead apostasy from New Testament terminology and usage of words, of which a postapostolic Catholicism was first guilty. The younger Roman and Greek Catholicisms adhered to the misuse of the Bible word *saint*. From that ancient, but far too young, Catholicism, the new Bible frees us, going back to the original titles of New Testament books, as we find them in the oldest and best manuscripts. Dr. A. T. Robertson well says that preachers who go around saying *Saint* Matthew are just clinging to that much Romanism, though Romanism has no monopoly or patent on the error. All believers are saints. Rome's monopoly of the noun for those its popes have canonized is just one more item of her apostasy from the New Testament. The new versions in general leave out this King James Catholicism. That is praiseworthy.

Look at another title, "General," which forms a part of the name given to the Epistles of James, Peter, John, and Jude. These were called *Catholic*. Of all writings, they least deserved that name. The latest Roman Catholic version I have of the NT (1950) says of them: "Catholic Epistles. This group includes seven Epistles, one of Saint James, two of Saint Peter, three of Saint John and one of Saint Jude. Since the second century they were called Catholic because not destined for a particular determined church but for all the churches of Christendom, even though some of those of Saint John are a bit private." I should say so: one of them being a few lines to a layman, another a few lines to a lady. Nothing in literature could merit less the name *Catholic*.

Such a word follows the principle of the camel's nose. Once within the flap of the tent, the entire animal follows and soon monopolizes the tent. The word *Catholic* got into the New Testament in this foolish fashion. Lo, it excluded all true Christianity. Just as *sacrament,* a word out of pagan

militarism, got into a false and wicked mistranslation of
Ephesians, and then could drag in with it all the seven
"sacraments" of Roman and Orthodox superstition. Today
no Catholic version translates any word of the Bible as
sacrament. But the poison is already deep in the system, a
gnawing medieval cancer.

Look, too, at the silly notes at the end of the KJ Epistles.
Galatians was not "written from Rome." Who believes that?
Yet it is a King James note after the Epistle. Look at the
end of the two Thessalonian Epistles, said to be "written from
Athens." That isn't so. Paul went on to Corinth and it was
there that Silas and Timothy joined him (Acts 18:5), brought
him news of Macedonia, and were his declared associates in
the said Epistles. Look at the end of II Timothy, where we
read: "The second epistle unto Timotheus, ordained the first
bishop of the Ephesians." That is ridiculous. Paul affirmed,
long before he wrote this Epistle, that the Ephesian Church
had a lot of bishops (Acts 20:18). Timothy was an itinerant
evangelist; he did not stop to be the bishop of any church.
That note is medievalism read back into the New Testament
in defiance of all the facts. Also Titus is said to be "ordained
to be the first bishop of the church of the Cretians." Silly
chatter. There was no "church of the Cretians." The New
Testament never knew of any provincial church, or of one
extending over a big island. Titus was instructed by Paul to
ordain bishops (Titus 1:5) all over Crete. There were already
a lot of churches, and bishops were their local officers. This
dogma of one island bishop is merely an "old wives' tale" of
early Catholic or medieval origin. Such notes are just as great
an anachronism as it would be to enumerate Gandhi and
Schweitzer among the twelve apostles.

Besides a lot of other erroneous notes and titles, many
Romish inventions are written into the text itself of the King
James version. *Easter* is a pagan word brought in by a false
translation of Acts 7:38. Furthermore, there never was any
Old Testament "Church in the wilderness." The connotations
of the word *church* forbid its use in any but the Christian
meaning of the Greek word it translates. In Jewish or civilian
Greek connotations, its meaning is its inherent sense, *congregation, assembly*. So the RSV correctly renders the word
congregation in Hebrews 2:12.

Now these King James elements of Catholicism are either left out or corrected in the RSV. And they are not light offenses of a version. Easter is nothing Christian. It has become a rival to Sunday, the "day of the Lord," the only Christian holy day. Together with a baptism that is itself burial and resurrection, the Lord's day is the great monument to the resurrection of the Savior and a prophecy of our own. With Easter comes the rest of idle, idolatrous "Easter" week. With that comes Lent. With that comes the old Roman carnival. I have seen more references to the promotion of carnival by Catholic institutions, on this furlough, than in all the rest of my life put together. Carnival is a three-day debauch during which an entire population, under the influence of such Catholicism, goes out on the street to "meet the devil." And a thousand Lents can never wash away the crime, anguish, shame, and tragedy caused by this willful removal of all moral restraints from a population, even for three days.

The moving over of the word *church* into the Old Testament meant the loss of New Testament churches and their pure Christianity, and the transference to Christianity of the Old Testament priesthood, altar, sacrificial idea, the family as the unit in religion, and many other falsifications of Christianity. And the loss of the word *saint,* as the proper name and title of every Christian, robs us of an ideal of that "holiness without which no man shall see the Lord," no matter how much Catholicism he absorbs in his mistaken mind here on earth. I read this in a daily newspaper recently: "When was Saint———canonized?" The answer was: "He was made a saint by Pope X," and a date was given. No pope ever made a saint. That can be done by the Spirit of God alone. When we lose the New Testament usage of that great word to a superstitious Catholicism, our Christianity has lost a great truth and a moral ideal of every Christian.

The uninformed may ask:"How came all that Catholicism in the King James version?" My friend, it still enslaved the European mind when our first printed Bibles began to appear. The first printed Greek Testament was the product of the genius and toil of a pet of popes and Cardinals, Erasmus of Rotterdam. He did not have a complete Greek New Testament at all; he translated some words into Greek from his Latin Vulgate. His Greek texts were of the poorest, and far

distant from apostolic times. But it set the style, and with
some later but very inadequate changes became known as
the Textus Receptus, a sort of "authorized" original. It was
copied till the modern era of Tischendorf, Westcott and Hort,
and the Nestles, who gave us texts much nearer to Christ and
the apostles in time, purity, and certainty. These critical texts
are the basis of most modern versions, and of much improvement in the RSV. Intelligent Bible students will rejoice in all
this, and will demand that the very use of such knowledge
shall be temperate, exact, and reverent, obeying that man-
date:

> *Be not the first by whom the new is tried,*
> *Nor yet the last to lay the old aside.*

It is not a fault of the RSV that it has cut out this grosser
Catholicism of the King James Version, but that it has left
some in and introduced other subtle elements of its own. But
of this, later. We are far closer to the original text in the RSV
and ASV than in previous versions, and fewer liberties of
Catholic inspiration are taken with the language now. Tyndale
used "Easter" in John 6:4, Matthew 26:2, and Mark 14:16.
He used "Good Friday" in Matthew 27:62 and "Whitsuntide"
in I Corinthians 16:8. And the Vulgate translates the Greek
word for mystery by its pagan term *sacramentum* nineteen
times. But Tyndale omitted this pagan word. We have come
a long way from the overhanging pall of Catholicism that
darkened the mind of translators when the world was emerging from the slavery of medievalism. God be praised. Let us
advance still more as God gives light and liberty.

CHAPTER THREE

ITS BODY BLOWS AGAINST MODERNISM

ONE OF THE MAJOR VIRTUES OF THE NEW BIBLE IS THAT IT has translated the meaning rather than the verbiage of the favorite Scripture of the modernist. We ought to thank God for that, and spread the knowledge far and wide. This is the verse that modernists now use to justify their irreverent indifference to revelation and truth: "God. . . has made us able ministers of the new testament; not of the letter, but of the spirit; for the letter killeth, the spirit giveth life." Behold the slogan of modernism for a generation or two: "The letter killeth, but the spirit giveth life." With that motto they easily repudiate all meaning of the Bible and rid themselves of its authority, even where they cannot deny its meaning or value. They allege a vague, indefinite spirit hovering over the Bible reader. But it must never take shape in any conviction of the fact of revelation of truth. If you insist that the Bible has meaning and that what it means is what God has revealed in it, they call out at once: "The letter killeth"; and that is for them the end of all argument or respect for the Bible as, in any real sense, the revelation of truth through that chosen literary channel.

But the RSV translation of II Corinthians 3:6 really gives Paul's meaning of the passage: "The written code kills, but the Spirit gives life." That is exactly true to Paul. *Letter* means legalism, the Mosaic law of ritual and ceremony. That kills; it always has, it always will. The Holy Spirit gives life in regeneration, and makes it more abundant in all his subsequent work of sanctification and grace. No mere "spirit," a vague sentimentality, can do that. The alternatives are a legal code: "This do and thou shalt live," which Paul repudiates utterly; or else: "Live through the Spirit, and then you will do his revealed will and truth."

The witness of this Bible about itself is coherent and fine. We read: "The First Book of Moses commonly called Genesis," "The Second Book of Moses commonly called Exodus," "The Third Book of Moses commonly called Leviticus," "The Fourth Book of Moses commonly called Numbers," and "The Fifth Book of Moses commonly called Deuteronomy." Nearly

9

seventy of the Psalms are declared to have been written by
David. That is the testimony of the early gatherers of the
collection, from the beginning. To Solomon are attributed
some of the Psalms, Proverbs, Ecclesiastes, in which in his
old age he testifies to the vanity of human philosophizings
and the eternal value of life in God, and the love songs, which
magnify the deep yearnings of sex life that mutually draw
"The Bridegroom and his Bride," as this Bible's running heads
declare the theme. There is one Isaiah, not a baker's dozen.
One Jeremiah presents lamentations in two books. Job,
Daniel, and Jonah are real; and, by title and text, the last
book of the Old Testament is by Malachi. The New Testament books are attributed to their authors, where that authorship is stated in the best ancient manuscripts. The witness of
Jesus and the New Testament to the Old Testament facts, as
set forth in the RSV titles, is preserved. The Holy Spirit is
the declared Author of both Testaments, "moving" these
authors to their literary witness given. Now this is the RSV's
witness about itself. It is what Robert E. Speer spoke of, to
the Baptist World Alliance, at its meeting in Atlanta, Georgia,
as "the Bible's Doctrine of Itself."

Except for a doubting note or two, you could not ask
for a better Bible, or a more conservative one, in regard to
its doctrine of itself—"conservative" of the facts, the truth,
the testimony given.

The question is whether these translators believe what
they solemnly publish and declare to be the Word of God.
What do you think? And if you had read their writings and
knew the teachings given in these translators' university departments of theology, what then would you be bound to
think? Would you believe that Moses, if he existed, was an
illiterate and uncouth Bedouin? Would you think there were
various Isaiahs, fragmentary or recurring on different pages
of the book? Would you believe that the fourfold Gospel
record was really "according to" Matthew, Mark, Luke, and
John, the current phrase that meant authorship? Or would
you agree that the Gospels were like tiny pieces of rock in
a mosaic? Are our Gospels made up of as many anonymous
bits as Carter had oats? "Oh," but someone might say,
"*according to* merely means that the Gospel was largely or

slightly indebted to the, or a, person who bore that name."
That is false. If *that* were so, then the second Gospel would
be "the Gospel according to Peter," for so the scholars think.
Is there any veracity in this precious Book the translators so
often call "the Word of God," in their Introduction and their
accompanying literature? What would you think of a bank
that continued to let circulate a forged check? What must
you think of the ethics of men who will let circulate, in their
name, a vast lot of literature that they consider forgeries,
fables, crude legends, anonymous folk stories, priests' lies,
and hoaxes of every shade and hue? There is the gravest possible ethical problem here. Is it presumption for men who do
not believe the Bible to assume to translate it for believing
men, women, and children? Can they do justice to it, under
the intoxication of their own heady subjectivism, which
denies it utterly? We shall see the translators' affinities later
on in this study. But, *if they mean what they say,* this is a
conservative Bible, almost entirely accurate in its doctrine of
itself, according to the original. And note that *according to*
means unhesitating fidelity to the Bible's witness to itself.

If we can believe this Bible, as the Nelsons printed it,
then it is a knockout blow to modernism. If the published
teachings of the translators will not let us believe it, then they
never faced a graver ethical problem as to the fountain springs
of their own characters.

CHAPTER FOUR

INDIVIDUAL TRANSLATIONS THAT I LIKE

ROMANS 8:1

"THERE IS THEREFORE NOW NO CONDEMNATION FOR THOSE who are in Christ Jesus." *Period.* That is exactly what Paul said, unconditionally. "No condemnation" is the beginning of that greatest of all his chapters, and "no separation" is its ending. Blessed fidelity to the original and to the truth. How much harm the false KJ addition to Romans 8:1 has done to the vital truth of the eternal security of the believer.

ISAIAH 52:15

"So shall he startle many nations." That is true and fine. "So shall he sprinkle many nations" is silly, false, and irrelevant. Just suppose he did. What would it matter? Would a national April shower, falling by some miraculous stunt on a nation, be capable of doing it any good? I know some have said that *sprinkle* here is a symbol for *purify.* But those who say it use the word to justify a false baptism, applied to infants, and that never purified a soul. Even if it were a true baptism, and even if it could purify the soul—which no baptism can do—nevertheless, salvation does not come by nations but by individuals. No nation ever has been saved, and none ever will be. My only change might be *"will* he startle," instead of the translators' mania for *shall.* The Basic Bible has *will.*

MATTHEW 28:18-20

How vital it is to have our Great Commission correct. The KJ missed the mark in the words *power, teach, Ghost,* and *world.* Baptists have been saying for generations that the Great Commission ought to read: "All authority in heaven and on earth has been given to me. Go therefore and make disciples of all nations, baptizing them in the name of the Father and of the Son and of the Holy Spirit, teaching them to observe all that I have commanded you, and lo, I am with you always, to the close of the age." I love a Great Commission with all its sturdy skeleton in evidence in its divine frame. "Authority . . . disciples . . . baptism in the triune Name. . . teaching. . . obedience to known commandments. . . and the Presence"—that Presence all day and every day for those who carry out the Great Commission, such as Moses pleaded for when he said: "If thy presence go not with us, carry us not up hence." And I like the certainty that this regime, mixed with human sin and the sanctity of divine grace, is just an "age" in progressive revelation and moves on to its climax and close. Has the risen Lord any rights in his own religion? The Great Commission says yes, and, calling in the Gospel records of his commands, defines those rights in all disciples.

Psalm 53:3

Total depravity is right there. Not that we are as bad as possible, but that the taint is through us wholly, though we are capable of redemption and of being better, by growth and by definite commitments in many matters. Hear it: "They (the sons of men) have all fallen away; they are all alike depraved; there is none that does good; no, not one."

Revelation 1:5, 6

The *present,* continuing love of the Savior is good to know: "To him who *loves* us and has freed us from our sins by his blood and has made us a kingdom, priests to his God and Father." Genuine, revealed and experienced Christianity is in a kingdom of priests, the universal priesthood of believers. It is the realization, in the believing heart, of the ideal God gave Moses for Israel: "Ye shall be unto me a kingdom of priests" (Ex. 19:6).

Exodus 20:6

I like the new ending of the second commandment: ". . . but showing steadfast love to thousands of those who love me and keep my commandments." That is the same sentiment expressed by Jesus concerning love and obedience in John 14:15,23;15:10; and other verses. The love that has no will

to obey is spurious, hypocritical, and wicked, however sentimental and mushy its pretense of sweet words, however impressive its ornate ritual.

I PETER 5:8

It is prudent to know that the devil "prowls around like a
roaring lion." Look out, you night revelers! Nor does this
lion sleep by day.

JOB 34:3

Elihu's poetry says:

> *For the ear tests words*
> *as the palate tastes food.*

So be it. That is one purpose of this study.

LUKE 2:14

The angels are Calvinists. They sang at Bethlehem: "Glory
to God in the highest, and on earth peace among men with
whom he is well pleased." God's glory first; man's peace afterwards. The "One World" in which alone there will be peace,
any peace worthy of the name, will be one in which Jesus
Christ is the absolute and only Lord. Only in so far as we
approximate that do we enter and travel together down the
road that leads to peace.

ECCLESIASTES 12:5

There is a solemn finality about death. "Man goes to his
eternal home." There is no second chance. "It is appointed
for men to die once, and after that comes judgment."

ACTS 2:1

This Scripture, properly translated, lays the dust of a lot
of silly unionism and folly. "When the day of Pentecost had
come, they were all together at one place . . . where they were
sitting." The Spirit came on a quiet, sitting, worshipping congregation, an already existing church. No "with one accord"

in the Greek. This Scripture repudiates the silly sentimentalism that today makes Pentecost a day on which a lot of discordant denominations quit their places of worship and gather at a city tabernacle, each abandoning, for the time being, all the truth it knows and its church obligations for an interdenominational or antidenominational propaganda of spurious evangelism. How often sentimentalism sallies forth in the devil's loveliest livery. There was only one denomination in the first century, as long as the churches paid attention to the revelation of God and "continued stedfastly in the apostles' doctrine." No excitement or energy of the flesh was there— all "sitting"—when the Spirit came as he sovereignly would in special mission.

PSALM 16:3

I love this estimate of humanity's elite almost as well as the beloved Sampey's translation: "As for the saints in the land, they are the noble (the "excellent," said J.R.S.), in whom is all my delight." David was not a Catholic by anticipation. His "saints" were not "dead ones." They were still living "in the land." No pope, let us repeat, ever made a saint. The Spirit molds such all over the earth, his spiritual elite.

ACTS 7:20

I like "Moses . . . was beautiful before God." Just so was John the Baptist "great before the Lord." He, the Judge; his, the criterion.

JOB 19:25

They have left us a hope. So many pulpit renegades of our day have reduced the kingdom of God to socialism and sneer at any hope for eternity as "pie in the sky." Such false leaders of men have turned the hands of the clock back beyond Plato and Socrates. They do not believe in immortality, so they take it out of the mouths of those through whom the Old Testament revelation came, or shuffle their dates so that they can attribute their faith not to revelation, but to their indebtedness to Persian paganism. These willful wreckers of Scripture are determined not to believe in hell, so they won't believe in heaven either, or any inherent immortality in man, as part of the image of God in him. But the new Bible permits Job to say: "I know that my Redeemer lives, and at last he will stand upon the earth; and after my skin has been thus destroyed, then without my flesh I shall see God, whom I shall see on my side, and my eyes shall behold, and not another."

EPHESIANS 6:24

It is good to think of "all who love our Lord Jesus Christ with love undying." Love undying manifests the life eternal.

GENESIS 9:3

How generous is the Creator! "Every moving thing that lives shall be food for you, and as I gave you the green plants, I give you every thing." Right there comes in mere Religion and says no to God. Look at India, covered with cattle that are of no use to men because of accursed priests who nullify the gifts of God. Paul classifies as "liars whose consciences are seared" men who follow "doctrines of demons," "who forbid marriage and enjoin abstinence from foods . . ." (I Tim. 4:1-3). Celibacy, Lent, forbidding meat on Friday, restrictions of food to its ritual preparation by rules of caste—all nullify the supreme words of history, God, Christ, and the Bible. Christ went back to Genesis in this matter, as he did in monogamy. "Thus he declared all foods clean" (Mark 7:19). This, too, is a vastly improved translation of the new Bible.

HEBREWS 2:1

It is truly the Bible's counsel that we "pay close attention to what we have heard, lest we drift away from it." There's the peril. Truth and right will stay right on—there in the Bible—but we may be slipping. How easy it is to drift, moving out into peril on deep and treacherous tides of thought.

JOB 36:15

This is an insight. "He . . . opens their ear by adversity."
True to life.

THE GREAT DOCTRINE OF IMITATION

This is hidden by the KJ translations. But we have it
clearly in the RSV. We see it in Ephesians 5:1, "imitators of
God"; in I Thessalonians 2:14, "imitators of the churches"
that are in union with Christ; "imitators" of Paul and of Jesus,
and so on in I Thessalonians 1:6 and I Corinthians 4:16. We
ought to imitate obedience and holiness purposely, not merely
following the styles of custom and thought. This is pure gain.

THE VISTA OF "FOREVER AND EVER"

This panorama of eternity comes on the horizon in Psalm
21:4. "He asked life of thee; thou gavest it to him, length of
days for ever and ever."

HEBREWS 2:9

In the Incarnation, Jesus was lower than the angels "for
a little while." Yet they knew their Lord, sang at his advent,
and ministered to him in the great crises of his ministry.

PROVERBS 12:9

Here there seems to be a vast improvement. "Better is a
man of humble standing who works for himself than one who
plays the great man but lacks bread."

GALATIANS 3:2,5

A vital part of the doctrine of the Holy Spirit is that he
is the possession of every believer and resides in all who hear
the gospel with faith. "Did you receive the Spirit by works
of the law or by hearing with faith? . . . Having begun with
(better: in) the Spirit . . ." That is the doctrine. You *begin* the
Christian life *in the Spirit,* at the very moment that you first
hear the gospel with faith. It is saving faith, faith in Christ,

which is our response to the gospel. When that comes, the Spirit comes into your life. There can be no worse translation than one which gives the Spirit, supposedly, on the basis of intellectual "faith," belief in dogmas, or even in Bible truth. The demons believe that way and tremble in lost terror. Yet Moffatt has the translation: "Did you receive the Spirit . . . by believing the gospel message?" The answer to that is: *No*. We receive him when we receive Christ. The Trinity is not divisible. "He that hath the Son hath the Father"—and the Spirit. He comes not outwardly, but inwardly. When you hear and faith comes, you then and there begin eternal life "in the Spirit."

PSALM 73:24-26

How easily Moffatt squeezes every bit of hope out of this, beyond life's little day. But the translator of these Psalms seems to have seen in them immortality. "Thou dost guide me with thy counsel, and afterward thou wilt receive me to glory. Whom have I in heaven but thee? . . . God . . . is my portion forever."

OUR ONLY REFORMER FOREVER

In Hebrews 9:10 the Old Testament regime is spoken of as lasting "till the time of Reformation." That is why Baptists will not tarry at the post of the Protestant Reformation, to take their origin or doctrine from there. We have an older Reformer, one Jesus. His Reformation repudiated much that the Protestant Reformation retained, canceling it on his cross (Col. 2:14). The whole sacerdotal, sacrificial-altar system, holy-days and sabbatic system, ceremonial and ritual system, family-unit and National-Church system, and the idea that a lot of things in Christianity have replaced a lot of things in Judaism—all that our Reformer has nailed to his cross. We return to Jesus as our Reformer and to the Reformation he made in the revelations God had given, in the preparatory, prophetical era of temporary religion, as set up in Israel. We want no part in man-made reformations of man-made religion. "Reformed theology" is merely Romanism reformed. We don't want it, reformed or unreformed. The new Bible correctly indicates another Reformation, promulgated at

Calvary, consummated in the New Testament, new wine in new wineskins, form and spirit new, not a few Christian patches on the Mosaic garment. This Reformation retained the God, the Bible, the morals (improved and perfected and purified), the history, the devotions, the Messianic hope realized, and the lessons in life, of Israel. But Jesus reformed, repealed, nailed to his cross its whole ceremonial, national, racial, sacrificial, and sacerdotal regime. There are no successors to it. It came to fulfillment and end in Jesus. It is very vital that any new Bible tell us the facts about this divine Reformation. Luther and Calvin, Knox and Henry VIII, are not our Reformers. Jesus is.

EZEKIEL 20:15

God, through the prophet, calls the land of Israel "the most glorious of all lands." And considering its adaptability for its mission, it is wonderfully worthy of that divine praise.

I JOHN 3:14

Listen to this. "We know that we have passed *out of death into life,* because we love the brethren." Take that into your deepest thought.

EZEKIEL 20:11,25

Much of the time Ezekiel was a prophet of the old covenant of works, modified by the sacrificial system of Israel's hope. You see that system, very different from the gospel of grace, in Ezekiel 18:21-28. The prophet himself senses the lack of reality there and says: "Get yourselves a new heart and a new spirit" (Ez. 18:31). But he offers them no such gospel in the old covenant and its ritual. Here is the theory: " . . . my ordinances, by whose observances man shall live." And finally God says: "I gave them statutes that were not good and ordinances by which they could not have life." No ordinances give life, except on the condition of absolute personal perfection in their total observance all one's life. The whole regime of the law was meant to educate Israel and the race in the futility of legalism. "Do and live" is a doctrine of despair. The system was not good; Jesus made a Reformation. He abolished it forever, nailed it to his cross, gave the gospel as the new covenant of grace. Now, men first receive the gift of eternal life, then live it. No man can live a life he does not have. That is the folly of the old covenant. God is getting Ezekiel ready now for the new covenant, which he rose to like one who sees a gleam of light afar.

JOHN 20:17

Jesus did not say to a noble, devoted woman: "Touch me not." Why should he be touchous? The answer is clear. He was not. He said: "Don't hold me," or "Don't cling to me." His resurrection task was urgent, as was her witness thereto.

EZEKIEL 36:27

There is a foregleam of the new covenant in Chapter 11, but the full glow of it, in an Israelitish setting, is in 36:26,27. Here God gives the new heart and the new spirit. The order is no longer "Do and live," but just the reverse, "Live and do." By this new heart, lo, "I will . . . *cause you to walk* in my statutes and be careful to observe my ordinances." The new life is an artesian flow, causing obedience.

SALVATION: PAST, PRESENT, AND FUTURE

The RSV makes all this very clear, repeatedly. "By grace you *have been saved*" (Eph. 2:5,8). And there are new and ever newer reaches of salvation, extending their claims to ever expanding frontiers of life and thought. "The implanted word," received with meekness, "is able to save your souls" (Jas 1:20). It is implanted, grows, has seasons, fruit. In the growth of the first church: "The Lord added to their number day by day those who were being saved" (Acts 2:47). Salvation has its *once-for-all* aspects, set forth in Hebrews, Romans, Galatians, John, and others. It has its progressive aspects. We are being saved; and we shall yet be saved, in salvation's final consummation in heaven. Our times need supremely the fact of salvation as a present possession, dating back in past time to the hour of our saving faith, reaching out to the panorama of "eternal life," here and hereafter.

PSALM 56:3,4

"When I am afraid, I put my trust in thee. In God, whose word I praise, in God I trust without a fear. What can flesh do to me?" Is that the way you act when afraid? That is the very time for praise of the Word of God, for that very hour and problem, not a time for looking toward some guilty conformity with the traditions of men.

COLOSSIANS 3:17

"And whatever you do, in word or deed, do everything in the name of the Lord Jesus, giving thanks to God the Father through him." "Do, in word." Fine thought. You do great things for God by *words*. American "activism," socialistic "do-goodism," works to gain Catholic merit, and all other works of that unholy breed are not doing "everything in the name of the Lord Jesus"; they are carrying out their own programs in their own way. And consider a queer praying custom that grows among us—men praying to God "in *thy* name." Who spawned that? "No man cometh unto the Father but by me." If you can't bring yourself to pray in Christ's name, you have spurned the Way, the Truth, and the Life. I wouldn't say to such as these: "Quit praying." You may stumble on a petition that is the will of God. But prayer is not primarily petition; it is communion. For that we have access only through Christ. "Whatever you do *in word*." Some of the greatest things Christian men have ever *done* they did in *word*, bravely, truly, opportunely spoken.

PSALM 22:3

"Yet thou art holy, enthroned on the praises of Israel." Your Sunday praises are God's throne. When you stop being Christian, in the calendar of every week, and steal the Lord's day for your own week ends, you dethrone your God from the praises on which he would be once more uplifted by your presence at church—were you not a deserter.

OTHER WORDS AND PHRASES I LIKE

I love the victory note of John 1:5, "the darkness has not overcome it," so it keeps on shining. How true is John 1:11,

too. "He came to his own home, and his own people received
him not." It is a motive for joy to read that we are "justified
in the Holy Spirit," not "by" (KJ, I Cor. 6:11). It is reassur-
ing, we repeat, to have the word *church,* always of a New
Testament connotation, erased from the Old Testament references, in Acts 7:38 and Hebrews 2:12. It is good to see
the far panorama of revealed Christianity, which is both
this-worldly and other-worldly, for "the present life and also
the life to come" (I Tim. 4:8), even "the day of eternity"
(II Pet. 3:18). The translators let Paul say once: "the *impending* distress" (I Cor. 7:26), though inconsistently with
their general record. There is great translation in Romans
3:21-24,27,28. Righteousness is wholly *"apart from* law,"
clean outside that realm, *"apart from* works of law." Men
are "justified by his grace as a gift." Tautology? Yes, there
in the translation, and deliberately so in Paul, in the Greek,
I appreciate Acts 4:13, where Peter and John are seen to be,
from the stand-point of highbrow scorn, "uneducated and
common men," not "unlearned and ignorant." It is interesting
to read of "some who belonged to the church" (Acts 12:1).
The Greek sense stands out in Acts 17:26, "allotted periods
and the bounds of their habitations," a divine determination
that is the Bible's philosophy of history. The peril of Christians
is well stated in II Peter 3:17: " . . . lose your stability." You
have a perfect picture of current liberalism in Matthew 5:19.
"Whoever *relaxes* one of these commandments." What about
those who say: "There is no difference"? Such teachers
"wander after myths" indeed (II Tim. 4:4). The idea of
"partnership" with a missionary by those associated with him
in prayerful co-operation is inspiring (Phil. 1:5). Again, it
helps immensely to know the New Testament's emphasis on
"the public reading" of the Scripture, for the Epistles and
the Revelation were to be "read aloud" (Rev. 1:3) to the
contemplated, worshipping audiences. And the command to
the public reader of Matthew 24:15 shows that the reading
of the Gospel in the public worship was contemplated also,
from the time of its writing. The public reader (the lector)
was to give the interpretation of certain apocalyptic language,
of immediate concern to the hearers. And, finally, to have
Paul's real thought, in I Corinthians 9:24-27, clarifies beauti-

fully the language of the Greek athletic games. You see the boxer and the runner of the race and you note the placards "Approved" and "Disqualified," whereby the winners and the losers were indicated. Those received a reward; the price, the crown. These were not approved for a crown, but did not lose their citizenship or lives. Farewell, old false translation "castaway." Good riddance! Hail to a better, truer translation!

These are, in every case, samples of like translations without number that could have been cited as worthy of admiration and praise, in the work of the translators of the RSV. Others, praiseworthy but not uniform in their usage, will appear also when that lack of uniform and coherent excellence is commented upon unfavorably. None of these really great and valuable aids to understanding the Bible ought to be lost from the treasures of the Bible student, or from the future stable English version the American public deserves.

Part II

What I Dislike about the New Bible —the Evil of It

CHAPTER FIVE

ITS PERSISTENCE IN A MULTITUDE OF KING JAMES ERRORS

SINCE THE RSV HAS COST GREAT EFFORT, MONEY, TIME, AND study, and has been given wide publicity, it seems reasonable to expect that its revisers would at least have avoided a repetition of the evident errors in translation in the King James version. This, in many and grave instances, has not been done. We give examples.

I TIMOTHY 6:10

Think of this translation still appearing in a new Bible: "The love of money is the root of all evils." That never was true at any time in human history. Paul never wrote such folly. It was not the love of money that made Adam eat the forbidden fruit, nor Cain kill his brother, nor Moses smite the Rock God told him to speak to, nor Aaron make a golden calf, nor David rape Bathsheba and kill Uriah, Herod kill John the Baptist. Nor is the love of money what the FBI often discovers as the motive of the darkest crimes. *A root of all* (or *all kinds of*) *evils,* yes; and that is what the Greek says: *a* root, not *the* root.

ROMANS 13:8

Paul never said: "Owe no man anything." It is the negative with a tense of continued action: *don't keep on owing.* Pay what you owe. The Bible, even Jesus, orders men to lend. And owing is just the other side of lending. Jesus compared himself to an owner who put out his money at interest and received his own with interest. That is basic commercial life in the Bible. There was never any excuse for such a translation. It is a careless repetition of King James' worst.

I TIMOTHY 5:17

Paul did not say: "Let the elders who rule well be considered worthy of double honor, especially those who labor in preaching and teaching." How would you go about *doubling* honor? This translation is a present to the Presbyterians, in

spite of well-known Greek considerations. This slavish following of King James has a bevy of errors. The persistence
of *elders* is misleading. The presbyter was no longer an elderly
person, but an officer, a counselor, whatever the age, and
that was as true in Judaism as in Christianity. It is not double
honor but double remuneration that Paul commands. That is
common knowledge now, confirmed by papyrus usage. The
two citations from Scripture in the margin treat of "wages"—
support. They are meaningless as a context, the way this verse
is translated. Then, too, Paul's very emphatic word is given
no emphasis. The contrast is not between one class of presbyters that is engaged in teaching and preaching and a layman
class not supposed to do these things. The two classes are
those who *toil* at their "preaching and teaching," and the lazy
ones who won't or the careless and diverted ones who don't.
Moffatt translates it as "ample remuneration." Phillips re-
peats this and makes the condition, "if they work hard." All
these men belong to one class, presbyters. All are paid of-
ficials. All have the mission of "preaching and teaching." All
are bishops. Paul really said: "Let the presbyters (not a question of age) who superintend (so Thayer—the office of a
bishop is indicated, and the identity of presbyter and bishop
has already been made evident in many Scriptures) well be
considered worthy of double remuneration, especially those
who *toil* in the Word and in doctrine." All are presbyter-
bishop pastors. All are paid. All have Word and doctrine as
their sphere of life and responsibility. Those who toil at it
are to have double remuneration. The highest-priced preachers I know are paid by intelligent churches just about that
way. The nontoiler is generally at the bottom. This text
ought not to be made a present to Presbyterians. Translate it
fairly, truly. There is no Bible presbyter who is less than a
bishop; no bishop who is more than a pastor. This is a text
for the support of the ministry. We need it. Somebody is being
liberal with what does not belong to him. Even the latest
Roman Catholic version in Brazil translates: *"dobrado
estipĕndio."*

II CORINTHIANS 8:18

Dr. A. T. Robertson often called attention to the natural force of the Greek article here, *his* brother. That description fits Luke. On the basis of the customary modesty of the New Testament writers about members of their families, the relationship would explain the otherwise strange silence of Luke, in Acts, about Titus, great comrade of Paul. The translators of the RSV sometimes translate the article by a possessive pronoun. But here they were content to stay on the King James level of discernment.

II TIMOTHY 3:16

KJ and RSV say with equal inaccuracy: "All Scripture," when the Greek has "every Scripture." It is never said that the Scriptures are inspiring. It is said that each one of them is "God-breathed," inspired. Such truth is too "conservative." The translators bar it from their Bibles and so make them diverge from our Bible, the original.

HEBREWS 11:3

The RSV erroneously retains "the world" which the KJ uses erroneously, but drops the Greek plural, respected by King James. It affirms thus the creation of the world, a good teaching. But that is not the point here. At this point, God is affirmed to be the Lord of history, the Creator of the moving panorama of "the ages" that run their course. These, in Hebrews 1:3, are also erroneously translated "the universe." The author of the Epistle is simply not allowed to say in English what he says in the Greek.

JAMES 5:3

There is no excuse for following the erroneous translation about laying up treasures *"for* the last days." The Greek preposition *in* is right there and it does not mean *for*. To translate that correctly would give us a New Testament name of our gospel era, "the last days"—"these last days" we read in Hebrews 1:2, the last epoch of revelation on earth.

LUKE 18:8

It seems to be generally agreed now that Jesus asked: "Will the Son of man find *the* faith on the earth?"—not just "faith," as in KJ and RSV.

JOHN 7:39

One of the boasts of the new Bible is that it was not going to use *which* about people, but *who*. Yet we read about "the Spirit, which" here, and "Holy Spirit which" in Romans 5:5, Romans 8:11, Titus 3:6, Ephesians 1:14, and other verses. Yet we have "the Holy Spirit, who dwells in us" in II Timothy 1:14, "the Spirit of God, in whom" in Ephesians 4:30, and "the Spirit himself" in Romans 8:26. It would have helped these gentlemen to have had a simple concordance to unify their translation when it appeared in a divergent fashion such as this. To some Bible readers the personality of the Holy Spirit is a vital doctrine.

ROMANS 6:4

My Baptist soul revolts against the sacramentalism of the mistranslation of this great gospel passage. You can't baptize a man *into* Christ, into his death, nor was Israel baptized "into Moses," (I Cor. 10:2). The symbolism follows the facts. You don't bury people *into* death, or *unto* death or *for* death. You bury them because they are already dead. And baptism is burial. The baptized have, by faith, already died to sin. Then comes the burial, because of death, not crudely *into* it. You cannot baptize a man into Christ. That is materialism, magic, superstition. You don't have to give it a Baptist translation: because of death, because of the remission of sins, (Acts 2:38), baptize because of repentance (Mat. 3:11), repent because of the preaching of Jonah (Matt. 12:41), and so on. The Berkeley Version found yet a middle way, neither Baptist nor sacramentalist: "Whoever of us have been baptized in union with Christ Jesus, were baptized in union with his death. So we are jointly interred with Him in death through the baptism." "All as companions of Moses were baptized." Baptists have been proclaiming to a sacramentalist world for a long time: "Blood before water; Christ before the church; salvation before baptism." The translator of the Great Commission got it right: "baptizing in the name." The general, root idea of this Greek preposition, in all nonmaterial matters, is *with reference to, in regard to, concerning,* which is one of the meanings of the KJ *unto,* given in the dictionary. Why this crude literalism about a preposition that all grammarians of note admit now may look either backward or forward, as to the cause or as to the purpose? The sense would prevent any sacramentalism. You do not bury people *in order to* their death, but *because of it.* To bury for the purpose of death is assassination. Reality comes before symbolism. Your man who has by grace died to sin and risen to newness of life must be there, happy and holy in purpose, before you can take the symbolic picture of him in baptism. Well did George Truett exclaim to the 65,000 present at the Baptist World Alliance in Atlanta, and to millions over the radio: "Salvation is always necessary to baptism: baptism is never necessary to salvation." A. T. Robertson repeatedly wrote that here what determines translation is whether you are evangelical or not. The Greek grammar, permitting either translation, lets the translator give it either the evangelical or the sacramentalist rendering. The RSV chose the sacramentalist rendering, saying virtually: "We will not give our readers any relief from the sacramental superstition that fastened itself on the King James Version as Europe emerged from the pall of medieval Romanism. If you want relief here from that crude materialism, then don't use our version." Now we have this preposition far more often with the verb *believe.* But do you ever see these translators render it *"believe into Christ"?* No. That would be evangelical. And, to excuse the obsession of this determined sacramentalism, the translators had to be consistent. So they have the Red Sea throw the whole multitude of migrant Israel and all its hangers-on right *"into* Moses." Indigestible.

JOHN 8:11

The KJ and the RSV got together again to put forth the monstrous error: "Neither do I condemn you." So Jesus did not condemn adultery? That delights the world's "intellectuals" whose intellectualism consists mainly of "wine, women, and song." How often have they exclaimed in Paris and other capitals: "Jesus did not condemn adultery." And I have read the sneer of agnostics to the effect that he looked longingly at her himself and found in Mary Magdalene a satisfaction of that longing, as her paramour. Irreverent? Hellishly so, but you may expect that from young university hellions whose university professors make Jesus say to an adulteress: "Neither do I condemn thee." But he did condemn her, then and there, and with stern forbidding of other sin.

Look at the scene. Tricky Jews put Jesus on the spot. The woman was caught in the act. But adultery is not a game of solitaire. It takes two to play it. Why did they not bring the *man* along? Because there was not the slightest moral concern in this little comedy. Rome did not permit the death penalty prescribed by the law of Moses. No need to bother to bring along their friend. Put it up to Jesus. If he says, "Stone her," he goes against Rome. If he says, "Don't stone her," he goes against Moses. He is caught and nothing can come of it. So they reason. Jesus outreasoned them. The jury was also the judge, under Moses, and the hangman. They asked Jesus to express that judicial decision. He was not a "divider and judge" among men; he had no right to pass judicial sentence. He said: "Neither do I pass sentence upon you." That was not his career among men. Now these translators use a similar translation of this same verb that gives the idea of "pronounce judgment" in I Corinthians 5:3, and use "pass sentence" in Matthew 23:33, and other passages. No "wicked and adulterous" generation needs a version that makes Christ seem indifferent to adultery. The Sermon on the Mount expands his moral reaction against it even to the lustful look.

II PETER 1:20

A persistence in fundamental King James error, in translation and idea, is seen in the apostle Peter's great words about the Scripture. Here is what Peter really wrote: "No prophecy of the Scripture becomes a matter of its own interpretation." The word translated *its own* must refer to the subject of the verb, and that is not any individual. "No prophecy of the

Scripture" is the subject. Peter affirms that not a single Scripture is to be given an interpretation which consists merely in some possible or apparent meaning of its isolated language. Scripture is to be interpreted by Scripture, not in contradiction of its immediate context, the intellectual context of the human author, elsewhere set forth, and certainly not in contradiction of the divine Author and his revelation of truth in the general witness of the Bible. This is Christian reverence.

Of course, this annuls the whole modernist point of view. Elsewhere in these studies it is shown that modernism hates the harmony of the Gospels, delights in the disharmony of the Bible in a multitude of alleged contradictions. It keeps the Bible in a state of civil war with itself, in an unending series of battles over its own misused pages.

Now King James said: "No prophecy of the Scripture is of any private interpretation." Romanism could hardly make a worse thrust against the Bible. That leaves you no alternative but to run to a priest or a professor or some other third party. But the RSV is just as bad, and at the same point. It denies freedom of interpretation, in similar language: "No prophecy of scripture is a matter of one's own interpretation." There is no excuse for such a translation. The Greek word *idios* is translated "his own" in Matthew 9:1 and most other places in the New Testament, because it refers to a masculine subject. It is rendered "thine own," in Luke 2:41, "its own," in Luke 6:44, "our own," in Acts 3:12; "their own," in Acts 25:19; Romans 10.3, and other verses; "her own," in I Corinthians 7:2; and in 7:4 it is translated twice—once "her own" and once "his own." The word has no reference in itself to gender, number, and person. It agrees in these respects with its noun, but its reference is back to the person, number, and gender of a noun to which the structure of the sentence makes the reference perfectly clear. In this case, the clear and only possible reference is to prophecy of the Scripture: "No prophecy of the Scripture is a matter of its own interpretation." It is never to be taken all by itself. It is a part of the Spirit's literary revelation, an organ or a cell in the body of revealed truth. Let it have its place in the living organism of the whole revelation and function in harmony with the rest. That is what Peter wrote.

But this Scripture denies the whole modernist position,

contradicts all its slogans and axioms of rationalism. These
say that the prophet wrote only to his contemporaries, that
there is no revealed truth, no Absolute from whom it could
come or in whom it could find its standard, no revelation but
the soft purrings of one's own subjectivism, one contradictory
theory being as true in its time and way as its opposite and flat
denial.

Now these translators know Greek. Why would they not
translate *idios* into *its own?* They did so in Luke 6:44. Why
persist in the King James error? There is a strange, ultraconservative reluctance to change bad translations to good ones,
after they entrench themselves in popular thought. The RSV
has a vast amount of this ultraconservative reluctance to be
right, especially when the right translation repudiates all the
premises of modernist thought.

To be sure, now we can see why Peter considered prophecy
thus interpreted in accordance with the whole movement of
progressive revelation a far surer way to know truth and reality than even to have seen Jesus on the Mount of Transfiguration. But both KJ and RSV wreck this testimony, and rather
destroy the freedom of the Bible reader to make his own interpretation, for which he can have all the resources of the indwelling Spirit's willing guidance and illumination. This great
Scripture, so favorable to private interpretation, setting it
above even presence on the Transfiguration Mount, is made
into a papal bull against that very thing.

The peculiar Greek idiom of Peter makes this a *positive*
tribute to the Scripture, like II Timothy 3:16. He said: "*Every*
Scripture is not (or does not become) a matter of its own
(isolated) interpretation." It is a part of a unified whole. That
being true, *revelation* through the written Word is a more sure
way to know the truth than to have been present at the Transfiguration of the incarnate Word. A frequent translation of
this word, in a special construction, is *apart* or *alone*. No
literary prophecy of the Bible is to be translated or interpreted *apart* from the rest of the Scripture, or *alone*. Have
enough respect for the revealing Spirit to reverence the unity
of his total revelation and the harmony of its parts. Moffatt
gave this free translation, or mistranslation: "No prophetic
scripture allows a man to interpret it by himself." Why could

he not have been true to the Greek and render it: "No prophetic Scripture allows a man to interpret it *by itself"?*

EXODUS 3:5

A simple blunder in the way of anachronism says that God told Moses to take off his "shoes." And the error is retained in Acts 7:33. Moffatt translates "sandals." Correct. Why, then, this curious anachronism in the RSV?

SELAH

Why does this meaningless word occur seventy-one times in the Psalms and three times in the prophecy of Habakkuk? If it had to be used, why not some explanatory note, or at least a helpful "conjecture" in the margin as the LXX had, which the Bagster translation of it renders "pause"? More clinging to King James obscurities.

SALVATION BY THE MATERNITY WARD?

A miserable and papist translation that crept into the King James Version and has again been perpetrated against womanhood by the RSV translators is found in I Timothy 2:15. Here is the monstrosity: "Yet woman will be saved through bearing children, if she continues in faith and love and holiness, with modesty." These are not Bible terms of salvation. Here is Romanism's biggest bonus for the huge Catholic families by which the Papacy aims to keep its control of the Latin world, and conquer Canada by the French midwife and the maternity ward. Of course, it is a futile hope. Infant baptism and a little catechetical instruction in error are weak sticks for a lame religion to lean upon. But why on earth should the Nelson translators give this unsolicited aid to Romanism? A Bible thus translated is not fit to put into any woman's hands, if it really aims to take away the mistakes of the King James Version. This is the crudest mistake of them all.

By this translation, the gospel is made a Humpty Dumpty that fell off the wall. Do any of these translators believe that women obtain salvation by repeated stays in the maternity ward? Is a midwife another mediatrix between God and man?

That a bachelor priesthood should crave this monstrous mistranslation for its unholy purposes in the ecclesiastical ex-
ploitation of mothers, we can understand. Europe was just
emerging from medieval darkness when the King James Version came along, keeping a lot of that darkness because its
deeds (a religion of sacraments) were evil. But why would any
gospel-enlightened mind surrender to that evil impulse?

The Berkeley Version approximates the truth here: "She
will, however, be kept safe through her child-bearing, if with
self-control she continues in faith, love and consecration."
That, too, destroys a *plural* which the Greek has: *they continue*. Let it mean *they* (the women in that hour), if you like.
But keep it. One translation I know in a Catholic land has
had the courage and the scholarship to say what Paul said and
not what a lot of unscriptural priests want him to be mis-
represented as having said. The great apostle of the marriage
ceremony said: "But she will be preserved through her child-
bearing, if they (husband and wife) continue (abide or per-
severe) in confidence and love and holiness, with good sense
(or sound judgment)." This is a promise of special providence
for the Christian mother in the holy bonds of matrimony,
where the responsibilities of parents are faced with mutual
qualities herein set forth and with the common sense that
studies and prepares for the blessed event. Such is the teaching
of the grand apostle of home life. To wreck it, and build up a
priest-spawned doctrine of salvation, forced on reluctant
Catholic mothers under the lash of this falsified Scripture, is
a wickedness that only translators can be guilty of. God blesses
motherhood. But he never promised it salvation. The maternity ward is not Calvary, or an open gate to heaven.

MATTHEW 10:22; 24:13, AND PARALLELS

The inventors of this salvation by maternity ward have
persisted in one other King James error in the misuse of the
verb *save*. The verb for *save*, in Greek, means *save, preserve,
deliver, cure*, and similar ideas. The RSV revisers, as we shall
later see, have squeezed out of our Lord's great pronounce-
ment: "Thy faith has saved thee," all but the physical cure,
where the "saved" were sick people. He both cured and

saved. In Scriptures that deal with cataclysmic times and events, great trials and testings of men's souls, eras that have to be divinely shortened for even the elect to endure them, we have declarations like this: "But he that has endured to the end, this man shall be kept," the literal statement of the Greek in both passages cited above. This is deliverance. It guarantees that the noble believer, put through the most horrible times imaginable, will not, after standing fast through all the persecution and suffering, just "fade away" like an old soldier. He will be kept through it, delivered from the defeat of attritions unending, come through with colors flying, will not merely survive, but *triumph*. He was saved at the beginning of his Christian life. This is deliverance, at the end of grave testing and on beyond. Nothing could be further from the context than to lay down a dogma of salvation by process, human process of human fidelity, human exit in lifelong perseverance in religious decency, "enduring" all through life, right up to the moment of death, with salvation conditioned on that endurance. That is just one more way of whipping the devil around the stump to teach salvation by self, by works of righteousness which we have done.

Jesus Christ has men who will endure, even though the heavens fall. He needs such men. He has promises for them. He never will let the gates of hades (the world of the dead) close on all such here. In the midst of apostasy (departure from truth, not loss of salvation), cosmic punishment of that apostasy, and all that men, demons, and God himself will bring upon men in the way of judgment, *still* the abiding heart is secure. God will preserve him to death, through death, escaping death, as he sovereignly wills. This is the promise. But if there is salvation only for those who endure to the end, in the sense of moral or ecclesiastical continuity of endeavor, then there is no gospel. All the paganisms believe that. There is nothing Christian in the idea. It is a King James error brought over from medievalism that the RSV translators did not have the judgment to see and correct. God promised to preserve already saved men, true in great trials, to be there and keep up their witness even to the end. But he never made salvation depend on continuous human endeavor. That puts the cart before the horse, man before God. The Greek parti-

ciple (*he having endured*) is the aorist tense. It looks at all life
as a snapshot. It is a once-for-all concept. With that understanding, it can be translated as a timeless present: not *he that
continually endures,* but *the endurer.* He who is saved once for
all, has eternal life, never comes into condemnation. The soul
that is so described, in brief, has deliverance guaranteed him
"though all hell should endeavor to shake" his security in
Christ.

PHILIPPIANS 2:12

Once again on salvation, the RSV translators followed
the KJ Anglicans off at a tangent, sidling away from the truth
Paul revealed. Here men spend millions of dollars and the best
years of brilliant minds to produce merely a version that per-
petrates all over again this old King James error: "work out
your own salvation." That is dead wrong, utterly unpardonable as a translation. The Berkeley Version sensed the meaning: "Cultivate your own salvation, for God is the Energizer
within you, so as to will and to work for His delight." Our
Portuguese revision says: "Develop your own salvation." It
is like the heritage of a son—farm, mine, bank, invention,
manufacturing plant, capital, investment, what have you. It
is a gift—already "your own." Develop it. It is a fearful responsibility, but you have infinite, adequate, divine backing,
and boundless hope and cheer. Why do we not deserve at this
point a Christian translation rather than a pagan one? Why
should Paul be forced, in Philippians 2:12, to contradict and
repudiate Ephesians 2:8-10? The Holy Spirit has not willed it
so. Phillips sees this truth in Matthew 10:22 and translates it:
"But the man who endures to the very end will be safe and
sound." That is it exactly. But Phillips saw the gleam one
time in four of these passages, and the Berkeley Version saw
it one time in four. The conception of the gospel that translators bring with them to the task will determine whether they
translate this verb as *save, keep, deliver, preserve,* or *cure.* The
whole translation must judge its parts and be judged by them.
This very version translates the word that often means *salvation* as meaning *deliverance* (Acts 7:25 and Phil. 1:19). It
could just as well treat of a "safe delivery," in I Timothy 2:15:

"She will be kept safe at the time of child-birth," says the Basic Bible. The verb meaning *save, cure, deliver,* and so on needs a gospel conscience in the translator, for to translate it *save* when it is not treating of salvation is just as grave a fault as not to render it *save* in the great gospel Scriptures. When you put your life into wrong doctrines, you incapacitate your mind to be a right translator, when they are concerned. There has to be an affinity between the truth on the sacred page and the truth within the translator. That is his greatest qualification, since spiritual things are spiritually discerned. That is where some of the RSV translators least qualify.

UTTERLY CONFUSING THE PENTECOST NARRATIVE: ACTS 2

Was Pentecost a movement of transients? It all depends on the translation of a key word in Acts 2:5. The KJ and the RSV both say "there were *dwelling* at Jerusalem Jews." But the confusion comes when these same people, in part, are described later on as *residents* of Mesopotamia and all the rest of the Dispersion, together with some *visitors from Rome.* The KJ has *dwellers* the second time, as the first. Now what did that word in Acts 2:5 mean? It means the dwelling of fixed residence, used of the Holy Family dwelling at Nazareth, of Jesus fixing residence in Capernaum, of the eight evil spirits fixing residence in a man, of all the inhabitants of Jerusalem, and of the residence both of Christ and of the Spirit in the believer (Matt. 2:23; 4:13; 12:45; Luke 13:4; Eph. 3:17; Col. 1:19; Jas. 4:5, and other passages). This very word the RSV translates in Acts 1:19, "all the inhabitants of Jerusalem"; and the same in Acts 4:16; of Abraham when he "lived in Haran" in Acts 7:2, 4; of Jews "who lived in Damascus" in Acts 9:22; and similar uses in Acts 9:32, 35; 11:29; 13:27; 19:10, 17; 22:12. Every Greek dictionary agrees that this treats of permanent residence. There simply is no possible doubt about it. And so all versions generally indicate. These who came together in Jerusalem were the regular inhabitants of Jerusalem who had moved there from lands of the Dispersion, where they were born. As in Portugal today, vast numbers of the sons of the land, born in colonies of their people abroad, returned to the "little land" of their fathers to spend their old age, their wealth, and die. The miracle of tongues had its verification in such inhabitants of Jerusalem. They are permanent residents in Jerusalem, but their previous residence in other lands gave them the knowledge of nearly a score of languages in which the miracle was by them verified.

Does the Greek, which demands this permanent residence, accord with the facts? It does. Pentecost was only a one-day feast. It was not the great international feast of the year. That was the Passover. Pentecost came only fifty days later. The vast throngs at the Passover, from so many foreign lands, would not have had time to get back home to other continents and turn right around and come to Jerusalem again. They would not come in such numbers to a one-day feast.

In like accord is the movement of the providence of God, what some would call the philosophy of history. God was building up first a great demonstration of Christianity in Jerusalem. Here a great First Church was to be a model. Here the risen Christ demonstrated, on the stage of the international life of Jerusalem, with its millions of pilgrims yearly, the gospel for the world. Now look at the theory the KJ and RSV unite in. By that theory, this entire Pentecostal crowd, there for one day only, vanished next day and left Jerusalem with a situation in no way better than if Pentecost had never happened, a city with only 120 Christians. People away from home must return, did return. But you say: "God would have missionaries for all these lands." There are things God cannot do. A man I knew, my theology teacher, used to say: "Even God can't make a bull yearling in less than twelve months." God never made a missionary in one day. Even Paul he seasoned for three years in the desert. No. The clear facts are that this Pentecostal audience, so far as it is considered of significance by Luke, was no overnight horde of transients in Jerusalem. They were the residents in Jerusalem who had come there in great numbers from the Dispersion, born abroad, now inhabitants of the Holy City permanently.

Does this agree with the Greek? It does when all the Greek is translated. How then do we have this same crowd, declared in the Greek to be people who *lived in, resided in* Jerusalem permanently, styled later on "residents of" so many lands and "visitors from Rome," as the RSV puts it? The reason is simple. The RSV translators simply threw out the clarifying language, which removes all difficulties. and made the confusion by the willful omission. The Greek says: "How do *we* hear, each in our own language *in which we were born,* Parthians, Medes, Elamites and *inhabitants* of nine more nations," and "those of us who were temporarily Roman foreign residents?" Now it is clear. "We were born Parthians, Medes and . . . nonpermanent residents in the Jewish colony of Rome," so we know the native speech in those lands and hear it now by this miracle, we who now are permanent residents in Jerusalem. The RSV cunningly throws away the entire declaration: *we were born* in former residence in Jewish colonies in those lands, and adds in place of the discarded Scripture simply the word "native"—"native tongue." That hides the vital fact that these adjectives all agree with the subject of the verb: *We were born—we were born Parthians,* formerly Jewish colonists in many lands, Roman colonists. The phrase *both Jews and proselytes* might cover the whole crowd, even though names of two more nationalities come to them at that point. The language is again doctored to fit the theory. We have "visitors *from* Rome." There is no such Greek in existence. The Greek has *"Romans* in temporary residence," "visitors *in* Rome," if you prefer. That is where they had been visitors, transients. Now in Jerusalem they are *permanent inhabitants of* the Holy City. This second word, for passing residence in a colony, we have in Luke 24:18, and the RSV translates it: "Are you the only visitor in Jerusalem who does not know these things?" These "Romans," whether Jews or proselytes, who had been temporary residents of Rome, were now permanent residents of Jerusalem. We have a similar word so describing them in Acts 17:21, where Moffatt translates it as "the foreign visitors at Athens." Remember, there is no *from Rome* in the Greek. These people had been born in Rome, were "Romans," though as members of foreign colonies, of course, that would not mean Roman citizens. I think that visitors is an inadequate translation. We have permanent foreign residents in Brazil. I have been one for thirty-eight years. We also have, in consular service or on business, temporary residents. Such had been these Romans, now living in Jerusalem, not mere "visitors in Rome," but families there on business. Children born there would speak Latin or Greek; and they heard it in the miracle of tongues on the day of Pentecost. There is neither contradiction nor the slightest confusion in Luke's narrative. Confusion has been artificially created in the RSV, following the KJ, by erroneous translation, by not translating at all a clarifying verb, and by making an adjective turn into a prepositional phrase beginning with *from*. None of this has the slightest justification in the Greek. All they needed to do was to translate the Greek just as they had uniformly translated the words elsewhere, and the story would have agreed with itself, with the history, with the philosophy of the missionary movement set forth in Acts, and with all sound missionary policy. No sensible person would ever think of baptizing 3,000 raw converts on the day they heard their first sermon, and turn them loose one day later to scatter over three continents. Nothing could be greater folly. These listeners of the day of Pentecost were the very crowd that had crucified Jesus, and had heard his sermons many a time. "This Jesus . . . you crucified and killed." The Jerusalem church was expanded by the addition of these informed, stable, radically converted residents of their own city, 3,000 of them in one day. There may have been transients in Jerusalem on the day of Pentecost, but they are not on the horizon of this story.

COMMUNISM REFASTENED ON THE BIBLE

Again we are faced with a matter of artificially created confusion, imposed on a clear record by the translators of the KJ and the RSV. Luke makes it abundantly clear that the principle of private property was neither abolished nor abandoned in Jerusalem among Christians, but there was voluntary giving. Genuine sales were made, and the money remained in private ownership till voluntarily given to church ownership and administration, just as are our gifts to churches today. Here is what the Greek says: "And all the believers had all common things *in the same place* (continually had, kept them there), and they were selling (began to sell, kept on selling, or intermittently sold now and then) their properties and goods; and, in so far as anyone might have a necessity, they

were distributing them to all." That is Luke's record. Now
what does the RSV do? First, it adds to the Word of God a
verb that is not there and has no business there: "all who believed *were together*." I have the Eberhard Nestle text before
me. It has no verb *were*. There is a variant that has it, the
Textus Receptus, basis of the KJ; and many modern translators prefer it because they come to the passage committed to
this communal idea of primitive Christianity, which came
down to us from the medieval communal life of monasticism,
not from Luke. The word *together* is a wresting of the sense.
The Greek has three words: *in the same*. There is no prepositional phrase, *in common*, as there is no verb *were*. Just what
would *were together* mean? What could it mean? A common
dormitory? A continuous meeting? A refugee compound for
all who made the exit from private property? It means nothing
that was possible. If there is textual-variant authority for adding the verb *were*, why did they not give the fact in a marginal
note, as they were so eager to do on the first page of the New
Testament, to discredit the birth of the Savior?

True it is that the KJ language is softened a bit. The old
1611 translators made it read: "All that believed were together and had all thing common; and sold their possessions
and goods and parted them *to all men*, as *every man* had
need." That adds the word *men*, making it a universal communism, and a universal drawing on the common funds
("every man"). *Man* is twice added. The *all* refers to the believers, naturally. Yet if the RSV softens a bit the KJ totalitarian conception here, it fortifies it elsewhere: "O Lord, . . .
who shall dwell on thy holy hill? He who does not put out
his money at interest" (Psalm 15:5). That takes us right back
to the heyday of popery, when only Jews could be moneylenders because the popes did not know the difference between
interest and usury. Of course, the popes themselves became
the heaviest patrons of Jewish moneylenders, to keep up their
vain and luxurious, sometimes lecherous, courts. They see-
sawed back and forth between patronizing them and burning
them alive. Well, this World Council of Churches, whose national branch makes money from the sale of every copy of the
Nelson Bible, almost went as far as the popes, at its initial
meeting in Amsterdam. Goaded by the fanatical communist,

Homradka, they nearly adopted a resolution condemning all capitalism, in the name of this New Catholicism, sponsor of the new Bible. At the last minute, they happened to remember that this was a pretty raw deal for the American capitalists, the Rockefellers, Tafts, and the like, who were putting up the money that made this New Catholicism click. So in panic and for very shame, they changed from the denunciation of capitalism they would have liked to give to the pet phrase of the current jargon, *laissez-faire capitalism,* which was a nose of wax every man could twist to his notion. Nobody advocates a *laissez-faire capitalism,* so all the rich unionists drew an easy breath and kept their necks in the noose. However, there will be a lot of American Christians who are not rich but have free minds and souls who will object to, and repudiate, this *laissez-faire* translation, which lets communism do as it pleases with the new Bible.

The passage in Acts 4:32-37 has similar treatment, favorable to the communal idea, though without such violent handling of the Greek this time. One of the main defects is that they translate imperfect tenses (which indicate something begun, in process, or intermittently happening) as if they were aorists, definite, once-for-all occurrences, embracing all life in the thing described. That gives a false impression. Men who know so much Greek might have given the facts here. It avoids this tone of finality just to say. "The heart and soul of the multitude of believers continued to be one (so linking this passage with the previous one); and not even one (man) was saying (would say) that anything of his possessions was his alone (his own), but all things were, for them, common." That can be fully expressed in a large stewardship, a great brotherly love, a sympathetic unity of fervent devotion to common ends. It is all set in its apostolic clarity by Peter himself: "While it (the land) remained unsold, did it not remain your own? And after it was sold, was it not at your disposal," or, to give the Greek: "While it remained (unsold) did it not remain thine (for thee), and, having been sold, did it not fundamentally continue in thine own authority?" The command "Thou shalt not steal" is not a greater declaration of the rights of private property. But besides the charges against the RSV of erroneous translation, tampering with the text or criminal silence as to variant texts, and omission of words or evident meanings, this translation, of course, is open to the charges, later studied, of *overtranslation* of the phrases favorable to communism, and *undertranslation* of language that makes impossible the communist version of things.

This second passage makes crystal clear where it was that the givers had "all common things in one place." It was at the apostles' feet, in the public giving, and under their administration until the deacons were appointed. These 3,000 baptisms, and successive ones in great numbers, included a lot of widows of those Jews who, from foreign colonies, had come to Jerusalem to die, *and had died,* and their widows came in for their daily succor from this common fund. A common stewardship and church treasury, but no communism, is all Luke's Greek affirms.

FIRMAMENT

The first thing I remember learning in Hebrew was that the Hebrew word translated "firmament," in Genesis 1:6, and other passages, does not mean that, and does mean *expanse.* Even Moffatt is fair enough to render it *"vault"* in Genesis 1, and "the sky" in Psalm 19:1. The Basic Bible shows the RSV obsession by translating Genesis 1:6 as "the solid arch." The new million-dollar commentary, which is part of this setup to conquer faith with confusion, gives its idea of "firmament" as "a solid substance," identified as "flat earth, mountains around the rim, dome of firmament resting on them as pillars, windows in it, water came through them as rain" summing up, vol. I, p. 472. People who get the consent of their minds to use that kind of a commentary will like this kind of a Bible. But let them not complain when they find their souls sick with a moral and spiritual leukemia. You can't trifle with truth and remain true. *Expanse* is just the picture that science now gives of the vast reaches of the universe, and it is what the Hebrew of Moses also says.

WHO WAS IT THAT FIRST TRUSTED IN CHRIST?

The RSV has wrecked the structure of Paul's great sentence about all the work of the Trinity in salvation, in Ephesians I (see other study), so it leaves rather misty the contrast between Jewish believers and Gentile believers, in verses 12 and 13. The King James Version at least kept the contrast clear: "we . . . who first trusted in Christ, in whom ye also trusted." That wanders off and is lost in the woods of the RSV translation. But the translation both versions give, *"first* trusted," seems to me unhappy. Who are these "first believers"? If it were clear that the Jew, all the way back through his history, who believed *formerly* (says the Greek), had been justified by his faith, as even Genesis affirmed of the believing Abraham, then the contrast with the Gentile gospel age would be clear. But will the reader not limit the application to Paul and the contemporary believers among the Jews? They were not the "first to trust" in the Christ. Abraham, David, Isaiah, and the holy seed of all ages "formerly trusted," and the Gentile believer becomes an *"also trusted"* group. Of course, the harmony of the two adjacent Pauline Epistles, Galatians and Ephesians, will seem a motive for the lifting of eyebrows to modernist university circles, eager, as shown elsewhere, for disharmony in the Word of God. But "first" is wrong, to begin with. And it can easily leave an inaccurate and an anti-Pauline idea, in the sense in which the unsophisticated reader will probably take the language. Why not accurately translate the Greek?

JOHN 18:37 AND PARALLELS

"You say" or "Thou sayest that I am a king" is just plain nonsense. That is crude literalism. The Greek has the sense of our slang: "you said it," meaning "yes." The translators know this. Why do they cling to an old KJ literalism rather than give the evident sense? It is an old idea of translating each word, rather than the total sense. The Berkeley version has "You say correctly that I am a king." And Phillips, far better, translates the real idea: "Indeed I am a king." This is undertranslation and both wrong and wrongheaded classifications that are discussed later on. In Luke 23:3, Phillips has "Yes, I am" *versus* the silly RSV, "You have said so"—he had not said so. Likewise in Mark 15:2 and Matthew 26:25 and 27:11. I confess, this naïveté by these university professors baffles me. You would think they were modest students in the first-year Greek class, translating a word at a time. See also Luke 22:70 for another case of the strange phenomenon, which Phillips renders "You are right; I am."

COMMON SIN AGAINST PREPOSITIONS

The RSV translates a Greek preposition just as it wants to, in a lot of passages, and not according to its meaning. It follows KJ in that, in Revelation 12:11. The Greek says: "And they themselves conquered him *because of* the blood of the Lamb and because of the word of the witness borne (of their testimony), and they loved not their life, right up to death." The ASV translates what is there, "because." But the RSV leaves off the emphasis: "they themselves" did the conquering. But their conquest was the effect; the blood and the testimony to it were the cause. The RSV adds a third cause, by the word *for* which it pulled out of the air.

ALSO ROMANS 4:25

This same offense gives us, in KJ and RSV, "for our trespasses . . . for our justification," a repetition of the KJ *for*. The Greek says *because of*. The sentence is a climax of the doctrine of justification as seen in the cases of Abraham and David. *Because* is doubly fitting, looking back on justification centuries past. The men are in heaven. Christ died *because* of their sins, was raised *because* of their justification, already affirmed, already a reality. Of course, their blessing is immediately extended, in the apostle's reasoning, to us. But to a Lamb slain from the foundation of the world, in God's eternal purpose, all the future is the consummation of Calvary. It was *because of* the contemplated results that he endured the cross and despised the shame. Why not let Paul say what he wants to say rather than force upon him the RSV ideas? "Who was handed over on account of our misdeeds and was raised, by reason of our justification" (Berkeley).

THE TRANSLATION THAT DOOMS US ALL

Here it is, the RSV aping the KJ: "He who commits sin is of the devil," "No one born of God commits sin," and "We know that anyone born of God does not sin" (I John 3:8, 9;

5:18). Do the translators have any hope of heaven? Do they leave the rest of us any? Now they are bound to know that this is false, by the testimony of every page of the Bible and by the universal testimony of holy men. It looks like more love of "disharmony in the Bible." Phillips freely translates the sense: "The man who lives a consistently good life is a good man. But the man whose life is habitually sinful is spiritually a son of the devil . . . The man who is really God's son does not practice sin . . .," but he forgets it all in the last passage: "the true child of God does not sin." It looks as if the translators are trying to make us all fall into that class of which John had already said (1:8,10) that they are self-deceived, have not the truth in them, but make God a liar and his Word is not in them. Such a translation is itself sin. John had already given warning not to leave that impression, in very stern language. Is this translation a present to the sinless perfectionist, as I Timothy 5:17 was to the Presbyterians, as Hebrews 6:6 is to the Methodists, as burial "into" death is to the sacramentalists, as baptize "with" is to the affusionists, as Romans 15:16 is to the sacerdotalists? Why not rather give the best present to the authors of the New Testament, and the Spirit, its Author, by letting their words mean what they wanted them to mean? Why revise King James and persist in its worst errors?

I Corinthians 11:6

Now we have a small present from the translators to those episcopal lords over womankind who force them to wear a covering on their heads, in order to be permitted in any church house, an outrage of trivial tyranny. The RSV is right in translating Paul, in Corinthians 11:6, "Let her wear a veil." That is what Paul said. That is the issue in Corinth. The *decent women* wore veils. The *hetaerae* (word in the dictionary) did not. A woman put herself in her place in the public eye by the presence or the absence of the veil. The Greek word describes the veil. It was not a covering *on the head*. It hung down in front of the face, the Greek preposition *down from* being a part of the very word. The RSV sometimes translates correctly, sometimes follows the errors of the KJ and the episcopal overlords who lay down laws in female millinery. There are "priests" on this committee.

Let us look at the facts. "Any man . . . with his head covered" (v. 4). Any justification for that? Not a bit. The Greek just has "any man having down from head," that is, having a veil hanging in front of his face, down from the forehead over the eyes. There is not a syllable about a "covering." That is just "priest" talk. Now the RSV attempts to teach Paul: "That is why a woman ought to have a veil on her head" (v. 10). The revisers confess in the margin that Paul didn't say that. The word is *authority,* and the veiling is the sign in the Orient of the man's authority over the woman. Here we have a preposition that might be *on.* Thayer, I believe, gives it various meanings, such as partial superposition, absolute superposition, or movement that aims at superposition. The case here would more likely indicate "partial superposition." A veil is *on* the head, as are spectacles, sideburns, whiskers, a goatee, or a double chin, I suppose. But the context must be respected. Then we read that "her hair is given to her for a covering." The Bible doesn't say that. It says a *mantle.* The Greek word means something thrown around one. Its first half is the preposition *around.* It is like a shawl or scarf. So a woman's long hair may hang to her waist. It is a lovely mantle. The translation is simply false, in v. 13, which says: "is it proper for a woman to pray to God with her head uncovered?" That is service to the priest, but a disservice to the Bible. Paul said: "with her head *unveiled.*" And so the RSV translators confess, for they translate it that way in verse 5. This confusion is amazing and utterly without any justification except the superstition of priests.

There are many, many other repetitions of KJ errors, throughout the RSV, such as writing the *Holy Spirit* in much of the Old Testament with a small *s,* as if we were translating a Jewish, not a Christian, Bible; such as substituting the covenant name of God—the KJ generally, and the RSV always, writing LORD—and a lot of other arbitrary and inaccurate translations, imbedded in what people are accustomed to in older versions. Much of this will be discussed under other headings. Those headings also apply to much here discussed.

CHAPTER SIX

ITS BANISHMENT OF MANY BIBLE WORDS, CHANNELS OF GOD'S REVELATION OF TRUTH

"NO DOCTRINE OF THE CHRISTIAN FAITH HAS BEEN AFFECTED by the revision," says Professor F. C. Grant (Introduction Booklet on the RSV New Testament, p. 42). That is a matter of opinion. To my mind, many of the most vital doctrines have been fearfully affected. Saying a thing is so doesn't make it so. Such an affirmation or such a denial must be judged by the facts assembled. To write *son* and *spirit,* instead of *Son* and *Spirit* affects doctrinal teaching, in the passages where this occurs, as to two persons of the Trinity, just as would the change of *Our Father* to our father. Doctrines are dependent on words for their literary revelation. Can you think of any way truth can be conveyed in writing except in words? What happens, then, when a lot of the key words of revelation are thrown overboard, some entirely, others to a large degree? In this study we shall see the utter abandonment of great key words of the Scripture, in which much of its most vital truth is expressed, and later we shall note other ways in which vital doctrines are altered, revoked, corrupted, confused, enlarged, or diminished. Speaking in the same booklet (p. 59) of the responsibilities of translators, Walter Russell Bowie says: "That responsibility in the first place is to truth."

"CONVERT" A BANISHED VERB

Two verbs are several times, and in great key Scriptures, translated *convert* and *be converted* in the New Testament —but not in the RSV. In it the translators utterly banished the verb *convert,* though by a strange inconsistency they preserve *conversion* once (Acts 15:3.) The Nelson revisers have banished from their Bible *being converted.* Older versions, and many just as modern, used the word *turn* for the translation when physical acts are concerned, but *convert* when the soul turns to God and the right-about-face is inward and spiritual. They certainly are two very different senses of the

50

verb and merit different translations. Other verbs obey this criterion. Why not the verb *convert*? *Turn* states a physical act. It might, in the process of time, be given great moral, revolutionary meaning. But it has not that meaning now, in itself. Here is a word that has been at the very forefront of conversion theology and evangelism. Now that is banished. We are given what very much looks like an anticonversion Bible.

The translators can hardly be unaware of the moral trends of their age. None are more aware. Professors Weigle and Craig are associated with the quarterly *Religion in Life*. In its first issue of this year (1953) is an article on "George Albert Coe: Revaluer of Values," a former teacher in Union Theological Seminary. Here are two or three revealing quotations: "In those days Methodist piety valued highly a conversion experience which could date the day and hour when one was 'saved,' and which attached much importance to the 'assurance' that one had been pardoned and 'accepted' of God." Sneering reference is made to "revival showers." ". . . he resolved never again to seek the internal witness of the Spirit." The article explains "Coe's virulent antipathy toward traditional religion" and attributes it principally to "his unsuccessful effort to achieve the standard form of mystical conversion experience." The article traces his advance in collectivism to a point "where there could be no *I* apart from the *Thou*." "In particular Dr. Coe deplored Protestantism's revived interest in human depravity." "Revaluing values once more, he came to the conclusion that we must look 'to the proletariat' for redemption from our capitalist enslavement." He speaks of "this Marxian religious perspective" and comes to this conclusion: "It was a long road that began with Methodist pietism and ended with Marxian pessimism, but Dr. Coe traversed it with a mental intrepidity that few Americans of his generation could match. Lowell's exhortation to keep open 'the soul's east window of divine surprise' found supreme fulfillment in this valiant revaluer of values." This current "revaluing of values" has banished the verb *convert* from our Bible. The above are spoken of, in the article referred to, as Coe's "basal contributions to American religious thought." We recognize them in the new Bible. Please keep in mind this "virulent antipathy." This attitude we shall see in "the hatred of gospel harmony" in one of the further studies of this group.

See how this works out. Instead of "Except ye become converted, and become as little children, ye shall not enter into the kingdom of heaven," we have "unless you turn and become as little children." Now read it without the verb *turn*. "Unless you . . . become as little children" has lost absolutely nothing by omitting the meaningless word *turn* in that connection. This is a major assault on the gospel by an anti-evangelical pyschology, cocksure of itself in proud university circles.

REMISSION

Nine times we read in our King James Version of the "remission of sins." But the word is banished from the new Bible. No converting experience for man; no remission from God. "Remission of sins," for our translators, is taboo. Thayer gives this definition: "forgiveness, pardon of sins (properly, *the letting them go, as if they had not been committed*), remission of their penalty." Now that has been a part of our Christianity for centuries. Is it suddenly to be banished, as it were, by an all-powerful politburo? There is a vast difference between the forgiveness of sins and the remission of sins, in many cases. Forgiveness, for example, for the faithful child of God, may have to do merely with the renewing of fellowship, interrupted by the offense of sin, or the initiation of such fellowship for the forgiven sinner who for the first time enters into it. That is one thing. It is quite another thing to cancel the whole record and all its effects from consideration by divine justice, just as if the sins had never existed. This comes into view in the great experience of conversion, now also banished from the new Bible. Remission of sins links up with the great once-for-all aspects of salvation. It solves the sin problem in its judicial and eternal aspects. The modernist does not believe in those aspects. So he shut out of his new Bible the remission of sins. Only subjectivism is left to salvation. In many Scriptures, however, there is a finality about the divine decision that inevitably means far more than a decision about the fellowship involved. It is a judicial cancellation, not a fatherly forbearance and yearning alone. This is based on that. Think of Hebrews 10:18; "Now where *remission* of these is, there is no more offering for sin." In such contexts, a stronger translation than *forgiveness* is welcome, to give this eternal, final tone. The KJ translators might even have added Colossians 1:14 to the verses having *remission* in the translation; for there *remission* is the equivalent of the whole "redemption"—"redemption (through his blood)" the Berkeley Version has. The RSV never even notices the Textus Receptus reading here, though so eager, at times, to put in the margin trifling variants, when they detract from the critical text. In the new Bible, instead of the canceling of our sins, according to this great doctrine, we merely have the arbitrary cancellation of the word that sets forth the doctrine.

PROPITIATION

The banishment of this great gospel word is another attack on the objective aspects of redemption. Paul represents the Lord Jesus, set forth on Calvary in his blood, as a propitiation, and declares it available through faith. Then he shows the bearing of this on salvation of the saints who lived before Christ. And he gives this blessed declaration of the divine purpose in it all: "that he might be just and the justifier of him which believeth in Jesus" (Rom. 3:25,26). That is the language of the temple sacrifices, and has a similar meaning. It joins the gospel of the Old Testament figurative ritual with the clear testimony of Paul's greatest literary exposition of his gospel, to the Romans. It is not easy for a just judge to forgive. The whole Bible witnesses to the objective need and the value before God of substitution by a sin-bearing sacrifice. It is folly and gross irreverence to try to make this aspect of divine justice degenerate into the false conception that God had to be made willing to save. God, out of his eternal willingness and the necessities of his universe as a reign of law in the moral realm, always felt the love that planned Calvary and accepted it, from the foundation of the world, as having atoning value, and so acted in view of its timeless meaning. All the Bible is eloquent with tribute to the eternal

Father's love. He planned, prophesied, and executed all the sacrifice of the Son, to make possible a just remission of sins. Yet now, for the new Bible readers, both the propitiation of Christ and its remission of sins are gone. And that majestic purpose, "that he might be just and the justifier of him which believeth in Jesus," is queered, too, in the new Bible. It is watered down into a mere accessory statement: "it was to prove that he himself is righteous and that he justifies him who has faith in Jesus." That is a false translation, guts the gospel. It may be said that "expiation," the word used instead of what the Greek means, has a similar idea. Maybe so. But it may take a generation or two for it to soak in on the popular mind. And you never know what any word means to a modernist who cares to twist it. Here, for example, is an exceedingly popular new book on *What the Jews Believe,* by Rabbi Philip S. Bernstein. It says: "Consequently, atonement must include not only *rapprochement* with God but also expiation toward our fellowmen. . . Acts of penitential restitution can alone clear the way for God's grace. The rabbis go beyond this and say: 'Whoever has a sin to confess and is ashamed to do so, let him go and do a good deed and he will find forgiveness.' . . . He who recognizes his sin has already begun to loosen its hold on him. Then, where possible, there must be expiation, restitution" (pp. 29,33). Now I notice that we have this word *expiation* in the RSV, in II Samuel 21:3, in the sense of restitution, in place of the KJ *atonement.* That looks exactly like "what the Jews believe." Of course, this is not Orthodox Judaism. The minds of modernists meet, whether Jew or Gentile. Rabbi Bernstein says: "Even God himself prays:

> *May my mercy conquer my wrath*
> *So that I may treat my children with love"* (p. 34).

The Father of our Lord Jesus prays no prayer. He need not persuade himself, for his love is eternal; he planned the incarnation, the redemption on Calvary, the gospel. His love made it possible, by means of Calvary, to be just and justify the believing sinner.

Not for a moment would I attribute to these translators the learned rabbi's ideas. I am merely showing that the word they fell upon in the place of Paul's word, so long in our gospel in English as *propitiation,* is widely used in a meaningless sense, so far as the ideas of Romans 3 are concerned. Theirs is not an unpremeditated offense. I shall show elsewhere that the boast was made, in Union Seminary, this version's "home of the soul," that the new Bible was going to be so translated that it would do away with the Godward effects of the death of Christ, in New Testament language. Banishing these great words of the gospel has woefully contributed to that unholy end.

CALVARY

Professor Craig boasts that the RSV has banished "Calvary" from the New Testament. Doubtful honor. I always remind my students: "You are not Adam." Someone might well have said to these translators that they are not Adams, at the beginning of all translations. Some translations have created the English geographical names of sacred places. Calvary is now the English name of the place of the crucifixion. "In Luke 23:33, the 1611 Bible kept the word 'Calvary' which had been used since Tyndale for the place which is called a Skull" (Introduction booklet on the New Testament, p. 18). Tyndale died four centuries ago. If Calvary has been the English name of that lonely hill that long, these new translators will never be able to banish it. Did it occur to you, gentle reader, that these translators seem to be men who never sing? Have they never sung about Calvary? The Berkeley Version puts the word in parentheses, by the translation. The ASV says in the margin: "According to the Latin, *Calvary,* which has the same meaning." Singing millions will veto the RSV's banishment of Calvary and keep right on singing:

> *Mercy there was great and grace was free,*
> *Pardon there was multiplied to me;*
> *There my burdened soul found liberty—*
> *At Calvary.*

ADOPTION

This is a sore word for modernists. If all men, by nature,

are the children of God, in any other sense than being created in his image, then how can they be adopted into his family? That, of course, is another judicial—"forensic," if I may use a hated and blessed word—word. It is vinegar in the nostrils of those who believe only in a subjective salvation, if any. Now the word *adoption* is found only five times in true translations of the New Testament. But in the new Bible the word has been banished from a majority of the passages where it occurs in the Greek, and it has been queered, as far as possible, in the substitute translation. (See Rom. 8:15, 23; 9:4; Gal. 4:5; Eph. 1:5.) Yet John Calvin made this one of the major truths he bore witness to as his hope, in his last will and testament.

IMPUTE

The doctrine of imputed righteousness, from Romans 4; II Corinthians 5:19; James 2:23, has fortified faith in the atoning Savior for centuries. It is also taboo in the RSV New Testament. But the Psalms were translated by a Canadian, and the Old Testament thwarted the New. What do we find in Psalm 32:2 but this blessed wording of grace: "Blessed is he whose transgression is forgiven, whose sin is covered. Blessed is the man to whom the Lord imputes no iniquity." Marvel of marvels. But, though they failed to banish the word there, they fell on it in their New Testament and exiled it with a vengeance. But the Old Testament comes out six years later and, lo, *impute* enters the back door of the New Bible and takes its place in the servants' quarters. Welcome, servant of Jehovah.

ABIDE

Again it would seem these translators don't sing. They delight in smiting Christian hymnology. They seem to have a deep hostility for the word *abide,* eliminated from our Bible many, many times, in the RSV. Ten Greek verbs were translated *"abide,"* one of them fifty-five times, in the New Testament of our homes and bosoms. But now the word is banished from such Scriptures as Luke 24:29; John 3:36; 8:35; 12:34; 14:16; II Timothy 2:13; Hebrews 7:3; and others, though retained in John 15 and I John 2. So often the mere physical sense of *remain* is all that remains. Are we to sing: "Remain with me, fast falls the eventide"?

GRACES

One of the Bible senses of the word *grace* describes the fruit of the Spirit as graces, gifts from him for use in the Christian life. Yet that is banished from the new Bible, in places. We read in II Corinthians 8:6, 7 of "gracious work" and in 9:8 of "every blessing," in place of *this grace also,* and *every grace.* To turn a *grace* into a "work" is the evil deed of a bad translator, and *every grace* in the Christian life is certainly not the same as "every blessing." There is thus a vast amount of tampering with the fundamental meaning of Christian words in this new Bible.

CONFESS

It seems to me utterly meaningless to change Matthew 10:32 to "So every one who acknowledges me before men, I also will acknowledge . . .," and so in Luke 12:8. Now the same Greek verb, in Romans 14:11, is translated, "every tongue shall give praise to God"; but in Philippians 2:11, "every tongue confess." Both passages are cited in the margin as quoting Isaiah 45:23, which is translated, however, "To me . . . every tongue shall swear." How does one *swear to* a superior being? Once more, as so often, the Old Testament committee contradicted the New, whose translators contradicted each other. *Confess* is banished also from the wording of Romans 15:9.

REWARDS

This is a great and blessed doctrine, but is frequently banished from the new Bible. King James translates one Greek word *reward* twenty-four times, and *hire* three times. The root idea is payment made, whatever the motive, whether salary, daily wage, premium, price, or reward. In this case, it is a voluntary tribute to the excellence of fidelity shown, or gratitude for services rendered. We are saved by grace, through faith. Then our salvation begins. We are rewarded for fidelity, after salvation has come to its fruition in heaven. When our Lord returns he will reward his redeemed according to their works. The word *reward* is retained in Matthew 5:12, 46; 6:1, 5, 16, and other verses, but it has been banished from I Corinthians 3:8. And though it is retained in precious passages, it disappears from the key Scripture of the doctrine in Revelation 22:12, which becomes "Behold I am coming soon, bringing my recompense, to repay every one for what he has done." It sounds like payday, a *quid pro quo* exchange in which we get value received in heaven for merit shown here on earth. How different it should read: "And behold, my reward is with me to give every man according as his work shall be." The new translation is sheer trust in human merit and activity, paid off in eternity. Often this version has these mixed translations, contradictory and mutually annihilating the respective doctrines involved. It is a major tragedy to close out the Bible with such a terrible translation as that, denying the whole gospel that so often went before.

SANHEDRIN

This is the great Jewish supreme court and senate. It is banished from the RSV, following the example of the KJ again. But it is retained even in the Basic Bible, at the cost of using another word, because it is essential as the name of an institution. There is no more excuse for calling the Jewish Sanhedrin merely "the council" than there is for calling the United States Senate that. The great, historic body is as much entitled to its name as you are to your name, or I to mine.

HADES

This word is banished from the translation of that key promise of our Lord, rendered merely "the powers of death shall not prevail against it." This is not translation. It tampers with the most important of all Scriptures in the meeting ground between Catholics and Protestants. Why have *Hades* everywhere else, if the word is incomprehensible, and then "liquidate" it here?

EARNEST

Next in the list of the banished is the noun *earnest*. It is a good word and not at all obsolete, according to the dictionary. But it is banished from the doctrine of the Holy Spirit, in which it played a notable part. An "earnest" is a partial payment, made in advance, sealing a contract to pay the whole. We receive now the Holy Spirit, a present "earnest", which both gives us in him, in advance, part of our heavenly inheritance, and seals the eternal covenant of grace. The Spirit, not any sacrament, is the seal of our covenant relation with God, and is the down payment of the spiritual riches promised us in salvation. In the place of this meaningful doctrinal word, arbitrarily banished from the new Bible vocabulary, we have only the word *guarantee,* in II Corinthians 1:22; 5:5, and Ephesians 1:14. Something like the theft of a jewel has been perpetrated. Its removal from the possession of the heirs of salvation, to whom it belongs, is a sin against them and against the Holy Spirit, whose revelation of himself is thereby impoverished.

WINE

Look at the mistranslation of Titus 2:3, *slaves to drink.* That would be an alcoholic, in a hopeless state, wouldn't it? Hardly a peril to saintly old women. That is a fearful overtranslation. Paul said: "not given to much wine" (KJ); "not over-fond of wine" (Phillips); "not given to taking much wine" (Basic); "not enslaved to much wine" (ASV). The slavery is in the verb. *Given* is an undertranslation. But the peril is wine. A lot of modern sociologists, for whom the supreme sin is ownership of private property, would scorn such bourgeois ethics. Paul knew women and wine. He barred from good women that pitiful slavery that wine produces in its victims. This isn't something you may leave to Alcoholics Anonymous. It is put up to the minister as morals for the weaker sex, the stronger one, too, and to the pastor of both. The minister, as example, is not to be one who "stays by wine" (1:7), also overtranslated by the word *drunkard.* Now look at the counsel for all, in the great Roman Epistle: "It is well to eat no meat and to drink no wine, no, to do nothing that would make your brother stumble" (Berkeley). Why is the Berkeley so positive, so strong? Because these are aorist tenses of the verbs. It is good not to drink wine. Period. Not to begin drinking it. It is not the present tense of only prohibition of continued drinking. Notice the cunning with which, in this antiprohibition version, the idea is watered down: "It is *right* not to eat meat or drink wine," and that would permit us to say "It is right to eat and drink" under the contrary circumstances. These translators well know that that adjective does not mean "right." How colorless and insipid! So it is not just the episcopal tipplers that Paul warned against wine. Then, too, the mistranslation of Ephesians 5:18 blots out the Bible's clear witness against wine as a beverage: "Be not drunk on wine, in which is debauchery." Ernest Gordon, in *Notes from a Layman's Greek Testament,* notes that the word *which* must agree grammatically with *wine*—"wine, in which is excess," "incorrigibleness" (Berkeley). The Jews drank wine, but mixed with water. The RSV waters down the Bible's witness, instead. Various passages simply banish the word *wine,* but not the wine. But even in this Bible it still stands written: "Do not look at wine when it is red" (Prov. 23:31). A new version cannot change New Testament morals.

VIRGIN

This sore subject so centers attention on the virgin birth of our Lord that many minor offenses, caused by prejudice against the word *virgin,* are overlooked. Take Acts 21:9. "Philip the evangelist . . . had four unmarried daughters, who prophesied." Luke did not say that. He said more: they were virgins. But the RSV translators banish that word, where they can do it without its being noticed, as the good housewife banishes cockroaches. Yet they are inconsistent, retaining the word when the NT cites Isaiah's great prophecy, but not in translating the prophecy. Banished is the classical parable title, "The Ten Virgins." When the next generation of students reads that in literature, they won't know what the author is talking about, provided this version also banishes the "virgin" versions. Inconsistent? Yes. They keep the abstract noun *virginity* (Luke 2:36). And they show what they think the

word means when they use it of men. There they translate it
"chaste" (Rev. 14:4). Well, if it means "unmarried," plus
"chaste," isn't that *virgin?* II Corinthians 11:2 shows how
hardheaded this fixed idea is. There they have rendered the
word "bride." The whole emphasis of Paul is on the tempted,
but unseduced, virginity of the Corinthian church. It is hardly
that he is taking John the Baptist's place in a spiritual wedding
as best man, "the friend of the bridegroom." Haven't the
translators rather rushed things, confusing the betrothal and
the wedding? They certainly overtranslated the word, in any
case, out of stark prejudice, trying to banish a great word of
revelation. The Psalms translator, where nothing is at stake,
gives us the phrase "her virgin companions" (Psalm 45:14).
While there was no celibacy in either Judaism or Christianity,
it seems to me there must have been a gentle connotation of
dedication to a career, on a voluntary basis, when Luke comments on a great evangelist's daughters, four of them, being
"virgins," in their dedication to their prophesying. But you
can't say that, brother Luke, not in the RSV. That is a banished word, so far as the RSV translators dared.

ONLY BEGOTTEN

This time the banishing has been eager. The word *begat*
is so sexual. We must not have it in our Bible, no matter what
the Bible itself says about it. So out it goes. And even John
3:16 is a bit mutilated, to speed the banishing process. One
of the beloved titles of the Son of God is lost in the shuffle. To
me, he is not just "a son of God" (Mark 15:39). His sonship
is set off from ours, in part, by his very title, *only begotten.*
Yet, strangely, the antimessianic campaign against Psalm 2
has left the objectionable phrase "today have I begotten
you." No earthly father ever could say that to his child. But
the eternal Father said that and far more to Lord Messiah.
Now the translators are great on fine points. They raise the
doubt as to that being the real meaning of the word, and
plump for *only.* Yet they know that the word *only,* in Greek
as in English, is a very common word, and not a compound
word. We have the simple word *only* forty-seven times in the
New Testament. Once more, in John 3:16, would have made

an even four dozen. But John did not want to say the simple word *only*. Why will the translators force him to? We have, in Greek, another compound word with *only*—*only-eyed, one-eyed*. Would they translate that *only?* No, they wouldn't dare. How dare they do this, then, to Jesus? Abbott-Smith says that the word is used in LXX and NT of both sons and daughters. The translators have never cared to say "only begotten daughter," "only begotten child" (Luke 8:42; 9:38). But I have no doubt that it is what the Jewish parents thought, with deep tenderness.

TRUTH

The translation of I Corinthians 13, whose English Dorothy Thompson so searchingly criticized as inferior, in *The Woman's Home Companion,* has this bit of disloyalty to the truth. It banishes the term. *Love rejoiceth in the truth,* Paul said, and Phillips not only preserves the word but gives it a capital letter, "it is glad with all good men when Truth prevails." "It sides happily with truth" (Berkeley). That is one of the notable qualities of genuine Christian love which distinguishes it from the counterfeit love of self-seeking sentimentality that is ready to run off with a multitude to do evil. Paul agrees with Jesus that love keeps both his words and his commandments, especially. *Speaking the truth in love* certainly is never less than love of the truth, and witness to it with joy. Paul did not say "love . . . rejoices in the right." That falsifies the Scripture.

A similar double prejudice is shown in II Corinthians 6:7. Paul is enumerating his spiritual assets in the witness he bears to the public. One of them is *the word of the truth.* That has been banished and in its place has been put "truthful speech." As a translation, that is not truthful speech. How often this Bible flees from the great objective realities to the subjectivism so precious to modernists. The language is again manipulated, in Ephesians 5:9, to get rid of the word *truth.*

Elsewhere a study is made of the mania of these translators for weakening or changing the testimony of the original by wrecking the grammatical structure. The frequency with which such liberties are taken with the Word of God is simply amazing. In III John 8 a peculiar case of this is seen, very untrue to the Greek. There the apostle wrote "fellow-helpers to the truth"; even Moffatt has "allies to the Truth," and Phillips has "co-operating with the Truth". The RSV puts it "fellow-workers in the truth." *Fellow-workers* or *co-operators* is a justified change, but there is no "in" in the Greek and there is a "with" in the nearby compound Greek word, very naturally understood with the noun. And this thought is companionable with both these short Epistles of John and the mental attitudes he shows in them. Very different is the avowed attitude of the RSV Committee, in its defense. Professor W. A. Irwin writes in *The Review and Expositor*, July, 1953: "Scholarship has no dogmas and no absolutes, save only the finality of truth, which in its absolute form is forever unattainable." That doesn't sound like one who said: "To this end was I born, and for this cause came I into the world, that I should bear witness to the truth." He was the Absolute, the Truth, and his witness was, and is, absolutely true. The professor's attitude reminds us of those "silly women" whom Paul describes as "ever learning, and never able to come to the knowledge of the truth." Pitiful state. The Bible has no sympathy with it at all. And nobody ought to give its authors, and its Author, a sort of brain-washing to try to bring them to the attitude of said silly women.

SEED

There is a lot of twisting and turning in trying to find some way to translate this seminal word of revelation and yet banish it from the translation. "The seed of the woman," in the proto-evangel, keeps the word (Gen. 3:15). From there on the mental gymnastics begin, to say it and not to say it. Any user of the RSV must feel an utter frustration in trying to follow the unity of messianic prophecy and its progressive revelation in the Scriptures. Here we are in a day of stark nakedness on the beaches, which is now transferred to home and streets. Never was there a time of such utter frankness of speech about all private matters of the world of youth. Courses are given in our universities concerning things only doctors used to talk about in private. Films and magazine

articles blazon abroad the most intimate sex matters. Nothing
is held back in conversation. And behold. A lot of university
professors, in translating the Bible, the frankest of all books,
act like a set of Victorian old maids and, with eyes averted,
banish from the Bible some of its key words of revelation,
because of what Dorothy Thompson calls their "prissiness."
"Radio and television can shout and sing the "Ave Maria,"
with its incessant tribute to "the fruit of thy womb," but in
the RSV the very God of heaven cannot give the simplest
revelation about the holy Seed of his promise. Nor can we
who believe any longer "remember Christ Jesus, of the *seed*
of David." That shocks our old-maidish translators beyond
endurance. But I still wonder why they could use the word
in Genesis 3:15, if they cannot bear it in the rest of the Bible.
Is it all right to be immodest, if it only occurs one time? Professor Millar Burrows says (Introduction booklet on NT, p.
29): "The word 'seed' becomes in our revision 'children'
(Mark 12:19-22 and parallels, Rom. 9:29), 'offspring' (Gal.
3:16,19,29; Rev. 12:17), 'descendants' (John 8:33,37; Rom.
4:13,16,18;9:7-8;11:1; II Cor. 11:22; Heb. 2:16), or 'posterity' (Luke 1:55; Acts 7:5-6;13:23; Heb. 11:18); elsewhere, as the context allows, it is paraphrased by a different
construction (Rom. 1:3; II Tim. 2:8), or omitted (Heb. 11:
14), or retained (I Pet. 1:23)." Of course, this squeamish
makeshift for a translation utterly wrecks all sense of many
of these passages. What is given as the translation is *not* the
translation and either makes no sense or a false sense. If words
could have a Siberia, the RSV must have an icy habitat to
which Bible words have been banished, and with sheer arbitrariness. And the version is in the "Authorized" succession,
so you have no option but to abandon great Bible words of
truth or abandon the RSV.

FORNICATION

It is typical of "a wicked and adulterous generation"—
and that describes all generations—that the very wickedness
it glories in, in practice, it seeks to make unmentionable in
preaching, or even conversation of a moral nature. So we

find a queer squirming and twisting as to the matter of the use or nonuse of the word above.

Fifty-five times, the noun and verb that state this sin occur in the New Testament. Yet the translators play hide-and-seek with its translation or banish it from their Bible. We read of "fornication" in Revelation 21:8;22:15. Elsewhere, such sinners are just "immoral." Now there is a vast lot of "immorality" that is not fornication. Such old-maidish subterfuges are a flight from reason and truth, and about elemental morality. I know that a lot of men utterly deprecate any preaching about such sins today, for to their minds, sympathetic with communism, the only sin is to be the owner of property, an obstruction in the way of the coming of the *own-all, be-all, do-all state.* Like Judas, they will go to their own place. But the Christian conscience will not abdicate. It will demand that we at least stand back and let God condemn fornication, and not a mere vague and nameless "immorality." In the RSV, the word that means fornication, every time, wobbles back and forth between translations and refusals to translate: "unchastity" in Matthew 5:32; "fornication" in Matthew 15:19; "immorality" in I Corinthians 5:1; "impure passion" in Revelation 14:8. Each of these translations takes its turn. How can a group of men retain their self-respect and be so fickle and unstable in their thinking and speech?

FAITHFUL

We can welcome the idea that sometimes, in either Greek thought or English, *faithful* may involve being "full of faith." However, I do not favor banishing the word when it has its normal meaning. The Greek word occurs sixty-eight times in the New Testament, and is rendered "faithful" fifty-three times in the KJ. Of course that version was far from infallible. But the word does ordinarily indicate fidelity to an objective norm, rather than to arbitrary subjectivism. We see in it fidelity, imposed by responsibility to another, especially to God. In the RSV, we no longer have the requirement that a "steward be found faithful." It is enough that he be found "trustworthy" (I Cor. 4:2;7:25). There is a vast difference. *Trustworthiness* reflects your own judgment of another's worth. *Faithfulness* would seem to be his fidelity, whether others knew about it or not. There is perhaps more gain than loss in the total translation of this word in the RSV, but what other goal can we have but that a version be wholly "faithful"?

GOSPEL

The Greek word for evangelize often means "preach the gospel," and it is so translated in the RSV in many cases. In KJ it is so translated forty-eight out of fifty-three occurrences. The new Bible banished the word *gospel* from the following passages:

1. The great word of Jesus to John the Baptist, giving the credentials of his Messiahship: "the poor have the gospel preached to them" (Matt. 11:5). That is repudiated—remember, this is a *revision,* not a new venture, unrelated to previous versions—and we merely have a vague "good news" preached to the poor. Of course, again that is pleasing to the communist sympathizers, who hold out numberless promises to the poor, till they get in power. To men who do not want their Bible twisted to suit atheists and their sympathizers, the banishment of the gospel from identifying our Lord's credentials is a terrible loss. Just what was this "good news" the messengers of the Baptist heard Jesus preaching to the poor? Revolution against Rome? Dr. Latourette recently said that "preaching the gospel to the poor" is the distinctive mark of Baptists. Now it is no longer in the Bible.

2. Luke 4:18 is another key passage, our Lord's program message to his home people in Nazareth. Again we see the gospel banished by the RSV translators and mere "good news" left.

3. Paul is robbed of the gospel in Romans 10:15. Yet the language is cited from Isaiah 52:7, where the good news is not revolution or totalitarian propaganda but "peace" and "salvation." Isn't that gospel?

4. Hebrews 4:2,6, perhaps because it establishes a parallel between an Old Testament "rest" and our "rest" of faith in Christ. Let it offend whom it will, still the New Testament finds all its gospel in the Old Testament. And it is offensive

for men who are unbelievers of that fact to exercise the authority of unbelief on great passages of faith.

5. Nor is Peter permitted to affirm that he had preached the gospel to his readers (I Pet. 1:12,25). Gospel is banished. He just told them good news, since it is definitely identified with Old Testament gospel.

But when we come to I Peter 4:6, there *gospel* comes right back into vogue. This is the passage about "the gospel" being preached to the dead. There let it stand. That might serve the cause of Disharmony in the Bible. So let it stand: *gospel,* for the dead.

Now why in the world should there be this hostility to the gospel, banishing it from such key Scriptures? It is outrageous. Luke also uses this word, preach the gospel, about John the Baptist (Luke 3:18). Is there any other gospel better than "the Lamb of God who taketh away the sins of the world" (John 1:29)? Or than repentance and faith (John 1:6; Acts 19:4)? But we must never be allowed to say, as Baptists, by the authority of the new Bible, that John preached the gospel. First thing you know, we might be confirmed in our doctrine that he gave all the apostles and thousands of others, including Apollos, "Christian" baptism. That would never do. So they take the gospel away from John. And just to make sure, take it away from Jesus too, in these key Scriptures. Leave both of them merely a vague "good news" about we know not what. No matter. They can thus uphold that silly fiction that everything Christian began at Pentecost. And so no one need go to the "Gospels" to look for the gospel.

There is also a change for the worse in a great Scripture that had better have been left alone. For some little verbal nicety, which has become an obsession, the RSV translators change some great Scripture that is the bedrock of an indescribably important doctrine. We had: "even so hath the Lord ordained that they which preach the gospel should live of the gospel" (I Cor. 9:14). This now becomes the awkward language of change for the love of change: "In the same way, the Lord commanded that those who proclaim the gospel should get their living by the gospel." Now what are you going to do with the current style which *proclaims* nothing? Just holds a mild conversation in the pulpit. Are they to be cut off from pastoral support? This is one of the worst translations of all. And once more, the mania against the word *beget* reduces I Corinthians 4:15 to this: "I became your father in Jesus Christ through the gospel." Instead of Paul's begetting them through the gospel, as he really said, lo and behold, they have merely made him a father in God. Alas for manias in the minds of translators.

INHERIT

Straight through the New Testament, sometimes, the RSV will faithfully translate a word, then banish it from some passage or passages as if it were poison, though the sense be evidently the same. So it is with the word *inherit*. It goes along with full value till we come to the Epistle to the Hebrews. Then, in 1:4,14 the word so often used is banished. There the translators jump to the verb *obtain*, then switch right back to *inherit* throughout the rest of the Bible. Strange.

COLLECTION

To please the advocates of Brethrenism or some such theory against collections, this word has been banished from I Corinthians 16:1. Now the word does not occur anywhere else but in this passage. Knocked out of here by prejudice, it is knocked out of the Bible, and from perhaps the most used verse in the Bible about church giving. What Paul said was *collections*. That is what he commanded in all the churches. And this inspired ecclesiology demands *collections,* by cooperation of the churches, as herein taught. Nor will they stop because the RSV translators made a present of this verse to opponents of Paul's doctrine. *Collections,* interprovincial, intercontinental, interracial collections, on the voluntary principles of co-operative life in the churches, systematic, prolonged, frequently added to—not mere offerings of the moment on Paul's arrival—these are the Pauline doctrine, not mere "contributions." Don't banish that vital word of revelation. You deal a deadly blow to Christian beneficence when you banish *collections*. And I speak from nearly half a century of watching and trying all kinds of measures and methods. Collections are exceptional, for extras. But they are there in the Bible and let no man cancel God's commands.

MEMBERS

Again we see a word accepted straight through the New Testament and then banished, just when it reaches the most important Scripture where it is due to appear, in I Corinthians 12:18-22. Then it becomes "organs," "part," and "parts of the body," and from there on goes right back to being "members" all the rest of the Bible. Strange.

SLAVES

This version is superior to many in giving, in some places, the word *slave or slaves* as it is in the Greek. There is a vast difference between *slave* and *servant,* and the facts ought to appear in the translation, either in the text or in a marginal note. It alleviates the contrast between those times and ours, if we know that in Matthew 18:23 the case is that of slaves. Naturally they could be sold for debt or treated as no hired servant could. What possible objection can there be to translating the facts? Doesn't everybody know that slavery was one of the evils of Bible times? Just so, in John 18:18, the abjectness of Peter's fall is seen in his companionship of slaves. Why not let the Bible say, *every time,* not just occasionally, its witness to the contemporary facts of life?

FLESH, CARNAL

Arbitrarily, unpardonably, frequently has the RSV substituted *body* for *flesh* and various adjectives for *carnal.* Ugly facts of human depravity and sin need the revealed vocabulary of their guilt and seriousness. Don't banish the vocabulary of evil. That doesn't get rid of the evil. We study some of these passages in other connections. One passage will illustrate both this term and *slaves*: "your earthly masters" (Eph. 6:5). The Greek has *your lords according to the flesh.* There is the contrast, between the lordship of Christ and the lordship that exists only according to the standards of the flesh. This both condemns slavery as a carnal regime and limits its sway to the physical. Translating the phrase as "earthly" loses the

suggestiveness of the comparison. The point is, the Christian
slave is free, in his inner being, *now* to have Christ as Lord.
It isn't a question of a fully comprehensive lordship of the
owner of the slave in this earthly regime or hope of a better
regime in eternity. Here and now the Christian slave is, in
the inner realm, though not in that of flesh, under the lordship
of Christ. Changing the sentence structure, abandoning the
connotation of the words, and banishing *slave* from the translation half the times it occurs (including the verb form once),
even in this passage, shows how slavish the RSV is to the KJ,
even at this point, and to the hesitations that cowed the KJ
translators and later ones. There is an unholy trinity: "the
world, the flesh and the devil," and you don't make moral
gains by denying the reality of the triple evil.

JEHOVAH—THE COMPLETELY BANISHED WORD

The most thorough and complete banishment of Bible
words to be found at all is the utter vanishing of the covenant
name of the God of Israel—Jehovah. To begin with, this is
one of the great boasts of the translators (p. vi of the Bible's
Preface). But in the text itself no trace of the word occurs.
It is a carefully planned and executed blackout of the covenant
Name.

Now the King James Version says: "I appeared unto
Abraham, unto Isaac, and unto Jacob, by the name of God
Almighty, but by my name JEHOVAH was I not known to
them" (Ex. 6:3). Psalm 83:18 says: "That men may know
that thou, whose name alone is JEHOVAH, art the Most
High over all the earth." And Isaiah sings: "Behold, God is
my salvation; I will trust, and not be afraid: for the LORD
JEHOVAH is my strength and my song; he also is become
my salvation" (12:2). And again, in 26:4, he sings: "in the
LORD JEHOVAH is everlasting strength."

Besides these, we have in KJ the compound names:
Jehovah-jireh (Jehovah will provide); Jehovah-nissi (Jehovah
is my banner); Jehovah-shalom (Jehovah is peace); Jehovah-
shammah (Jehovah is there); Jehovah-tsidkenu (Jehovah
is our righteousness). These are great doctrinal revelations
(Gen. 22:14; Ex. 17:15; Judg. 6:24; Ezek. 48:35; Jer. 23:6).

These translations, or their meanings, are given in the KJ text or in the margin, and in the abundant KJ helps in the study Bibles that are in general use. Then the KJ uses the device of *Lord* with small caps. Thus the user of the King James Version is not wholly robbed of the revelation of the covenant Name.

The ASV changed that. Its preface says: "The change first proposed (by the American revisers to the British Revision Committee, W. C. T.)—that which substitutes Jehovah for Lord and God (printed in small capitals)—is one which will be unwelcome to many, because of the frequency and familiarity of the terms displaced. But the American revisers, after a careful consideration, were brought to the unanimous conviction that a Jewish superstition, which regarded the Divine Name as too sacred to be uttered, ought no longer to dominate in the English or any other version of the Old Testament, as it fortunately does not in the numerous versions made by modern missionaries. This Memorial Name, explained in Ex. 3:14,15, and emphasized as such over and over in the original text of the Old Testament, designates God as the personal God, as the covenant God, the God of revelation, the Deliverer, the Friend of his people;—not the abstractly 'Eternal One' of many French translations, but the ever living Helper of those in trouble. This personal name, with its wealth of sacred associations, is now restored to the place in the sacred text to which it has an unquestionable claim."

Of this the OT Introduction booklet of the RSV Committee, page 24, says: "We dissent from their innovation in using Jehovah for the Divine Name." To return to the effort to translate the original an "innovation"? That the decision occasioned qualms of conscience is very evident, for we are informed that the decision had to be made three times, in 1930 (they started out to do this), in 1937, and in 1951, "on each occasion, after full discussion," by unanimous vote. Even Moffatt's last-minute copying of the French, "the Eternal," would have been better. But their banishment of the Name is total. Other versions at least gave some relief to the situation by some marginal information as to the original and its meaning.

Note how stubborn and obstinate is this blackout of the

Divine Name. In the key Scripture, Exodus 6:2, the RSV gives in the margin "El Shaddai" in explanation of the original of "God Almighty," but never a whisper of the vastly more important fact, in that context, of the original of the more important Name. It is an obsession. On page 58 there is this queer note: "The word LORD (last three letters small capitals) when spelt with capital letters, stands for the divine name YHWH, which is here connected with the verb *hayah, to be.*" That is both unpronounceable and meaningless.

Let us look now at the highbrow alternative, seen in the Basic Bible: "I am Yahweh" (Ex. 6:2,8); "Yahweh-yireh" (Gen. 22:14), with the transliteration of the Name but no translation of it, and so on. It might give our theological highbrows pause if they lived in Brazil. We have no letter *Y*, no *W* and no silent *H* in our alphabet now. So see what becomes of *Yahweh.* The *Y* becomes *I*, each *H* falls out, and the *W* becomes *V*. So the word is printed IAVE. Our theological professors who cannot bring themselves to pronounce the word *Jehovah,* of our plebeian English, would have to be content with IAVE. In nearly every other language there would probably be complications in this theological gobbledygook, if its use were attempted where the people could get at it. No. It is kept as a Star Chamber pronunciation. The name God gave himself to Israel has become, in English, Jehovah. "Ah, but that was not the way the Hebrews pronounced it," you will say. My reply is: Who cares? No other proper name we use is what the Hebrews said. They wouldn't recognize Joshua or Jesus or Mary or any other of our English names, so far as either spelling or pronunciation is concerned. Why on earth shall we suddenly become jittery because our spelling of a name, or its pronunciation, is not that of a language a long time dead? Who cares? And I would add: How do you know? As the great scholars of the ASV said: "A Jewish superstition" lost the pronunciation, from overreverence. How will you prove that you have recovered it from centuries of silence? You don't know it is Yahweh, any more than I know it is Jehovah.

The fact that the English word *Jehovah* is unlike the lost Hebrew word that it translates is true of virtually every other ancient name in our Bible. Who cares? Why get worked up over that? I notice four Greek ways of spelling *Moses* and none of them is our English word. What difference does that make? I notice *Maria, Mariam,* and *Miriam* as originals of *Mary.* Are we going to change the name of our Lord's mother on that account? Who cares? *James* is in Spanish *Santiago,* in Portuguese *Tiago,* in popular Brazilian speech *Jaime,* formerly *Jayme.* Who cares? It is *James* to us, with no apology, as it is their way with them, in just as great freedom.

The fact of the business is we have *Jehovah* looking us in the eye straight through our Bible. It went into the making of a lot of compound names. First and foremost is *Jesus,* which is the same as the older name *Joshua.* Every time you say *Jesus* you say *Jehovah.* Will the intellectuals tell us it must now be *Yahsus?* But the Greek ends in *sous.* Maybe it should be *Yahsous,* then. *Jesus* means "Jehovah is salvation." And *Joab* means "Jehovah is father." *Jochebed* means "Jehovah is glorious." *Joel* means "Jehovah is God" *John* means "Jehovah has been gracious." Now if *Jehovah* should begin with a *Y,* how did all those words happen to begin with a *J,* just like *Jehovah?* And where is any *Yah* in their spelling? Why go off at a tangent on the name *Jehovah* and keep to the main English highway, as far as all the names compounded with *Jehevah* are concerned? There is no sense to it. And the people haven't budged.

There is a reason why a lot of university professors feel as guilty as Judas Iscariot about this word *Jehovah.* Two currents of irreverent thought swept over the rationalist part of the nation. One came from the movement of rationalist criticism which split the Old Testament into the shattered shale of *J, E, D,* and *P* fragments, with maybe *H, K,* and *C* fragments of the fragments. It became the custom to call Jehovah a fictitious god of Israel, in a certain stage of nationalist evolution. All the professorial wrath was poured out upon him. One of the heads of the New Catholicism, which owns the new Bible, called him a "dirty bully." This sort of smart-aleck blasphemy gave a man a high rating among the "intellectuals." Then came pseudomissionaries who were more disciples of pagan Gandhi than of Christ and reduced the remains of this rationalist Christianity to pacifism. Along came Schweitzer, who used his missionary career to renew men's doubts as to whether Jesus ever existed or not. And both these irreverent currents poured all their wrath on "the old war-lord Jehovah." I heard, on two different furloughs, Northern-trained Southern preachers preach to students and warn them sneeringly against said "old war-lord Jehovah." The effect of all this near-atheism and brutish cynicism can be seen in the book *God and Man at Yale,* by William F. Buckley, Jr., if you want a contemporary picture.

Now, as I show elsewhere, this Bible is produced largely by men from the theological departments of an axis of Northern universities that have been cursed with this century-old blasphemy. You can understand how men who have lived in that environment, even if not guilty of this rationalism, would feel a longing to hide the Name of Israel's covenant-keeping God from university readers, fed on that kind of pabulum. (I may say, in justice, that the book just mentioned pays tribute to teachers from Yale's theological department, especially Professor Latourette, in helping withstand this evil propaganda. But it laments the smallness of their classes in the university proper.) There is a moral cowardice that comes from being in a theological department of an infidel university. There ought not to be a single man from any such environment on a committee of translators of the Bible for Bible-loving people in this country. Let the Bible be translated by its friends. They will never be ashamed of the revealed Name of the God and Father of our Lord Jesus Christ, for Jesus is Jehovah and all the opprobium cast upon Jehovah falls on Jesus. "I and the Father are one."

Now, of course, you have *Lord* as an Old Testament name of deity, which must go into the translation, in its own right. To have the same name, printed in a queer fashion, so that you could never quote such a Scripture on your typewriter or by pen, as the translation of another name of deity is a source of maximum confusion. Even a child will notice these two *lords,* Lord and LORD. How can his mother tell him the latter is for Jehovah, Yahweh, or Iavé, or what have you, if she doesn't know it from her Bible? Even a child will stumble up on such language as this and wonder: "the LORD your God" and "O Lord GOD." He will say: "Mama, what's the matter with my Bible? Here in Deuteronomy (3:21-24) it first spells

Lord with two sizes of capital letters and *God* with a capital
G and small letters. Then it turns around and does just the
opposite, spells *Lord* with only one capital letter and *God* with
all three capitals, of two sizes. Mama, what's happened to the
Bible?" Could she tell him? You can. You know that you had
Lord, in its own right, followed by *Jehovah;* so, to avoid saying Lord LORD, the small capitals were switched this time to
GOD, put in to save the situation in an emergency. The Bible-
to-be ought to find some better way than this, more sensible
and more reverent. And if it refuses to translate the sacred
Name, it ought at the very least to give full information in the
margin. Cut out a few conjectures and put in this major fact.
This blackout, a vindictive intolerance of God himself as revealed, is a scandal before the bar of the American conscience.

Sometimes God chastens his people with pagans. Just
when the infidel universities of this land thought they had
laughed out of court the very Name Jehovah, up surges that
plebeian and outrageous movement that glorifies the Name
as their name, "Jehovah's Witnesses." And they gather in
assemblies under the very shadow of Columbia University,
one hundred and twenty thousand strong. And they baptize
(real meaning of the word, too) over three thousand converts
to their Jehovah in one day, and next year over four thousand
in a day. And one of their lawyers goes before our august
Supreme Court and defies the Catholic judge on it to hold
back their liberties, and that judge votes for him. And with
considerable scholarship they get out their own New Testament and, lo and behold, they put Jehovah into the New Testament two or three hundred times. And then our curious
America says: "What's it all about? I bought a copy of the
new Bible. But I didn't find that word even in it. How come,
professor? Weren't you on that committee of translators?"
Then will the professor-translator have to confess: "We are
guilty of suppression of that Name. It ought to be there many
times. We banished it, from professorial pride and self-suffi-
ciency. And God has judged us with these pagan barbarians
and brought it back into the thought of all the people. We
ought not to have made that wrong and arbitrary decision.
The next Bible, I assure you, will not repeat our folly." God
said: "This is my name forever, and thus I am to be re-

membered throughout all generations" (Ex. 3:15). No. Not to the generation of readers of the RSV. But wait a minute. Enter Jehovah's Witnesses. He is remembered, in judgment if not in grace.

EPHESUS

Can you beat this? We have still, in the RSV, "The Letter of Paul to the Ephesians," yet no address, in its text, "to the saints that live in Ephesus" (Berkeley), "to the saints that are at Ephesus" (Basic), "to all faithful Christians at Ephesus (and other places where this letter is read)" paraphrases Phillips, and similar words in the ASV, and so on. This address, I say, has been dropped down to the margin and put on the same level with so much spurious stuff, all equally described by the set phrase, "Other ancient authorities read: *who are at Ephesus and faithful.*" This is what I call elsewhere "Delight in Disharmony of the Bible."

WORDS, THE WORD

Word itself is one of the most important words in the Bible. And there is a deliberate and constant effort to banish it from the RSV or diminish or confuse its meaning. Remember our praise of the RSV blows against modernism, especially in translating the modernist slogan, "The letter killeth," so as to show that it is legalism of which Paul there treats, the confidence in divine law and human morals to save men by their works. There is also the constant effort to confuse the figurative use of *Word,* as one of the names of Jesus, with the Word of God, in the sense of the content and meaning of the literary or oral revelations God has given us. It makes not a particle of difference whether you say or write *John* 3:16. Its meaning is the same, and the meaning, set forth by the words, is the Word of God we read in our Bibles and preach or witness to, in pulpit and private talk. In its simplest form, the Word is the words that compose the revelation, whether oral or written. The Ten Commandments were first spoken, then written. Either way, they are the ten words, set forth in all their God-given language. Note how Jesus identifies *Word* and *words.* The *Word* is the *words*: the *words* are the *Word.* Look at the identification: " . . . keep my words: the word which ye hear . . ." (John 14:24). "Remember the word" (John 15:20) —it is a whole sentence, given in quotation marks, but those words are "the word." In John 10:35, Jesus very definitely calls "the Scripture" he cites "the word of God." Yet only last week I heard a man solemnly affirm that such a thing is never done in the Bible. How can men say that? If I had said anything as patently false as that, I couldn't enjoy shaving for looking at the face of a guilty soul. Not only is the statement made in one verse, but straight through the Bible it is the whole point of view. What is Scripture but written words, so often called "the Word"? The Gospel of John has as definitely an expanding doctrine of the Word, as equaling the words, of God, as it has of the signs that progressively identified Jesus as the Son incarnate. "He whom God has sent utters the words of God" (John 3:34). Note the identification of "the word" and "the Scriptures" (John 5:38, 39). Note the affinity of belief of "his writings" (the Mosaic Scriptures) and "my words" (John 5:46,47). Hear Jesus say: "The words that I have spoken to you are spirit and are life," and Peter unconsciously echo his Master: "You have the words of eternal life" (John 6:63,68). "He who is of God heareth the words of God" (John 8:47). "The words . . . I do not speak on my own authority"; "if a man loves me, he will keep my word"; "he who does not love me does not keep my words" (John 14:10,23,24). "If my words abide in you . . ." (John 15:7). "I have given them the words which thou gavest me," Jesus says to the Father in prayer, and he had just said, "They have kept thy word." Everywhere the *Word* is the *words*: the *words* are the *Word*. And don't mouth an old modernist slogan about there being anything "mechanical" about inspiration of the Scripture, the written words. What is there in all life as far from being mechanical as a word?

Now I rejoice to see, in John's Gospel, that the RSV has been true, translating *word* where the original has that, when other versions put *saying,* or some other term. But in other parts of the New Testament that fidelity is not maintained. There seems to be a mania to banish the very term *word* as often as possible. You see that in Acts (the worst bit of translation in the RSV) 5:32;10:22;10:44 (where *words* and

the *Word* would again be identified, if words were translated);
11:14 (*words* being changed to *message*); 26:25 (where
words of truth and soberness is watered down to *the sober
truth*). See also 28:25 and elsewhere. "The Bible's doctrine
of itself," as Speer would phrase it, fares badly in the RSV,
for the Bible's doctrine of itself is its doctrine of its words,
the Word, the Scriptures (words written).

DOCTRINE

In Matthew 7:28, both *words* and *doctrine* are banished
from this vital comment on the Sermon on the Mount. There
are two Greek words translated *doctrine* in the New Testament. In the KJ version one is translated *doctrine* nineteen
times out of twenty-one; the other, twenty-nine times out of
thirty-one. Bear in mind the RSV translators' insistence that
theirs is not a new version but a revision. In the revision they
banished from their New Testament the word *doctrine* thirty-
four times. They have translated the two words as *lesson* once,
precepts once, *instruction* twice, *doctrine* fourteen times, and
teaching thirty-two times. One wonders why they left the word
at all. Evidently a sop thrown to Bible-loving Christians who
are not going to be led astray by this antidoctrinal carnival.

What do they put in the place of *doctrine*? Principally,
teaching. Of course, that can mean the act or art or career of
teaching or it can mean the content of the teaching—*doctrine*.
The whole version camps in this no man's land. Take, for
example, Acts 2:42. "And they devoted themselves to the
apostles' teaching and fellowship." Death loves a shining mark.
So when the RSV picks a Scripture to kill, it often picks one
of the most vital. The RSV translates this very word: "continue stedfastly" (Col. 4:2). The RSV, in Acts 2:42, sounds
like an instant decision. It is, rather, a periphrastic imperfect:
"they kept on continuously persevering in the doctrine of the
apostles." Meaning and tense both emphasize *stedfast* continuing in doctrine, not an *instant* commitment. Of course,
this could mean that they were organized into catechumen
classes, the apostles being the teachers. But that is hardly to
be conceived of, knowing how busy the apostles were in a wide
public ministry, even though maintaining their center in Jeru-

salem. But if they continued stedfastly in the apostles' doctrine, that can indicate fidelity to what they learned of truth from these very meetings in the temple of daily witness by the Twelve. Then it is simply incompetence to translate "in the apostles' teaching and fellowship." The Greek simply forbids that rendering. It says: "In the doctrine of the apostles and in the fellowship." These are two distinct things. The apostles went. The fellowship abides.

Join this banishment of *doctrine* with that of *truth, gospel, word,* and the other great vital words driven out of this Bible. It makes you wonder if we are dealing with a lost generation, so indifferent to truth as to be hopelessly committed to apostasy. But I keep my faith. No matter how many knees bow to Baal, he never wins. And I cheer my spirit with a promise: "If they kept my word, they will keep yours also" (John 15:20). That is neither sarcasm nor cynicism. It is the faith of our Lord in the truth, in doctrine revealed. He knew there would be those who *kept* his word. There will be those who keep ours, as we help them to keep his.

CHAPTER SEVEN

TRANSLATIONS THAT ARE WRONG AND SOMETIMES WRONGHEADED

MATTHEW 1:6.

HERE IS A MONSTROUS TRANSLATION AT THE VERY BEGINNING of the New Testament. "And David was the father of Solomon *by the wife of Uriah.*" That is an outrageous slander. No woman is a man's wife after his death (Rom. 7:2). Solomon was the child of David's wife, born in wedlock, however previous crimes may have figured in the case. He was not the child of fornication. Here the KJ and ASV are far superior versions.

I PETER 2:13

We are hereby commanded, by the RSV, not by the Bible, to "be subject for the Lord's sake to every human institution." Amazing. The papacy is an institution. But "for the Lord's sake," I refuse to be subject to it. God never commanded that, and Peter wrote no such folly. There are thousands of "human institutions" that no Christian ought to be subject to. And they are so many, nobody could, even if he wanted to. A better Scripture than this falsified one is: "Be not conformed to this age." Why would the translators put something there that they would not respect, would not obey, would not want anybody else to obey? It is incomprehensible.

JUDEA IS NOT IN TRANSJORDAN

Yet we read: "he went away from Galilee and entered the region of Judea beyond the Jordan" (Matt. 19:1). There is no such region. There is a simple principle of Greek grammar that teaches us to take adverbial phrases with the verb, not with the noun that happens to be close, unless the context forces that translation. Then it is clear. Thus translated, the Greek says: "He went away from Galilee and came across the Jordan into the regions of Judea." The normal Jewish way of travel was to cross over into Perea, to avoid Samaria. From that Transjordan region you would cross the Jordan to get into Judea. That course of travel is so familiar to Matthew and his Jewish readers that it needs no expansion or clarification. This is a pet offense of the RSV against Greek grammar and accounts for a number of its errors.

YES, BROTHERS

In Genesis 13:8, we hear Abraham say to Lot: "We be brethren" (KJ); "we are brothers" (Basic Bible). Now we read: "we are kinsmen" (RSV). That seems to me picayunish about trifles.

MARY WAS NOT A WIFE WHEN THE INCARNATION HAPPENED

She said so. "How can this be, since I have no husband?" (Luke 1:34) That to one angel. But the RSV makes an angel say to Joseph, while Mary is still unmarried: "to take Mary your wife" (Matt. 1:20). The Greek just has the word *woman*. It can be translated either *wife* or *future wife, betrothed,* as the facts demand. A little good will to make the evident meaning clear is enough. Or a little ill will, to promote disharmony in the Bible, can force a translation that is contrary to the known facts, stated in the immediate context. The Berkeley Version has: "When His mother Mary was engaged to Joseph, before they were married, she was found to be pregnant through the Holy Spirit . . . an angel . . . said: . . . be not afraid to marry Mary . . . When Joseph awoke from his sleep he carried out the angel's command from the Lord. He married Mary but conserved her virginity . . ." That is perfectly true, fair, and accurate. Yet look at the next step in promoting disharmony. Right on the eve of the birth of Jesus, Mary is called by the RSV "Mary, his betrothed, who was with child," (Luke 2:5). Amazing. Only betrothed, in Bethlehem already? Even Moffatt is not guilty of that folly. He translates: "Mary, his wife." Here the verb is in the perfect tense. The betrothal, which among the Jews was almost marriage, had been brought to that consummation. I doubt that there is another version in the English language that treats the infancy narratives of the incarnation with such arbitrary ill will.

SHALL WE STARVE THE RETIRED?

The RSV has, in II Thessalonians 3:10: "If any one will not work, let him not eat." That's bad. How about our retired ministers, Sunday rest, men on strike, vacationers, convalescents, and so on? The Greek is clear: "If any one wills not to work (present tense, as a habit, custom), let him not keep on eating." Dr. A. T. Robertson often translated such presents, with a negative, by the word *stop*. "If any one wills to stop working (and go stargazing into the heavens in expectancy for the second coming) let him also stop eating." That we can understand and approve.

TWO MISTAKES AGAINST THE INCARNATION STORY

One is to translate Matthew 1:23, "*a* virgin." She was *the* virgin, the only one in the history of the world to whom that language could apply. Moffatt, Basic, and Phillips all have the article. There seems to be a RSV focusing of ill will on this narrative. Then why would they spell *Immanuel,* in the Old Testament prophecy, but *Emmanuel* in their translation of Matthew? Are we trying to glorify Emanuel Swedenborg's name or that of the Savior?

TARES, NOT WEEDS

It seems utterly childish to me to translate the word that means *tares* by the word *weeds*. *Tares* has been made classical English speech by the parable of Jesus, for centuries. *Weeds* ruins the story of Jesus. You don't sow weeds. Nor do you fail to root them up when they appear. The whole point of the counterfeiting work of the enemy, the similarity between wheat and tares, goes down the drain. I can't understand why translators of the beautiful story of our Lord could consent to make it commonplace and senseless.

MATTHEW 13:44

A peculiar translation is "The kingdom of heaven is like treasure *hidden* in a field, which a man found and *covered up*" (Matt. 13:44). The verb is exactly the same, permanently *hidden* (perfect tense)—*hid*." Why *cover up*, if already hidden? In either case, it may have been hidden in a cave, or in a hollow tree, or cached in various ways, or buried deep. The man found it hidden in one way, then hid it in his own way, so only he would know it, then made the great transaction by which he could take possession. *Covered up* is a thoughtless translation.

"EARS" OF WHEAT?

We have wanted for generations a translation that got rid of *corn*, in our Bible, in the English sense of *wheat*. Now we have it. But the RSV still talks of plucking "ears" of what we know to have been wheat (Deut. 23:25; Matt. 12:1; Mark 2:23; Luke 6:1). Strange to say, the Basic Bible, translated by English scholars, shows deference to the American public and speaks of "heads," as does the Berkeley. But the RSV uses *ears,* as if of corn. Of course, the word *can* be used, according to our dictionaries, in that connection. But would we not expect *heads* in an American version? Is this not the undue influence on the Committee of Moffatt, who still has "ears of corn," in a Bible published in the United States?

"GOD FORBID, LORD"

It is the boast of the Committee that they removed the frequent use of *God forbid* to translate an exclamation in Greek that is equally strong but does not have either *God* or *forbid*. Well, neither word is used here, in the Greek, which merely says: "Mercy on thee, Lord" (Matt. 16:22). The translation "God forbid, Lord," besides being inaccurate and exaggerated, is repulsive to me. And whether on purpose or not, in throwing in erroneously the word God here, it seems to reduce the word *Lord,* applied to Jesus, to less than deity. The Gospels never make that contrast, but lead us on to a day in which one of these very men exclaimed: "My Lord and my God," to our Savior. It is futile to discuss whether Peter rose to that height at Caesarea Philippi. In any case, what he said was beyond the meaning flesh and blood might give it. The term *Lord* grew in content as faith grew. In the mouth of some who had not faith, it is merely a courteous *Sir*. But in progressive Gospel revelation of our Lord, in the days of his flesh, as told in our Gospels, the Name rose to the full New Testament meaning, which we give it always when applied to our Lord.

MATTHEW 10:23

The RSV translates: ". . . you will not have gone through all the towns of Israel, before the Son of man comes." That seems deliberately to promote a Schweitzer propaganda against our Lord, as a thoroughly deluded revolutionary. (See the section on Love of Disharmony in the Bible, and Hatred of Harmony in the Gospels.) The Greek says nothing about "going through . . . towns." It says that the apostles will not have completed, or perfected, the work of evangelizing the cities of Israel that constitute their field till this coming of the Son of man. It is not anything current at that time. They are yet to go before kings and governors—a thing no apostle did at that time. Children are to betray Christian fathers. That is not a phenomenon of the time of Jesus. Our Lord sees far into the future, and beyond it his coming. No evangelization of any cities ever was complete. Wait a few years and a new generation will be here. The RSV tries to give the impression of some hasty "coming." The whole sense is just exactly the opposite, the far view, tension of the great historic persecutions, Christianity a world factor in the life of nations, and a still future coming of Jesus. That makes Jesus a far-visioned prophet, which, of course, no modernist will admit. So the translation is doctored to suit modernists, and our Lord is forced to say a senseless thing. This translation is a present to the detractors of our Lord. If Jesus was a false prophet he was no Savior of the world.

MATTHEW 7:17

"A sound tree" does not bear "good fruit" unless it is a good kind of tree. Nature tells. Who has not seen a *sound* mock orange or wild cherry tree give perfect fruit, such as it is, but fruit nobody wants? And I have seen many an old tree that was rotten give marvelous peaches. These gentlemen seem to know neither horticulture nor Greek. They inexcusably translate the Greek word for *good* as if it meant *sound,* and they make Jesus say a lot of horticultural nonsense. It is nature that decides the kind of fruit, not the state of the tree. And who would cut down a good tree if it had a bad crop of its proper fruit, due to drought, blight, insects, or lack of fertilizer? Failing to translate the Greek before them, the RSV Committee produced bad translation, bad horticulture, bad theology, and a fair amount of nonsense. The tree illustration goes with the animal example, too. Is a wolf less a wolf because it is sound of limb and lung? Nature tells, not soundness. The Bible has a doctrine of soundness, even "sound doctrine," (Titus 1:9). If they love soundness, let them look out for it, where the Bible really demands it.

EMPEROR OR KING?

The RSV translates I Peter 2:13 with the word *emperor* where the Greek has *king* (so the Berkeley, ASV, KJ, and Basic versions). Of course an emperor is a king, of sorts. Now this translation serves a theory. All this New Catholicism, which owns this new Bible, wants Rome to be meant by Babylon, in I Peter 5:13. As a matter of fact, Rome was not in Peter's covenanted territory. He gave his word to Paul (Gal. 2:9) that he would confine his ministry to the Jews. That he faithfully does. He went to Babylon, wrote from there to the Jewish Dispersion. But it is a dogma with such translator-interpreters that Peter was the bishop of Rome. So they turn the word *king* into *emperor*. That seems to turn the exhortation to respect for the emperor. Uniformly, the New Testament refers to the emperor as Caesar (*render to Caesar, Caesar's household* and so on.) It is possible, but not natural, to make this forced translation. The Dispersion Jews were partly under Caesar, partly not, but were often under their own regional kings, even where Rome had general sway. Their direct obedience would be to these kings. An inferior translation is given to bolster up an inferior interpretation, and help on the Catholicisms of the world, worldly. Again we read: "Honor the emperor" (v. 17) Peter said "king." Now if you translate *king*, that can include the emperor; if you say *emperor*, that excludes kings from this reference.

GENESIS 10:13

"Egypt became the father of Ludim," says the RSV. That seems a bit crude. We know that genealogies of those ancient times jumped generations, and sometimes dealt with regional descendants rather than individuals. In fact, verse 5 has promised that the list would be of "nations." It seems crude, and ill disposed toward the Bible itself, to say "Egypt," a nation, "*became the father of*" a people. The Basic Bible is more reverent: "Mizraim was the father of the Ludim." If you want to put a note: Mizraim, *Egypt,* that would be fair to a Bible you are translating, not just for university professors, but for the inexperienced and uninformed, who have a right to expect reverence and friendliness to the Bible on the part of its translators.

ONE LANGUAGE AND FEW WORDS: GENESIS 11:1

That certainly is not in sympathy with the book's long history of the human race, already told. Even Moffatt doesn't so translate, but reads it as "one language and one vocabulary." The LXX has "one lip" and "there was one language for all."

DEUTERONOMY 30:4

What a strange reading: "Even if your outcasts are in the uttermost parts of heaven, from there the Lord your God will gather you." Moffatt has "if your outcasts are at the end of the earth." The LXX said: "from one end of heaven to the other," a phrase we know as meaning universal reach. This seems like a purpose to make the Bible incredible or bizarre.

II TIMOTHY 2:13

The RSV tends to build up the Methodist doctrine of apostasy. (See discussion of sectarian bias against Baptist truth.) I do not mean that only Methodists believe that theory, but I thus identify it as over against the Bible's own doctrine of apostasy, meaning departure from revealed truth. Here we have two possible translations, as so often. One is as given; "faithless." That, too, has two meanings: *unfaithful,*

unbelieving; and *unfaithful, disobedient.* It is a choice between promoting the Disharmony of the Bible or its Harmony. No Christian ever becomes utterly faith-less. In all his
doubts, there remains a basic faith, perhaps even in his sub-
consciousness, which will spring to affirmation at a given
stimulus. He may be like that man: "Lord I believe; help
thou my unbelief." That is not totally faithless. Our hope is
that when we become unfaithful he remains faithful. The
covenant of grace is not a contract between man and his
Savior, but within the godhead itself. His faithfulness chastens
us, seeks us, woos us, and brings us back. This could have
been translated in accord with the facts of grace, and not as a
doctrine of salvation by fidelity to contract, by unfailing good
works, by either unflagging faith or fidelity on the human
side. The RSV might have bettered the prevalent translation
of this passage but did not. Note the contrast, in Romans 3:3,
where the call is evidently for a comparing of *unfaithfulness*
(rightly translated), but at once departed from (*faithlessness*)
even though the word *pistis* itself is here given its less common
meaning of *faithfulness,* to make sense.

II Timothy 4:15,17

Here is part of the banishment of the term *words.* The
hostile coppersmith strongly withstood Paul's *words.* Why not
say what Paul said here? His "message," like that of our
Lord's, was his *words.* Then we have a sudden preference
shown for the term *word*: "The Lord . . . gave me strength to
proclaim the word fully." This both banishes a word of Paul
and changes the sentence structure, which is an obsession of
the RSV. What Paul wrote is "The Lord . . . empowered me,
in order that through me *the preaching* might be brought to
its full measure and that all the Gentiles might hear." Strange
to say, this word *preaching* is now being brought over into
gobbledygook English in its Greek form, *kerugma.* If they
want to fill their learned books with this foreign term, why
could they not let Paul have it, and fairly translate it? Paul
himself says his imprisonment provoked preaching, by friend
and foe (Phil. 1:14-18). He here affirms that *preaching* came
to a new reach, as the great apostle to the Gentiles spoke in

their very world court itself. It is *the preaching,* the content
and substance of his apostolic witness. There is no excuse for
this juggling with the words, the translation, and the grammatical form, weakening at every turn what Paul said.

PSALM 37:37

My father's funeral was preached from this text: "Mark
the perfect man, and behold the upright: for the end of that
man is peace." The context shows a comparison of men, not
qualities: "the wicked" . . . "the upright" . . . "the righteous."
Our version seems to weaken the tribute needlessly. The Basic has "Give attention to the good man, and take note of the
upright; because the end of that man is peace." Moffatt seems
to follow the LXX, and he is followed by the RSV in making
the promise consist in posterity.

ROMANS 13:11

Salvation is a present possession and a future hope, all in
one. In this Scripture Paul really wrote: "for our salvation is
now nearer than when we became believers" (Berkeley); "for
now is your salvation nearer than when you first had faith"
(Basic). The RSV changes the structure deliberately: "For
salvation *is nearer to us now* . . ." There seems to be a textual
difference, with no note as to what was at least an alternative
reading, and given by Eberhard Nestle as the true text. The
effect is to cancel this double truth; salvation already ours,
but destined to future consummation in glory.

II CORINTHIANS 13:5; ROMANS 14:1

"Examine yourselves, to see whether you are holding to
your faith." That is untrue to the Greek. Paul's concern here
is about *the faith,* the sum of Christian truth, as so often in
his writings. "Test yourselves, whether you are in the faith;
give yourselves an examination" (Berkeley). Moffatt has "the
faith." How could anyone have anything else? The same ob-
stinacy against the idea of *the faith* is seen in Romans 14:1.
Welcome is an overtranslation. *Receive* is the word, but that

might make clearer the Baptist doctrine that the church is the judge (I Cor. 5:12) as to who is either received or retained in its fellowship. If that were not true, how could *fellow-ship* be maintained? The weakness of this faith in Romans 14 consists in scruples. And nothing more weakens and sometimes destroys fellowship than for a weak but exacting faith to come in and wreck what was a peaceful fellowship. *The faith* is a thing to banish, however, from the Bible, wherever the RSV can bring it about.

MATTHEW 26:64 VERSUS LUKE 22:69

One of the earliest memories I have of Dr. E. Y. Mullins is his emphatic insistence that, in the first of these Scriptures, Jesus said: *"Henceforth,"* or *"From now on."* The New Testament teaches many comings of Christ: for fellowship (John 14:23); in judgment on the churches (Rev. 2:5,16); kingdom manifestations of his coming, such as the transfiguration, Pentecost, and so on (Matt. 16:28); in providential judgments (Luke 20:16); in judgment on nations (the book of Revelation); and his final coming to raise the dead and reward and punish (John 21:22,23; Rev. 22:12). The verb *come* is used as much about one of these comings as the others.

Now, during his trial, Jesus affirmed of himself a constant coming. *from now,* says the Greek: *"Henceforth,* ye shall see the Son of man sitting at the right hand of power, and coming on the clouds of heaven" (ASV). That means the double function of Jesus in the exercise of his "all authority." First is his lordship, seated on the throne of the universe; second is this multiple, contemporary coming, or repeated comings, into human life in omnipresent decisions, contacts, blessings and judgment, with their climax in the final coming. Of this double function Jesus said: "From now on" both would be seen.

It so happens we have this declaration of Jesus partially repeated by Luke: "From now on the Son of man shall be seated . . ." He does not quote the "coming" clause. But he begins the sentence as Matthew did, only in an incontestable phrase: "From the *now*." Not even the RSV translators dared

translate that any other way. There is no excuse for their
going back to the King James error and translating it "hereafter," in spite of the ASV "henceforth."

PAUL A PRISONER, AND AUTHOR OF EPISTLES IN HIS OWN HOUSE IN ROME

So states Luke, Acts 28:30: "Paul dwelt two whole years
in his own hired house" (KJ); "in his own hired dwelling"
(ASV); "in his rented lodging" (Berkeley); "in the house of
which he had use" (Basic); "private lodging" (Moffatt). The
RSV gives this in the margin, but "at his own expense" in the
text. The Greek Lexicon of Abbott-Smith gives the meaning
of the Greek word as "hired dwelling," even though saying
that no other case has been found in which it has this meaning. The context demands it. Paul there "welcomed (received)
all who came to him," says even the RSV. That is not prison
protocol. Compare now the fairness of other versions with the
love of Disharmony in the Bible, of which I write in another
section of this study, on the part of the RSV. Twice in the
Epistle to Philemon we have "whom I have begotten in my
bonds . . . minister unto me in the bonds of the gospel" (vs.
10,13,ASV). But the unfair RSV wrote *imprisonment* both
times, not clarifying by any reference to the close of the Acts,
which they have already queered. The tender plea of "Paul
the aged" and prisoner of Christ Jesus has passed into the
showy rendering "Paul the ambassador" and prisoner "for"
Jesus. Paul was chained to his guard and thus evangelized
Onesimus. A prisoner treated with such distinction would
hardly have been in chains in addition to being in a prison
cell. But the RSV translators are content to create this false
impression. In Ephesians the RSV preserves *chains,* but on
the very next page has *imprisonment,* unexplained, where the
Greek has *bonds,* four different times (Phil. 1:7,13,14,17).
In Colossians 4:18 they relent a little and translate: "Remember my fetters." Why didn't the RSV translators remember
them?

HEBREWS 13:13

The KJ is so much better than the RSV here: "Let us go

forth therefore unto him without the camp, bearing his re-
proach." That is like the Marys and the beloved John on the
Day of the Cross. The RSV managed to get that down to
"bearing abuse for him." That is a wretched abuse of grammar and meaning, inelegant—change for change's sake—and
wrong besides.

A Bit of Deception and Trickery

"God be thanked that ye were the servants of sin, but . . ."
says the King James Version in Romans 6:17. But the RSV
has this wording: "But thanks be to God that you who were
once slaves of sin have become obedient from the heart to the
standard of teaching to which you were committed." Let us
see where each one is right, where each one is wrong. "Thanks
be to God" (RSV) is the Greek of it. The KJ changed the
sentence structure. But "that ye were the *servants* of sin" (substituting *slaves*) is what Paul wrote in the Greek. Now not a
a soul supposes that Paul approved sin or gave thanks for it
in any life. No danger of that. But what he said, he felt; and
we often feel the same way, but the RSV won't let the apostle
say what he and we feel. Often you feel a sense of relief that
a Whittaker Chambers was a communist, though you come,
with him, to hate what he was. You feel that legalism is a
slavery, too, but give thanks that Paul went through it, to be
able to guide a lost world away from it, to the gospel of grace.
The *who* of the RSV here is both false and cowardly. They
can't understand the bolder reaches of the human spirit. The
RSV "standard of teaching" is a part of its antidoctrinal bias
which, as we have shown, almost banished the word *doctrine*
from the New Testament created by them for our times. The
"form of doctrine" ("rule of faith," says Moffatt) is Paul's
idea, not a "standard of teaching," as if in an intelligence
test for normal-school teachers. And *you* are committed to
it, delivered to its witness, welfare, and promotion, not it to
you—though that idea, too, is apostolic. We "belong to a
church," and to true doctrine as well.

An Old Testament Jesus in Luke 3:29

This is a queer anachronism. We had that sense-destroying

error in the KJ in Acts 7:45 and Hebrews 4:8. Why turn the hands of the clock back to that mistake?

II PETER 3:2

" . . . remember the predictions of the holy prophets and the commandment of the Lord and Savior through your apostles." So the RSV has it. It seems strange that a conservative should have to remind these "liberals" that all prophecy is not prediction. Nor does the Greek have *prediction*. The original is ". . . remember *the words spoken beforehand* by the holy prophets and the commandment of your apostles, of the Lord and Savior." Of course, the RSV would banish the term *words*. Its hatred of verbal inspiration impels it to that action, on every possible occasion. Now the *words spoken beforehand* include law, history, psalmody, poetry, devotion, prediction, ethics, national and international issues on the panorama of Israel, theocracy, and so on. I put down just what the Greek has. Translating freely, I should either repeat "the commandment of your apostles, commandment, I say, of your Lord and Savior," or simply as the RSV has that part. The wrongness, and wrongheadedness, of the RSV is its mania of not letting the *words* of revelation appear in their version, where they appear and are emphatic in the original. "Your apostles" would be the Twelve, sent to the Jews. That division of territory was effected between Paul and Barnabas, on one side, and, on the other, Peter and John. Of course, they would go to all in that territory, and to all nations after the destruction of Jerusalem, when the Jewish field was closed by the hatreds of the Jewish War. Or it is possible that *apostle* is used in its general sense of *missionary,* as in the case of Barnabas. They knew. We don't.

PHILIPPIANS 1:6

The RSV scholars sin against the Greek in many ways, but more against its prepositions, I think, than in any other way. Paul said: "I feel sure that the One Who has begun His good work in you will go on developing it until the Day of Jesus Christ" (Phillips). That is a bit free and has a lot of capitals, but is just the idea. *Until,* not *at,* is the idea. The perfecting of the believer goes right on until the Day of the

Lord. He grows in grace in this life. At death, his spirit leaves
all sin behind, for none enters heaven's gate. There, however,
he is not infinite. Though without imperfections, he has room
for growth. The return of the Lord brings the resurrection
and a new era. Our redeemed personality will keep right on
growing till the Second Coming. Now the RSV translation
gives the idea that the completion of this blessed development
will come all at once. It is not so.

GALATIANS 1:8,9

"But even if we or an angel from heaven should preach
to you a Gospel that differs from what we have preached to
you—a curse on it . . . if anyone evangelizes you with a
Gospel that varies from what you have received—a curse on
it!" (Berkeley). That seems to me the idea, except that "on
it" seems to me possible but unlikely. Lightfoot has a classic
discussion of the issue in his great Commentary. Now the RSV
goes against the ASV, raising to the text what was in the
margin. This is a case, as Dr. Robertson said of the sacramentalist interpretation of Acts 2:38, where your interpretation depends on your evangelical attitude. The Greek can be
contrary to or *different from*. The Greek preposition is *alongside*. Is it *alongside* in the sense of *extra, supplemental, com-
pleting* the evolution, or of going *against, in direct opposition,
contrary to?* Here we have two types of Christianity. One says:
"If it is not openly and unquestionably *contrary* to the gospel, it is permissible." The other says that any addition to the
gospel nullifies it; you can no more add elements to the gospel
than you can to a chemical formula. Changed at all, it is
something else, an accursed counterfeit. Now the New Catholicism owns this Bible. The affinities which brought about
this phenomenon naturally tend to make anything licit that is
not directly *contrary* to Paul. And so they have translated.
That leaves the door open to most anything. It largely nullifies the whole message of Paul to the Galatians. But it mighty
well serves the purposes of the New Catholicism.

I PETER 2:2

The RSV revisers like to break sentence structure to cut
a sentence in two. Now we have a sentence beginning in

I Peter 2:2. Here is what is given us "Like newborn babes, long for the pure spiritual milk, that by it you may grow up to salvation, for you have tasted the kindness of the Lord." Peter said "if," not "for." The prepositional phrase about salvation was not in the KJ, not being in their Textus Receptus. But it seems to be the correct text. You note at once " . . . grow up to salvation . . ." Is it the phrase *grow up?* Or is it the verb *grow* modified by the phrase *up to salvation?* The verb is the common verb *increase,* often used of *growing.* But I do not remember seeing it translated in the significance of *growing up.* This translation seems to me to be slanting at infant baptism and church membership, even though these folks show faults of adults and are "babes" only in the sense of newborn, by regeneration. If they are regenerated, they are already saved. But there are three tenses of salvation. From the past salvation, you grow in the present, progressive stage of salvation. You could hardly be said to "grow up" to the final stage of salvation. The RSV has shown a like bias in translation the other times we have salvation in this Epistle, especially in 1:9. The Greek has "receiving the end of your faith, even the salvation of your souls" (KJ). But that is queered and becomes a separate sentence, thus twisted: "As the outcome of your faith you obtain the salvation of your souls." That slants toward no salvation in this life, but only as the final "outcome of your faith." By the smart handling of words, a present salvation seems to be disappearing completely from the RSV in this Epistle. I think anyone who believes in salvation by grace will feel that Peter has been mistreated and robbed of part of his witness by the doctrinal prejudice of the RSV translators.

ACTS 21:8

We have a contradiction of the facts in the translation here given: "Philip the evangelist, who was one of the seven." The Greek has *being out of the seven.* There is no "one." *Being from the seven* is literal and does not contradict the facts. "He belonged to the seven" is the Moffatt rendering. Now priests, of whom the Committee has some from its Episcopal constituency, want the diaconate to be an initial priesthood, rather than an office of laymen, as the New Testament teaches. So they want Philip to be an evangelist-priest, baptizing in that capacity all over Palestine. Sometimes this phrase is a case of the partitive genitive of Greek grammar; but more often the numeral is expressed, and often without the preposition, in other cases. The translation is not true to the facts, nor does it show that Philip was *from* the seven. While that *could* mean *one of the seven,* it says to the original reader, by the very preposition: *out of the seven.* Philip ceased to be a deacon the day he left Jerusalem, for that was a local task. Then he became an evangelist, a wholly different career. The RSV clings tenaciously to literalism, in the part favorable to its views, in translating a passage to which ecclesiastical value is given, but will not allow other literal meanings to appear that are in disaccord with its views.

Honors or Gifts?

The RSV translates a word as "gifts," in Acts 28:10, which it refuses to translate "remuneration" in I Timothy 5:17. It is translated "money" the very first time it occurs in the New Testament (Matt. 27:6), but I Timothy 5:17 is an ecclesiastical passage, a gift to the Presbyterians, as we have already shown. So the evident financial sense of the word is refused in that great Scripture on discerning support of the ministry.

Tendential Wrecking of Grammar and Sense of the Greek

Such a case, one of a multitude, is Titus 1:1. The Greek says: "Paul . . . an apostle of Jesus Christ, *according to the faith* of God's elect and the knowledge of the truth which is *according to* godliness (based) on the hope of eternal life, which the never lying God promised before eternal times, and manifested at the proper times (as) his Word in the preaching with which I have been entrusted *according to* the commandment of God our Savior, to Titus, legitimate child *according to* (the) common faith." Never did Paul say so much in so little. Now see what the RSV has done to it. We have the Greek preposition that sets up a standard four times in this passage. Once they transfer it into a verb *to further,* as if it were a preposition of purpose. Even if it were, that is very arbitrary—but very RSV-esque—as a translation procedure. The second time, they again presuppose a transmigration of the soul of the preposition, this time into a declarative verb *accords.* The third time they simply repudiate the sense of the preposition and substitute *by.* And the fourth time they substitute another preposition, *in.* The RSV doesn't like standards to which we should bring our thought into conformation, standards of revelation, the Absolute, unchangeable truth, permanent commands about it. It sins against this preposition many times.

Now note its attitude toward *the faith,* the sum of revealed truth. Paul was tenacious about that: *I have kept the faith.* By wrecking the sentence structure, the RSV gets this: "to further the faith of God's elect and their knowledge." That seems to make both faith and knowledge their own personal experience, instead of leaving both of them objective in content, as in the Greek. *Their,* before knowledge, is invented out of whole cloth, brought in to make possible the false impression given. It is futile to say that the Greek does not have the article, for it has qualifying genitives, which give the same effect, according to Greek grammar, as the context may clarify the meaning. Paul sets up this twofold standard: the faith, the knowledge of the truth. Then he makes this affirmation about the truth: which is according to godliness, on the hope (based on the hope) of eternal life. The RSV translation leaves it to be supposed that it is the personal faith and the subjective knowledge of the elect that brings them into accord with godliness. That may be true, in sanctification, *if* faith and knowledge are according to these standards: *the faith* and *the truth.* But Paul makes it crystal clear that it is *the truth* that has such affinity with godliness, and that it has, furthermore, its basis *upon* the hope of eternal life. The doctrine of apostasy, so dear to the hearts of these translators, belies that hope, says that if we have sure and known eternal life we will "take our fill of sin." Paul belies that in Romans 5 and 6 and here affirms that the very basis of godliness is the certainty of eternal life, which gives stability to all holy purpose, character, and motive power in the Christian life and experience. *The faith* and *the truth* have affinity and motivating kinship with godliness. Let modernism prevail today, and tomorrow you have no basis for morals, no Absolute.

The verb *manifested* is swung aloft between two words that seem to be direct objects. That is not as hard for the Greeks as for us. God manifested (to eternal beings, the Son pre-eminently) or promised, as his covenant of grace before all time, *eternal life* (belied by men every time the RSV forces the doctrine of apostasy on its version) and he promised *the Word,* language so familiar and so precious in Paul and all other apostles. I translate: which the never lying God (or God un-lieable, God who cannot lie, in Paul's so compact Greek) promised as his Word. The Word, as summarized in John 3:16 and here, makes eternal life of the believer sum up all the gospel. That is why Baptists do not want to see every kind of trickery employed to get rid of the doctrine, which is *the Word* in its essence, of the eternal life and security of the believer.

Let us come back to the prepositional phrase *according to.* Paul's ministry is one of preaching. The Greek makes clear again, by necessary concordance of the gender of words, that it is *the preaching* (again objective content of *the preaching,* as of *the faith* and *the truth*) with which he had been entrusted *"according to* the commandment of our Savior God." *The Preaching* is never at the disposal of subjectivism. It is not a nose of wax. It is defined by divine command, in the Word.

Again we have a standard, this time even of the new birth. Titus is a *legitimate child* according to "the common faith." Not every doctrine abroad will lead men to regeneration, but only the gospel of eternal life through Jesus Christ the Savior. There are a lot of nominal sons of God, spiritual "bastards," in the language of the Epistle to the Hebrews. Titus is a *legitimate child of God.* The common faith of revealed Christianity is the standard by which sonship of the children of God is judged and certified to, in biblical assurance. According to *the faith* of the gospel, life and sonship legitimately come only through personal faith in (utter trust on) Jesus as the only and all-sufficient Savior. These two senses of the word *faith* are essential to any Christian understanding of sonship and eternal life by the saving faith, and discipleship and education in Christianity by the once delivered faith (Bible doctrine). All this, in Paul's great preface to the Epistle to Titus, has been simply slaughtered, as if the translators thought nobody in America knew Greek and so no one could hold them responsible for the mutilation of a great Scripture.

Good Works are More Than Good Deeds: Titus 2:15

Good works have been trimmed down to the size of *good deeds,* in the RSV. *Good works* is a great Pauline doctrine in this Epistle. The term, established for centuries in Christian doctrine, on both the negative side, "not by works" as in any way a means of salvation, and positively, everywhere the doctrine of good works, the outlet of the inner grace of eternal life. As a great country Baptist preacher used to say: "We are saved *apart from* good works by a faith that produces good works." No doctrine changed in this version? The whole gospel is confused and cluttered up with all sorts of tendential and antievangelical translations in some of the most vital of all Scriptures. We have *good works,* in the negative and positive doctrine, eight times in this Epistle, every time translated *works* by the KJ. But the RSV renders the word *deeds* seven times out of eight. The exception is in 3:1, where the idea has been moved over into another thought realm, *honest work,* which is simply a refusal to translate the Greek and a deliberate departure from the time-honored doctrine of the Epistle, in spite of the boast that no doctrine anywhere has been affected by the RSV translation.

Other Arbitrary Decisions in Titus

Faithful is changed to *sure,* a very different idea (3:8). In 3:11, instead of *sinful.* the Greek has a verb that translates *lives in sin,* present of continual or habitual action. *Love us in faith,* Paul has in the final greeting. When he writes *faith,* they want to put *the faith.* When the apostle writes *the faith,* they rebel and change it. Love and faith are twins, born in the same new birth of the spirit. The RSV seems utterly blind to the realities of the Christian experience (3:15). *Which,* when used about the Holy Spirit, is either bad English or irreverence (3:6). Paul did not say (2:14) that the grace of God appeared "for the salvation of all men." As usual, the sentence structure is wrecked and something else than what Paul said is put down for translation. *Salvation* is really a part of a predicate adjective, agreeing with grace, and there is no separate noun *salvation* in the sentence, much less in this connection. The grace of God appeared for all men, saving, educating us. . . . Or, as I sometimes paraphrase it: "Once in the course of human events there was an epiphany of the grace of God, bringing a salvation destined for (offered to) all men, disciplining us, to the purpose that we should say, once for all, an emphatic *no* to irreverence and the lusts that loom large in life like a cosmos, and that, positively, we should set ourselves to live (the verbs are aorists, once-for-all attitudes decided upon) sensibly, morally and reverently in this fast speeding age, waiting eagerly for the blessed hope of the Christian, that other epiphany, this time not in the weakness of incarnation but the glory of his majesty as God and Savior." And still it goes on and on. Other sins of this translation appear elsewhere, as to this Epistle. If we took the whole New Testament, book by book, as we have Titus, it would take many books to show the mistakes so ruthlessly made by this version. But this gives the main faults seen in the translation of Titus.

RESPECT OF PERSONS

Repeatedly (Rom. 2:11; Eph. 6:9; Col. 3:25; Jas. 2:1; Acts 10:34; Gal. 2:6; and Jude 16) we have *partiality* substituted for *respect of persons,* in this version. "God is no respecter of persons" has become proverbial language. The RSV cannot displace its meaning in literature. That is secure. *Partiality* is simply not the idea. If you and I were alone on an island and, because of your bearing, haughtiness, or majesty of form, I showed some deference to your will that was unethical, that would be sin. It is not that *partiality* is involved. There is no thought of modern slogans of the dignity of the person. Such questions are not on the horizon here. God is no respecter of persons—doesn't look at the *face* and then and thus reach his conclusions.

CHAPTER EIGHT

ADDING TO THE WORD OF GOD

HOW GRAVE A SIN THAT IS, YOU SEE IN THE EMPHASIS OF BOTH the Pentateuch and the Revelation of John, at both ends of our Bible. It is a pet sin of the translators of the RSV. I should not like to face that charge at the judgment bar of God.

INSPIRATION EXTENDED TO ALL AND SUNDRY

Once only do we truthfully have the doctrine of the inspiration of the Scriptures stated by the use of that word. That is in II Timothy 3:16. If the translators would only swap us a dozen conjectures they made, for the simple truth, in one marginal note, they would say "inspired, *God-breathed.*" That is what Paul really said: "Every Scripture is God-breathed." Robert E. Speer, speaking to the Baptist World Alliance, in Atlanta, in 1936, called this "the Bible's doctrine of itself." Inspiration is never affirmed, in the Bible, about men, but only about Scriptures. That is the heart of the doctrine. The men were "moved," as prophets, organs of divine revelation, which they gave forth in this literary form. God moved men, prophets. He inspired Scriptures.

Our translators could never let that by. They spread inspiration out into a far wider use, simply adding it to the Word of God wherever it suited them to do so. That is a grave offense. In I Timothy 1:18, Paul is made the author of this doctrine of a vague and undefined inspiration of man. This is the forged Scripture: ". . . the prophetic utterances which pointed to you, that inspired by them you may wage the good warfare." There is not a thing in the Greek that corresponds to that addition to the doctrine of inspiration. Then Luke 2:27 adds more inspiration of man: "And inspired by the Spirit, he came into the temple." More addition to the Word. Mark (12:36) is drawn into the conspiracy and is made to say "David himself, inspired by the Spirit." Mark did *not* say it. They added it, to suit their own purposes. Now Matthew is made to join the chorus: "David, inspired by the Spirit," another forgery, in a parallel passage. Paul is obliged again to testify this false doctrine: "All these are inspired" (I Cor. 12:11), like a radio announcer who beams with the news that "there are prizes for all." Again, inspiration is made universal, "for there are varieties of working, but it is the same God who inspired them all in every one" (I Cor. 12:6). Certainly translation of the Scriptures is one of the varieties of working. Are our translators then "inspired"? And is that the reason why the Nelson Bible is "authorized"? Colossians 1:29 adds inspired energy. And the Thessalonian Christians, at the very outset of the Christian life "received the word in much affliction, with joy inspired by the Holy Spirit" (I Thes. 1:6). I do not know how many more times there are additions of man-invented inspiration, which these translators have tacked onto the Word of God, destroying the Bible's doctrine of itself and substituting their own, invented out of whole cloth. That is just like having the dairy trucks dump their milk supplies into the municipal swimming pool. It is an addition, yes, but an addition that spoils both the milk and the water. It does not result in an increase of the city's milk supply. Far better retain our true Bibles, whose originals were God-breathed and given literary form by men moved of God. If you spread out the doctrine of inspiration so thin that it covers the whole earth and everything in it, it will evaporate while you look at it.

GENESIS 10:5

Here the translators confess that they added the declaration: "These are the sons of Japhet," which, they say, is "supplied from verses 20,31." It is a rather artificial criterion. The Basic Bible doesn't adopt it and is just as clear. The context shows that the sons of Japhet are under discussion. If this were the only case, it would hardly be worthy of notice. But the habit is confessed here early in the new Bible and is followed lots of times without notice being given and in cases not so innocent as to the results.

"THE PEOPLE" ADDED

Democratic? No. Just plain wrong. In Matthew 8:4, Mark 1:44, and Luke 5:14, the RSV adds *the people* to the story: "Show yourself to the priest and offer the gift that Moses commanded, for a proof to (them) the people." The RSV retains *them* in Leviticus 14, where it occurs various times without saying to whom it refers. There is a possibility that it refers to the leper's family, or to the priest's assistants, Levites or co-operating priests. The whole priesthood was the health department of the Jewish theocracy. A man did not deal just with the individual priest. He was responsible before the hierarchy and, as the process was long, sometimes he might be before one, sometimes before another. There was absolutely no democratic phase of the procedure. When the priest put the ex-leper back into circulation, he was restored to society. This addition to the record, *the people,* is not justified. It takes liberties with the Bible.

MORE "PEOPLE" ADDED, AND WORSE CONSEQUENCES

Another case of this addition to the text of the Gospels is found in Matthew 19:14, Mark 10:13, and Luke 18:15. Strange to say, with an identical Greek pronoun, nevertheless the RSV translates the pronoun *the people* only in Matthew, and gives it the true translation, *them,* in the other Gospels. You wonder at the difference. It is not hard to see the reason. The sentences are organized differently in the three Gospels. In Matthew's, there is just one subject of the verb, later the object of the next verbs: "Children were brought . . . lay his hands on them (the children) . . . The disciples rebuked them" (the children). Why not let that stand? Because this is the pet text for the advocates of infant baptism, and so it had to be doctored. The identical pronouns, one right under the other on successive lines of the Greek, show clearly that the disciples rebuked the children themselves. But, if that was the case, they were big enough to walk and be shooed away, on their own responsibility. That does not fit in with infant baptism. Luke has even three identical pronouns, with the same reference. Luke refers to the aim "that he might touch *them* . . . they rebuked *them* . . . Jesus called *them* to him." In all three cases, the same pronoun clearly refers to the children.

The Lucan account has been exploited by pedobaptists because it has a word that can mean *infants,* even *fetuses.*

Well, clearly, these children were already born. And it was to them Luke refers: "But Jesus called them to him." But, shutting their eyes to both the context and to the word for children in the parallel Gospels, the advocates of infant baptism fasten on the possible meaning of *infants* here. Yet Luke's word is not limited to infants in arms, at all. It is the word used in II Timothy 3:15, "from childhood" (RSV); "when you were a child" (Basic); "from childhood" (Moffatt); "from infancy" (Berkeley), "you have known the Holy Scriptures." Clearly it is an infant that can learn the Bible. Luke considers it a synonym for the word of Mark and Matthew, for he probably had both before him when he wrote. And always let it be remembered that the effort to implant infant baptism here is a lost cause. Jesus never baptized. "Jesus himself did not baptize." If he didn't, then he didn't. Period. If he never baptized at all, then he didn't baptize these children. And to add *the people* to the Gospel text is a cheap sectarian trick, to try to insinuate that he did what he didn't do.

ADDING A WORD THAT CHANGES THE WHOLE REFERENCE

The word is *his* (Jas. 2:14). It takes the place of the definite article. There is always a bit of the demonstrative pronoun in the article. It defines, points out. But James did not say: "Can his faith save him?" That implies it cannot, and merely fosters the cheap trick of trying to promote a civil war between one part of the Bible and another. A purposed "disharmony," as I later show, is the driving motive of much of this kind of translating, between parts of the Bible made to appear contradictory when they are not. Here all possible antagonism is made to appear to exist between James and Paul, whereas no antagonism exists. The New Testament affirms that a man is justified by grace, by blood, by faith, by words, and by works. And he is, each in its own sense. The word *justify* always means *declare righteous,* never the Latin etymology of the English word *justify,* which is *make just.* None of the five things mentioned *make* a sinner just. They *declare* him just, whether that be the judicial decision

of God, as Judge, on the basis of his own grace, the blood of
Christ, and the instrumental faith of the saved believer, or
by words and works as the demonstrating, proving testimony
in this saved man's life that he is progressively righteous. Such
words and works declare him so to be, prove it.

The same James, who has only the one sense, as Paul, for
the phrase *to declare righteous,* has two common senses for
the word faith. Belief, opinions, system of doctrine and its
mental approval—that is one sense. Trust in Christ, rest in
and upon him, inner reliance on the crucified and risen Savior
and his finished work on Calvary and on his priestly propitiation and pleading—that is the other sense. James said, in
2:14; "Can *the faith* (the belief of truth, such as the unity of
God, v. 19) save him?" His illustrations that follow show the
sense to be *belief.* Can the belief of truth save? The answer is
always, everywhere, and totally: No. Right opinions do not
save the soul. They do not declare a man righteous before
men or God. To God they lack all that he has offered as the
gospel. To man they lack all proof of reality, power, or value.
Faith, in the sense of opinion, gets nowhere in this whole
realm. It has its realm, in the sphere of obedience, loyalty,
orientation, and witness. But your opinions do not *declare
you righteous* before either God or men. They are like a foreign currency in a native market.

Now what do the RSV translators do to this delicate translation problem? They queer it right from the beginning, to
promote Disharmony between James and Paul. They translate: "Can *his* faith save him?" Jesus had said: "Thy faith
hath saved thee." This translation seems to take a contemptuous attitude of cynicism about the very center of the message
of Jesus and Paul and John. The *his* is an RSV addition.
James said "the faith" (just referred to) is evidently spurious.
Can *that* faith (mere Jewish belief in divine unity, as he goes
on to show) save? Some have translated the article *that,* "Can
that faith save?" And this device the RSV translators themselves adopt openly in Romans 3:31: *this faith.* When they
say *his faith* they leave the impression that it is the usual
saving faith of a believer. This the context shows clearly that
it is not. The addition is antievangelical.

DESERVING WORKS: REVELATION 2:23

The addition of the word *deserve* is also antievangelical. There are no meritorious works. Jesus said: "according to your works," the prepositional phrase the RSV seems to hate to translate truly. The version "as your works deserve" is utter buncombe. It falsifies the Bible. This is sheer Romanism.

REVELATION 2:24

In spite of its being the book of Revelation that says such stern words about adding to, or subtracting from, its message, the RSV does just that again in the very next verse, 2:24. It speaks of "what some call the deep things of Satan." Satan has a lot of deep things. The Bible recognizes that. He held Jesus himself at bay for forty days and found a momentary incarnation in Peter, a permanent one in Judas. It is shallow thinking that discounts the devil. "What some call" is spurious. God never gave a word of that cynicism in The Revelation.

REVELATION 14:12

The RSV has added to the Word of God "a call for," translating: "Here is a call for the endurance of the saints." There is no such Scripture. John wrote: "Here is the endurance," not just *a call* for it. There was the real stuff. Why flee from reality to theory, from glorious endurance to merely the call for it?

A CONTEMPTUOUS ADDITION ABOUT BAPTISM

"Jesus himself did not baptize, but only his disciples" (John 4:2). The word *only* is not in the Greek. It came out of the heads of the RSV translators. Not even Moffatt has it in his version. There is just *one baptism*. God sent John the Baptist to introduce it. Jesus received it, taught it, practiced it, through his authorized administrators, perpetuated it, baptized more than John had, incorporated it in the Great Commission, and demanded it stay where he put it, till the end of time. But there is an utter contempt for "John's baptism" in the New Catholicism, as in the Old. So they added the *only* contemptuously to the Word of God, as a matter of sectarian prejudice.

"JESUS PRAYS FOR THE CHURCH"—JOHN 17

The word *church* is not in John's Gospel anywhere. That makes Catholic heads ache. It seemed a sore handicap to the New Catholicism, to the new Bible translators. So they put it in. If they couldn't get it in the text, which is God's Word, they put it in the page title, which is man's word. But the fundamental principle that ought to rule these titles is that they ought not to introduce into the title some pet idea *which is not in the text itself.* Now the New Catholicism has no similarity to anything for which Jesus prayed. It consists mostly in union of Church and State, Religion and World, which is just exactly what Jesus repudiates in that prayer. His prayer treats only of saved people, not of the amalgamation of the hordes of victims of infant baptism, that incorporates whole populations into *"The Church"* of the Old and the New Catholicism, in Europe and its colonies. That is nothing Jesus either prayed for, revealed, or tolerated, in the way of his revealed will. But not to have *The Church* of their invention in the center of John 17 gave the RSV owners a sense of an aching void. So they reasoned: "Isn't it our Bible? If it is not there, let's just put it there, right at the head of the prayer." So there they added it to the Word of God.

ROMANS 9:18

"He hardens *the heart of* whom he wills." There is another addition here. Paul never said that. It is Old Testament talk, true to life. Old Pharaoh hardened his heart a lot, then God judicially set the seal of judgment on the self-petrifying process. But that is not the language of this text. Why add to the Scripture?

I CORINTHIANS 10:14

"Therefore . . . shun the worship of idols." Paul really wrote: "Shun idolatry." That is a far larger order than the narrowing enlargement of the command we have in the RSV. Most of idolatry is not worship of mere idols. The second commandment of the moral law forbids the making of images or pictures as aids to religion, their service in any way, and every act of bowing down to them (Ex. 20). All that is idolatry, beginning with image-making, which is a vast profession—as witness the guild of shrine manufacturers of Diana of the Ephesians; the mighty priesthood that serves images; the employees of temples; and the big business of the manufacture, spread, and sale of images and pictures of God, Christ, and the Virgin—to say nothing of that invention of the Old Catholicism: the "Saints", canonized by mere ecclesiastics and put upon altars on earth and, supposedly, in heaven among the mediators between God and man. The most futile and immoral capitalism on the face of the earth is image manufacture, service, sale, and worship—all of which the moral law sternly forbids. In Corinth there was no danger of worship of the image by the saints. Their contamination with idolatry would come from the banquets of the labor guilds in the big temples. Flee from it. Now when you add words that narrow idolatry down to the actual worship of idols, you nullify the Scripture. Most of idolatry is not worship. It is conformity with the habits of others; and, in the shadow of earth's great temples for images, are the worst centers of gambling, prostitution, and drunkenness, with attendant crimes, that can be found on the face of the earth. Don't whittle away Bible morals by adding to the Word of God expressions that reduce sin to nothing tangible. Even Moffatt has "Shun idolatry." Shun it then, in all forms. Hold to that. Idolatry includes all uses of images in any religion, and that Paul has in mind in this Scripture.

GALATIANS 4:9

This is a question of insight. The RSV adds to the Word of God *spirits,* when spirits are not in discussion. The issue is judaism and its ceremonial legalism, which Paul calls "weak and beggarly rudiments" (Berkeley).

EPHESIANS 2:3

The RSV adds *mankind,* "rest of mankind." A rather large addition.

"Us" Added Twice: Ephesians 2:14,16

Paul is contrasting the Gentiles and Israel, as figuring in the panorama of the divine purpose in the program of redemption on Calvary. God's own law had set up the wall of division between Jew and Gentile. Christ knocked it down with his cross. It is far larger in scope than the mere relations of any "us"-talk. That narrows it in a most undesirable fashion. Additions often restrict meaning.

Philippians 3:12

Adding *this* to that Scripture weakens it. It seems to say that Paul had not obtained the resurrection yet, which will seem to the casual reader a very obvious statement about a man still alive. The KJ is far better: "Not as if I had already attained." Period. This is the true humility, about all the goal just stated.

I Thessalonians 5:4

Adding *that* weakens. It is far stronger to let Paul say: "*The* day," for which all other days were made, or "the Day."

"Rules" Added: I Timothy 5:21; II Timothy 2:5

How often have spiritual men said that the New Testament is a book of principles, not of *rules*. Now all that is washed down the drain. There is no excuse for the addition in either case. I suppose these "rules," which the RSV invented, are part of the new "inspiration."

Innocent Enough but Inconsistent

The RSV has added *hearts* and removed the reflexive force of the verb, in I Timothy 6:10. Passing strange, in view of its rather hostile attitude toward heartfelt religion, shown by its banishment of vital Bible words related to the Christian experience.

Postponing Salvation Till Beyond Death

This is an obsession of the RSV translators, as we have

already seen. In II Timothy 2:10, Paul said: "On this account, I endure all things for the sake of the elect, that they
also may obtain the salvation which is in Christ Jesus with
eternal glory," the salvation which is now in union with Christ
and which will have, by-and-by, the blessing of eternal glory.
Now the RSV adds, in a tendential context, the words *which
goes.* It then becomes "salvation which goes with eternal
glory," seemingly, therefore, a postponing of salvation till
the eternal glory with which it "goes." This habit is sinister.

EPHESIANS 2:22

The inexcusable addition of *into it,* in this passage, is
a willful change in the meaning of Paul, for a doctrinal purpose. That I shall discuss under the head of a sectarian bias
against Baptist truth. It wrecks a great doctrine, to the liking
of the New Catholicism, which owns this Bible and does as it
pleases with its property.

ACTS 2:39

To him is an addition which confusingly and needlessly
weakens the great meaning of the verb *call.* We have already
shown how the addition in verse 44 helps on communism.

THE "BLESSED AMBIGUITY" OF THE ORIGINAL GREEK

It is a pity to destroy that where it really exists. "The
love of Christ constrains"—the love we have for him or his
for us, which? Either is true. Better to leave it. If either is
true, both may be in the text in consideration. The RSV often
forces a choice where the Greek leaves it open. Take Ephesians 1:19-23, one of Paul's greatest prayers. It is fine that
the RSV shows that the "heart" has eyes. That is where our
godless intellectuals are blind. Now with those eyes of the
heart you see three things. The first is "the hope of his calling," KJ and the Greek. The RSV added the interpretation,
as well as the translation, "the hope to which he has called
you." Many of the greatest interpreters take the other alternative. "The hope of His calling" is the hope Jesus has in the
believer when he sounds in his soul the effectual call of grace.

The thought moves right along in the enumeration of his assets in our redemption, the riches of the glory of his inheritance in the saints. Jesus is rich in those he owns, by inheritance from his Father. And this chimes in with the riches of his power *toward* us, hardly *in* us. Once again, it is the potential resources and possible invasion, from without, of the objective power, rather than the subjective, inherent power. The bounteous supply of the reservoir is our guarantee, rather than the water that is in the pipes and immediately on tap. All that is on tap comes from the reservoir. The supernatural is natural, in the realm of grace.

AN ADDITION THAT PROMOTES DISHARMONY

In Matthew 27:62, the Greek says: "On the morrow, which is after the Preparation." The Jewish sabbath was the very center of Jewish life, every seven days. It dominated Friday as well as Saturday. So the very name of Friday in Greek is Preparation. Jesus was crucified on Friday. Eberhard Nestle, even in the Greek, spells Preparation with a capital letter. It ceases to be preparation and becomes Preparation, the very name of Friday. Mark, in the parallel narrative, explains to the Dispersion Jews, in their Gentile environment: "It was the day of Preparation, that is, the day before the sabbath" (Mark 15:42). That makes it perfectly clear and absolutely certain. But in a Love of Disharmony and a Hatred of the Harmony of the Gospels, which I shall examine in detail later, the RSV adds four words: *that is . .. day of.* The Disharmonists like to promote the idea that it was the preparation for the Passover, which was already past, throwing John into civil war with the other Gospels, with regard to what day Jesus was crucified on. Here even, we read in the Basic Bible: "on the day after the getting ready of the Passover," which is sheer nonsense. Some say Jesus ate the Passover the night before his death, others that he was crucified at the hour of the Passover sacrifice. But nobody supposes that he was crucified on the sabbath, which Mark definitely affirms to have been the day for which this preparation was aimed. Yet the Love of Disharmony begets translations that are in Disharmony with its own theory. So here, in the Basic.

The RSV doesn't openly make that blunder, but its four words put in to clarify, seem to slant toward this Disharmony. Why not leave it as Matthew left it? The emphasis is not on day, so much. The priestly class, the superguardians of the sabbath, first of all completed preparation for that, even in an hour like this of our Lord's death, in which they had so great an interest. Once finished with the Preparation, they hurried to Pilate on unfinished business. It was an awe-ful day. The earthquake may have made the beginning of the new day, at sunset, confused. And, after their supreme religious concern, the Preparation for their sabbath, they edge in, on the borderline between Preparation and Sabbath, their pleas for a guard for Messiah's tomb. This addition is either tendential or worthless.

Let me say that in none of these studies is there the slightest objection to adding words not in the original, *if they contribute to making clear the sense of the original*. Often the subject is not in the Greek and has to be supplied from the inflected verb. Often the verb has to be supplied, sometimes the object, and so on. This is proper translation. But these cases and many others are additions that confuse, deny, or modify the *sense of the original*. It is to that I object.

CHAPTER NINE

DEBUNKERS OF CHRIST, THE BIBLE, AND ITS AUTHORS

NO RSV TRANSLATOR IS AN ADAM, I INSIST. HE IS NOT AT THE creation of the English Bible. For three and a half centuries we have had an "authorized version." The RSV very definitely set itself, by solemn public promises, not to prepare a new translation. Its preface (p. ix) affirms: "The RSV is not a new translation in the language of today. It is not a paraphrase which aims at striking idioms. It is a revision which seeks to preserve all that is best in the English Bible as it has been known and used through the years. It is intended for use in public and private worship, not merely for reading and instruction. We are glad to say, with the King James translators: 'Truly (good Christian reader) we never thought from the beginning, that we should need to make a new Translation, nor to make a bad one a good one . . . but only to make a good one better.' "

So be it. If, then, the conception of Christ the Lord and Savior is deliberately reduced from the KJ level, that represents a debunking of the Name that is above every name. That is what I charge. The revision has reduced the worship and meaning of Christ. Let us see the facts.

The New Testament is a library with a purpose. That purpose is to bring men to worship, serve, and obey, in spirit and in truth, Jesus the incarnate Son of God. The New Testament is the history of how that worship came about and grew. The RSV banishes much of that worship from its pages. That is a serious offense against the very genius of Christianity. Benjamin Warfield has somewhere stated that one of the most remarkable phenomena of all time is this. A group of utterly monotheistic Jews began to worship another Jew, to pray to him and to attribute to his Name all the meaning and value of God. That is indeed an insight into history. I doubt that Toynbee has discovered anything in the philosophy of history as meaningful as that movement of thought, the creative thought that explains the force of Christ in history. Now the RSV tries to set in motion a countercurrent, diminishing this witness to the worship of Jesus. The RSV sets as its goal to "preserve all that is best." If it banished the worship of Jesus from many passages, then clearly it thinks that is "best" for Christianity.

There are seven words, nouns and verbs, in the Greek New Testament, which are translated *worship* in the KJ a total of seventy times. The RSV preserves the record of worship given by the cultured Athenians to cold and lifeless idols (Acts 17:23); by sophisticated Gnostics to angels (Col. 2:17); by apostate Israel to the stars (Acts 7:42); by the Roman world to creatures versus Creator (Rom. 1:25); by the "whole world," allegedly, to Artemis (Acts 19:27). Nor does it deny the worship of the devil as proposed to Jesus in his temptation. The RSV does not hold back the word *worship* from being legitimately used of human devotion and prayer to all kinds of frauds and freaks of superstition. Rather it increases both the number of words it translates *worship* and the number of times it so translates the chief ones thus. But there is one exception. To Jesus it permits less worship, removes the word from passages about him in nearly a dozen cases. That is my charge of debunking the Name.

The principal verb is used sixty times and always translated *worship* in the KJ Scriptures. Eleven of these sixty times the accompanying statement is made that the worshipper *fell down and worshipped*. Here is the crux of the matter. The Gospels represent men as worshipping Jesus, in hours when he revealed his majestic power or person. Is that to be, by any debunking process, diminished and rendered unbelievable, wherever a trick of translation can banish the testimony?

Now this does not involve, in every act of worship, a deliberate philosophy of reasoned interpretation of the nature of Jesus. It is rather the question whether his majesty, miracles, and redemption were such that men, women, and children instinctively, spontaneously, and gladly gave him their worship, without, as Warfield said, ceasing to be monotheists in so doing. Long before the studied New Testament evaluation of the full meaning of their act, if followed out to its logical conclusions, would naturally occur to these worshippers of Jesus, they *worshipped him*. This spontaneous, unreasoned worship is more significant than the studied, official Caesar cult, in the Roman emperor (and empire) worship, which

lost the war of "Our Lord God and Savior Caesar," waged
against "Our Lord God and Savior Jesus Christ."

Our Gospels affirm, but the RSV, because of its debunking purposes, denies, in the following cases the worship of
Jesus: (1) the leper of Matthew 8:2; Mark 1:40; Luke 5:12;
(2) Jairus the ruler of Matthew 9:18; Mark 5:22; Luke
8:41; (3) the Syrophenician woman, Matthew 15:25; Mark
7:25; (4) the case of a great farsighted kneeling mother,
Matthew 20:20; (5) the Gerasene demoniac, Mark 5:6
parallel to Luke 8:28, which does not have the word *worship;*
(6) the mocking soldiers, Mark 15:19.

Here is a leper who calls Jesus "Lord," believes he can
cure leprosy by a word, kneels and falls prostrate before
Jesus, prays to him, becomes an enthusiastic herald of Jesus.
Yet he is not allowed in the ranks of worshippers of our Lord.
The second case is of a man who knew the Scriptures and had
faith to receive from Jesus his daughter by resurrection from
the dead. The Syrophenician woman shows knowledge of
Messianic truth, so addresses Jesus and he calls her faith
great, but she is not allowed among the worshippers of our
Lord. The mother of apostles James and John worshipped
him, asking places of honor for her sons when he comes to
be enthroned. The other cases are the frequent phenomena
of demon recognition of our Lord and the *mock worship* of
the soldiers. It takes no great insight to recognize that these
soldiers, contemptuous of the Jews, understood the issues and
gave Jesus mock worship, as a rival to Caesar, even as they
were accustomed to give Caesar the worship the State required of them. Neither of the last two acts were sincere, of
course. The others were deeply so.

Now why single out these as debunking cases, refusing
them the right to be worshippers of our Lord, in Gospel
history? These same RSV translators say the "Wise Men"
worshipped the baby in the manger, and that Herod proposed
to. Are they superior spiritually to the principal recipients
of our Lord's great miracles? The RSV translators give the
full testimony that Jesus was *worshipped* by the man born
blind whom Jesus cured. Why the distinction? I confess it
seems to me utterly arbitrary.

Now please note that the RSV is willing to say that Cornelius would have worshipped Peter, (Acts 10:27), and that John would have worshipped an angel (Rev. 19:10; 22:8). In every case, kneeling or prostrating oneself to a man or an angel is condemned and forbidden. How do they explain, then, that these people fell down before Jesus, and it was not forbidden, unless it was legitimate worship?

THE "SON" IN PROPHECY

For me the most detestable translation of the whole RSV is Psalm 2. With the decision to use *you* for all who are not God, the Messianic reference of the Psalm is rudely "liquidated." The language can have no possible reference to any human being. Then the climax comes in the exhortation to kings and rulers of the earth to kiss the Lord's feet. The margin says the Hebrew here is uncertain. So the translation chosen is the worst possible. Now there sets up a discord between the RSV in the Old Testament and in the New. For we have this Psalm quoted in the language of the divine *thou,* in Hebrews 1:5; 5:5; and also in Acts 13:33. Three to one, the RSV repudiates its miserable job in Psalm 2. Couldn't somebody get them together somehow, before publishing such a shameful contradiction? Why have two contradictory RSV committees?

Moffatt has an interesting translation here: "Do homage to him truly." Do you know what the verb most translated *worship* by the RSV in the New Testament means? It means *kiss,* says Abbott-Smith, in his Lexicon. That is the etymology, yet it is never once translated by that literalism. But, instead of following Moffatt from the literal to the figurative, in their translating Psalm 2, they go all out for the crudest literalism, precisely in the Psalm of supreme Messianic witness. The New Testament Committee corrects the Old; but, as the New Testament was published first, the Old Testament Committee members win the victory where they can, denying the New Testament citations of the Old.

Another of these victories in reverse, of the RSV New Testament Committee over the Old, is in this same great tribute to Jesus in Hebrews 1. "Thy throne, O God" is said to the Messiah by Psalm 45:6,7. But when we get back to that Psalm, lo, anti-Messianic unbelief has conquered the New Testament faith once more. And this Messianic Psalm has been "liquidated" by the translation: "Your divine throne endures for ever and ever," which, of course, is nonsense as referring to any man.

FOUR SON - SIGNS IN ISAIAH

The Psalms have the Messianic King Son. Daniel has the glorious Son of man. Isaiah, as in all other phases of prophecy, reaches the climax of prophecy as to the Messianic Son. There is a march of Son-signs in the ongoing of Isaiah's message. All of them are signs to expectant spiritual Israel, timeless, one with all those who are even today the Israel of God. See those sons dawn on that Israel as signs.

Son-sign one. Isaiah never had the slightest hope of his nation. From the dawn of his call, all was doomed "until the cities lie waste without inhabitant, and the houses without man." He sees nothing on the horizon of prophecy but a "stump" of Israel's tree. Always this is the prophet's outlook. The scenes of the captivity are as much in his mind in the language of his call as in his vision of the land forsaken and then inhabited again of the later sections. Now this faith of doom takes prophetic shape in a son-sign. He and his wife name a boy Shearjashub (a remnant will return). Would you name a boy that? Isaiah called out his postcaptivity message of Israel's return and Messianic future every time he called his boy, in the capital city of his people. He was living son-sign number one. (Isa. 7:3).

Son-sign two. Ahaz, mulish king of Judah, was invited to accept a sign from God. He haughtily refused. Period. God turns from him to the nation, or rather to Israel, independent of its nations and divisions, "the house of David." He gives the house of David a sign, timeless jewel in the temporary setting. That sign is: *the virgin* shall conceive and bear a son, and shall call his name Immanuel. There are two witnesses by whose mouth this sign should be established for every believer in revelation. One is the Septuagint (LXX). It was the Bible of the Jews and of Jesus. It said "the virgin," as its translation. It was so evidently a prophecy of Jesus that the

Jews repudiated their own translation and made others. The New Testament cites it. The second witness is Jesus himself. He drilled the apostolate, and their companions of the post-resurrection forty days, in the things in the Scriptures about himself. This, their testimony, was the result of the risen Lord's interpretation of the Scripture concerning himself (Luke 24:27,32 and Acts 10:43).

Of course, no modernist would ever accept this sign. I shall not argue it. I simply say that if the language did not mean *virgin,* it has no place in the RSV margin. Certainly the margin is not a list of false readings or interpretations. The Union Seminary's theological journal classifies the whole new Bible as conservative, and especially their putting *virgin* here in the margin. Professor W. A. Irwin (*Review and Expositor,* July 1953, p. 350) says: "But doubtless I may be asked: 'Then what about that footnote?' In reality, I am at a loss to answer." Certainly so. And all concerned will be at a greater loss than that, before the discussion and decision by American Christianity are over. "I offer the opinion that it was a sort of concession to tradition, which only since publication we have realized was entirely wrong." So the Committee now repudiates its own Bible at that point? Certainly the Committee must be made up of innocents abroad. Professor Irwin says they did not even talk about this vital passage that lies at the very door of the New Testament and of the Christian hope. That is naïve to the superlative degree. Are men that unaware of the realities of life, and of thought all about them, fit to translate a Bible?

Of course, they miss the point entirely who labor the meaning of the word as being *a young woman.* To be certain, she was that, and all so believe. The question is as to her purity. Now one of the most common defects in translators with fixed ideas is that they confuse what a word often, or generally means with the question of what it *can* mean, in a given context. The known minimum of meaning is often not the correct translation. The context adds facts, and these have to enter into the one-word concept and its translation. Jewish children tended to be, officially, the children of their fathers, not primarily of their mothers. There is unquestionably no father in the picture. We don't know the name of Isaiah's wife. *He* gives value to the son-signs, as part of this prophecy. Now just how could the humdrum fact of an anonymous young woman, harlot or married woman, being pregnant and being about to give her baby, with no father in the picture, the pompous name of "Immanuel," I say, how could that trifling incident be a *son-sign* to "the house of David"? *There is no sign in the high-sounding names of nonentities.* It is only in the reality of a virgin birth in which God really comes into humanity and is with us that the house of David can see its timeless sign.

While writing this, I came across, in my reading, a third witness. One of the RSV Committee, in a new Bible dictionary, while repudiating any relation between this passage and Messianic prophecy, says that Micah made the same mistake that the New Testament makes, in taking this passage as referring to the virgin birth. Lo, we have another comrade in our faith, admittedly, Micah 5:3. Welcome, brother Micah, to the ranks.

Son-sign three. It is another boy of Isaiah, Maher-shalal-hashbaz (the spoil speeds, the prey hastes). The same prophecy of doom, hopelessness in Israel after the flesh, Messianic light alone for the hope of the soul is the meaning and message of this boy.

Son-sign four. Here all this is brought to a glorious climax of faith: "The people who walked in darkness have seen a great light . . . for to us a Child is born, to us a Son is given; and the government will be upon his shoulder, and his name will be called Wonderful Counsellor, Mighty God, Everlasting Father, Prince of Peace. Of the increase of his government and of peace there will be no end . . . The zeal of the Lord of hosts (Jehovah of hosts, the covenant God of Israel) will do this" (Is. 9:2,6,7).

Now think of Isaiah's great prophetic drama as *son-signs* in four acts, two of his own sons, and a Son twice predicted who transcends human proportions in all these majestic and redemptive manners and meanings, on a vast future scale, beyond the contemporary horizon of Israel, which is utterly doomed and hopeless, by prophetic testimony. There is always local verbiage in Messianic prophecy, even as in the parables of Jesus. The prophets did not say one conquering nation would succeed another, and in yonder time and under the yoke of yonder people, so many years hence, Messiah would be born. They wove into current phrase and contemporary talk, some of it lost to us in its application, this great picture of Messiah's features. And when it is all painted we see Jesus, virgin-born, the Suffering Servant of the Cross and all the rest of the "Gospel According to Isaiah." When nobody any longer remembers that there was once a Revised Standard Version, Isaiah's gospel will still stand. There is nothing to keep it from standing. So great a Hebrew scholar as R. Dick Wilson said that every time the word translated *virgin* in Isaiah 7:14, in the Bibles of the world—and that includes the margin of the RSV—is used in the Hebrew Old Testament, the reference is to a virgin. If those are the facts, maybe they regulate the meaning intended.

JOSEPH EXALTED TO THE FATHERHOOD OF JESUS

This note on page 1 of the New Testament belies all the witness of the Gospels as to the incarnation, even if the page above it retains what the RSV will not allow to have been a correct translation of the virgin-birth prophecy. "Joseph, to whom was betrothed the virgin Mary, was the father of Jesus who is called Christ." There is the leveling note: "Other ancient authorities." You do not know from that that they are a very, very small, later, and less valuable group of manuscripts. It is a miserable debunking of the Savior. Once again he is betrayed in the house of friends. This New Catholicism is tremendously fanatical about a united front for shaping up a vast ecclesiastical totalitarianism, such as Rome already has, and fastening it upon the world. But it seems to have no conception of the value of a united testimony of the witnesses as to facts. If at the top of the page some "ancient authorities" allege that Jesus was virgin-born (proving it by a "false" translation of an Old Testament text), and if "other ancient authorities," unclassified as inferior, late, and few, give a self-contradicting testimony at the bottom of the page, you have no "catholic gospel" left. You introduce contrary testimony into your Bible and you have a house divided against itself. Some anonymous schemer invented this terrible farce. But he is allowed to contradict Matthew right on the front page of Matthew. The men who perpetrated this sin against the Savior will certainly answer for it to him, but they must also answer to the Christian public in America.

It takes a pre-existing being to experience an incarnation. We don't speak of our incarnation, unless we are spiritualists. Our beings began when begotten. If Jesus thus began, there was no incarnation. He is just like you and me, if he is the mere son of Joseph. Furthermore, if the beginning of his being came when Joseph was still just "betrothed" to Mary, then Christ is himself the product of sin. Two young hot bloods, who couldn't wait a decent time, would be the authors of the being of the Savior. Sin is the author of his very being. This is the royal highway to infidelity and, have no doubt about it, it will serve that end—and probably already has.

"TRULY . . . A SON OF GOD"

Here the Greek cannot determine. It has no article with either noun, *son* or *god*. The context determines whether either or both nouns are definite, according to Greek grammar. In a noun modified by a genitive of another noun, both may be. If I say: "Lincoln's Tad was a dear boy," and I am writing about President Lincoln, then it means *the* Lincoln and *the* boy Tad, even though there are a lot of Lincolns in history and maybe other Tads. I wonder why these RSV translators said "a son of God." God, with a capital *G* is definite, for the Christian. If they don't want any articles, why did they not represent this man, whom I count as one of the converts of the Day of the Cross, as saying: "Surely this man was a son of a god"? Why follow a rule at the beginning of a short line and then refuse to follow it *just two words further on?* Many of us believe Simon of Cyrene was saved on the Day of the Cross. In spite of its demolishing all sacerdotalism and sacramentarianism, we believe the converted bandit, on a second cross, was saved that day without church, priest, sacrament, merit, or morals, and went to heaven with Jesus that afternoon. And we also believe this centurion saw the light, along with these other two, and lifted Jesus to the category not of *a son of a god* but of *the Son of the only true God.* Why would Matthew be putting in the idle chatter of a soldier who, on the modernist hypothesis, would have merely made a remark that did Jesus no honor whatsoever? Willful debunking is the only explanation of this version.

There are several considerations that back up the expression of this centurion's faith as genuine. He had heard the gospel that the bandit also heard on the cross. Just above this passage, the RSV permits the chief priests, the scribes, and the elders to say: "He said: I am the Son of God." The centurion has heard this all day. Why, then, at the end of the day must we suppose him to say only "He was a son of God, or a son of a god?" What would Matthew be doing putting *that* into a Gospel? Eberhard Nestle shows his faith by printing both *Son* and *God* with capital letters, in Greek. Thus he expresses his faith and witnesses to the faith of another. And, too, the whole emphasis of the Greek is noteworthy. *God* is the very first word, after *truly*—"Truly God's Son was this one." There are two words for *son* in Greek, and this is the high, noble one. So, of the two possible meanings, that of *faith* seems far more natural, in the man, the hour, and the Gospel which records the event.

Much more of the same nature appears in other sections of this study. Now let us turn to the debunking processes against the Bible and its authors.

DEBUNKERS OF THE BIBLE AND ITS AUTHORS

We begin with the apostle Paul. He is at once both modest and even shame-faced over his record as a persecutor and belated believer. But he is the channel of the grace of God and adds: "I labored more abundantly than they all." Look at the map and the record and you see that. The whole Twelve toiled at the world task of missions far less than the one Paul. Now see how the debunker-translators treat the apostle: "I worked harder than any of them." *Any of them* is singular. The Greek doesn't have the singular. It has the plural: *they all*. The translation simply falsifies the record here. The Greek has *toiled more abundantly. I worked harder* diverts the point of view to the effort, as you measure effort in a gymnasium by certain machines. This isn't a machine-like calculation. It means the toil was fruitful beyond compare. Moffatt has "I have done far more work than all of them." The Basic has almost the same. Paul fares badly with the RSV.

WAS PAUL A STUPID HOLY ROLLER CHATTERER?

He is so presented. The total effect of the translation of I Corinthians 14, the classic Scripture on the developed use of the miracle of speaking with tongues, is to give Paul just that value before men. He speaks with tongues more than all Corinth. He recognizes the gift as of God. He does not restrict its use, when tongues are interpreted. He affirms the intelligence of the message so delivered when he demands interpretation. You can't interpret chatter, monkey whine, pig grunts, hen clucks, or the shrill cries of bird and beast in the forest. All this gift must have the meaning of known music, the clarity of a military bugle call, the ready acceptance of a familiar voice. It is the "tongue" which must be one of four things, in its understandable contents: "revelation, knowledge, prophesying or doctrine" (v.6,KJ); or, "revelation, knowledge, prophecy or teaching" (RSV and Moffatt). By this miraculous gift, then, God could send to some hearer or hearers one of these four messages, in his native tongue, other than Greek, just as he sent perhaps all of these things to nearly a score of nationalities on the Day of Pentecost. Prophecy itself could come through a foreign tongue, just as truly as through the native speech of the audience.

It is only elementary fairness, always, to look at the Bible's own presentation of its case, see what it means and then judge the possibility and coherence of the hypothesis by the context, local or larger, and all the facts. Let us look at this situation. A great miracle, new to Christianity—Jesus and John the Baptist spoke with no tongues—came on Pentecost as the public credential of the Advent of the Spirit, as the Advent of the Son had its credentials in Bethlehem's miracles. The speaking on Pentecost was just what Paul sets forth here, not understood by those who spoke but by those who heard. That is the miracle. For a man to speak to a foreigner in his native speech is no miracle and no wonder. For him to speak intelligent language that corresponds to intelligent thought that he has in mind but in a language he does not understand, is the miracle. That is a great equalizing miracle. So it happens to the Twelve and to Paul. It happens to Jews on Pentecost and to Cornelius and his Gentile comrades in Caesarea. It happens to the outlanders who show up in Ephesus, perhaps from Africa. It shows up in Corinth. Now all these places were great international centers. "All Asia" came to Ephesus. Corinth had two seaports on two seas, and countless tourists, sailors, and delayed travelers from all lands were there for considerable periods. Caesarea was a capital of a bilingual native population and a multilingual transient population. These are the places where the miracle was natural and had its witnessing value. Now just suppose, as some hold, that there was a real miracle in Jerusalem at the Pentecost of Acts 2, but the rest of these cases were just chatter. Don't you suppose that the nationalistic pride of the Jew, jealous of his superior prerogatives in Christianity and aggressively so in the Judaistic controversy, and with a faction right there in Corinth, would have cried aloud to the four winds: "Yes, but look. We Jews spoke with real tongues at Pentecost, and Paul and these Gentiles just chatter." The equalizing miracle closes all mouths to such a comparison. But an inferior miracle in Caesarea, Ephesus, or Corinth, which is no miracle at all, reduces the Christianity of these Gentile centers, and of the Gentile apostle, to a sham and a disgrace.

There is no debunking propaganda quite so disastrous as to present Christianity's foremost spokesman, writer, apologist. and missionary as a perpetrator of sham miracles, a Holy Roller of base pretenses, a parrot in apostle's clothing, a hypocrite who would demand interpretation of that which had no meaning. That great scholar, A. T. Robertson, took the Corinthian tongues as of the same nature as those at Pentecost. Anything else falsifies the record and reduces the Bible itself to the level of approving an idiotic chatter.

Few versions are free from fault here. But the truth could be given to the people. The Berkeley Version has these items of a true translation. It recognizes in verse 2 that the speaking is "in the Spirit" (not merely in the human spirit). This is the special and supreme miracle that served as the credentials of the recent advent of the Spirit to that age. Once accredited, the credentials ceased. But they had to be accredited (not to a pope, for none existed) to all elements of international Christianity by the same genuine miracle appearing to all elements and the apostles of all elements. This truly took place.

The Berkeley Version again and again puts in parentheses the word *unknown* before tongue. That brings to focus the issue. It is a real tongue, but unknown both to the speaker himself and to the regular Greek audience in Corinth.

Note the distinction in verse 14. "For in case I pray in an (unknown) tongue, my spirit prays, but my mind is unproductive." Just so. The longings in the praying spirit go up to God. God's Spirit puts them forth in the speech of a foreigner, in the prayer uttered audibly. But the man praying does not understand the petition. That is of the nature of the miracle. His spirit meets God but his mind does not grasp the message God sends out through his lips.

If you believe in miracles, let the Bible testify the facts. These are of the very essence of the nature of the miracle to which Paul testifies here, and Luke in Acts 2. If you don't believe in miracles, it is a terrible impertinence for you to thrust yourself forward as a translator of the Bible of believers who do accept the Bible witness and want it translated as the miracle took place. The special, temporary, and geographically limited possibilities and usefulness of such a miracle are evident and, in this very connection, Paul prophesied that "tongues will cease, prophecy pass away." Both things came to pass as he prophesied. Neither tongues nor prophecy exist today. The Berkeley Version also saves Paul's statement in verse 2 from incoherence: "no one catches the meaning." Meaning there is, but it can be perceived only by the hearer to whom the Spirit directs the miracle message, in his native speech. The Greek has "No one hears." It means *catches the meaning,* for meaning is there. It is just the Corinth audience of Greeks that doesn't catch it. The tourist or sailor or traveling Jew, who wanders in, will hear.

We cannot put Paul down as a babbling Holy Roller. He commands exactly the opposite of such a program. Only one talk at a time. That is not Holy Roller procedure. *Interpret or shut up.* That would silence Paul himself and all others, if there was nothing to interpret. The subjection of the gift to the control of the one endowed with it and the decency and order in its use are all evidence that Paul had in mind absolutely nothing of the meaningless chatter, *which is never any tongue at all.* When Paul said *tongue* he meant *tongue,* and no debunking process can truthfully reduce him to those horrible proportions. I wrote a tract once on the subject: "The Sect to Which God Said: Hush." That is the command, through Paul, to all who had this gift, unless, first, they had the real gift of foreign speech, miraculously, and, second, it could and would be interpreted for all to understand.

The Incisions from RSV Surgery Left Open

I have been through a lot of surgery, but all the incisions are sewed up. Good surgeons don't leave them open to bleed or to suppurate. Look at the incision on page 113. There is a great hole, from John 7:53 to 8:12. Something has been removed but left lying on the operating table, handy at the foot of the page. When surgeons cut things out they don't leave them lying around. If that does not belong in the Bible, then leave it out and begin the first verse of Chapter 8 with verse 1. When they put the first verse of the chapter as 12, they either confess to removing something that belongs there or confuse the reader. Some manuscripts have this section in Luke. If they think it belongs to Luke, why not have the courage to insert it in Luke? If it has no right to appear anywhere, then don't let it appear anywhere. What would *you* think of a Bible from which surgery had removed that Scripture just as if it were a tumor? Most scholars think we would lose a piece of genuine record of a real happening in the life of Jesus. Well, then, if you are going to leave it in the Bible, leave it in the text, not in tiny type at the foot of the page. The RSV said it was not going to use italics. But it did. It made them a sort of purgatory for purged Scriptures. Basic leaves it in. So does Berkeley, with this note: "Although 7:53-8:11 is not in older found manuscripts, the incident has such a Christlike ring to it, the omission of it would be a great loss. We accept it as a true report." The RSV has cut out two spurious verses of I John 5. They left no open incision there but just stretched the language left over the same verse system. Why not do that elsewhere? That is good surgery—stretching the remaining parts and sewing them together.

Why didn't they do that to the "Good Confession" of Alexander Campbell? Alexander is gone but not quite forgotten—unmourned, though. But there his "Good Confession" is, in a footnote: "Other ancient authorities (the leveling textual criticism of the RSV that makes all cats brown in the dark. W.C.T.) add all or most of verse 37: *And Philip said, If you believe with all your heart, you may. And he replied, I believe that Jesus Christ is the Son of God.*" That's not a good confession and entitles no one to baptism. Why, it takes more than that to get into the World Council of Churches, even. This spurious confession has no more right on any page of any Bible than the Trinitarian invention, properly left out of I John 5, with the incision sewed up.

LOOK WHAT HAPPENED TO MARK

On the last page of his Gospel is major surgery, nearly half a page left on the operating table. The Gospel is left without an end. I don't object to all the facts being told. Tell them. But wait for more light, for more is coming every day, before throwing away the end of a Gospel and one form of the Great Commission. My objection here is not to the facts, but to the RSV scholars' dogmatism. When they doubt, they doubt dogmatically. Samuel Zwemer wrote a book, whose title I do not now recall (I am away from my library), in which he goes to great length to argue for the genuineness of this Scripture. And he says that the antimissionary drive just now is not against missions in itself, openly. It is against the genuineness of the Great Commissions of our Lord, denying them to him, from preconceived notions of the critics' subjectivism.

JOHN R. SAMPEY'S OPINION

Some years ago I was serving as interpreter for the beloved Sampey, staying with him in the home of Doctor and Mrs. A. E. Hayes, in north Brazil. One day we spent much of the day together, sitting under a tree and talking of all things that occurred to us. He asked me: "What do you think of the ending of the Gospel of Mark?" I replied: "I think the judgment of Broadus is best. I rest no doctrine on it till it is proven genuine Scripture, but I defend it from the false interpretations of sacramentalism and pentecostalism." He gave many reasons why he thought it to be genuine, and I agreed, and agree, that it ought to hold its place with the admittedly genuine Mark till some proven different ending is found. Yet, bear in mind, the RSV promoters are trying to make Sampey and Robertson serve as a blind for this spotted version.

Consider the theory that suddenly, one day, there was just one copy of the Gospel of Mark, and the last page broke off. No one thinks that was in Mark's lifetime. He would have tended to it. No, it is held to be in a time of persecution. But that brings the Gospel to a day of its wide, general use. Anyone who knows anything at all of the early Christianity knows the feats of memory it showed and used in its educational processes. Suppose the last leaf broke off. How many men, how many women, how many children would have been able to say this: "You say we have just one copy of Mark's Gospel left and the last sheet of the papyrus broke off and has disappeared. Don't grieve. Tell me where what you have ends. *I can quote the rest by heart.*" A modernist can screw up his courage to believe anything, if it is against the Bible. Debunking.

Now, the conservative Bible scholars have not hidden the facts. Benjamin Warfield and A. T. Robertson, John Gresham Machen and W. Hershey Davis taught more men the facts of textual criticism than all these RSV translators put together, many times more. They will go with the facts anywhere they lead. But not beyond the facts, out into the pathless depths of the swamps of speculation, subjectivism, and dogmatic unbelief. Did not the ASV put all these facts in their proper place in its margins? Absolutely. Why not be content to stay with the facts and avoid dogmatism, in this the greatest day of discovery of manuscripts and papyri in the history of the world?

Again, I would ask this. For us who are conservatives, these facts are not blinked, and they are grave. But we are not running ahead of the facts. But what difference does this

all make to the modernist? Does he consider any of the rest
of Mark's Gospel as any more genuine than the present ending of it? Not a whit. Does he not think the rest of John just
as spurious as the beginning of Chapter 8? He certainly does.
Is not the *Formgeschichte* criticism all the style now, which
makes the Gospels, all and altogether, just a collection of traditions, legends, myths, editing, and what have you, like little
stones put together from many quarries to make a mosaic?
If none of John is genuine, why worry about this little piece?
Mark 16 and John 8 and the rest of the marginal Scriptures
are just as good as any of it, according to the current hypothesis. I fail to see the reason for this enthusiasm for purity in
a situation these critics currently regard as hopelessly corrupt.
When a surgeon finds the whole interior permeated with cancer, he sews up the incision and doesn't operate. Why then this
surgery only on one or two spots, if all the organism is similarly affected?

Debunking Paul Again

Begin with I Corinthians 7:40. The RSV has "And I
think that I have the Spirit of God." That seems to make Paul's
guidance of the church a matter of his own opinion. A word
has been deliberately left out, to debunk Paul in that fashion.
It is also very emphatic in the Greek: "And I think that I *also*
have the Spirit of God." The alternatives are not do I, or do I
not, have the Spirit when I teach? The burning issue is: Does
some factional leader there in Corinth, who boasts of his spiritual graces, have a monopoly on the Spirit, or do I *also*
have the Spirit and guide you by his revealing light? Just as
the RSV turned on the hose of additions to the Bible and
scattered *inspired* all over the New Testament, in order that
there might be nothing unique in the Bible's being inspired, so
they often turn off the spigot, by subtractions from the original
Greek, and stop the flow of revelation, which they ought to
let flow on into the English fully. The effect here is to cast
doubt on Paul's being the Spirit's revealing organ of revelation, in I Corinthians and on.

Again Debunking Paul

In I Corinthians 14:37, we read: "If any one thinks that

he is a prophet, or spiritual, he should acknowledge that what I am writing to you is a command of the Lord." Note the debunking process. A stern imperative command is debunked into a soft "he should." Paul wrote the plural, "the things that I write to you." They include all his Scriptures. This is debunked into the singular, restricting it into *what I am writing,* just that where the ink was still wet. Paul did not always give commands. When he did command the churches, it was Christ issuing the command through him, or else he quoted commands of Jesus already known.

ONCE AGAIN DEBUNKING PAUL

In I Corinthians 7:17, the preoccupation of the RSV revisers with setting up a Christianity of *rules,* or of misrepresenting Christianity as being that, makes them utterly misrepresent Paul. The apostle said: "And so I command in all the churches." This has been watered down to rules, as if Paul were writing a discipline or a prayer book: "This is my rule in all the churches." Paul had no ambition to rule, in any sense. That is why it is vital to preserve his words, for he is transmitting the revealed will of Christ, when he issues commands. Now the RSV translators are as free to believe that or disbelieve it as I am. But let them not blur Paul's affirmation of his apostolic authority as an organ of divine revelation, authoritative over the Christian conscience. That is the issue. The wrongly translated command of I Corinthians 16:1 is also watered down: "I directed," in place of *I ordained* or *commanded.*

DEBUNKING LUKE IN HIS GREAT PREFACE

Luke wrote more of our New Testament than any other man. His preface is vital. But its great witness is watered down in the RSV. It is one of the most vital Scriptures in the whole of apologetics. It is not something for amateurs to try out their hand on. The verb *accomplish* seems to me inadequate. This is not a tribute to somebody's achievements or accomplishments. It is not a boast of a successful program. The ASV scholars were right in feeling the inner sense to be that of the verb *fulfill.* The Greek doubles up that idea, as if it were a verb *full-fulfill.* The tense (perfect) intensifies that idea, *perfected* in full-fulfillment. You see why the KJ translators overtranslated the word: "things which are most surely believed" (mg. *are fully established*). Moffatt has "the established facts of our religion." This is a case where the subjective joins the objective, the things prophesied or predestined came to the fullest fruition and brought the Christian community to full assurance of these facts. How much the RSV lost of the verb's meaning. Then there comes the usual change of sentence structure. Luke gives a positive, active statement: the eyewitnesses *delivered*. The mania to change the construction passes it to a passive verb, with a different subject. "The things which were accomplished . . . were delivered to us." Hardly that. Not the *events* were delivered, but the conviction of the witnesses that they are the truth, the whole truth, and nothing but the truth. You see why the KJ scholars felt impelled to "the things most surely believed." You can't deliver an event: you can a gospel, news, testimony of convictions as to facts and their meaning. The RSV missed the bus here. Spurgeon commented on the ASV: "Good Greek but poor English." Often one must feel that the RSV is neither good Greek nor good English.

So far the RSV may have failed, trying. But now it gives up trying and deliberately goes off from trying to translate and puts in ideas of its own that it likes better. The Greek has twice in a row the language *from the beginning,* phrased differently. That is very vital. First, did the Gospel come to Luke and the whole Christian community in such a way as to make certain the *origins,* from both God and man? Or did Luke pick up a lot of traditions floating in the air, sift and harmonize them? Luke says no. All the Gospel facts came directly from eyewitnesses. And they came from a special group of eyewitnesses. They were not laymen. They were eyewitnesses from among one small group, the group composed of those who had been preachers of the Word from the beginning.

Who are these so important witnesses? The Twelve, surely. There are not many more in this class. Luke begins his second book, The Acts, with this same problem of witnesses. Probably under the command of Jesus (Acts 1:2), led by Peter, the church of 120 chose a successor to Judas. He had to be one of the "men who have accompanied us during all the time that the Lord Jesus went in and out among us, beginning from the baptism of John until the day when he was taken up from us." Luke is an expert on witnesses. We see here the Twelve and two more who measured up to the preface to both his books. We see where the Christian movement began, with the ministry and baptism of John. Luke searched out accurately the united witness of these who were eyewitnesses "from the beginning." Jesus said to these same witnesses: "You also (as well as the Holy Spirit) are witnesses, because you have been with me from the beginning" (John 15:27).

That is one thing, to *have available* witnesses from the beginning, capable of giving certainty as to both origins and developments, the whole march of the supreme phase of all progressive revelation. It is another thing to have used fully the witnesses and have drawn from them the testimony "from the beginning." Now here the RSV falls down, out of sheer carelessness or plain ill will. When Luke says he followed all things accurately, in drawing up his narrative, *from the beginning,* the RSV revisers won't let him say it, in their English. They repudiate him and change his record to read: "followed . . . from some time past." It is unpardonable.

There is more debunking in Acts. Luke gives great emphasis that Jesus goes on in Acts, in continuity of "*all the things which* Jesus began *both* to do *and* to teach." The two elements of the Gospel record, doing and doctrine, receive special emphasis, *both . . . and.* It doesn't please the RSV. The plural is reduced to the singular and the emphasis is thrown in the ash can. Emphasis, always notable in the Greek Gospels, doesn't please complacent souls.

Too Much to Tell

I cannot go on, though there is much more of the same. All this banishing of Bible words is a debunking process to which the Bible vocabulary of revelation is submitted. We shall see the grave love of Disharmony, hatred of harmony of the Gospels. We shall see the aftermath of letting the camel's nose into the flap of the tent door. We shall see the linking up of the translation with a vast propaganda against the Bible from the same faculties and many of the same men. We see irreverence and unfaith acting as *squeezers* of many, many Scriptures, squeezing out all the supernatural, and much of the natural meaning. We see ignorance and detrimental opinion in the introductions and the margins. We see much more that is offensive against the majesty of the Savior. All this is done with impunity and full confidence that they can get by with it. Can they? If so, our American Christianity is doomed. It remains to be seen. Speak to us again, Tennyson:

> *Let knowledge grow from more to more*
> *But more of reverence in us dwell;*
> *That mind and soul, according well,*
> *May make one music as before.*

CHAPTER TEN

CUNNING SECTARIAN ATTACKS
AGAIST FUNDAMENTAL
BAPTIST TRUTHS

AN ILLUSTRIOUS LEADER OF AMERICAN PROTESTANT THOUGHT has thus defined the difference between Church and Sect. You join a Sect; you are born into a Church. I should say rather that you have there the difference between Christianity and the pagan mind, made pagan by the European idea of infant baptism, which incorporates into the State Church the entire population, while it cannot help itself. Such a Church persecutes New Testament churches and styles all nonconformists "sects." Contemptible insolence!

Now I do not use the word *sect* in any contemptuous sense. Baptists glory, like Paul, in "the Way, which they (the Catholics, and the New Catholicism, in our case. W.C.T.) call a sect" in which we "worship the God of our Fathers," though it be now, as then, "the sect . . . everywhere spoken against" (Acts 24:14;28:22). Paul told the Corinth church: "There must be factions among you in order that those who are genuine among you may be recognized" (I Cor. 11:19). Paul stirred up divisions wherever truth was being sacrificed or imperiled, even what the Greek calls an "insurrection" (Acts 15:2). In I Corinthians 11:19 he used this same word, there properly translated *faction,* for it was just in that one church; but over a vast area, affecting many churches that would have to show fidelity in division against falsehood in doctrine and life, Paul's meaning would be: "It is necessary (the Greek says that) that there be sects . . . ." Christ divides, came with that in view (Matt. 10:34). It is never right to be wrong. A Catholicism or Council of Churches composed mostly of those who are wrong is no right Church, or group of Churches. Each is as wrong as its false doctrines. The massing of doctrinal wrongness under a persecuting hierarchy, unknown to revealed Christianity and set to stamp it out of existence, never made anything which has the right to the name *church*. Every Catholic Church (and I believe the federal statistics show some eighteen Catholic Churches among the denominations in the United States) is a sect, which means a group following a certain system. Are you and your group *all* of nominal

133

Christianity? You know you are not. Then you are a sect. Baptists are a sect who have set as their standard the New Testament faith, in New Testament churches, loyal to Christ. You can be a sect just as loyal to the pope of Rome or Mrs. Eddy or the Mormon Apostles or Luther or Wesley or Alexander Campbell. All parts of nominal Christianity are sects in it. It is a pitiable blindness and insolence when one of those parts assumes, by the word Catholic, to be the whole. It can't even aspire to say: "I am holier than thou," for that delusion never produces holiness. It has to say: "I am unholier than you, but bigger than you; and, since I am leagued with Caesar, I'll stamp you out in blood." This contempt of our ecclesiastic eggheads for sects is the prelude of the persecution they will perpetrate when they dare, *if* they get the power.

The eggheads are right, half right; "You join a sect," of your own free will and accord. But they are half wrong; nobody was ever born into a church. This said, it will be clear what I mean by saying this RSV harbors cunning sectarian attacks on fundamental Baptist truths. By Baptist truths I do not mean anything that we invented, but truths that we love and preach that are peculiar to us, as distinguished from other sects. This is what I charge and shall proceed to prove.

SECTARIAN BIAS FAVORING SPRINKLING FOR BAPTISM

Translators are forbidden, by the rules of all Bible societies that render general service, to translate either the word for church (congregation) or the word for baptism (immersion). When you take any English Bible in your hands, you know those words are not translated. Now, in the providence of God, on the ASV Committee, in 1901, there were men who were great scholars—men with a sense of justice and fairness as well. Though they could not translate the verb *baptize*, they every one knew what it means. They were not forbidden to translate correctly the prepositions that go with the verb. With a great lexicographer, Thayer, and others of like scholarship and spirit, on the Committee, they made a decision of fraternal justice that warmed the hearts of the Baptists of the nation. With no Baptist on the Committee at the time, I think—the only Baptist member had died, I believe, before that—the wholly pedobaptist committee voted to translate the preposition with the verb *baptize* by our preposition *in,* when the place or element in which the baptizing was done was referred to. That is simple truth, scholarship, and justice. The long Bible Union controversy was over. Both sides were drawn closer together in the impartial decision. Fellowship was deepened and broadened.

Now the RSV turns the hands of the clock back. All that is overturned. Where the American Revision has *baptize in* the river Jordan, *in* water, *in* the Holy Spirit, *in* fire, the RSV brutally undid all the scholarly fairness and fraternal good will of their predecessors and put that back to the 1611 *status quo,* and now we read *baptize with* in Matthew 3:11; Mark 1:8; Luke 3:16; John 1:26,32,33; Acts 1:5, 11:16, and in all the baptismal descriptions, literal and figurative. The Brazilians have a proverb with which they describe this ruthlessness: "They had the cheese and the knife in their hands." So they carved it to suit their own interests. It was a shamefully sectarian trick.

THE SACRAMENTALIST TREASON TO THE GOSPEL

We have already commented the stark folly of the dogmatic nonsense of *baptism for repentance, baptism into Christ, baptism unto death*— burial in order to kill, and much other similar folly of the sectarian RSV. These are mortal offenses against the gospel itself. They wound every Baptist heart in all it holds most dear.

BANISHING BAPTISM FROM FOUNDATION DOCTRINES

Six elementary doctrines, foundation truths, were enumerated in Hebrews 6:1,2. The Christians are exhorted to go on to maturity in their doctrinal outlook, beyond this elementary belief, to such doctrines as the sacrifice and priesthood of Jesus, the New Covenant, and so on. Now, one of these six elementary doctrines is "the doctrine of baptisms" (KJ, ASV using teaching of baptisms, Basic, Phillips, and so on). With its mania for banishing things from its Bible, the RSV issued one more edict of banishment. *Baptisms* are out. *Ablutions* are rushed in to take their place. But there is no Christian doctrine of ablutions. Once more sectarianism walks abroad.

AN ANTI-BAPTIST TRICK OF SECTARIAN JUGGLING OF THE VARIATIONS OF THE TEXT

The New Testament Greek text is quite uncertain when it describes certain Jewish ceremonial acts. Some manuscripts refer to Jewish ceremonies of sprinkling, some of immersion, for purification purposes. Both acts were ceremonies among the Jews. The uncertainty has absolutely nothing to do with baptism. Whether it should be sprinkling or immersion in the text has nothing to do with baptism, since it is a Jewish ceremony. But now comes the trickery. The RSV gives the preference in the text to sprinkling, which is probably correct. But they don't put sprinkling. They put "They do not eat unless they purify themselves" (Mark 7:4). In the margin it is stated: "Other ancient authorities read *baptize*." That simply isn't so. The intelligent Bible student knows it isn't so, but the casual reader does not; there will be eager friends to exploit this false note. The RSV puts in the margin: "Other ancient authorities read *baptize*." They don't. They read *immerse, dip*. If it pains the translators to say *immerse*, then let them follow the custom elsewhere and put the Greek in anglicized form, *baptidzo*. This takes us back to the tricks of baptismal controversies of last century. Syllogism: "Our New Bible says: The Jews do not eat unless they purify (sprinkle) themselves. But it also says in the margin that other authorities say *baptize*. Therefore to sprinkle is to baptize." I need not call attention to the several fallacies in this. The second premise is simply a falsehood. The Greek does *not* say *baptize* for *baptize* is a transliteration of the word into English, not a translation, and probably ninety-five per cent of the times the word was used it referred to other immersions rather than baptisms. This was a special use of the meaning of the word and cannot apply to Jewish tradition. Whether the Jews baptized at all in Christ's day is a debated question. *If they did,* it was only a once-for-all baptism of proselytes entering Judaism, not a purification rite practiced every time they came home from market. This is just a cheap sectarian trick, involving a lack of veracity.

A Version Meant to be the Handmaiden of Infant Baptism

We have called attention already to this tendency-translation of the Gospels about the children coming to Jesus. He said: "Let them come." They were big enough to come, did come, and *they* (the children) were rebuked by the apostles but received by Jesus. Now look at the wresting of the language of Acts 16:33,34. The intense thought that has been put on the wording of the RSV, to make it serve the interest of its pedobaptist owners and their Council of mainly Pedobaptist Churches, is amazing. Look at it. "He brought them up into his house, and set food before them; and he rejoiced with all his household that *he* had believed in God." Clearly, by this sectarian trick of cunning mistranslation, we have one man's faith serving as the ground of a household baptism. The pedobaptist owners of this version have made millions from it, and it is worth millions to infant baptism. But what does the Greek say, if not tortured by sectarian brainwashing to force it to say something else?

The sentence structure is violently wrenched. Here is what the Greek says: "And he himself was baptized and all his at once, . . . and rejoiced *whole-house-ly* having come to believe in God." The Greek has just one word for our expression *with all his house*. It is an adverb. It can modify the first verb, or the second, or both of them, since the second is a participle, subordinated to the first verb. The subject of both main verb and participle is *he,* but his action is modified by the accompanying phrase *with his whole house.* The adverb *whole-house-ly* is like a bridge between the two verbs. The Basic Bible (by British scholars from the universities of London and Cambridge, with Mr. Churchill and American scholars as sponsors) says: "He was full of joy, having faith in God with all his family." Moffatt has "overjoyed, like all his household at having believed in God." The Berkeley has "Extremely happy with his loved ones for believing in God." And the Oxford Shorter Bible approves the KJ: "Believing in God with all his house." Both text and context show that he was not alone in hearing the message of evangelism, in the subsequent baptism, or in the previous salvation. In every case the house

is unanimous. Baptists are accustomed constantly to evangelizing and baptizing whole households. I have done it in this
country and in Brazil. And Jesus found an entire household
of believers in Capernaum, in his early ministry (John 4:53).
Let the reader judge by the facts.

BREAKING INTO THE SAVIOR'S BAPTISMAL WITNESS:
LUKE 7:29,30

The RSV has set a parenthesis in a discourse of Jesus.
That is possible, where the author of the book makes an aside
explanation, as in Acts 1:18,19. But here the continuity of the
thought seems to demand that these words be taken as those
of Jesus, not of Luke in an aside to the readers. Note the
march of the thought. Verses 24-28 contain only praise of
John the Baptist by Jesus, but no criticism of the Pharisees
and lawyers. At once there follows a criticism of these ruling
elements in Israel for their rejecting of John and his baptism.
Immediately there follows the scorching condemnation of
these elements by Jesus by an illustration that makes them ridiculous, like pouting children.

Two questions arise. First, what call is there for the biting
sarcasm, making the Pharisaic element ridiculous, if no fault
of theirs has been mentioned? And, second, why should the
RSV translators wish to interrupt the discourse of Jesus, which
they report in quotation marks, doubly subtracting this declaration from the word of our Lord both by a parenthesis and
by leaving it outside the marks of quotation? Let us see the
facts.

First, the part in question is exactly the motive Jesus had
for bringing in the criticism given in verses 31-35. Read it
now as part of the speech of Jesus: "All the people, when they
heard, likewise the publicans, justified God (vindicated God,
declared God to be right in his commands and Messianic program) by being baptized with the baptism of John; but the
Pharisees and lawyers rejected the counsel of God concerning themselves, by not being baptized by him. To what, *therefore,* shall I liken the men of this generation, and to what are
they really similar?" My translation here takes this hearing,
"when they heard," as referring to the times of John the Bap-

tist and his ministry. He fills the whole previous horizon. That is the natural course to take, for it is the decision made after hearing John that brings on the action and attitude Jesus condemns in these two classes. Now taking these as words of Jesus, you see him draw a conclusion from them: *therefore.* His criticism flows from his statement about those criticized. Otherwise, it surprises us out of a clear sky, with no connection with what went before and no provocation for such an outburst, one of the most severe in all our Lord's public ministry.

The second question arises. Why would the RSV translators wish to extract these two verses from the midst of a discourse of Jesus that they are putting in quotes? Why give the authorship to Luke and refuse it to Jesus? Look at what is removed from the speech of Jesus: *strong approval of the baptism of John.* It isn't hard to see why a committee of translators hostile to the baptism of John would hate to hear Jesus say it was the counsel of God and from heaven. The baptism of John was evidently immersion. Even the anti-Baptist RSV says it was *in* the river Jordan. And it was evidently not infant baptism, since fruits of repentance were demanded for it, even if the RSV folly does state the demand of fruits before baptism, of a repentance *for* which baptism is supposed to be a commitment. For pedobaptist purposes, far better subtract this high tribute to the baptism of John from Jesus, and leave it discounted as merely a parenthetical remark of Luke in passing. So it is broken off from the quotation marks, shut up inside the parentheses, and a pronoun not in the Greek is added, "when they heard *this.*" Now note also the abrupt and improbable movement of the RSV thought: "the Pharisees and the lawyers *rejected* the purpose (another spurious translation, to avoid recognizing the baptism of John as a doctrine) of God." But how on earth could they be doing that at this late day ("when they heard *this*")? They did it when they heard *him,* (John). This treatment of the continuity of our Lord's discourse registers a bias against his doctrine, which happens to be a Baptist truth, one we have from his divine revelation and authority but in loyalty to which we stand almost alone.

It is Jesus who says this. By inventing the parenthesis, the

RSV took the words away from Jesus, making a breach in his remarks, which they renew right afterwards. Moffatt, though using parenthesis, has this translation: "all the people and the tax-gatherers acknowledged the justice of God, as they had been baptized with the baptism of John; but the Pharisees and jurists, who refused his baptism, frustrated God's purpose for themselves." Have not most of these translators done exactly that same thing about the baptism God commands? Now they set themselves to dishonor and repudiate this same baptism by their sectarian translation, directed against it. And they shunt off into a parenthesis, attributed to Luke, our Lord's very words in condemnation of earlier "scholars" who did this same thing.

A LITTLE PREPOSITION, THE BIG CHANNEL OF SACRA-MENTALISM

The supreme glory of Baptists is their unsacramental gospel. We are almost the only great denomination that holds that baptism neither saves, helps save, keeps saved, or avoids the loss of salvation. It professes a salvation obtained in Christ previously to baptism and sets forth in beautiful picture the great redemptive acts that are its objective causes, and by the same picture and at the same time sets forth its subjective effects. Catholics have seven sacraments; Protestants have two; Baptists have none. *Sacrament* is a word of pagan militarism, alien to the New Testament and to apostolic Christianity. Even the new Catholic Bibles do not have the word. Nor do we want its pagan idea thrust in by wrong translation. It took centuries to get the false translation of the word out of printed Bibles; if it takes centuries more, Baptists will still insist that the sinister ideas of sacramentalist superstition follow the exit of the word that expresses them.

A battle for the centuries is the effort to get an evangelical, unsacramental translation of the preposition *eis.* Sacramentalists are determined to have it a preposition looking only to the future, and expressing purpose but never cause. The context determines whether it looks forward or backward. Its general idea is *reference,* either way, and the context determines what the reference is. That is why Dr. Robertson says it is not Greek grammar that determines such translations but whether a man is evangelical, or not. Some day, as "knowledge grows from more to more," and also reverence for revealed truth, however it may affect creeds, we will have Acts 2:38 translated: "be baptized on the basis of the remission of sins," previously obtained by repentance. We shall see that Nineveh repented *because* of the preaching of Jonah, not in order for him to preach nor merely *at* his preaching. Some day it will be held ridiculous that translators ever let themselves put "I baptize you for repentance" in any Bible. It is medievalism's anachronism, still exploited by sectarian bias. And it would still be sectarian, even if the vast majority of the sects approved the wrong, as they probably do. There is a cloud the size of a man's hand on the horizon. Phillips, an Anglican priest, nevertheless translates Matthew 3:11: "I baptize you as a sign that your hearts are changed." And in Mark 1:4 he gave us: "John came . . . proclaiming baptism as the mark of a complete change of heart and of forgiveness of sins." Why could not the RSV have had that moral courage? Why couldn't *they* tell the people the truth, too?

Silly Slavery to Sacramentalism I Peter 3:21

For the superlative extreme, listen to this: "Baptism, which corresponds to this, now saves you, *not as a removal of dirt from the body* but as an appeal to God for a clear conscience." That is a wicked torture of the Word of God, false at every turn. The Bible does not say that. These words are not there. And what the Bible does say is not translated. Trivial substitutions have been made, to serve the ends of ecclesiastical magic. There is no word in the Greek that means *body*, none that means *dirt*, no verb *corresponds*, nor is there any appeal *for* a good conscience, as if it were a rabbit some magician is to pull out of his hat. Sacramentalism has put the mask of salvation by holy water over a great gospel Scripture.

What, then, does the Bible say? It says *flesh*, not *body*. That is a very different word, and its frequent apostolic meaning is nothing physical, but the moral turpitude of human depravity. Water cannot take that away. But sacramentalism says it can. So the translators would not let Peter say that water cannot take away human depravity. They think it can, even removing original sin. The *flesh*, in Scripture, does not mean avoirdupois. It has a mind, the carnal mind (Col. 2:18). The *flesh* has a will (John 1:13). The fl*esh* has a line of judgment (John 8:15). The *flesh* has laws and principles that govern its spiritual operations, (Rom. 7:25). Think how translation has degenerated when serious men can reduce all this to mere *dirt* on the *body*.

Now this Scripture denies sacramentalism. Water can remove dirt from the body. But believers do not come to baptism for that. They come already bathed and clean, in more senses than one. Dirt is not the issue. Water cannot take away sin, moral filth of unregenerate human nature, which in the New Testament goes by the name of *flesh*. When Peter said that (I Pet. 3:21), he denied all the sacramentalism of the apostate centuries.

Now go back and look at Noah. Was he saved by water? No. Through it. His old world lay on one side of the flood, his new life on the other. That baptism can signify, mark, and portray in life. Noah was saved by the ark. The ark is Christ. Water only drowned the race, and it will damn every sacramentalist who trusts in it. Peter called baptism a *figure*. The translators assassinated that testimony. Evil scheming. Baptism is a figure, not a sacrament; a symbolic representation of truth, not a channel of grace. Nor is baptism an appeal for a good conscience, either. You don't get a good conscience that way. "The blood of Christ purifies the conscience from dead works to serve the living God" (Heb. 9:14). Baptism is the question of a good conscience, cleansed by the blood of the Savior, asking: "Lord, what wilt thou have me to do?" "Art thou a teacher in Israel and knowest not these things?" Then Jesus would say to you again: "Ye (you and your like-blinded colleagues) must be born again." Sacramentalists are not competent to translate a nonsacramental gospel. As well might a blind man pilot an airplane.

BAPTIST TRUTH ABOUT THE MINISTRY ALSO TAMPERED WITH

This Bible teaches celibacy for widowers who are either ministers or deacons. "Leave that to the popes," you say? You spoke too late. Here it is in the new Bible: "Now a bishop must be . . . married only once" (I Tim. 3:2). And the demand reaches even to laymen and orders likewise the deacons: "Let deacons be married only once" (v. 12). Any reason for translating the Bible in this semi-Catholic way? Not the slightest. Both times the translators themselves put in the margin: "Greek: *the husband of one wife*," Greek: *husbands of one wife*." Now were translators of the new Bible once married men? Two of my greatest teachers were thrice married. Should they have resigned from their theological chairs? I suggest that before any deacon decides to use this new Bible he either get rid of his second wife or resign as a deacon. Now if the Greek doesn't say that, as is confessed in the margin, why should the translators say it in the text of what they propose as our Bible? This is an "authorized" version. Who authorized that folly? This celibacy of ministerial widowers is a little better than Romanism, I agree. Paul says that forbidding to marry is a doctrine of demons, (I Tim. 4:1,2). I am interested to know this. Does that include forbidding second marriages? If so, this false translation is of demonic "inspiration." Who wants a silly translation?

A FORTY PER CENT BANISHING OF BISHOPS FROM THE BIBLE

Baptists believe in bishops, in the Bible meaning of the term. An illustrious prelate asked Dr. Truett, in England: "Do the Baptists have bishops?" "Yes, indeed," said the great preacher. "I did not know that. How many bishops do the Baptists have in the United States?" queried the prelate. "Some sixty thousand, more or less," replied his Baptist guest. The prelate paled and trembled. " 'Pon my word, I didn't know that." To be sure he didn't. He doesn't even know what a bishop is. Truett did. Truett was my guest a week and told me this in my own home. A bishop is not the boss of anybody. He is the servant of one church, its pastor. That is New Testament Christianity. Now that being a very vital part of Baptist doctrine we resent the arbitrary banishment of the word *bishop* from the new Bible twice out of the five times it ought to be there. Every bishop was a pastor, every pastor a bishop, all of them presbyters. Accustomed to that beloved figure, the New Testament churches gave Jesus the beloved title

Pastor (Shepherd) *and Bishop of our souls.* The RSV translators robbed the Savior of that title of love. I resent that. It is a name infinitely dear. What did they put in its place? "Shepherd and Guardian." That could be true, of course, but it is not what the Bible said. The dear name of the pastor of each reader, who was both pastor and bishop in that Baptist Christianity of the first century, was given to Jesus, the example of that ministry for us all. It dishonors our Lord to rob him of one of his dearest titles in the New Testament.

The second place where they banished *bishop* from the Bible is in Acts 20:28. There Paul said, as quoted by Luke: "the Holy Spirit made you bishops." Paul said that to the presbyters of the church of Ephesus, all of them. There were not two classes, ruling and teaching presbyters. Every elder was a bishop. And, too, every bishop was a pastor, for Paul told them to *pastor,* as you hear people say who make a verb out of the word *pastor,* the church of God. So here you have some very important Baptist doctrine; all presbyters (elders) are bishops and pastors, title of endearment also given to our Lord (I Peter 2:25). The three names of the ministry belong to every minister. As presbyter he is counselor, as were the old men (presbyters, etymologically) in Israel. As bishop he is presiding officer, administrative official, overseeing the organization. As pastor he is guide and intimate friend and shepherd soul for his dear flock. Now the RSV destroys this part of the Bible. It goes off at a tangent and, twice out of five times that the Bible has the word bishop, it banishes it to the RSV Siberia. Thus there disappears the Baptist truth versus Catholic apostasy, that a bishop is never more than a pastor, that there are many of them in a great and numerous church, where that is necessary, and that they are not bosses over other ministers or over a diocese of churches but can be several in one church. By substituting this false translation —the name in itself is not false, but as translation of this word it is false—the edge is taken from a very important and wholesome truth.

THE RSV MAKES PRIESTS OUT OF THE MINISTRY

That is never done in the New Testament. *Priest* is not the name of any official in Christianity. Never. Figuratively the term can be used in the sense of the universal priesthood of believers—a vital doctrine that is always nullified by the invention of any official priesthood. But when the officers of the Christian church life are enumerated and summed up, you never find Christian priests among them. Thirty-two times do we have the word *priest* in the New Testament, but always it treats of Jewish or pagan priests, when literal officers of a religion are referred to. Other use is figurative.

But one time we have Paul using the verb *to priest*, just as he used the verb *to pastor*. This gives the RSV its opportunity to render a great service to its owners, the New Catholicism (World Council of Churches). When this New Catholicism finally gets back with Rome, in one great apostate Catholicism, which is what it covets, it can then make this boast: "We first injected this New Catholicism into the new Bible. Then the rest was easy. Accepting that, they had to accept the rest. Had they rejected the New Catholicism, they would have rejected the new Bible in which it is 'authorized.'"

Here is how figurative language of Paul is given a priestly twist: " . . . the grace given me by God to be a minister of Christ Jesus to the Gentiles in the priestly service of the gospel of God, so that the offering of the Gentiles may be acceptable, sanctified by the Holy Spirit" (Rom. 15:16). The figurative language here draws similitudes from both State and Theocracy. Paul is a public figure in the service of the Divine State (the kingdom of God), its service to the Gentiles. That is the first figure. But the comparison did not make Paul really a public servant of the Roman or Jewish State, did it? He was not a diplomat of Caesar or Herod. The second figure is the Jewish Theocracy. Its responsible figures were priests. So he uses the figure which corresponds to the noun *priest* and makes a verb out of it: *"Priesting* the gospel of God." Such a *priesting of the gospel of God* ends up in another *priesting* by the apostle of God. He offers up the whole Gentile world as an offering to God, in so far as it becomes Christian. By the first figure ("minister," public employee, Minister of State, the State being the kingdom of God), Paul classifies himself as what we should call today "a statesman of the kingdom of God," part of its diplomatic corps of ambassadors for Christ. So, in the spiritual realm, he *priests* it, offering up as a sweet savor to God the whole body of Gentile converts. There is here no more a literal priesthood than there is a literal clerical bureaucracy of a political nature, in the union of Church and State. Paul uses the figures of both bureaucracy and priesthood, without belonging to either. Incompetent translators have introduced this language, in cold literalism, without clarifying its use by the apostle. Yet it was very clear to the readers of that day. It tragically misleads the public that has no Greek.

Paul's language is always full of similitudes. Any great teacher's is. The vital thing is to know that figures of speech are to be taken figuratively, not literally. Paul calls himself a slave, figuratively—he was not one literally. He calls himself an ambassador, figuratively—he was not one literally. Paul described himself as a mother giving birth to children and cuddling them—he was not of that gender. Paul uses of himself boxer language—but he was no pugilist. Paul affirms he has begotten (*been made a father of,* say our timid, old-maidish gentlemen of the RSV) workers—he never had a son that we know of. Paul was an architect and carpenter spiritually—but not literally. He merely built well on the sure foundation. Paul compares himself to a planter—he was not one, just a "sower who went forth to sow." Just so the great literary apostle spoke of himself as *priesting* on a cosmic scale, *priesting* all the Gentiles (all nations) to God as the priest offers up the firstfruits of the harvest to God, in Jewish temple ceremonial sacrifice. *But he was not a priest,* any more than he was a slave, an ambassador, a diplomat, a soldier, a farmer, a pugilist, a bureaucrat, an architect, a carpenter, or a woman, both mother and nurse, *except figuratively, in Christ.* The learned priest Phillips correctly saw here no symptoms of a literal priesthood so his translation did not try to force it in. But subservient translators sold their souls to the World Council of Churches, whose largest element is the Greek Orthodox Church (the ancient Eastern Catholicism) and made them an ecumenical present of priesthood, in supposedly revealed Christianity. So they have a Bible, at this point, that is all sacerdotalism and sacramentalism could desire. Does some one say: "But if Paul used this figure, they had to put it in." No. They left out countless figures. In the vital passage of Matthew 16:18, they left out the figure of the *gates of hades*. Right here they left out the figure of the *leitourgos* (from which our word *liturgy* comes), merely translating it *minister* (not minister of the State). They could have omitted the figure *priesting* (they don't *translate* it) and said *ministering,* as other versions do. No. They preferred to put the figurative language in, to be taken literally, by such sacerdotalists as would use this unethical gift of the RSV.

A THIRD BANISHING OF BIBLE BISHOPS

This is in the note on Philippians 1:1 about *bishops* or *overseers.* Of course, when you say overseers, your first thought is of slaves. In any case, including the margin, this leaves the word *bishop* on its way out, sixty per cent repudiated. Yet all these Anglican, Orthodox, and other sectarian "bishops," the "lesser breeds, without the law" of union of Church and State, are not abandoning their titles, so unscriptural, when they go to the World Council. They strut their stuff in the gaudiest robes of a half-Jewish, half-pagan priesthood, that now can find comfort in the new Bible. The hurt that is caused only wounds Bible bishops, pastors of Bible churches.

LENDING THE LORD'S SUPPER TO SACRAMENTAL SUPERSTITION: I COR. 11:24

The Supper is made to be, according to the RSV: *"Participation* in the blood . . . the body of Christ" (I Cor. 10:16). The ASV has *communion* and the Berkeley, *fellowship. Koinonia* suits either word better than the RSV sacramentalism. Wrong on one ordinance, wrong on the other.

SHATTERING THE SUPPER LANGUAGE

The classic language of Paul's narrative of the supper has been dehearted. Could anything sound flatter than "this is my body which is for you." The prepositional phrase is *in your stead,* or *on your behalf,* not just our preposition *for.* It especially invites a verb. And there is a verb right in the context, easily supplied. Immediately before, we find the declaration *broke it.* How natural, then, to supply that verb here, where one is lacking. The RSV has supplied a lot more, when it wanted to, in other connections. Now, strange to say, even Moffatt has here "broken for you" and defends it with a note.

As we shall see later on, the RSV Committee didn't just publish a Bible and introductory volumes. They published "Gospel Parallels," a Disharmony of the Gospels. Nevertheless, that Disharmony gives I Corinthians 11:23-25 this way: "when he had given thanks, he broke it and said. This is my body *which is broken for you.*" But that Disharmony leaves Luke's narrative of the Supper wholly without the account of the cup, ending with the words: "This is my body." Now will these ritualist denominations celebrate the Supper with no cup? No. And they will go on saying: "This is my body which is broken for you." Their Scripture for their ritual will come out of prayer books, disciplines, and so on. They can use this Bible and not have their Supper meaningless. Just the denominations that use the Bible itself in their ordinances will have their celebration of the Supper wrecked by deficient wording.

It is futile to say that Christ's body was not broken. Not a bone was broken. But his flesh was broken by scourging, his brow with the thorns, his hands and feet by the spikes driven through them into the cross, his heart burst, and the soldiers opened a gaping wound in his side, still there after the resurrection for doubting Thomas to put his whole hand in. *His body was broken* and that is the point of the first half of the Supper, and the second half, too. For how was his blood "shed" or "poured out" if the body remained whole?

THE TRUE DOCTRINE OF APOSTASY BANISHED

The New Testament has no doctrine of apostasy in the sense of saved people's losing their salvation. But it has a doctrine of apostasy in the sense of a falling away individually, or in mass, from revealed truth, a doctrinal lapse. This RSV is a part of the current apostasy of that nature, in much of its language. We have that doctrine in II Thessalonians 2:3: " . . . the apostasy is to come first" (before the Day of the Lord), as the Berkeley Version well renders the Greek. Now this is disguised by the RSV as "the rebellion," so as not to postpone the idea of Christ's coming. For if a general apostasy had to come first in Christianity, then of course a Schweitzer idea of the speedy advent of the Savior in cataclysm eschatology would be impossible. So the translators won't let Paul prophesy *"the* apostasy," even though the Greek itself is almost our English word.

BANISHING THE TRUE TO INTRODUCE THE FALSE DOCTRINE

Perhaps the most basely sectarian translation of the whole RSV is to be found in its Methodist rendering of Hebrews 6:1-6. We have noted the banishment of the "doctrine of baptisms." Now, in verse 6, we read this amazing language: *"if they then commit apostasy."* There now. The easiest way to put in the Bible a doctrine that is not there is to translate it into it, if you can get translators under enough control to bring that about. That is what happened here. All surrendered unconditionally. "Commit apostasy" becomes official Methodist doctrine, right in their favorite Scripture, twisted for this purpose. Of course, it reduces the Bible to a state of civil war with itself. "Eternal life," "eternal comfort," "eternal salvation," and the "eternal covenant" are all wiped out like chalk marks from a blackboard. The negative declarations that go with these positive promises pass, too: *"never* perish," *"never* leave thee nor forsake thee," *"never* hunger," *never* thirst," *"never* see death," *"never"* cast out, and all the "for ever and ever" promises of our gospel. If anybody believes the RSV falsification of Hebrews 6:6, much of the New Testament is destroyed for him. *There is* condemnation for those who are in Christ Jesus. We have *not* passed out of death into life, but keep bobbing back and forth like rats that leave the hole slick where they come and go. We *are* separated from the love of Christ. He has *not perfected for ever* those who are sanctified. He is *not* able to keep that which was committed unto him (promise also falsified). John 3:16 is false.

Is there any excuse for this partisan Methodist translation? None in the world. We don't have the Greek word *apostasia* here, which they allegedly "commit." And we don't have *commit.* What do we have? We have a simple phrase: *fall by the wayside, fall alongside.* That any believer can do; most have done. So my Greek teacher translated this as referring to backsliding, but not loss of salvation: "cannot renew them (to the repentance that should follow backsliding) *while* they crucify afresh the Son of God and put him to an open shame." I cite that, from C. B. Williams, a great teacher of Greek, to show that the RSV was not limited to the *interpretation* they wrote into the record. My own interpretation follows that of the notable evangelist, T. T. Martin, who preached to lost men from this text: "Where the lights go out on the road to hell." For many Jews, at the crisis of the Jewish War, the light did go out forever. They had come to the very door of salvation, but turned back. Hellish politicians, risking all on the gamble of a fool's war with Rome, has forced men to that awful decision between patriotism and the choice of Christ as Messiah. It was a commitment. The decision was momentous, forever. They turned definitely aside from the Way and went off at a tangent into hell on earth and in eternity. The RSV translators see a Methodist camp meeting, and men losing salvation right after it is over, and getting it all over again every August. That really is not the message of Hebrews. This is the most awful crisis human beings ever faced. They rendered a once-for-all decision. It is the unpardonable sin. There is *only one* unpardonable sin. Since these can never be brought again to the door of repentance, they have committed that sin. They did not "commit apostasy," in the Methodist sense, for they were never saved, in spite of inner drawings to their Messiah. This is the context of history. The literary context is exactly the same, for these men are described as "land that had drunk in rain, brought forth never any useful vegetation, but only thorns and thistles, worthless, near to be cursed, whose end was to be burned." How much more fully could you say that these men were never for an instant saved? But of the Hebrew believers he says: "Though we speak thus, yet *in your case*, beloved, we feel sure of better things that belong to salvation." Clearly, then; verses 4-6 do not belong to salvation. The eternal security of the believer has in Hebrews one of its greatest exponents. And there is no civil war of contradictory thought in the Epistle.

A FURTHER STAB AT THE TRUTH OF THE SECURITY OF THE BELIEVER

This time it is in Paul's great utterance of assurance, "For

I know whom I have believed and am sure that he is able to guard until that Day what has been entrusted to me" (II Tim. 1:12). While possible, this seems to me one of those smart aleck translations, showy and making changes for the love of making changes. Not even Moffatt made that change. Paul immediately commands Timothy to "guard the truth," an overtranslation but the idea. Would he tell Timothy to guard the truth if he himself had just said that Jesus would do the guarding, in his own case? Can you put off on Jesus a personal responsibility like that? And if you do, can you then turn right around and hold a colleague responsible for guarding what you yourself hold Jesus responsible for guarding, in your own task? The real motive here seems to be to get rid of one of the great elements of the truth, the majestic affirmation of the security of the believer. It is part of the campaign to promote the doctrine of apostasy.

DENYING LUKE'S CHURCH HISTORY

Luke tells the story of a church session, electing a new apostle in the place of Judas, to start off his story of apostolic life and leadership. It is his way of connecting up what Jesus *began to do and teach* with what he continued in his resurrection ministry, with that formerly itinerant church life which he then localized in Jerusalem, with a beginning of 120 members. Luke says there were 120 *names* together—a church roll, responsible membership, all moved there from Galilee to live under Christ's orders. Because they don't want a church before Pentecost, with a roll of names, (in spite of erroneously using the verb *enroll* in verse 36) they change the Scripture to suit themselves and put it "company of persons," where Luke wrote "number of names" (Acts 1:15). This word *name* is used 224 times in the New Testament. In meaningful phrases, it does indicate all the worth and dignity and value of a man, or a person of the Trinity. But it is almost uniformly translated *name,* in any Bible. Once or twice, in Revelation, sometimes in the papyri, it means *person,* or *people* as the RSV translates it in the Revelation.

Ecclesiastical bias has by its prejudice blacked out the fact that a real election was held when Matthias was chosen apostle. One of the most beautiful tributes to democracy in

church life and organization in all literature is that of Professor W. O. Carver, in writing about this passage in his Commentary on Acts. He pictures the meaning for history of this
first church election, placing it far above the most significant
things that men usually glorify in the history of democracy.
The King James Anglicans and the Nelson Pedobaptists
slaughtered this Scripture, which is against their way of life.
The KJ says of the election: "He was numbered with the
eleven apostles." The RSV says: "He was enrolled"—though
they banish the idea that 120 *names* were "in the same place"
on a church roll. It is rather hard to think of a man's being
enrolled as an official when there is no roll of the organization
in which he holds the office. If no roll, then how does the
book of The Acts of the Apostles report so accurately the
number of additions, from time to time, or of membership?
The cynicism of a false episcopacy has reduced this event,
which Luke thought worthy to be his first picture painted of
apostolic Christianity after the ascension, to the level of a
cheap gambling stunt. I have seen and heard just that blatant
irreverence toward the Word of God. And some of the union-
ist conservatives join the modernists in this irreverence, because they are determined to have their Church beginning on
the day of Pentecost, turning their backs on all that was nor-
mative in the earthly life of our Lord. Professor Carver shows
the election to have been majestic and pondered, under the
guidance of the Holy Spirit. First, they established the proper
qualifications of the office. Then they examined the possibilities
and found two men who had the qualifications, and narrowed
the election to these two. Then they asked God to show his
choice. He replied through the classic method of the Scriptures, the casting of lots. That was never gambling. I saw
the same method used in a church I visited on this furlough.
A great church, with the rotating diaconate, had two names
tied. They did not ask the pastor to prefer one over the other,
on which the church was evenly divided. They cast lots, and
all were satisfied. That is done still in our Baptist life. The
casting of lots is not the election. At once, the vote, now unanimous, is taken. So it was in Acts. But, you say, did they
not already know the will of God? Yes. But how many times
people know that will and refuse to do it. They accepted the

providential guidance and voted to make God's chosen their choice. So Luke wrote: "He was voted a place with the eleven apostles," which is exactly how the Berkeley Version has it. There is no excuse at all for the RSV translation. The Greek verb is not *numbered,* as in verse 17, or *enrolled.* It is *elect.* But the election is banished by an anti-Baptist sectarian bias, tampering with the Word of God.

TURNING THE CLOCK BACK ON A COMMAND OF CHRIST

Jesus seems to have talked much and often about his purpose for church life, during the days of his flesh. There is no curiosity manifested by the disciples. When he made the momentous deliverance, *"my* church," Peter did not say: "What's that, Lord?" Furthermore, our far-visioned Savior, even in the days of his flesh, saw clearly that in every hamlet, village, and town, and also in many synagogues, during the solely Jewish phase of Christianity in Palestine, there would be a definite congregation of his disciples. To each of these he gave the name *church,* using the word congregation, as he had before. He issues a very clear, definite command about corrective discipline in those churches-to-be. And that is one of his commands, which he incorporated in the Great Commission, to be both practiced and taught till the end of time. Very few except Baptists either teach it or permit it or recognize that our Lord made such a church the supreme court, in judging the life of the membership.

Now Baptists love the churches of Christ, commanded in the days of his flesh, and that command reaffirmed in the days of his postresurrection Great Commission. We love the churches of Christ, and what the Spirit has said to the churches, either through their Lord on earth, or through the revelation of his will by apostles in Epistles and Revelation. We love the churches of God and distrust the adjectives of men, tendential all of them—national, catholic, ancient, local, modern, protestant, ecumenical, and so on. Matthew 18 treats of congregational life and activity in church discipline, but congregation, in the New Testament, never shrinks up to the narrowed proportions of "local" churches. That is a term of inevitable contempt, even if not so meant. No churches have any right to be *local* churches. They meet in a certain locality, each one of them, to be sure, but not one is *local* in its horizon, outlook, sympathy, missionary obligation, inter·cession, fellowship, co-operation, or potentialities in beneficence and evangelization through *messengers of the churches, the glory of Christ* (II Cor. 8:23). No New Testament writer ever felt the least necessity of saying "local church," though the Berkeley version has "the local Antioch church," in Acts 13:1.

The offense of the RSV in Matthew 18 is to narrow the sphere of individual initiative for the fraternal correction of sin in the life of a brother in a church. The younger Nestle goes back to a number of readings that for a generation have seemed to competent textual experts on the Greek text less probable, and that his father had put in the margin. Westcott and Hort, Eberhard Nestle, and other great authorities do not have *against thee,* in Matthew 18:15. The RSV has preferred to go back to a persistence in a KJ error of text just there, which to me seems strange. It narrows the scope of this passage to personal offenses. God's will is that *for any offense, for every sin,* personal initiative be undertaken to bring the sinner back. To narrow the scope of the command to personal offenses is almost fatal to its meaning and scope. Jesus said: "If thy brother sin," nothing more in the conditional clause. He had just taught searchingly that every Christian is his brother's keeper, duty bound to leave the ninety and nine and go after the straying, personally. This is the doctrinal definition of the duty taught in that parable. Only in case of, first, individual failure, then, secondly, group failure, is the matter to be taken to the church for action. But that action is final. It is heaven's own way of settling this issue.

Here, as in Matthew 16:19, Jesus did not assure either Peter or a judging church that their decisions would be infallible and God would ratify them, irrespective of ethical considerations. That is false and base. God never said to Peter: "Now go ahead and make any kind of decision you like, binding or loosing, and heaven will ratify, God will approve anything you say, do, or teach to do or not to do." God never put himself in such a silly subordination to man. Such a translation, though long fostered by episcopally controlled translators, is utterly false. What Jesus said, in both instances, was that whatever should be bound or loosed on earth (prohibited or declared licit or a matter of indifference) *should have been "previously bound or loosed* in heaven." Earth is to follow heaven's revelation of truth and duty, not heaven blindly to ratify the will of a man or a church. Among the forty versions I use, at last I have two that so translate these passages. The RSV might have advanced to that fidelity to the words of the Savior. But it preferred to persist in the errors of King James and even turn the clock back to its narrowing the scope of church discipline to personal issues. And, with all these authorities on textual criticism affirming the difference in the readings, the RSV doesn't even give a note. They can drag in a worthless variant reading to declare Jesus a bastard, right on the front page of the New Testament. They can sow conjectures all over the Old Testament margins. But when they reject the true reading, they don't even put in the margin the reading preferred by such authorities at Westcott, Hort, Eberhard Nestle, Warfield, and A. T. Robertson. This happens a number of times. Just to cite one more notable case, Westcott and Hort have as their text, in John 14:17: "For he (the Holy Spirit) abides by your side and is within you." Now that doesn't please men. The man-made theory is that nobody had the Holy Spirit resident within, until the Day of Pentecost. So the preferred Westcott and Hort text, which affirms the residence of the Spirit within, as well as his abiding companionship with the apostles in our Lord's earthly ministry, is coolly disregarded and ignored even in the margin of this translation, though given by both Weymouth and Goodspeed. It is another case of bias against a truth. Both of these truths are Baptist specialties of interpretation. The RSV virtually says to Baptists: "If you want to give out your distinctive truths in your continuing witness, don't use our version." It might serve Baptists who are *on their way out,* but not *permanent* Baptists.

ANOTHER OFFENSE AGAINST CHURCH AUTHORITY BY OVER-TRANSLATION

The same doctrine of ultimate authority by a church for

the discipline of its members, which our Lord commanded in
Matthew 18, Paul sets forth in I Corinthians 5:9-13. God
judges the outsider. Every church is the judge of its insiders,
barring them from the Lord's table (restricted communion
demanded, by church authority over the Supper) for quite
a number of reasons, all moral. But Romans 1:17 demands
restrictions of the Supper for doctrinal reasons, for the language of the original is exact Lord's Supper language of *reclining* at the table to eat, as Jesus and the early churches did.
Here the RSV translates "avoid them," but the Greek literally
says *break off reclining with them* (at the Supper). However
that may be, the overtranslation of the command of I Corinthians 5:13 ("Drive out the wicked person from among you")
is evident when we compare the translation of the same verb,
also in a case of expulsion of a member, in verse 2. Here the
RSV merely has "Let him . . . be removed from among you."
But, in this demand by Paul for judging the members by
refusing them the Lord's Supper, it is translated: "Drive out,"
as if violently, rather than the serene judgment of disciplinary
action. It seems an effort to hide the strict communion and
the obligatory church action in guarding the table of the Lord,
which are so clearly taught in the New Testament and not at
all practiced by open communion ecumenicalism.

HIDING THE DOCTRINE OF A REGENERATED CHURCH MEM-BERSHIP

Nothing has been a more emphatic Baptist doctrine than
that. All the members of New Testament churches are called
"saints" because such, ideally, they were and, actually, sought
to be. It did not deny the entrance of a Judas, an Ananias or
Sapphira, a Diotrephes or a Demas, but there was no infant
baptism to bring the unregenerate in wholesale, as when
Catholic and Protestant Europe alike baptize their whole
populations in a nation. Now see the blow to this New Testament ideal and doctrine. It falls on two Scriptures like a
guillotine, Galatians 1:22 and I Thessalonians 2:14. Paul
said: "And I was unknown, by the face, to the churches of
Judea which are in Christ Jesus"; and again: "the churches
of God which are in Judea in Christ Jesus." So spoke Paul.

By a cunning trick, the RSV translates the first Scripture: "the Churches *of Christ* in Judea." That effectually guillotines the New Testament doctrine that a church, as a church, due to its being made up only of declared believers, could be supposed to be "in Christ Jesus." And look at the second cunning trick of ecclesiastical trifling with the Word of God and purity of church life and ideals: "the churches of God in Christ Jesus which are in Judea." That willfully inverts the order, transposes phrases, takes away the *which* clause from where it belongs, kills the great truth in the Greek. Paul said: the *churches* of Judea *which are in Christ.* The RSV says:" the churches of Christ which are in Judea." The problem of any translator who could be guilty of that is moral, not intellectual; a matter of ethics, not of scholarship. The same miserable trickiness shows up again in "the churches of God which are in Judea in Christ Jesus" of Paul, by the inspiration of the Spirit of God. When it gets translated by the RSV, it degenerates into a transposition of phrases that removes the doctrine of the union of churches with Christ, "in Christ Jesus," and we read merely: "in Christ Jesus" this side of the *which* clause. Paul said *the which* (churches) are two things: geographically, "in Judea"; spiritually, "in Christ Jesus." This latter *in* clause is wrenched out of the *which* clause completely and thrown into the sentence vaguely where it could mean: "Ye became imitators . . . in Christ Jesus." This, too, is a sin of the tricky heart as well as the conniving head. It is ethically wicked, not merely grammatically incompetent. And it is sheer sectarian prejudice against the truth of God. The translators are trying to build up the New Catholicism and changed the Bible where it would condemn its vast hordes of unregenerate members, such as the 200,000,000 of the Greek Orthodox, immersed three times in their infancy, and the sprinkled hordes of the State Churches of Europe that know as little about the grace of God as a kitten, if infant baptism is all the regeneration they have.

THE EFFORT TO WRECK THE WORD "CHURCH" AND GET A PROVINCIAL CHURCH

This cunning trick is seen in Acts 9:31. What God has

joined together, the RSV men put asunder; and what God put asunder, the RSV men join together, and make new meanings, to their own liking, countless times. One case is Acts 9:31; one other, for we just saw two cases of it. At the beginning, Christianity was just one church, a pilgrim church, assembling constantly with its wandering Master and Head. The RSV aims to turn the clock back twenty centuries. One church became many, by the will of God. Now they want to make many *one*. There is not a hint of a Catholic—National, Provincial or State—Church in the whole New Testament. Ah, could that just be broken down, then the New Catholicism could say: "See. The word *church* can mean anything. It is not just *congregational* in its meaning. It described all the Christians in a province or nation. So we can use it in a sense that has these wider reaches." The new Bible, and the New Catholicism built on it, would be failures forever, if the word *church* retained its congregational meaning, even though, like *baptism,* it is never translated in our versions, it being against the Anglican rules of the King James era. The battlefield where this attack on the truth is launched is Acts 9:31. It is easier here. The order of the Greek words, which in translating is never a criterion, except as the Greek grammar is to be interpreted by the relations of words to the article, to the verb, or to clauses or phrases that have a determined unity within the sentence, is here made an excuse for translating right on, as the words come, without looking at their order as determined by the Greek genius of sentence structure. So we have "So the church throughout all Judea, Galilee and Samaria had peace and was built up; and walking in the fear of the Lord and in the comfort of the Holy Spirit it was multiplied." That is RSV order, to promote its Catholicism, by giving the word *church* the apparent geographical meaning of an entity with a triune-provincial area and meaning. Such a translation banishes the congregational sense definitely, without even a kiss of farewell. What does the Greek *say,* by what it *means?* It means *congregation* when it says *church.* And it means adverbial phrases to be taken with verbs—adjectives modifying nouns, adverbs (including adverbial phrases) modifying verbs. Thus translated, we have "Therefore, in contrast (*men*), the church had (began to have) peace throughout the whole of Judea, and Galilee, and Samaria, being edified (or built up); and was multiplied, as it kept on walking in the fear of the Lord and in the comfort of the Holy Spirit."

Let us study the translation. Notice that word *men* in parentheses. That is the Greek word *men*, which is a device for sharp contrast, even though often untranslatable. What, then, is the contrast here? It is Paul. He had no peace. He was run out of Damascus. And when he came to Jerusalem, nobody believed in him. And he was soon to be assassinated there. *In contrast with Paul*, the church he had persecuted had peace.

Now what church was that? The Greek says "the church which was in Jerusalem" (Acts 8:1). That church, about which the previous history of the Acts has been told, was scattered all over Palestine. It was still scattered when Paul came back to Jerusalem, in vast numbers. It took root and became *many churches* soon. Like other live things, it brought forth after its kind. Where there had been *one church*, there came to be many. But while it was still in this state, in contrast with its persecutor Paul, now converted, *it began to have peace*. Clearly Luke does not need to say that he is talking about the very same church he has been talking about, in Chapters 1 and 2 without using the word but using kindred words, and by the word *church* in 5:11; 8:1, 3. No other church is on the horizon till a second church appears in Antioch, so far as Luke speaks of churches. So this is that church which was in Jerusalem, during the events of Chapters 1 to 7, but scattered all over the land during the Pauline persecution. *This one congregation*, though hounded out into far places, was still the Jerusalem church, and it was this, in contrast with its persecutor, which had peace all over the land.

Now besides this being the natural way to read the history and respect the Greek grammar in exegesis, we have a parallel statement by Paul. Here it is: "I was still unknown (says Paul about his leaving Jerusalem for Tarsus) to the churches of Judea which are in Christ Jesus." This proves that the persecuted Jerusalem church multiplied, reproduced after its kind. This phenomenon was on the horizon of Paul's memory of developments, but not in the march of Luke's history just at this point (Acts 9:31). It came into view later in the plural of the word *churches,* Acts 15:41; 16:5 and the two passages discussed before. And here is a page without a note, in the RSV. They don't tell you at all that "other ancient authorities" do have "churches" right here in Acts 9:31. They save their notes for worthless testimony that Jesus was Joseph's son, fruit of the betrothal with Mary, or for what it pleases them to record. *Church* is the correct text, but it is the Jerusalem church, still largely in exile from home, scattered by persecution.

BRETHRENISM IN THE POT

Plymouth Brethrenism says there is no church, if by that you mean an organization. There is just *one mystical church,* the *body of Christ,* also mystical. For Brethrenism, when the New Testament talks of a church, or churches, it means nothing organized, but merely local elements of this one mystical church that happen to be under consideration, a part of the mystical church which, in its perpetual state of flux, happens to be the group in consideration. The church in Jerusalem, then, would be just like the air in a room. It was the part of the mystical church that happened to be at that moment in Jerusalem, just as the air in a room is part of our total atmosphere around the earth. The church in Priscilla's house, in Rome, was nothing organized, but rather as the water in the Gulf Stream or the Panama Canal is part and parcel of the water in the oceans. This disintegrating, disorganizing propaganda that slips into all organized Christianity and preys upon it, preys also upon the New Testament translation, wherever possible. Its leaders have always been great on translation, naturally tendential. Brethrenism is only one of many approaches to the destruction of the doctrine of New Testament churches in modern thought, but it has its part in the RSV. Note Acts 8:1; 11:22. The Greek says crisply: "the church which was in Jerusalem"—*the . . . in Jerusalem* (church), doubly definite. The whole of a church, definite, identified by name. But the RSV, whose translators are capable of saying "the Holy Spirit which . . .," cannot bring themselves to say "the church which." They say "the church in Jerusalem," as we say the space in this ship. Just so, Paul says: "to the church which is in their house" (Rom. 16:5), and "the church which is in Cenchreae," two verses before. But the RSV takes these doubly definite references and reduces them to Brethrenism, "the church at Cenchrea," "the church in their house." The RSV won't let the Bible say what it wants to say. To get what it wants to say, you will have to own another Bible or Bibles.

FURTHER ANTI-BAPTIST BIAS IN ECCLESIOLOGY

An important word in Greek is the one we may translate *all, every, whole, entire, any, each,* according to its relation to the Greek article. It is translated all those ways in the RSV, and often rightly so. Where it does not affect ecclesiology, the RSV has advanced over previous versions in translating the Greek word *pas* right. Unhappily it is not uniform in its fidelity to the original. Dogmatic or sectarian influences have affected the rendering of phrases in which the word *every* ought to appear, but does not. One such is II Timothy 3:16, where Paul said : "Every Scripture is God-breathed," but where no modernist would ever consent that the apostle single out every one of the Scriptures and make that great affirmation about each one of them.

Now, biblical ecclesiology is kept true, in part, by not making a nose of wax of this generalizing word *every,* changing it arbitrarily and falsely into a catholicizing *all.* This is the anti-Baptist trickery back of much modern translation, and the interpretation it makes possible. Such translation-cunning concentrates its powers on the Epistle to the Ephesians. The RSV, for example, utterly falsifies Ephesians 2:21, rendering it "Christ Jesus . . . in whom *the whole structure* is joined together and grows into a holy temple in the Lord, in whom you also are built *into it* for a dwelling place of God in the Spirit." Paul did not say that or anything similar to that. To bolster their New Catholicism, the translators made this Scripture to order, forming their English doctrine with no Greek to back it. Paul's Greek utterly denies this perversion of truth. There is no word here for *temple.* The translation is unpardonable. The words *into it* are a sheer dogmatic addition to the Bible, to help out a weak exegesis. Paul did not say: *the whole structure;* he said *every.* Paul did not say: *built into it,* as if they were a unit in the vast temple area of conjoined buildings that formed the whole. The picture is false, utterly and inexcusably false, invented to bolster up the false Catholicism of the owners of this Bible and their Council of Catholicizing Churches.

Paul and John both wrote books of the New Testament to the "churches of Asia," whose capital of that Roman province was Ephesus, also the foremost of those churches. Neither in Paul's day nor in John's was there either a *church of Asia,* nor a bishop of Asia, nor any general organization or officer of a provincial nature. To get these circular messages out to the churches of Asia, Paul and John adopted two different devices, both demonstrating the perpetual congregational nature of New Testament church life. Paul wrote a circular letter, sending copies to each church. Each letter was the same. A blank space was left, filled in with the name. One, probably the original copy of this circular Epistle, became the Epistle to the Ephesians, in our New Testament. Another is probably the Epistle to the Laodiceans, mentioned in Colossians 4:16. That it should have been called the Epistle *from* Laodicea indicates that it belonged to that church and circulated from there among the other churches of the region. This explains why the Revelation is only to seven churches, each being the natural center of other churches in its zone. So Paul had many copies of the same letter sent, each with a different address. One with the blank space, without the name of the addressee, copied later without allowing for the blank space, seems to have fallen into the hands of Origen, and the RSV follows old Origen instead of the better authorities that have our Ephesian Epistle addressed to Ephesus. That is just another bit of perversity, changing things for the sake of change. But the fact of the circular letter remains clear. John used the system of a joint letter, letting each church read both the praises and the blame which Jesus, their Judge, assessed to every other church also. Each could learn from all, all from each, so the same document went to all alike, even as to the address. In any case, there is nothing on the horizon above co-operating New Testament churches, in Christianity's organized life. What was added in the second and subsequent centuries is apostasy, copied after different fashions by each of the constituent members of the New Catholicism of the World Council of Churches such as the Bible knows nothing about and nothing similar to.

Nowhere is the congregational nature of churches so evident as in what I sometimes call First and Second Ephesians, the First Epistle by Paul, the Second by John, or by Christ through John (Rev. II). Yet here is staged the great battle for Catholicism. The *church* is called "divine" and the continuation of the incarnation and is almost added to the Trinity—as the Virgin Mary is the fourth person in the Catholic Trinity—and we see men nominally Protestants now let their mouths say those most abominable words in human literature: *Extra ecclesiam nulla salus* (Outside the Church there is no salvation). That is medievalism of Stygian darkness, an Egyptian plague of darkness that rolled over the land from perversion of the Epistle to the Ephesians.

Now, if Paul did not say the New Catholicism of the RSV perversion of Ephesians 2:21, what did he say? Here it is: "*Every* building, as it is being harmoniously framed together, grows into a holy sanctuary in the Lord, in whom ye also are being built together for a dwelling place of God in the Spirit." This is as exact a statement of Baptist doctrine about church life as words can frame. Note it: "Christ Jesus . . . in whom (the doctrine of the regenerated membership of the churches held aloft as our banner and ideal) *every* building (each autonomous, independent church, of a congregational nature), as it is being harmoniously framed together (organized life, obedient to the plans of the divine Architect) grows (both organism and organization, framed and grows, rooted and grounded) into a holy sanctuary (not the vast, sprawling temple collection of houses, courts, porticos, military barracks, treasury, dwellings, synagogue, altars, sanctuary and all, but *the sanctuary* alone) in the Lord (the sovereign Christ commanding and being obeyed), in whom (doubly emphatic about the union with Christ of a regenerated church membership as the church ideal—not a conglomerated Council of the State Churches made up of the hordes of unregenerate victims of infant baptism) ye also (the particular church to which this copy of the circular Epistle was addressed) are being built together (edification and sanctification of an imperfect membership) for a dwelling place of the Spirit" (every believer having the Spirit resident in him and so their collective life indwelt by the guiding Spirit in each church). That is as magnificent a statement of Baptist truth as can be found on earth.

Now suppose we study the RSV perversions of this truth, for its catholicizing purpose of sectarian propaganda. First, the word *whole*. The RSV was not content with being moderately wrong. With the cheese and the knife in their hands, they cut themselves a superlative advantage by a maximum wrong. The Greek word *pas* may mean *all, whole,* or *every*. It depends on the article and the position of it, if used, in relation to *pas*. The article, followed by *pas* and the word for *house,* means the *whole house*. That is not the *Greek* here. The article followed by the word for *house* and then the word *pas* means *all the house*. We do not have that Greek here, either. But *pas* and the word for *house* with no article means *every house,* and that is what we have here. Not a man on that RSV Committee is ignorant of Greek grammar on this point. They willfully mistranslated the Greek, for partisan purposes. All this, about these very words, is clearly set forth in that great classic on the subject by Hort, *The Christian Ecclesia.*

To get this and other erroneous translations. the RSV makes a false translation, overriding elementary Greek facts, all through the New Testament. The Greek has two words; one means *temple,* all the buildings on the temple mountain. That is what the RSV wants here. Then each member of the World Council of Churches may be taken as one contributing building in the Catholic whole, in this passage. That word *temple* does not exist here. There is a second word which means the *sanctuary*. It is not a complex structure, made up of other structures. It is the inner shrine, the holiest of all. This is the basis of the most beautiful figurative language in the New Testament. Now the whole RSV is utterly wrong in its translations along this line, throughout the New Testament. This is another case of following the errors of the King James Version. Every Greek dictionary makes the distinction perfectly between these words. But to translate them correctly is one of the worst possible blows to any Catholicism, so sectarian policies have thus far prevailed and the "authorized" versions have authorized a false translation.

Where the word occurs in the New Testament, the KJ translates it wrong all forty-five times. The ASV translates all of them right by a note in the margin, and twice in the text (Matt. 23:35; 27:5), but otherwise keeps the wrong translation in the text. The RSV translates the word right one time about the sanctuary in the temple in Jerusalem, once about Diana's imitation shrines, and the rest wrong. All but the RSV take care to translate the fact that Judas went to the priests and threw their thirty pieces of silver *into the sanctuary,* a despairing gesture of mockery both to them and to God. Why be right only one time? The teaching is so beautiful. Each church is a Holy of Holies (I Cor. 3:16; II Cor. 6:16; Eph. 2:21). It is not just this passage that so teaches. Our Lord's body and our bodies are Holy Places, sanctuaries for the divine indwelling. All the imagery is beautiful, august, sanctifying. But it is thrown to the winds so ecclesiastics can build a Catholicism.

Look what folly this mistranslation gives. It says that a priest could only enter the general temple *by lot* (Luke 1:9). *No indeed.* "My house shall be called a house of prayer for all nations." Any pagan could enter the temple, freely, if he stayed in his place. It was the sacrifice center the priests entered by lot. Then we hear that the people wondered at the delay of Zacharias in the "temple" and saw him "come out" of it. Then where were the people, pray? Off down in the streets of Jerusalem or the Vale of Hinnom? *The people are in the temple,* down in their lower, proper courts. Zacharias delayed in the sanctuary. The whole meaning is wrecked stupidly by the will to mistranslate. Happily, the ASV does justice to the word *pas* in Ephesians 2:21, "in whom *each several building,* fitly framed together, groweth into a holy temple (but in the margin, *sanctuary*) in the Lord, in whom ye also are builded together for a habitation of God in the Spirit." That is Baptist Christianity of the first century. Sometimes, and in Ephesians, the word *church* is used of all Christians, considered under the figure of a congregation of the redeemed, and destined to be just that before the Throne one day. But the Ephesian type of church life, organization, and ministry are all of a congregational organizational nature, in the wide fellowship of the churches of Christ, under "pastors and teachers," also called bishops and presbyters, in Acts 20, by Paul.

Kindred studies to this appear under nearly all the other titles of this investigation.

CHAPTER ELEVEN

THE CAMEL'S NOSE IN THE TENT

THERE IS A PROVERB FROM THE NEAR EAST TO THE EFFECT that once you let the camel's nose inside the tent pretty soon all there is in the tent is the camel. That is the inevitable effect of this new Bible on faith. Once you put on its pages the testimony of unbelief, the basis of faith is destroyed. The Christian mind can no more remain half skeptic and half believing than this nation could remain half slave and half free. Skepticism may leave in the Bible every witness to its Savior and its truth, except an occasional expression of unfaith. Still it will be perfectly sure of its victory. One contradiction of a positive doctrine by negative disharmony is enough to create doubt, distress, and maybe the silence of suppressed witness or the cynicism which believes nothing for certain. The doubter will hark back always to that one expression of contradiction of the general message of the Bible. There he will find his Waterloo, in his struggle to keep believing the Bible. A Bible that has ten affirmations of a truth and one denial of it is a book of uncertainty and contradiction. The RSV has let the camel's nose in its tent. The camel will take care of the rest. Better not count on that tent.

GOING BACK TO TAW IN THE FIRST GOSPEL

Just look at the first page of this New Testament. On page 1, an inch below the beginning of the New Testament, you find an *e* referring to a note which says: "Other ancient authorities read: *Joseph, to whom was betrothed the virgin Mary, was the father of Jesus who is called Christ.*" The effect of that on the reader is to affirm the ordinary origin of Jesus, instead of what is about to be said about his virgin birth. The denial of the truth gets attention before the New Testament gets a chance to affirm its truth. Doubt takes precedence over faith. Before Matthew is allowed to say: "Worship the virgin-born Savior," the RSV says: Attention, please. Note well. Before you believe that Jesus was born of the virgin, be sure to note that other ancient authorities state that this is not so. They give it out that Joseph was his father, while bethrothed to this same virgin Mary. If you give credence to that note, you simply cannot believe the New Testament. Jesus was no more God with us than you are God with us.

Some eager modernist asserts: "Oh, but people can believe that there was a real incarnation, the Word becoming flesh, through the usual channel of procreation, by two parents. I refer you to Dr. John Doe who so believes." I don't doubt it. Men are capable of all sorts of intellectual stunts, especially when they want to be. What we want to know is the answer to three questions. First, did not this learned modernist, still a believer in the virgin birth of Jesus, become such a believer while he still accepted the Gospel narratives of that birth? In such case his true belief may be a mere hangover from a time of faith, but his son, in the house or in the ministry, may well be incapable of such a faith, on his father's and preceptor's premises. Second, just what is the nature of the *authority* of these *other authorities?* There is the authority of government. And there is the authority of truth. Now there is no dictator over translators who could force them to put this note in, if they believed it to be untrue. If they believe it to be a lie, there is no authority of the truth which would force, or consent to, its inclusion in a New Testament for the public. Third, if the translators do not believe Jesus was Joseph's boy, and if they are not forced to put this in the New Testament, is their criterion that of textual criticism, giving out the alternative readings where serious manuscripts differ?

"No lie is of the truth" (I John 2:21). What is this lie doing in the Book of truth, then? Let us look at the studied, cultivated, professional, and boasted neutrality of a lot of theological professors who think that they must give both sides, lie and truth, or else Dr. Dryasdust won't consider them scholars. Is the RSV New Testament a textbook of textual criticism? Well, it certainly isn't. Many, many times, where there is important divergence of excellent manuscripts, it never even hints of it. Sometimes it puts the true reading, as attested by such authorities as Westcott and Hort, Nestle (father), A. T. Robertson, and Benjamin Warfield, in the margin and adopts a novelty that suits its passion for novelty or its tastes otherwise. Sometimes it does not give the text of these great authorities in textual criticism, even in the margin. We gave an example of that in John 14:17: "He (the Spirit)

. . . is in you," as is the Westcott and Hort text, and as the
translation is given outright by Weymouth (cited) and Goodspeed ("is within you"). But the RSV never even hint at
this better text. It does not suit their Pentecostal theories. It
is precisely some of the most worthless variants that they put
in the margin, to contradict the text they give above and
where there is a serious and excellent difference in the text,
on good authority, they don't whisper the facts. This is not a
textbook on criticism of the Greek New Testament text. There
is no obligation in the world that rests in any way upon the
translators to put in this lie about Jesus unless they want to
circulate it. *Men are mighty careful how they insinuate anything about a woman's reputation, yet these men virtually
assail the character of the mother of our Lord,* when they
well know this slander merits no sort of respect and has no
right to a place in any Bible.

Textual criticism is another matter. There we give all the
variants, however silly. We show that Aleph and B (the
Vatican MS) both say that men light a lamp to *put it under
the table.* That and a thousand other variations of manuscripts
were made by sleepy scribes, in the drear task of copying vast
quantities of script. But no translation on earth puts that in a
version as an alternative reading to *on the table.* Why, then,
should this insult to the Savior and his mother, blessed among
women, soil the front page of the RSV New Testament? It is
baseless perversity. Now the KJ, the ASV, the Berkeley, the
C. B. Williams version, Goodspeed, the Basic Bible, and so
on give this stray slander no place on their pages in any shape,
form, or fashion. Moffatt incorporates the slander in the text
itself: "and Joseph (to whom the virgin Mary was betrothed)
the father of Jesus . . ." That seems to me unutterably wicked.
He does not even give any notice to the almost unanimous
witness of the thousands of Greek manuscripts. But he cou-
rageously made his choice. He did not leave the matter in
doubt. The RSV half adopts his mania. Pitiful and incompetent indecision. Even as textual criticism, both Moffatt's rash
decision and the RSV indecision are indefensible. The camel's
nose in the RSV tent will, for every skeptical mind, go all
the way in and fill the tent to the exclusion of the possibility
of faith in the virgin-born Son of God.

ANOTHER WORTHLESS VARIANT DISHONORING CHRIST

This one is in the note to Luke 3:22: "today I have begotten thee." The RSV even gives up its mania of using *thee* only of God the Father and repudiates its translation of the Second Psalm, which has *you,* in order to fasten this adoptionism on the Gospel narrative. If the equalizing phrase *other ancient authorities* can be put back of applying the Second Psalm to baptism, then Christ is robbed of his real Sonship and baptism is put on a sacramental throne as having power the incarnation itself had not till then had. Such a fake Scripture disturbs your faith, either in the Bible that has it or in the Son who didn't have his Sonship till thirty years of age.

WRONG ONCE, CONFUSED FOREVER ABOUT THE GOSPEL

"The righteous shall live by his faith," said Habakkuk (2:4). You have exactly the same Greek words in the LXX, in Romans 1:17, in Galatians 3:11, and Hebrews 10:38, except the addition of *my* in the last passage. Now in the first and last of these four Scriptures the RSV translates: "The righteous (my righteous one) shall live by (his) faith." And in the two middle ones it translates: "He who through faith is righteous shall live." Now the margin in Habakkuk 2:4 has a note, "Or, *faithfulness,*" while notes in Romans 1:17 and Galatians 3:11 have, as notes, the correct translation, which they refused to allow on the pages of the text, and Hebrews 10:38 has no note at all. That is four ways to translate half-a-dozen Greek words that are unvarying and keep the same position. The mistranslation in Romans 1:17 and Galatians 3:11 is the utter ignorance or disrespect for the Greek principle of grammar, which does *not* translate words just as they come along in the sentence. But the worst, the Arminian camel's nose, puts human *faithfulness* right in the most glorious of all testimony as to justification by faith. That is horrible. That is the "mark of a falling church"—or World Council of falling Churches. Justification by our own faithfulness— all the demons must have giggled in glee when that was printed in the RSV. Are we to count the various ways the RSV translates the same sentence and decide what the truth is by their majority vote? No matter how much the natural man may be impressed by the great words of Habakkuk, Paul, and Hebrews, he will go back to that margin and say: "Better play safe and trust in my own faithfulness. In this confusion, how can I be certain that faith in Christ will justify?" Now two objects can't occupy the same space at the same time; and faith in Christ to save and faith in self to save can't occupy the same heart at the same time. That is the woe of this unbelief. The man who trusts in his own faithfulness is a lost soul unaware of the existence of the gospel. It is supremely tragic that this camel's nose should have been allowed near the tent.

LETTING THE CAMEL'S NOSE INTO ISAIAH'S GOSPEL

The unbelieving theologian wants to make "the Gospel according to Isaiah" shrink away from a prophecy of Jesus, crucified, risen, and atoning, to a mystic reference of some vague kind to Israel or a remnant in Israel or the spiritual Israel. That is wholly impossible. The garment of revelation does not fit those lean and little beings. It fits only the majestic person of Jesus the Redeemer. Of this Suffering Servant of Jehovah we read: "there was no deceit in his mouth." There never was a day in Israel's history when that was true of the nation, or of the best remnant the nation ever had, or of any Jew but Jesus, or of any Gentile. Paul, gathering up from the Old Testament his indictment of the entire human race, denies that utterly of us all. No. This Servant was sinless; he bore others' sins. He died, he was buried, he rose, yet he sees the travail of his soul and is satisfied. He had "made intercession for the transgressors," and will justify many. That language describes Jesus alone.

The Hebrew said, by the testimony of the RSV itself in the margin: "Thou makest his soul an offering for sin." That is the atonement, set in the Trinity and in the meaning of Israel's sacrificial system. What does the RSV do? Two things. It discards the Hebrew, rich in meaning, and betakes itself to the Vulgate, confessedly preferring wrong Latin to right gospel. Then it destroys the divine agency whereby God could "be just and the justifier of him that hath faith in Jesus." Now he merely "makes himself an offering for sin."

We notice the banishment of the word *soul*. We feel its loss. Right here is the explanation of Gethsemane: "My soul is exceeding sorrowful unto death." Where it can, without violence, the RSV eases the word *soul* out into banishment. It does here. We are told by Ferm's *Encyclopedia of Religion*: "Modern psychology has, for the most part, lost the soul and substituted terms less encumbered by traditional theologies and metaphysics. The soul now becomes the self or the person or one's spirit or the id or the psychophysical or a mere SR (stimulus-response), depending on the particular brand of psychological theory" (p. 729). It doesn't matter now if a man loses his own soul by gaining the world. The transaction, in the RSV, is otherwise stated. And here we lose the soul of Jesus from Calvary, though it is retained in other verses. But that God should make the soul of Jesus an offering for sin is intolerable to such theologians. So they run off from what they ought to translate and borrow some mistranslation, gotten up in Latin many centuries later. That is how we got this "he made *himself* an offering for sin." Protestants ran to Rome and borrowed it. It is false. When one takes to himself the career of both Priest and Sacrifice, it is God-ordained. "No man taketh this honor unto himself" (Heb. 5:4). He did not "make himself" this sacrifice, on his own.

You say: "Well, admit that the RSV refused to translate Isaiah 53; that is just one time and place." But it is a nose in the tent, and a long gangling form follows. God and the soul of the Savior were here banished from the panorama of redemption. To be sure, they are left elsewhere, but we miss them here. This is not a place for originality or self-orientation. If God came into human life, in Jesus, for our redemption, we want him God-guided as to what to do.

Furthermore, we miss the soul. That is the shallow stuff Good Friday superstitions are made of, the mere sufferings of his body. So Romanism drags out its most horrible images and parades them to and fro, and men pitch pennies before one on a street corner as an alms, and buy merit thereby. They kiss another's toe. Romanist sculptors have carved horror in stone, in their Stabat Mater, and it is sung in shrieks. All this is shallow, superficial stuff, Good Friday stuff. The suffering of Jesus was not primarily that of the body. He suffered little in life, physically. We do not read that he ever had the finger of man laid on him to hurt him before the Day of the Cross. He was young and strong. He suffered physically only a few hours. Many a mother suffers more than that *in her travail,* when her baby is born. Many in the hospitals today suffered more than Jesus on the day of his crucifixion, or maybe all his life. His physical sufferings were the fringe of the garment. They are not to be emphasized. God made his soul, his mysterious infinite being, for our finite beings, an acceptable offering for sin. He bore our sins in his own body, but on his soul, on the tree. Let no translator falsify the prophetic record here. We are on sacred soil. Translate as "it stands written."

The Nose and the Edge Are the Things to Watch

It is the nose of the camel you want to keep out of the tent. "It is the thin edge of the wedge you want to watch" in divisive issues. And no matter how much hush-hush prominent theologians may whisper, a Bible this wrong is divisive. It is the *start off* at a tangent, easy to come back from now, but which will some day reveal our people on widely and rapidly diverging roads, if they follow men instead of the Word of God, and a new Bible for a New Catholicism instead of loyalty to New Testament churches and revealed truth.

One time wrong is enough to wreck life on. The Romanists falsified the word *mystery* one time and got the nose of the camel called *sacrament* into the tent of translation. Once was enough. Once the word, now abandoned by all new Catholic versions, got into the Bible thus mistreated, there came the whole brood of seven sacraments into the tent and nestled down for centuries and are still a curse to nominal Christianity, leading millions to hell by their false sacramental gospel. The word *Catholic* got its nose in the Bible tent as the name of individual little letters, and some group missives. And where is there a word that has drawn in its wake more falseness, more cruelty, more intolerance, and more crime? The word *congregation,* which is what both churches and all other congregations were called in Greek, got the name *Church in the wilderness,* one time. And that camel has been in the tent of Catholic and Protestant Christianity and has corrupted ever since their Christian life by Old Testament ritual, priest-craft, and legalism, dragged in under the pretext of the Old Testament Church, a thing that never existed. And does not this RSV command us to *obey* our leaders, a camel's nose of hierarchical tyranny, in the wrong translation of Hebrews 13:17? And just one superlatively figurative reference by Paul to *priesting* the Gentile Christians, like an offering of firstfruits to God, is a nose that will be followed in the tent by an army of men who dress like women. They can fill a tent as big as Barnum and Bailey ever stretched. You don't need to say "commit apostasy" but once, in a falsified Scripture, and every word in the Bible about eternal life is at once scrapped and belied. Beware of the camel's nose, edging in.

CHAPTER TWELVE

OVERTRANSLATION

THIS FAULT CONSISTS IN GIVING A WORD THAT IS BEING TRANS-
lated into English a meaning far beyond that which it had in
Hebrew or Greek. Take these cases.

MATTHEW 21:46; JOHN 10:39

Tried to arrest is overtranslation. They made not the
slightest effort to arrest Jesus. "Though they were seeking to
arrest him, they feared the multitude." They made no open
attempt.

ACTS 1:7

It is an overtranslation to say *fixed*. The tense is not perfect. "It is not for you to know the times or the seasons, which
the Father put (or placed) in his own jurisdiction (or placed
in the sphere of his own authority.)" There is no fixedness in
the verb's idea.

ACTS 6:2

Luke wrote simply this: "Then the Twelve called the multitude of the disciples and said: It is not fitting that we should
leave the Word of God to serve tables." With their eager emphasis on the church as a body, they overtranslate the Greek
thus: "The twelve summoned the body of the disciples and
said: 'It is not right that we should give up preaching the
word of God to serve tables.'" There is not the slightest reference either to *the body of the disciples* or to *preaching,* in
the Greek. Preaching is not, and never has been, a monopoly
of the ministry. All those deacons preached, two of them
seemed notably gifted along that line, one probably the most
gifted and advanced witness to gospel truth in Jerusalem,
forerunner of Paul. Yet he preached as a layman. That is the
universal witnessing of the disciple, as occasion affords, telling
what, and of Whom, he knows. That is not the issue. The
official ministry of teaching, however, needs time for *study*.
Study and prayer were what the apostles had in mind. The
multitude, not *body,* of disciples reminds us that *three thou-*

sand resident Hellenists were converted on the Day of Pentecost, now became vocal in church life and, judging by the
names, furnished all the new officers of the organization. This
is the second great Baptist election told of in Luke's history.

ROMANS 3:4

False is an overtranslation. "Every man a liar" is a far
less serious state than "every man false," through and through,
in character and profession. What Paul said was *liar,* not the
deeper, wider state of being false. Peter swore and lied. But
he was not false, either as a man or a disciple, so he wept
bitterly over his lie. Being squeamish about a word, the Committee overtranslated it, making it worse.

ROMANS 9:22

Made for destruction is an irreverent overtranslation. It
attacks the motives of the Creator in creation. God fitted them
for the destruction that was their due. Here are how other
translators saw the meaning: "ripe for destruction" (Goodspeed), "stand ready for destruction" (Weymouth)", "matur-
ing for destruction" (Berkeley), "ripe and ready to be destroyed" (Moffatt). Would the RSV translators wish to multi-
ply infidels?

ROMANS 10:9,10

There is in the RSV a threefold overtranslation in this
great Scripture. (1) "The Lord Jesus" is expanded into
"Jesus is Lord." It is either "the Lord Jesus" or, more probably, "Jesus as Lord." The Greek just has the two words *Lord
Jesus,* destined right there to be the rival confession to *Lord
Caesar,* and maybe already approaching that issue, in Rome,
where this Epistle was sent. The Berkeley has "the Lord
Jesus"; Weymouth, "Jesus as Lord." (2) "Believeth unto
righteousness," by the usual RSV breaking up of the sentence
structure, is changed to this: "and so is justified." Paul did not
say that. He said: "believeth unto righteousness" (or *into
righteousness* might be the translation for those who insist on

baptism *into* the Name or *into* death; far more often is the translation possible *faith into, believing into.* Would the idolaters of a sacrament give more value to a physical act than to an inner experience?). But the RSV didn't even want "believes unto righteousness," so it changed the structure to separate as far as possible the verb *believes* from its purpose, or object in view, and utterly removes *righteousness* from the scene. Now *righteousness* is a far wider concept than *justify*, for it has phases of it that treat of morals, inner experience of right relations with God, providential justice on God's part (the problem in this section of Romans—the whole subject of Romans—is this varied *righteousness*) progressive righteousness in life and conduct (sanctification), and in relation to the complex problems of Romans 12—to the State, to social fellowship in wide areas of life, to benevolence, and so on. The RSV translators seemed not to see the epistolar panorama and wanted to free themselves of the very theme of the Epistle, the *opus maximum* of Paul. (3) Then Paul said: "and with the mouth confession is made concerning salvation" (obtained by faith, as just set forth). That is changed, in this mania for change for change's sake, to "he confesses with his lips and so is saved." We had heard of "lip service"; now the RSV has invented "lip salvation." It is incompetent translation and frivolously seems not to care to be right. One of the great Scriptures has been given a run-around.

ROMANS 16:1

Both overtranslation and anachronism are the words for the translation *deaconess,* in Romans 16:1. There may have been women among the deacons—the word here is *deacon*—but the order of deaconesses seems not to be on the horizon. The early churches used their widows greatly for Christian work; there seems a great stress on the importance and place of deacons' wives, in the Pastoral Epistles, and, in general, women have a vast place of service in the Scriptures that reveal to us how both Jesus and Paul worked. *Deaconess* has connotations that are not those that go with the case of Phoebe, either, who, like Lydia, was a business woman.

I Corinthians 7:14

Here we have a new kind of "consecration." "The unbelieving husband is consecrated . . . the unbelieving wife is
consecrated . . ." Strange consecration, in unbelief. Lost souls
consecrated? Now even the casual reader of the Old Testament constantly runs across the verb *sanctify* used of material
things, of days set apart, of acts of ritual and worship, of
legitimate relationship, approved by the law or legal provisions. That is the situation here. In spite of unbelief in the
united hearts and lives of the married couple, their marriage
and their offspring are legitimate, sanctified by law, hallowed
in the sacred bonds of matrimony. That is Paul's idea. But
it is not that of those who would exploit the passage for the
defense of infant baptism. They look on longingly to the declaration. "Otherwise, your children would be unclean, but
as it is they are holy." Wrenched from its context, that seems
to be a doctrine of the essential holiness of the newborn baby.
Born holy. So any new birth before baptism is out. That which
is born of the flesh, our Lord to the contrary notwithstanding,
is spirit, needs no second birth. Take it in the church and
train it up so it will never be lost. Starbuck, writing in Ferm's
Encyclopedia (p.622), on "the Psychology of Religion,"
speaks of "The Perfection of Childhood. Development and
evolution can, with the aid of selection, become anticipatory.
The child, at birth and after, bears so many indications of its
superiority . . . A sort of 'Heaven lies about him' and is incarnate within him. He usually stumbles out of this Heaven
of perfection into a rude world of specificities and jobs . . .
Is it not possible, through right culture and training, to build
the racial highway, straight and sure, from the Paradise of
Childhood into the land of the All-Pervading Beauty and
Righteousness of an adult world?" The answer is *no*. Compared with that kind of a flighty mind, Alice in Wonderland
was a Wall Street broker. And the end of that folly is juvenile
delinquency, with eighteen years as the major crime age. And
the people who live in the same home with these pets of perfection and paragons of such a paradise live in a veritable
purgatory. We have cited this Bible's very praiseworthy
doctrine of human depravity already. It contradicts this idea

of inherent holiness of babies. They are "holy" in their legitimacy, not in inherent perfection or guaranteed character.

I CORINTHIANS 1:12

I belong to Paul is overtranslation. You can favor a man, even in a partisan, factional way, without *belonging* to him. Factions are more apt to think the favorite belongs to them: "He's *my* man."

I CORINTHIANS 16:2

Why add to the Bible the word *every,* with week? The usual preposition for a standard procedure is here again. "As the norm, then, let each one of you, on the first day of the week, place something aside, treasuring it up, according as he may have prospered, in order that, when I come, there may be no collections *then.*" This Paul wrote. But it was not a permanent plan. It was the campaign plan for the collection for the Jerusalem poor. We may see Sunday worship in stewardship and offerings, and weekly, systematic giving, and the folly of waiting till the last minute and *then* give your loose change. All that is there. But Paul did not say *every* week, and there is no excuse for translating it that way.

ROMANS 11:32; GALATIANS 3:22

I protest that God never "consigned all men to disobedience" nor did he "consign all things to sin." That is little short of blasphemy and there is nothing like that in the Greek.

GALATIANS 4:5

That we might receive the adoption, or *the position of sons* is permissible, but "adoption as sons" omits the defining article and uses a needless tautology.

GALATIANS 6:4

Paul wrote simply *the other* and it is overtranslated "neighbor."

GALATIANS 6:16

We have as translation: ". . . mercy be upon all who walk by this rule, upon the Israel of God." That unduly exalts all who happen to obey that rule—*rule* is one of the obsessions of this RSV—and identifies the rule-walkers as "the Israel of God." Paul doesn't. He separates them, in his Greek, as far apart as possible. And instead of this juxtaposition and identification by a comma, he had a big *and,* indicating another group introduced. "The Israel of God" is not a synonym of *the rule-walkers,* but something entirely different.

I TIMOTHY 1:18

Paul wrote: "This charge I command you, son Timothy, according to the prophecies that led up to you, to the intent that you wage the noble warfare within them." There were prophets in the churches. They took the place of a written New Testament by their oral revelations to the churches. One of such prophets had pointed out Timothy as one who should enter the career of the ministry, as Paul came to his church. Those contemporary prophecies, perhaps repeated, led to Timothy and identified him as God's choice. Now Paul tells him they also defined his mission, and that he should not stray from his goal but fight his good fight of faith within those limits. The RSV gives this translation: "This charge I commit to you, Timothy, my son, in accordance with the prophetic utterances which pointed to you, that inspired by them you may wage the good warfare." The RSV destroys the authority of the revelation. God's prophetic revelation defined the career of Timothy and he should unfold that career within those bounds. But we have that changed to a vague inspiration of Timothy. We have shown at length that the Bible never says men are inspired, using that word only of the Scripture. What difference does it make to us whether the prophets were inspired or dull, amiable or unattractive? They are dead. It is not their personal qualities that give value to their words. *We have the Word* and it is of that that God assures us that it is his Word, God-breathed and authoritative. What the man experienced is millenniums gone.

Some time ago I preached in a suburban church in Rio

de Janeiro, in a new, overcrowded slum district. I had to use my flashlight to read my Bible, yet the electric lights were on in the church. The pastor explained to me: "We do not have connection with the city lighting system yet. A single line was run in here to light fifty houses. Five hundred hooked on to it and so there is no force to make the light shine." That is just what happens when the RSV, on its own professorial authority, adds to the Word of God inspiration for men, and hands it out to all and sundry. With this diffused inspiration, everything is inspired, nothing is inspired, and inspiration degenerates into personal impulses instead of being the revelation we need of the truth and will of God.

ROMANS 9:3,5

The RSV likes to bring in current talk. It got *homosexual* into the Bible (I Cor. 6:9), and now it exalts the Pauline word *flesh* to mean *race*. That brings us right up to date, except for one thing. There is no such word in the Greek. Paul's point, of course, is not that the Jews are of the same race. His contrast is with kinsmen according to the *flesh,* whereas in Christ he is akin to every believer. The second racial insertion is this crude. Instead of *of whom,* with reference to the patriarchs, there is inserted *of their race.* Just there, at the mention of Christ, Paul exclaims: "who is exalted above all, God blessed through all the ages" (Weymouth). This is changed, in accord with the debunking spirit already discussed. A period is inserted, and Moffatt even adds parentheses for the isolated remark: "Blessed for evermore be the God who is over all. Amen." Just what satisfaction the RSV gets from inserting the word *race* these two times in the Bible I cannot conceive, unless it may make them feel good just to have the word on the horizon.

ROMANS 5:11

To me there is a tremendous difference between the Berkeley translation of this verse and that of the RSV. The Berkeley follows the Greek: "We also exult in God through our Lord Jesus Christ, through whom we have now received the reconciliation." That is the finished work of Christ on the cross, *the reconciliation,* that which brought peace with God to our souls. It is not true that God was already reconciled, and only man needed to be. The propitiation wrought by the Savior on Calvary enabled God to be just and the justifier of the believer. When we receive that finished work, *the* reconciliation, we have ratified that reconciliation, objectively wrought on the cross, subjectively now effective in us. The RSV changes that to "our reconciliation," as if it were only a subjective change wrought in us. So few ever complete citing the great reconciliation classic, II Corinthians 5:18-21, which defines the reconciliation as God's "not imputing their trespasses to them" (not some inner subjective change in them) and gives the ground as "he made him to be sin who knew no sin." Why rob the Greek of its *the* and insert *our?*

JOHN 1:42

John wrote: "Jesus said: You are Simon, the son of John; you will be called Cephas,—translated Peter." John, writing at the end of the century, wants his readers to know that Cephas and Peter are one and the same. They all spoke Greek so they knew perfectly well what Peter means. You wouldn't need to explain to an American the common meaning of the name of a boy named Noble. John doesn't explain. But the RSV adds to the Bible an item meant for their readers in the United States explaining that Peter means rock. Now that needs qualifying. Peter does not mean the rock of proportions for a foundation. But in their addition of these words to the Bible are they not identifying on purpose Peter as the rock of Matthew 16:18? If they wanted to add this in a Bible with notes, well and good. The Berkeley has frequent small notes, and comments here: "*Petros* means a piece of rock; it is Peter's future name. *Petra* is the great rock foundation. The disciples stood on rock and they saw pieces of rock lying loose. The Church . . . is founded on the rock Jesus Christ." But the words the RSV adds to the Bible seem to be lending the aid of the New Catholicism to the Old Catholicism, insinuating that Peter was the *petra,* which is false. Why not stick to the Greek and leave off additions and tendential interpretations? To be sure, they have just as much right to their opinions as I have to mine. But why presume to write these *opinions* into the Bible as a part of its translation? It is to that I am objecting.

II THESSALONIANS 2:11

Sometimes I feel like asking the RSV translators: "What have you got against God?" Take this: "God sends upon them a strong delusion, *to make them believe* what is false . . ." It seems to me that it is to the RSV translators that the strong delusion has been sent there. What can they be thinking about? The Greek is strong language but why make it stronger, strongest? The subject is that judicial decision of God against willful disbelievers of truth revealed, men who refused it the love that truth merits. We often find that divine judgment on hardened men, devil driven, in hatred of truth and right. But the Greek only says: "that they may believe." Given their confirmed attitude to truth, it is certain they will choose to believe the lie. God's judicial decision works that way, "that they may believe the lie," just mentioned, the devil's lie for which alone they have shown affinity. But that is vastly different from saying *to make them believe* the lie. Their belief was voluntary, in accord with long affinity. There is no hint of God's *making* them believe any lie. It is again time to plead that "more reverence in us dwell."

II THESSALONIANS 2:2; I Corinthians 7:26

Here we have a verb very easily overtranslated. The reason is that its participle, in the perfect tense, can mean either *impending,* as the RSV translates I Corinthians 7:26, or *present,* as we see in the phrase *things present,* in Romans 8:32 and I Corinthians 3:22. Since either meaning is possible, the *context* must be relied on, in an unusually necessary manner, to clarify the *text* in study. Paul is evidently counseling abstention from much normal life because of the *impending* distress. What a distress it held in the near future we see when we remember the expulsion of all Jews from Rome by the stroke of an emperor's pen, the Jewish War against Rome with its chapters of unequaled horror and the perse-

cutions of Rome against Christians in that same decade.
Paul sees home life under this peril and tension. *Impend* is
of Latin origin meaning *to hang over.* The Greek verb means
to stand over, be upon us. It was the distress *that was almost
upon them* that Paul thought dread. Is that the situation also
in the context of II Thessalonians 2:2? The RSV translates:
"the day of the Lord has come," as the false rumor he is
combating. Now the context requires us to examine if that
rumor would have caused the situation Paul was correcting.
Here are men stopping their work and going out to look for
Christ from heaven, coming in the Day of the Lord, for
judgment on the world. If these idlers thought the Day at
hand, you can see why they would rush out in the open to
meet it. But what crisis could there be, if the rumor spread
that the expected Day had already come and they hadn't
noticed it? Why would that cause anybody to stop work?

What causes this strange translation, so alien to its context? Thereby hangs a tale. Modernism holds that the New
Testament was utterly unthought, unplanned, undreamed of.
They seem sometimes to feel that it was a surprise to God
himself. In this obsession it is important to give the impression
on every hand that all and sundry in the apostolic circles
are looking for Jesus right away, so nothing like a Great
Commission or a New Testament or a permant ethic or doctrine or organized church life is on their minds when they
write these hurried "letters." That is why the RSV doesn't
even dignify this great literature of the faith with the name
"Epistles." They are held to be just overnight notes, of passing
and local concern. Read them, Christian, for yourself, and see
if they look to *you* like that. But to the issue. Was Paul likewise wrapped up in this apocalyptic, eschatological mania?
Nobody agrees with Schweitzer, not even Schweitzer, but
sentimental modern thought lends value to his valueless
opinion of the Jesus he is not sure ever existed, as an eschatological enthusiast, whose John Brown's body soon lay mold-
ering in the tomb. All this spells out an apostle Paul, too, who
must have been looking for the end of the world before the
break of day. *Now to have this Paul assure the Thessalonians,
who have exactly this same mania, that he taught them better
when with them, never veered from that idea by letter, and*

never had thought the Day of the Lord was impending is a death below to any Schweitzer-like theory. So it cannot be tolerated by modernists that Paul said: "Touching the coming of our Lord Jesus Christ . . . be not quickly shaken from your mind . . . as that the day of the Lord is just at hand" (ASV). That repudiates the whole eschatalogical school, in a few words. Now modernism likes a "reduced" Jesus and a "reduced" Paul. We have seen their reduced Paul of the Corinthian Epistles. He is a glorified Holy Roller, capable of getting off a ten-thousand word outburst of senseless jargon, and then demanding that the meaningless chatter be interpreted, in the case of other people. Now take this cheap fraud and make him a stargazing apocalyptist, expecting the end of the world before day, and you have a complete picture of the crazy fanatic that no one needs to take into account. Exit Paul from the life of contemporary thought.

Here is the case, now and then found, where so far as a single word is concerned it can have either of two meanings. Can it mean "the day of the Lord *has come?*" Yes. Undoubtedly. And means also a senseless II Thessalonians and a not really bright apostle. Can it mean "the day of the Lord is just at hand?" Yes. And that translation means a harmonious text and context, an explained situation that is historical, and an intelligent apostle Paul who was such a man as did more to change human history and thought than any other except Jesus. But if this is the meaning, then modernism is a fraud, without insight of either literary or spiritual nature, and the New Testament reassumes its real proportions and meaning. Choose your Bible. It is your choice, with the consequences.

I CORINTHIANS 16:12

Again we choose between two possible meanings. The RSV made the irreverent choice, by inserting the word *God.* The Greek simply says: "It was absolutely not (   ) will to go now." What will you put in the parentheses? It should be some word in the context. The theme is Apollos. The only natural decision is *his.* That makes sense. There was a bitter faction of the city highbrows, all out for him. We can see his noble spirit revolting against them and against giving them any leeway by a return visit. He repudiates it. That is what putting *his* in there means. It is the choice of KJ, ASV, Williams, Goodspeed, Berkeley, Weymouth, Basic, and so on. It is the reverent choice. Now put *God* in. At once you have a breach between God and Paul. He has been very insistent on Apollos' coming. But it was absolutely, utterly, altogether not God's will. Paul, as usual with modernists, is off-color. Now is *God* in the context? The word is not to be found even once in the entire chapter. Arbitrariness rakes it down out of a blue sky and puts it in as contrary to Paul. But does not Paul's and Apollos' disagreement amount to the same thing? Not at all. Both are agreed against the factions. Each is sure of the other. Each would yield to the power of the other's suasion. It is a beautiful mutual confidence. But it is wrecked by the RSV translation, and a *deus ex machina* is thrust into the problem, as in the old Latin dramas. Moffatt and the RSV favor this, or Moffatt did before he died. Now I am sure he has changed a lot of his ideas, in the home of truth and reality. How much modernism will you believe five minutes after death?

I would translate further along: "He will come when the time is ripe." That is the meaning. To say "He will come when he has the opportunity" is misleading. He had the opportunity right then.

ROMANS 8:28

We have lost that anchoring conviction and hope: "All things work together for good." To me it is a tragic loss. I see the loom from this under side. It looks ugly to me. But I have faith that it follows a pattern, and that, seen on the other side, it is beautiful. How many have rested their heads on this pillow of faith. Now the RSV takes it away from us. Here, as in the last case we studied, adding *God* is not more reverent, just as turning the translators' hose loose to scatter inspiration (by them invented) among all and sundry is not a more reverent view of inspiration. Just the contrary. Now certainly it is true that God makes all things work together. No one would deny that. Its very weakness is that it is the obvious. And faith does not break into hallelujahs over the obvious. Then, too, there is a big difference. Once all things worked together *for* us. Now God works *with* us. No chain is stronger than its weakest link. This one is no stronger than *we* are. *God,* with *us,* does the working. That is a doctrine of divine co-operation. It is not the Romans 8:28 doctrine of Divine providence that includes everything in the universe. The doctrine of divine co-operation was not lacking. You did not have to kill the great doctrine of divine and all-embracing providence, gentlemen, to get the doctrine of divine co-operation with human effort. And the two doctrines are not the same nor are they equivalent. Look also at the literary effect. "God works for good to those who love God." That is worse than it was. So, having put *God* in, where the word did not belong, they took God out of where he did belong, substituting *him.* I know no change in all the RSV with all its changes for change's sake that saddens me so much at this one.

Luke 16:16

Seemingly to make the Bible either false or repulsive we have this: "every one enters it (the kingdom) *violently.*" Name three. I never saw or heard of a man's entering the kingdom violently. I can think of no man in the New Testament who entered it violently. Paul was the most violent enemy of the kingdom on the New Testament's horizon, but he did not get in the kingdom thereby. He was captured by a simple voice of protest from the risen Savior: "I am Jesus whom thou persecutest." I insist that the Bible ought to be translated so as to make sense. This is another aid to the eschatalogical mania which aims at a revolutionary conception of Christianity, which inevitably ends in communism, whether the Kerensky liberals had in mind all the resulting bloodshed and tyranny or not. The well-meaning, blinded by theories whose destination they do not understand, are the world's worst guides, sometimes.

James 4:8

One of the obsessions of the RSV is to introduce the

word *men* every time the Greek has a masculine adjective that
is used as a substantive. That is not Greek thought. Even its
generic word *man* included both genders. James said: "Ye
double minded," masculine or feminine. Now, as a matter of
diction, *you double minded* sounds a bit cheap. So they put
in "You double minded *men*." Gallant, but not true to life.
Are there no double-minded women? No Delilas? No Jeze-
bels? No Salomes? No Drusillas? This is not the only case in
life where less gallant is more faithful. Perhaps it is this gallan-
try that gave the world the translation: "these women, for
they have labored *side by side* with me in the gospel together
with Clement . . ." (Phil 4:3). There is nothing in the Greek
that justifies the overtranslation, "side by side." "And I ask
you, true yokefellow, cooperate with them; for, in the gospel,
they shared my struggle (were fellow athletic contestants),
along with Clement, also and the rest . . ."

PHILIPPIANS 2:1

Once again we have *fellowship* banished. *Participation*
is not the idea here, though a true idea, to be sure. In the
midst of "love, sympathy, affection" and unity, certainly the
social side of the Christian is to the fore, "the fellowship of
the Spirit," not "in the Spirit." The Spirit is the Author of
our fellowship. They have not dared to change the benedic-
tion: "The grace of the Lord Jesus Christ and the love of God
and the fellowship of the Holy Spirit be with you all" (II Cor.
13:14). Yet they wanted to, for even here they put "the
participation in" the Holy Spirit in their marginal note. Strange
obsession, perhaps a fruit of sacramentalism, where the
"communion" is tangible, material, magical, the participation
of the "Host," the "real body, blood and deity of Christ."
Yet, though that is where this New Catholicism is headed, it
is far from being there yet.

COLOSSIANS 3:9; EPHESIANS 4:22; ROMANS 6:6

The RSV says: "you have put off the old nature." That is
a false doctrine. The two natures continue till death. This is
classic language that has entered all modern tongues from
the Bible. A few favored university professors cannot banish

it. "The old man" and "the new man in Christ" are our Dr. Jekyll and Mr. Hyde. You can and must mortify the old nature daily, but it revives every morning and breakfasts with you, and once more has to be put in its place and kept there. Nor does it aid to translate it *self* (Rom. 6:6). We see two selves at war within us, in every hour of temptation and doubt. Life would be easy indeed if all our foes were without. Look at I Corinthians 9:25-27. We are to deny ourselves, say no to self, daily, as Jesus taught us.

HEBREWS 4:1; 12:15

A gross overtranslation is "lest any of you *be judged* to have *failed to reach it.*" *Be judged* is passive; the Greek verb is active. The verb means *seem, appear,* and the RSV so translates it in 12:11. But a version that invented out of whole cloth *commit apostasy,* in 6:6, does not tolerate here the idea that believers only *seem* to have failed. It wants them to be *judged.* The Bible warns its people to be careful of appearances; the modernist likes to shock Christian public opinion till it becomes numb. Here judgment is to be given, to the effect that maybe some one of these Hebrews "failed to reach" the Christian's rest in Christ. And in 12:15, "fail to obtain" is the translation. These overtranslations are all dictated in the service of the Methodist doctrine of apostasy. But the RSV itself translates this latter verb "fall short" in Romans 3:23 and "be inferior" in II Corinthians 11:5; 12:11 and I Corinthians 12:24. But the translators want it to be an utter failure to obtain, failure to reach the *rest* in Christ which is salvation. Again they had the cheese and the knife in their hands and cut themselves a greedy slice of sectarian advantage. The context would have helped the translators, if they had wanted the help it offers. "We who have believed enter that rest," *"do* enter," the KJ says firmly—no doubt about it. But the faithful Christian watches appearances, lest he even seem to fall short. The exhortation in 12:15 is a plea for holiness as our constant pursuit. As usual, the RSV breaks the sentence structure and can thus alter the meaning better. A series of participles follows and we ought to give their meaning. "Follow steadily after holiness . . . constantly keep-

ing watch lest any one be falling short of the grace of God,
lest any constantly defiling root of bitterness"—now a sharp
change to the aorist tenses—"spring up and cause trouble."
We all do fall short of this watchfulness, not using the ample
supply of grace available, to be and do and say what we
ought to. These participles speak of the day-long, life-long
aspects of life in Christ, and in the pursuit of holiness. Reduce
these overtranslated verbs to their proportion and the truth
will be restored as before. So will

> *mind and soul, according well*
> *make one music, as before.*

REVELATION 11:8

". . . the great city which is *allegorically* called Sodom
and Egypt." This is the version that has invented a vast lot
of "inspired" people, without benefit of the Greek's saying
so, and a religion of "rules"; and now it brings into the Bible
another word that is not there, *allegorically.* What a vast
amount of harm allegorizing has done in Bible interpretation!
The word occurs only once in the New Testament. Williams
translates: "figuratively" (marginal note, "spiritually"). It is
not a literal meaning, so it is a spiritual one, for John. Now
every man who has a mania for allegorizing all the Bible
will feel that he has justification and a great reinforcement in
the RSV.

I CORINTHIANS 16:17

Here we have the noun that corresponds to the verb just
discussed. Strange to say, the RSV translates it "absence."
Certainly that is possible. But KJ, ASV, Williams, and Weymouth translate it "what was wanting on your part." That
would ordinarily mean financial help, and it is certainly not
contrary to Paul's custom of taking nothing from the advance
field, just being entered, but teaching the already established
churches to contribute, and definitely to help in his opening of
new fields. At least, the group who were strongly his partisans
would have sent him something by the committee that went
to consult and visit him.

In verse 16 we again have the idea of absolute *subjection* to the ministry, as in Hebrews 13:17, but it weakens in verse 18 to merely "give recognition." Again *men* is added, when the whole household is in the picture and all co-operating Christians are, too, making this *subjection* an overdrawn exhortation, and not for men only. In verse 19, Aquila and Priscilla and the church they house are a numerous group and send "many" greetings, but the *many* is changed to "hearty." Of course, that is more serious as revealing the methods of the RSV than for the change itself.

I PETER 4:7

"Keep sane and sober for your prayers." Sounds like said prayers, "vain repetitions." The usual breakup of sentence structure. "Be serious minded and be awake to the practice of prayer." So the Berkeley version grasps the thought. If a paraphrase were wanted, Moffatt's would be better: "Steady then. Keep cool and pray." Are we going to stop singing "and watching unto prayer"? Which is larger, the army of those who sing "Stand up for Jesus," or the army of those who use the Revised Standard Version?

MATTHEW 26:31, 33; 13:21; MARK 14:27, 29; JOHN 16:32; ROMANS 9:32

In accordance with the official apostasy doctrine of the RSV, the apostles are all made to "fall away" and to flee away to their "own homes," go back to fishing and be saved, or made of some account on the Day of Pentecost. This is every bit a vast overtranslation. The apostles were to stumble over the crucifixion. Is it to be wondered at? But not one of them left Jerusalem. They did not go home to Galilee. The entire Christian body was at the crucifixion (Luke 23:49). The Passover was a week-long festival, and they stayed through. They stayed on still further till they were unanimous, with the reassurance of Thomas. They were in regular meetings while Christ was in the tomb. This theory is just as fanciful as the Arabian Nights tales. The overtranslation *fall away* helps make possible the slander on the great witnesses.

Acts 15:25

"It has seemed good to us in assembly." Is this meant to suggest a Presbyterian General Assembly? Well, it wasn't that. Messengers from the Antioch Baptist Church came up to the Jerusalem Baptist Church and lodged a complaint against some of the members, accusing them of meddling in other folks' business and teaching false doctrine. The Jerusalem Church and its ministry met, heard, studied, and resolved, having heard the visiting committee. Now they reply. It being a doctrinal matter, the apostles, of both sides, met in study privately and agreed on doctrine and on distribution of mission fields between the two groups, but Luke doesn't treat of that. See Galatians 2. Here the point is that they all come to one accord, after hearing and study, repudiated the Judaizers and upheld Paul, Barnabas and the Antioch Baptist Church. Bringing a General Assembly in here is sectarian hocus-pocus, partisan buncombe. This is neither Assembly, Conference, College of Cardinals, nor World Council. It was the Jerusalem Church and a protesting committee.

I Corinthians 7:1

Out of the many that clamor their protest against the RSV, I cite one more Scripture. It is I Corinthians 7:1. Paul is supposed to say: "Now concerning the matters about which you wrote. It is well for a man not to touch a woman." Not even shake hands? This is amazing, even with full cognizance of the special sense of the verb *touch*. Now the RSV separates the first seven words as a title of this section of the letter, the various questions raised by the Corinthian church itself. So far, so good. Let that be a kind of title for the Epistle division. Now the RSV sometimes uses quotation marks. Why not use them right here, in quoting? David Smith does. This, then, becomes the opinion of the ascetic element in the Corinthian church elements. They were the ones who proposed: "It is well for a man not to touch a woman." Paul gave this reply: "Rather, because of the (prevalent) fornications, every man have his own wife, and every woman have her own husband." Then he insists that no religious fervor shall withdraw husband or wife into any celibacy, but each shall carry on, in full loyalty and generosity, in their marital relations. Now how can you introduce a doctrine of universal marriage, and constant sex use and fidelity, by saying: "It is a noble thing for a man never to touch a woman"? It can't be done. Paul did not say those words, just as a lot else in this Epistle is properly in quotation marks, cited by him from others. It was the Corinthian ascetics who said. "It is a beautiful thing for a man never to touch a woman." Paul immediately said exactly the opposite, beginning with an adversative conjunction, which I translate "rather."

CHAPTER THIRTEEN

UNDERTRANSLATION

UNDERTRANSLATION IS PERHAPS THE MOST INEVITABLE AND the most excusable fault of a translator. It is inevitable because a foreign word or phrase may have a foreign significance that is hard to reproduce in English. It is excusable at times, because, to translate all that is in the original may give a cumbersome, confused, or complex wording to the English Bible that defeats its mission and purpose, with the general reader. Nevertheless, with all due allowances, we must consider how undertranslation, at times unnecessary, belittles and impoverishes the message from God which the Bible has for men. Certainly never should unnecessary undertranslation win the consent of a translator.

WRITING "SPIRIT" WHERE "THE SPIRIT" IS MEANT

There all undertranslation is needless. And if the Spirit of God is meant, it is never overtranslation to say so. It is easy for us, for we make the distinction by a small or capital letter. And here the RSV is greatly at fault and utterly inconsistent with its own standards.

Let us never forget that the Old Testament is the major part of the Christian's Bible. It is the Christian's by rights. It was the Bible of his Lord. It is the preparatory, prophetic, and progressive revelation that is a meaningless torso except as it comes to its completion in the person, work, authority, redemption, mission, and revelation of Jesus Christ, all known only by the New Testament. If we can't translate the Old Testament as Christian Scriptures, then we had better not translate it at all. If it is merely a lot of Jewish national literature, then let the Jew have it. I do not want it in my Bible. The Jews are precisely those who have the least right to the Old Testament, for they deny its central meaning and leave it headless and unfulfilled. The Old Testament is a Christian body of Scriptures. It is not a question of reading back into the Old Testament our full Christian vocabulary or thought, based on the New Testament. But it is a question of seeing and recognizing, in the Old Testament, the persons of the Trinity, the Messiah, Calvary, and the gospel, as Christ himself identified them all for us. Translators must decide whether Christ is their Teacher of the Old Testament, before they go into the translation of it. If he is not, then they are not Christian translators.

In Hitler's most triumphant hour, I never wavered in my personal friendship for Jews and defense of their full religious rights in the community and their right to translate as they please, believe as they please, and disbelieve Christ and Christianity as they please. What I say here is not a hedging as to those convictions of religious liberty. Nevertheless, when all is said, it strikes me as a very revealing fact that a Jew is on this RSV committee of translators, even though conservative scholarship of this land is virtually unrepresented in the Christian group of translators. And, of course, the whole thing was submitted to British modernists before its final form took shape. The simple fact is that the RSV Old Testament is neither a Jewish nor a Christian Bible. It is a half-breed.

JOEL 2:28-32; ACTS 2:17-21

"This is that," I heard F. B. Meyer once preach to the Southern Baptist Convention. So the Spirit interpreted prophecy on the day of his Advent as Christ's Vicar, the Leader of the World Missionary Enterprise. Was Peter Spirit-led, Spirit-infilled, Spirit-baptized when he so interpreted Joel? Or is this a mere reactionary conservatism that we have to give up to get liberals to call us scholars? Peter quoted Joel, saying twice that God fulfilled on Pentecost Joel's prophecy of the pouring out of the Spirit. But when we turn back to Joel, in the RSV, there is no such prophecy. All we read is something about a being called "my spirit." That could be a special spirit, who acted as God's agent, much as if he said "my angel." Or it could be merely "my spirit" in the sense of my attitude, my point of view, my character and sympathy, a promise to imbue others with his own spirit, his own mental outlook and spiritual purpose. The two things, "my spirit" and "my Spirit" are as different as Judaism and Christianity, as Unitarianism and the apostle Paul, as Emerson's *essays* and Spurgeon's sermons, as a false prophet and a true prophet.

"Oh, but we've got to imagine what the words meant to

the man who wrote them and give them that meaning." That
is atheistic chatter. *We have to see what the Spirit of God
means in the words he inspired as Scripture when he moved
that prophet to write.* You can't discover by imagination the
content of a prophet's mind millenniums ago. And the New
Testament definitely affirms that the messages of the prophets
went far beyond their own understanding of them, and
awakened even the curiosity of angels (I Pet. 1:10-12).
Peter there affirms that the Spirit was in them, leading them
to make timeless predictions of grace, which they did not
understand, but we may.

Now suppose that Joel did not have the clear idea of
Father, Son, Holy Spirit, one God. Suppose that to him the
Spirit of God was God, just as to us the spirit of a man is the
man. Nevertheless, a reverent Joel would have considered
that Spirit of God to be God. And we write that thought with
a capital letter, in Christian English. In either case, the small
letter with spirit is a repudiation of the Trinity. If there is no
Trinity in the Old Testament, none can be believed in the
New. If Peter said that Joel prophesied the outpouring of the
Spirit of God, the Advent of the third person of the Trinity,
then Joel prophesied the coming of the Spirit, else there is no
veracity in either apostle or prophet. You cannot have Jewish
unbelief translating Christian Scripture. The Old Testament,
I repeat, is Christian Scripture, our Savior's Bible. He and
our New Testament tell us what the Old Testament prophecy
meant. The Christian translator accepts that or goes off at a
tangent, away from Christ himself and the Holy Spirit, resulting in a non-Christian Bible, deliberately so translated.

The same conflict of veracity is seen in Matthew 12:18:
"I will put my Spirit upon him." Jesus says it. The RSV belies
our Lord, giving the prophecy in Isaiah 42:1-4 as "my spirit."
Can you trust a being as Savior who would not give to his
own Bible a truthful meaning? I could not, would not. If
Jesus said Isaiah declared: "I will put my Spirit upon him,"
that is the Christian—the Christ-ian—faith. It will so appear
in any Christian Old Testament men may print.

LUKE 4:18; ISAIAH 61:1,2

Now, marvel of marvels, we run into a Christian Old

Testament in one spot in the RSV. Both Old and New declare: "The Spirit of the Lord is upon me," in a great Messianic prophecy. That is why I say there is no consistency in the RSV translation principles. Also we have the Spirit of God in Isaiah 11:2, one time *Spirit* and three times *spirit* in that one verse. In Psalm 139:7, we read: "Whither shall I go from thy Spirit?" And in Psalm 51:11; "Take not thy holy Spirit from me." In Nehemiah 9:20, we find: "Thou gavest thy good Spirit to instruct them." And "the Spirit of God was moving over the face of the waters" (Gen. 1:2). Why we should have *the Spirit* on either side of the great Messianic Scriptures that treat of the Advent of Jesus and the Advent of the Spirit, but find only *spirit* in these key, vital prophecies, according to the RSV, is to me a mystery of mysteries. I understand how late some of these Scriptures are held to be by modernists. Still there is no consistency in an Old Testament that is Christian on one page and mere Judaism on another. It is a half-breed.

MATTHEW 3:16; JOHN 1:32; ACTS 8:16

Amazed, we read: "he saw the Spirit of God descending like a dove and *alighting* upon him." Is that frivolity or ignorance of the Greek? The Greek has Spirit (neuter) descending (neuter) like a dove (feminine), coming (neuter) upon him (Jesus). There is no possibility in the wide world of associating the *coming* of the Spirit on Jesus, anointing him for his Messianic career, with the action of a bird alighting. The Greek does not mean *alighting*. Physically, in detail, that is overtranslation, and in spiritual significance vastly undertranslating. It was that coming that showed Jesus to be the Christ. It cannot be reduced to a mere bird gesture of alighting. Maybe this "alighting" idea of the Spirit of God explains why he is called *it* in John 1:32 and Acts 8:16, inconsistently with the masculine personal pronoun in other cases. Of course, this is doubly emphatic in Greek, where *Spirit* is gramatically neuter in gender, but a masculine pronoun will be used in referring to him.

STANDARDS: "ACCORDING TO . . ."

In other connections I have noted a time or two that the

Greek preposition *katá* sets up a standard. To that idea the
modernistic mind is often hostile, for God's standards are not
its standards. Its prime obsession is against the *status quo*.
Just say *status quo* to a modernist and he sees *red,* maybe his
color predilection anyway, and foams at the mouth. His
gospel, even though he be a pacifist, is revolution even though
that means bloodshed, militarism, and totalitarian autocracy.
Not caring for some of the standards the New Testament sets
up, especially truth, the faith once delivered to the saints,
doctrine, and the like, he deletes the *standard* idea by mistranslating the prepositional phrase *according to.* Thus the
divine standards vanish away and the unwary public, which
has no Greek, never knows what it was robbed of by the RSV.
When the public life and safety have been undermined and
wrecked, it will be too late to ask: What became of our
standards that ought to have been a bulwark against this
enemy? Which reminds me that one of the Scriptures we
utterly lose in the RSV is Isaiah's great battle cry: "When
the enemy comes in like a flood, the Spirit of the Lord shall
lift up a standard against him" (Isa. 59:19). Well, now the
Spirit is dissolved into "breath", "wind"; and the standard to
which men might rally falls from its place. Even if not accurate in translation, the words are, in themselves and in
history, true and timely and rather urgent.

Here are the facts about standards. The preposition that
sets up the standards is found in that sense in the New Testament 177 times, translated in the KJ "according to," "after,"
and so on. It is not a very common preposition, in this sense,
in the Gospels, having that meaning only seventeen times,
mainly in Luke. Now the translators of the Gospels were
generally faithful, conserving "according to" where it belongs. The translator(s) of Acts, which seems to me the
worst in the New Testament, kept the phrase five times and
varied from it three, but not in grave fashion. But it is in the
doctrinal Epistles that the word comes to the fore and is most
often found in this sense. It is found in Romans about fifty
times and half of them in the sense of a standard raised. And
in the brief Epistle to the Ephesians it is found twenty-four
times and raises a standard in more or less a score of the
passages. Hebrews has it forty times, the majority of them
raising standards of revelation and life. Peter has it in his

Epistles fifteen times and mostly as indicating *standards*. Let us go to cases.

1. Here's one they threw in the ash can and got rid of. Paul said: "So, *as much as in me is,* I am ready to preach the gospel to you that are in Rome also" (Rom. 1:15). Paul really said: *according to the standard me.* The Paul standard? You see it in II Corinthians 11. The *me* Standard, of the greatest Christian. He was ready to look at his best and equal it in Rome. Did we sustain no loss when the RSV threw that in the ash can?

2. "We know that the judgment of God is according to truth" (Rom. 2:2). How vital, then, to conserve the truth. The RSV despises the standard, saying only: "The judgment of God rightly falls on those who do (*practice,* Greek) such things." But the standard of the judgment has been destroyed by willful or incompetent mistranslation.

3. "According to thy hardness and (thy) impenitent heart (the standard of judgment, in defining the degree of blame —just as judges distinguish between first-degree murder and involuntary manslaughter—even as the truth is the Absolute, as the standard of law and duty) dost thou treasure up for thyself wrath?" That is the Greek of Romans 2:5. Truth, the standard of law; hardness and impenitent hearts, the standard of responsibility in sin. It all disappears from the RSV: "But by your hard and impenitent heart"—no, the human heart is not the *agent* of divine wrath and judgment, but its purposefulness in sinning is the lost standard of judgment.

4. "It is of faith, that it may be according to grace" (Rom. 4:16). It is by that standard that Paul there affirms the security of the believer, the standard of grace. The promise is to the spiritual "seed," those born again. But the RSV discards it all: "That is why it depends on faith, in order that the promise may rest on grace and be guaranteed to all his descendants." All Jews are descendants of Abraham, and a lot of Arabs. So they are all in on this. *Rest on grace* lends itself to all sorts of interpretations, including the right one, but in no way excluding wrong ones.

5. "The purpose of God according to election," (Rom. 9:11), becomes "in order that God's purpose *of election* might continue," a confused and wholly different idea.

6. "They have a zeal for God but not according to knowl-

edge" (Rom. 10:2). Zeal must obey standards. Zeal for wrong is very wrong; zeal for truth is very true and holy. The RSV dissolves it in thin vapor: "They have a zeal for God but it is not enlightened." It was lit up with culture, but not with the knowledge of the truth. "Every man that comes into the world is enlightened" by the moral law written on his heart, by impulses of the broken image of God within him, and so on, but light by the standard of knowledge was not theirs.

7. "A remnant according to the election of grace" becomes the standardless "remnant chosen by grace" (Rom. 11:5), simply a false and unreasonable translation.

8. "Now the God of patience . . . grant you to be of the same mind one with another *according to Christ Jesus*" (Rom. 15:5). Our Lord is the standard of our mental attitudes. And we are to cherish the ideal of mental unity rather than senti- mental and disobedient unionism. Mercy! That will never help on the New Catholicism. So we keep a similar-sounding phraseology in part: "May the God of stedfastness . . . grant you to live in such harmony with one another, in accord with Jesus Christ . . ." Here all that appears is "harmony with one another," which glides smoothly into "accord with Jesus Christ." No *standard,* and the *mind* is tucked away out of sight. True, in the phrase *be of the same mind,* in Greek, the verb takes *the same* as object. But this involves the thought life and "bringing every thought into captivity to Christ," our divine *standard* of thought life, which comes before unity.

This in the Romans Epistle alone. Now see Ephesians 2:2; 3:20; 4:16,22; 6:5 for similar banishment of standards, God-given, RSV-suppressed. See II Timothy 1:9 also, where *according to* becomes *in virtue of.* Would you think there was no difference between interest paid according to the amount of your deposit, and merely in virtue of your deposit, without any standard? See II Timothy 2:8; 4:14. Note this tremendous lack of fidelity. The Greek says: "The Lord will pay him back according to his works," the standard of judg- ment. The RSV says: "the Lord will requite him for his deeds." See discussion of Titus 1:3; 3:5,7 elsewhere. See this error of Hebrews 7:5. The priests were to take tithes from the people *according to the law.* How different from the un-

restricted robbery by most priestly systems. The RSV makes
it all merely "a commandment in the law," no standard there
set up. See the difference in Hebrews 9:19. In I Peter 1:2;
"Elect according to the foreknowledge (which means far
more than prescience, in Bible terminology) of God . . ."
becomes merely "chosen and destined" (without saying to
what). No standard. Similar wrecking of the meaning is
found in I Peter 1:3; Revelation 20:12,13. It is a gruesome
total.

GRACE BANISHED OR REDUCED

A word that is greatly stressed in the Bible is *grace*. In
the RSV it has a varied fate, passing to mere *favor* in Luke
2:40; to *blessing*, II Corinthians 9:8; to *thankfulness*, Col-
losians 3:16; *gracious work*, II Corinthians 8:6,7,19 (already
discussed); to *approved, approval*, I Peter 2:19,20, and
other instances. The structure of Hebrews 12:28 is wrecked
and *grace to serve* is blacked out, while in I Corinthians 3:10
grace has become merely *commission*.

POOR ESAU: HEBREWS 12:17

"He was rejected, for he found no chance to repent,
though he sought it with tears." That is so wrong and blind.
What was denied Esau, as a simple matter of history, was
not a chance to repent but any change in his father's mind.
Now change of mind is the basic meaning of repentance. The
Berkeley version has "he found no place for recalling the
decision, although with tears he sought for the blessing," with
this note: "He could not persuade his father Isaac to change."
The ASV is familiar reading: "He found no place for a change
of mind *in his father*," the last three words in italics. There
is simply no question that it was the father's mind that could
not be changed.

TABERNACLE CUT BACK TO TENT

The word *tabernacle* is almost banished from the RSV
New Testament, but it is in good company, with a host of
great Christian words. It remains in the New Testament only

in John 7:2, "feast of Tabernacles." Yet that was when they used *tents* of the crudest fashion. But the great center of Hebrew worship in the wilderness and early kingdom of Israel becomes a mere tent. This is a matter of taste. It seems to me wretched taste, sprung from irreverent attitudes. We even read of the "temple of the tent of witness" in heaven itself (Rev. 15:5). They feel that themselves in Revelation 21:3 and modify it to *dwelling*, which is not the meaning, but an escape translation. Life is cheapened by calling our body a *tent*, when for centuries the *tabernacle* language of the Bible has been in use in this precious passage. That is the trouble. The RSV seems to have no background, in so many of its translations. Several times the revisers simply cannot bring themselves to translate *tent*, but having brought themselves determinedly to repudiate *tabernacle*, they change the word *tent* to *body, habitation,* and other terms (II Pet. 1:13,14; Acts 7:46; Ps. 84:1). Can you read now publicly: "Lord, who shall sojourn in thy tent?" (Ps. 15:1).—a highbrow word *sojourn* with a plebeian word *tent?* Yet in the less read portions of the Bible, *tabernacle* is retained, as Exodus 25:9; Leviticus 8:10, and other passages. Such measures cheapen the Bible.

More Than Custodian: Galatians 3:24,25

In this highly figurative passage there are three possibilities: (1) discard the verbal dress of the figure and translate the essential idea without figurative language; (2) retain a word that translates part of the figure and explain the rest in a note; (3) adopt a similar figure from modern life. The word, from which we get *pedagogue*, means a capable slave who is in charge of the child between school and home and with disciplinary authority over him, during his minority. Now we have the word twice. In I Corinthians 4:15 it describes Paul as related to the Corinthian church, or rather all the ministers (slaves) who had been their *pedagogues*, in the Greek sense. These great men were slaves to the Corinth church, as minors, but Paul was the father. No figure could be bolder. Here he makes all Jewry the minor; the law, the slave; Christ, the Teacher; God, the Father. Of course, neither *guide* nor *custodian* is an adequate translation, and the RSV, so abounding in notes and conjectures, gives no aid to the reader here. So much for the first method, a grave undertranslation by the RSV. Now, in the second, see the combination of partial translation and note. Williams has "our attendant"; note: "usually a slave who cared for the Greek child on the way to and from school." Only a very partial success. Berkeley is far better: "The Law served as our tutor Christward"; note: "*Paidagogos,* boy's leader, tutor. Jews under the Old Covenant and Gentiles under sin were like minors. Jews under Law and Gentiles under sin were like slaves. Through Christ we become sons and heirs." There are three notes, to different words. The reader must get, by all this, much of the idea. It is too much for a Bible without notes, but a better single note with *paidagogos* could suffice. In the third, the equivalent, cut loose from Greek life and terms, is sought to be expressed by these figures: "governess" (Phillips), wrong in gender, occupation, and as a figure, but very suggestive of the facts; "attendant" (several); "servant" (Basic: "So the law has been a *servant* to take us to Christ," very simple and rewarding, but inadequate). Moffatt transfers the whole figure to the ones under Law: "The Law thus held us as wards in discipline."

Bear in mind that the translation of this Scripture serves a great purpose in missionary modernism. The less meaning it has, the better, for such purposes. It is the dogma of all eclecticism that the Old Testament was the "pedagogue" for the Jews, Confucius for the Chinese, the Vedas for Hinduism, the Koran for Islam, and so on. All these "scriptures" are introduced as parallel sacred books in Ferm's *An Encyclopedia of Religion,* in which the leading translators of the RSV take a leading part. Nothing could be more antimissionary than the viewpoints and propaganda of such a book.

HOUSEHOLD SLAVES AND THEIR HUMAN LORDS

In Romans 14:4, the RSV translates the Greek word *Lord* as "Master." The reason is a bad consistency. They translated it "master" about the human *lord,* in the case of slave relations. So having translated *lord* as "master," they

consistently translate *Lord* as "Master". Would not the reverse be the better policy and give clearer meaning? It would
be true and faithful translation. The RSV uses the word *lord*
in translation in Matthew 18:24-34 five times, though it
ought also to use *slave* in the context. Now it is very poorly
translated, to hide the institution of slavery. It never seems to
enter the mind of many translators that *the Bible is history,*
even its parables giving the true history of the times, but that
faithfully giving the history of slavery is no endorsement of
it. So, like other versions before and currently, the RSV falls
into a sentimental evasion of reality. The RSV has *lord* also
four times in Luke 10:16-25. Also in Acts 25:26. We do
find that the RSV, in a lucid moment of insight on this problem, translates properly *slaves* (Eph. 6:5; Col. 3:22; 4:1;
and other verses), but shuns the word *lord* it used in such
contexts, at times, in the Gospels. "Other ancient authorities"
have *God* where our text gives *Lord.* They certainly could
not translate *God* by the word *Master,* and it would be better
not to do so when the meaning is *Lord.*

The New Testament makes very clear distinctions also
in both the classes of slaves and the classes of servants. Why
not preserve these truths? What is the use of a new translation
that goes right down the beaten track of conformity with
old errors of previous translations? Now let us look at this
slave-servant word of Romans 14:4. Distinctions are of the
essence of exegesis. The servants in Cana were paid workers
(the word for *minister* of the gospel), and it is the word in
Christ's command that he who would be greatest should be
the servant of all. Great New Testament saints often went
beyond that and considered themselves voluntarily the slaves
of their brethren. The distinction should be made, especially
in certain Scriptures, at least in the margin. Leave off a lot
of conjecture and give us a lot more vital facts.

Now look at this term for household slave-servant. The
New Testament uses it only four times: Luke 16:13; Acts
10:7; Romans 14:4; I Peter 2:18. Matthew is very plain in
the parallel passages (6:24), saying: "No one can live in
slavery to two lords." Luke cites the words: "No household
slave can be a slave to two lords." Now the common translation is not true. I have been pastor in Brazil of people who

were servants in other people's homes. Often they served two
employers well, as wash-women, as gardeners, and in other
ways. But a household slave in two homes, that is impossible
—as cook for two families, nurse for two sets of children, or
doubling in other exacting household duties. If you remember
the stories of slavery, you know the household slaves were
generally people of great intimacy with the family, and trustworthy and proven in every responsibility. Now you can't
hold that position to two lords, nor to our only Lord Jesus
and any rival. Two such intimate household slaves and a
devout soldier went after Peter for Cornelius. Undoubtedly
the Spirit fell on those slaves as they heard Peter preach. To
household slaves Peter said: "Be subject to your *despots*
(lords, without the idea of despotism that our word has) with
every fear" awake, and he recognizes the good and the bad
among slaveowners (I Pet. 2:18). Now, coming back to
Romans 14:4 again: "You, who are you that pass judgment
on the household slave of another? To his own lord he stands
or falls." Then Paul's great love and understanding and sympathy for slaves, perhaps the majority of the members of
churches he founded, makes him add tenderly: "But he shall
stand, for the Lord is powerful to make him stand." To be
a successful slave, true to God and man, was perhaps as great
an achievement of grace then as to be a successful Christian
in any freedom. These slaves in even a "despot's" household
were also in the intimacy of the household of God as slaves
to his Son our Lord. And the good Lord backed up the good
household slave. These facts of translation, if revealed even in
the margin, would relate us to Christ very intimately, both
as to his authority and his tenderness.

PHILEMON 9; TITUS 1:4; I TIMOTHY 1:2

Paul wrote: "Therefore, even though I have much bold-
ness in Christ to order you to do what is fitting, yet I rather
beseech you, for love's sake (because of the love you have
for me), because I am in the category of Paul the aged (such
a one as . . .), yet at this very moment even a chained captive
of Jesus Christ, yes I beseech you for my son Onesimus, whom
I begot in my chains, formerly useless to you, but now useful

both to you and to me." The undertranslations of the RSV
are *Paul an ambassador*. That is wholly figurative and rather
meaningless without the direct connection: *ambassador of*, or
for, Christ. Paul is within a few years of death, feels his age.
William Carey thought Felix, when he accepted diplomatic
service of Great Britain, "degenerated into an ambassador."
This tender appeal means far more from an aged friend than
from a mere "ambassador." Onesimus was not a *child*, but a
son. Either word for *son* may be so translated, though the
other one has higher meaning. But that is not the issue here.
The same consideration applies to *child* about Titus (Tit.
1:4), and Timothy (I Tim. 1:2). It is not the tender age of
Onesimus that is in question, but the tender relation, son of
Paul, outranking the claims of ownership by Philemon. *For*
Christ is not the Greek. There is the evident double sense of
captive, of Caesar in Rome, in his own hired house, chained
to a soldier, and *captive* of Christ in his thought life, bringing
every thought gladly into that slavery of discipleship. I have
already discussed the overtranslation of which this version
is guilty in rendering *chains* as *imprisonment*, as if they had
never read the conclusion of the Acts of the Apostles. This
seems to be a purposeful "disharmony" translation.

Angels Preferred to Church: Hebrews 12:22-24

The undertranslation of this passage is a great loss to
New Testament thought, doctrine, and theology. Contrasting
the two covenants and eras of law and grace, the author says:
"You have come" to Mount Zion (the spiritual Israel) and
the city of the living God (the center of spiritual life and
worship, as Israel's capital was, in a national sense, under
the old covenant), the heavenly Jerusalem (the mother of us
all, our supernatural, life-giving hope), to tens of thousands
of angels (servants of the heirs of salvation), (this comma
is even in the Greek of the elder Nestle) to the general
assembly and church of the firstborn (*general assembly* is
one word, which begins with the Greek word *all* as first
syllable in a compound word, and is between commas with
the word *church*, one concept) who have been enrolled in
heaven (they were not there when that happened), and to

God the Judge of all, and to the spirits of the just who have been made perfect (they were just by faith, and at death they were made perfect and permanently remain so), and to Jesus the Mediator of the new covenant, and to the blood of the sprinkling (fulfilling all the promise of purification in Mosaic emblems) blood speaking something far better than Abel (had to say)." This is the Greek, with my comment in parentheses.

The RSV removes the *church general* utterly from this Scripture, substituting twice the angels alone. It makes the panorama of the New Covenant too utterly otherworldly. The firstborn, were it singular, would be Jesus. But it is plural. The author has definitely classed the angels already as heaven's servants of the heirs of salvation, but the believers as the sons Jesus is bringing to glory. *They are his brethren,* of 2:12, and constitute the heavenly *congregation* that centers around him. In that very connection we have: "it is not with angels that he is concerned." How, then, could they fill the whole panorama of the congregation, which already has been defined as being constituted of his brethren, who are also his sons brought to glory? John says: "as he is, so are we in this world." How much more so in heaven. The firstborn in the Jewish system was the priest of the family. We are of the universal priesthood of Christianity. The firstborn in the royal family was the king-to-be. We are both kings and priests. The firstborn was the double heir, got as much as two other children. We all have a double portion in the inheritance of grace. It is believers who, in Christ, are joint heirs with him of his firstborn privileges and functions in the heavenly family. It is a general assembly of the heirs who have come into their inheritance of glory.

How useless it is to say that the RSV changes no doctrine. It would be nearer right to say that it has left no doctrine intact. This passage gives no place in the panorama for a Protestant Purgatory, a dear idea to hell-repudiating modernists. We here see the difference between the just and the perfect. Here we are just by faith, righteous in Christ, perfected by the one offering of Calvary, so far as our standing is concerned, but utterly imperfect in our state. At death, that instantly changes, in our glorification, and the just by faith become permanently and utterly perfect. This is great doctrine, vital theology, glorious hope. Don't pass out to the angels the heritage of sons, Dr. Modernist. That is not their standing in this context. Hebrews is not a part of Job's poetry, or *vice versa*.

There is nothing about either "the sprinkled blood" or "more graciously" or "the blood of Abel" in this passage. Such translations are made up in the minds of the translators and brought in. If they think some paraphrase helps in such figurative passages, drenched with Old Testament terminology and New Testament theology, they ought at least to put the Greek truth in the margin.

"THE SCARS OF CALVARY": REVELATION 5:6

The greatest sermon I ever heard was preached from this text, unmutilated. "I saw a Lamb standing, as it has been slain." The preacher was the unique educator-missionary, E. M. Poteat, president of Furman University. He said: "Why are the scars of Jesus evident in glory?" And answered: "They are the marks of his continuing human personality. They are the receipt of our redemption. They bear witness that sacrifice is heaven's first law." Don't make a pretense of all of that, modernist translator, by putting it: "I saw a Lamb standing *as though* it had been slain." We know that Lamb. He was slain. And we shall see him as did Thomas and exclaim in adoring wonder: "My Lord and my God."

A CONSECRATED FETUS: JEREMIAH 1:5

"Before you were born I consecrated you." We are used to Bible meaning for Bible words, and we know that *sanctify* means *to set apart, separate unto*. That can be the divine decision as to the unborn. But a consecrated fetus is meaningless chatter. Maybe this consecrated fetus is getting ready for infant baptism in I Corinthians 7:14. The sectarian vision of these pedobaptist translators reached afar.

TWO ONCE-FOR-ALL DEATHS: HEBREWS 9:27, 28

Generally, the translators of the Hebrews-Jude section of

the Bible are very faithful to translate the great *once-for-all* Scriptures. They failed in these two important Scriptures: "And according to the standard that is laid down for men (or by just as much as it is appointed unto men) to die once for all, and after this judgment, just so also the Christ, having been offered up once for all, in order to bear aloft (in his own body on the tree, as the Lamb of God that taketh away the sin of the world, is the idea. W.C.T.) sins of many (or the sins of the many), a second time will appear, for salvation (the consummation of it), without a sin offering, to those who are awaiting him." Now it is very important that this once-for-all truth be not suffocated by prejudice. It is well not to obscure the testimony to Spiritualists that there is no reincarnation. Death is final. There is no second earthly life, no second chance. *Once for all* is the description of time and of eternity. Nor is there any repetition of Calvary's offering, in the "Eucharist." That is the very heart of Hebrews, *once for all*, no other offering, none other needed.

One Sunday morning, a little before my own hour of worship in a church nearby, I stepped into a Catholic church. The priest was talking about death, Purgatory, and "the judgment that takes place while the body is still warm." Like most of Romanism, that idea did not come from the Bible, and it has no place in revealed Christianity. You can't fit the Mass, meant to take people out of a place where they *are not, for the place does not exist,* or the Purgatory it is the patent medicine for, into the *once-for-all* truth of Hebrews. Why should the RSV play into the hands of Spiritualists or Romanists by suppressing the truth at this point?

ACTS 13:39

Paul preached: "Through this man the remission of sins is proclaimed to you, and by this man every believer is justified from all things. You could not be justified from these things in the Mosaic legal regime (or from which things you could not be justified by the law of Moses)." I have commented on the unpardonable banishment of "the remission of sins" from the new Bible. In their translation they now banish twice the verb *justify* from this Scripture. They are almost as bad about banishing as czarist or soviet Russia. There is no sort of excuse for translating this verb "free." That is neither the meaning nor the resultant sense. And if the RSV really wanted to make doubly clear the sense, given their habit of breaking up the structure of a sentence, they would have done it here, as indicated. The idea is not that the law of Moses could almost entirely free you, or justify you. But Christ steps in, like a relief pitcher in the ninth inning of the ball game, and saves the situation which you almost saved yourself, but lacked a little. The law of Moses was absolutely impotent to save you, a failure in the whole realm of moral responsibility, "all things." The believer is justified wholly, forever, at the moment of faith, from "all things." Paul was preaching in a synagogue. He did not becloud his gospel there, Moses being presented as mostly the Savior, Jesus as supplemental. He gave the same message as in Romans 4.

JOHN 8:31

My translation of the Greek is: "If in the future *you* abide in my Word, truly you are *now* my disciples, and you will know the truth and the truth will liberate you." The future, continuous-life attitude toward the Word, from faith on, proves the reality of the professed present discipleship, and guarantees the progress in truth that is a liberating force in life, a liberating force that *they* (the emphatic you of the Jew public) would supremely need in the trials ahead. Here the often excellent Brekeley erred utterly: "If you adhere to my teaching, you will truly be my disciples." No. The future discipleship tests and proves the present faith. The tree that in the future doesn't bear the right species of fruit, doesn't have now the right species of root. I have fully translated the sense; the RSV half missed it. "Make you free," in the thinking of those who use this text in the educational world, does not refer to an attitude toward Jesus; it refers to the slow progress from freshman to sophomore and on through the discarding of sophomoric ideas. That itself is a miserable cheat of a sophomoric interpretation, utterly false to the whole liberating gospel of Jesus, which he then announced to countrymen who would be faced with the choice that ended in his crucifixion.

To turn it into a slogan of college professors is of the same moral caliber as turning over the translation of our Bible to university professors in a Chicago-New York-Boston axis of modernism.

I Peter 1:11,12

The sum of modernism as to prophecy was that the prophet spoke primarily to his own time and people. That is false. The prophet was always the organ of revelation and gave the revelation God gave him, without philosophizing. Peter said: "searching to whom or to what manner of time the Spirit of Christ within them was manifestly referring when he testified beforehand the sufferings of Christ and the glories that should follow thereafter; to whom it was revealed clearly that not to themselves but to you they were ministering the things which now have been announced to you by those who preached the gospel to you by the Holy Spirit sent from heaven, which things angels long to stoop down and look into." Words could not more clearly deny the fundamental postulate of modernism about prophecy, but it is blurred, confused, and denied by the RSV translation. The prophets did not simply "predict" the sufferings of Christ; they gave them dramatic portrayal in the whole sacrificial system of Israel, and all comment on it. What a tragedy that men will deliberately conceal from the public what the Bible has to say to them. The prophets were not simply "ministering" to their generation. They were ministering the gospel of the sufferings of Christ. "To him give all the prophets witness."

Hebrews 11:33

Now "enforced justice" is a forced translation. What was really God-breathed into this Scripture was "wrought righteousness," a vastly wider and deeper concept of faith's achievements.

Hebrews 11:35

What the Greek says is "a better resurrection," not "rise again to a better life." I believe in a general resurrection, but

I believe the difference in the praises of Christ and the rewards he brings with him will make the resurrection of the faithful believer far "better" than that of the neglectful one. Furthermore, we have no right to mistranslate this Scripture in order to shut off the premillennial interpretation of two resurrections. That takes an unfair advantage, "with the cheese and the knife in hand."

Hebrews 13:5

This has been called the strongest utterance in the Bible. It has the strength of five negatives in the Greek, and gave rise to the great hymn of the security of the believer:

> *The soul that on Jesus hath leaned for repose,*
> *I will not, I will not desert to its foes;*
> *That soul, though all hell should endeavor to shake,*
> *I'll never, no never, no never forsake.*

But the RSV, all of whose enthusiasm is for the doctrine of apostasy, leaves the statement as weak as it can possibly be and still be a translation at all.

CHAPTER FOURTEEN

THE TRANSLATORS' LOVE OF DISHARMONY IN THE BIBLE AND HATRED OF THE HARMONY OF THE GOSPELS

Look at each end of your Bible. The RSV states that its first five books were written by Moses. Modernist criticism denied Moses could write till archaeology forced it to concede the possibility. The contradiction between modernist unbelief and the new Bible it likes is obvious.

In point of time, the last five books of your Bible were written by John. John could write, but modernist theory holds that he could not tell the time of day. If we have a Bible whose supposed first author could not write, and whose alleged last author could not tell the time of day, then it is no wonder that Christianity is lapsing into paganism where such views prevail. Such a Bible is merely a fairly interesting antique, an outmoded superstition. A Bible forged by anonymous nonentities loses all moral driving power. It can no longer be a book of motives. That is why the population of the State Churches, which bulk so largely in the New Catholicism that sponsors this new Bible, is only nominally Christian, really pagan, never sets foot in its pompous cathedrals. *The British Weekly* recently spoke of its own national proletariat thus: "as pagan as India and more difficult to be evangelized." And, around the Chicago-New York-Boston axis of the translators of this new Bible, does not the same popular alienation from evangelical Christianity exist? Have not Romanism and Unitarianism swept the day? Are not their "intellectuals" and their "proletariat" also a unit in unbelief in either the Bible or the Constitution, and a menace to the morals and the liberties each enshrines? The infidel universities where these translators shine have in recent generations grown themselves an infidel environment, largely by their infidel attitude toward the Word of God.

COULD JOHN TELL THE TIME OF DAY?

Our new Bible has left John in open contradiction of the

Synoptic Gospels on the most important subject in the Bible or in the world, the death of Christ. The time setting of Calvary's cross is too important to be left in Disharmony by hostile translators. The Synoptics tell us that Jesus was crucified at the third hour (9 A.M.) and hung on the cross till the ninth hour (3 P.M.) (Mark 15:25, 33, 34; Matt. 27:45, 46; Luke 23:44). The testimony is coherent and is validated by three witnesses. Mark was a resident, most probably an eyewitness. Matthew most certainly was. Luke gives the testimony of all the great eyewitnesses and ministers of the Word, carefully sought out. There is no possible question of the hour.

Now John 19:14 says: "it was about the sixth hour." Does that mean noon? No. It can't. The trial was still on, before Pilate. The further trial, the scourging of Jesus, the mocking by the soldiers, the slow march through narrow streets, the crushing crowd obstructing the way, the weeping women, the falling Savior, the impressed Simon, the delays for the nailing of the victim—all would combine to project the beginning of the crucifixion far into the afternoon. The gospel story fades away into a silly tale, contradictory at every step of the way, unworthy of faith. So this Disharmony closes the door to reasonable faith and opens it wide to infidelity.

Why could not the translators omit ninety per cent of their idle conjectures and tell us what the Harmony of the Gospels reveals and demands to be stated? John's different hour system, later terminology, time setting in a different environment, language for different readers is all perfectly established by great scholars like A. T. Robertson, and classic Harmonies of the Gospels. What is far more, A. T. Robertson and his peers did not invent that Harmony. It is all there in your own Bible, in the RSV, in all Bibles, if you only read. You do not have to know a letter of Greek. All you need is a seeing eye and a thinking head. John uses the word *hour* frequently enough to make crystal clear his meaning. He began his count from midnight or noon; the earlier Gospels begin from sunrise, about 6 A.M. That is the difference. No use to quibble as to secular data concerning the change in system. The facts as to the already effected method of reckoning time in John are self-evident. In John's very first chapter you

have the meaning (1:35-39). John and Jesus were early
risers, were early pray-ers. Only two disciples seem to be
with John when he points out Jesus as the Lamb of God.
They are ready for the day, but the crowds have not come.
These two leave John and follow Jesus. Jesus turns and wel-
comes them and the three go on, "and they stayed with him
that day, for it was about the tenth hour." By Synoptic time
system, the tenth hour would be 4 P.M. How could you
arrive at a place at 4 P.M. and still spend the day?

Friends came to spend the day with us in Rio de Janeiro
a short while ago. They lived in the suburbs and arrived at
10 A.M. and stayed till 4 P.M. and left, having "spent the day."
But suppose I should go to your house at 4 P.M. a spring day,
nearly dark, and say: "I came to spend the day with you."
Would I not need to be, as our fathers used to say, "tapped
for the simples"? Yet that is the folly of the RSV. It gives no
note to clarify John's time system, half a century later and
half an empire away, from the Palestinian time system.

Clear confirmation of this hour system comes from the
Samaritan woman at Jacob's Well, at "about the sixth hour,"
6 P.M. That goes with the weariness of Jesus after a day's walk.
It accords with our oriental Bible. Sensible women did not
carry heavy jars of water a long way under the midday sun.
"At the time of evening, *the time when women go out to draw
water*" (Gen. 24:11).

The Jewish Encyclopedia says that Babylonian Jews had
already discovered the sixty-sixty measure of seconds and
minutes and carried the news to Jerusalem at the feasts. But
some say there were no clocks. If you have ever been pastors
of farmers, you know that those who tell time by the sun tell
it accurately and don't need a clock. John was a fisherman,
lived in Galilee. There never was a day in his life when he
would have been capable of confusing 9 A.M. and noon.

STILL JOHN 19:14

It seems, to some, that John could neither tell the time of
day nor knew the day of the week, for they make him say:
"Now it was the day of Preparation for the Passover; it was
about the sixth hour." Modernism seems to feel that both all

the apostles and all the persons of the Trinity were utterly unacquainted with each other and no one knew what any other had done or was going to do. The Greek doesn't have *for* the Passover. It has *of*. The word *Passover* had three meanings; the Passover lamb, the Passover Day, and the Passover Week. It has the last sense here. It was the day of Preparation, of the Passover week, Friday before the sabbath of Passover week. There is not even a difficulty about the verse. And *Preparation* became the Greek name for Friday and is to this good day. With nothing but elemental fairness, the translators could have left the Word of God in harmony. They love rather the Disharmony, hate the Harmony that Broadus, Robertson, and countless others have given us. Broadus knew this theory, advocated in his day by German scholars. He knew it and thought it worthless, expressed his horror that men could accept Disharmony in the Gospels. Sir William Ramsay early wrote out the same theory. It is old stuff. But A. T. Robertson saw through it and gave the Harmony, rather than Disharmony, of the Gospels. Our translators could have given us a translation in our language, which they so much pretend to want, in "o'clock" terminology, with perfect harmony between John and his predecessors. Some day the rest of them, who have not already died, will stand before the Savior and give account for this misdeed and hear him say: "But ye *would* not."

THE OFFICIAL DISHARMONY

The RSV Committee have not limited themselves to translating the Bible. They are tremendously active in getting it disbelieved after their own hearts. No sooner had they gotten their New Testament out in 1946 than they got out a Disharmony of the Gospels, officially. It is called *Gospel Parallels: Revised Standard Version* (1949). It begins: "A thorough study of the gospels is possible only when they are printed in parallel columns for comparison. Therefore, the American Standard Bible Committee requested a sub-committee to prepare a synopsis based on the Revised Standard Version so that the new version might meet the needs of students." College and

seminary professors were consulted, evidently of similar lean-
ings. The usual combination of two Union Seminary men
and one each from Harvard and Yale did the work. The
centers of infidelity spawn it. It repeatedly pretends that it
publishes in parallel columns "each gospel," "the gospels,"
"study of the Gospels" (the indecision as to the capital letter
is theirs), "canonical gospels," and so on. Yet they have a
different canon from the rest of us, for the Fourth Gospel is
not in it. They speak of "the Gospel of John" entering into
consideration, placing it on a level with the "Gospel of Peter."
Yet John is never in the parallels. It ranks with the apochry-
phal literature cited and has no voice at all in the makeup of
its Harmony. In fact, no Harmony is even pretended to be
in view, just "Parallels," mostly without John. Choppy bits
of the noncanonical "part of our tradition" are put not as
parallels to the Synoptics but as footnotes, stuff ranging as
far from Christ as the twelfth century. Why not add the
Union Seminary anthology of unbelief, as "Gospel Parallels"?
It would make the Disharmony more systematic.

Ashamed of the gross stupidity of coming at 4 P.M., to
spend the day— which, at that time of the year, would be
nearly night—the latest translators are now beginning to try
for some Harmony of the Disharmony. So Phillips translated
John 1:39: "So they went and saw where he was staying and
remained with Him *the rest of the day.* (It was then about
four o'clock in the afternoon.)" Goodspeed had already done
the same. It shows to what ethical depths modernism can sink.
The primary consideration in the choice of translators is
whether they can get the consent of their consciences to bend
the Scriptures to suit their theories, as is ruthlessly done here.
Some day we shall have a Bible that tells the truth in modern
speech as this one so blatantly advertises that it does. That
Bible will read: "It was then about ten o'clock in the morning."
The Basic Bible is more fair-minded. It reads: "They were
with him all that day: it was then about the tenth hour of the
day." The Greek has the accusative of extent of time:
"throughout that day," and the placing of the phrase is meant
by John to give stress to the fact of the all-day-long visit.

THE WICKED, DELIBERATELY PARTISAN CHOICE

It is revealing to know that the RSV Union-Harvard-Yale axis committee (How did Chicago get left off?), when they foisted this Harmony of crooked Gospel Parallels on the unwary public, to promote the RSV Disharmony more effectively, had to reject and repudiate openly a friendly and scholarly gesture of a Lutheran Colleague of Dean Weigle, Professor Ralph David Heim, of Gettysburg Seminary. In 1947, two years before this Disharmony of crooked Parallels got out, Professor Heim published *A Harmony of the Gospels, for Students,* in the language of the RSV. That is a Harmony, in purpose and makeup, as I recall. I obtained a copy at once. but it is in my library in Rio de Janeiro. My memory of it is that it followed the normal Harmony standards such as you see in the Broadus-Robertson *Harmony of the Gospels* or most Bible dictionaries that are not out also to wreck faith or follow the styles of those whose aim is just that. To repudiate a real Harmony, given them in friendly co-operation, and go all out for a partisan Disharmony, concocted on an old German model of the last century, simply shows the factional, divisive, unethical, and determined spirit of the RSV Committee. They are gambling with loaded dice. Will they win?

Let us see how the dice are loaded against the Gospels and any possibility of believing their witness. First, the whole Gospel of John is kicked down into the footnotes. Mostly it is banished. Out of 978 verses in John's Gospel, 109 verses, in 47 parallel cases, are cited, and there are 32 other passages mentioned (references given) but not quoted. Second, the preface makes a pretense of being more fair than the German model they are following, alleging that they cite the Gospel of Peter and, so, why not the Gospel of John? That levels the fourth Gospel with the Apocrypha. Third, that is just what is done in the general makeup of the book. Such silly superstitions as fire on the Jordan when Jesus was baptized are put parallel to the whole decimated citation of the Gospel of John. The whole structure of the book is calculated to wreck any possible faith in miracles, both by the Disharmony and by putting the true miracles on the level with apocryphal puerilities. Fourth, it all stretches out over twelve centuries of documents, whereas Luke cited oral or documentary evidence of only eyewitnesses who were ministers of the Word, and wrote within a score of years after Christ ascended on high.

Now to Cases

Their first section is the "Infancy Narratives." But not in a Gospel Harmony. No. The real beginning is: "In the beginning was the Word and the Word was God . . . and the Word became flesh and tabernacled among us." It is a headless harmony, a torso whose head they threw away, clean out of sight. The whole thing starts out with a false beginning.

The second section is "The Galilean Section." And the first eight items have nothing to do with Galilee and did not take place there and are utterly unrelated to that province.

The Sermon on the Plain follows the Sermon on the Mount, each cited in parallel columns opposite the other, in two successive sections. That aids the Disharmony. The fact that Jesus spoke to many crowds, all forming an international crowd, and repeated undoubtedly many, many times these sayings that day, leaves abundant room for different language, testified to by many witnesses, as heard at different times. There is no need for this breach in the Harmony.

Then follows "Luke's Special Section," with parallels from the other two Gospels admitted as parallel witnesses. Why not just leave each Gospel complete in itself, without attempting to make either Harmony or Parallels?

Then follows the "Judean Section." That is a question of the veracity of the apostle John or these apostles of modernism. John says there was a Judean ministry of great meaning and length before the Galilean ministry. These gentlemen make the Judean ministry consist mainly of the journey to the cross and the crucifixion. This is singularly perverse, a brazen false witness.

Skipping to the final section, we find under "Appearances of the Risen Lord" this very weak organization: "The Bribing of the Soldiers. The Command to Baptize." You see the import of that, a suggestion of denial of the Great Commission, and that issue is all that they are willing to let the student see in the Great Commission. Being unwilling to allow our Lord to perpetuate to the end of time the baptism he received from John and administered through the Twelve, they stage the whole Great Commission for rejection. The Road to Emmaus is the third item of "Appearances." Then comes "The Appearance of the Risen Christ in Jerusalem," as if there were just one. Then comes "The Ascension" and "The Longer Ending of Mark" (of course, a climax of evidence staged for rejection). Can you imagine a weaker outlining of the evidence for the resurrection? Why no more? The answer is simple. Under the head of the "Passion Narrative," the Disharmony places, under the title "The Empty Tomb," 29 verses of Matthew, Mark, and Luke, describing the first appearances of our Lord. Isn't it strange they should be dislocated from where they belong, and be counted in as part of the Passion? Accidental, are we to believe? What respect can sincere people have for a book like that? Yet that is a willful part of this new Bible movement, engineered to create this impression even before the Old Testament appeared, and in opposition to a friendly and real effort at a Harmony of the Gospels. A Harmony they hate: a Disharmony they love and promote by every influence at their command.

INTERPRETATIONS: DISHARMONY AS TO PAUL'S CONVERSION

It is a commonplace in Greek grammar that the verb *to hear* with one construction may mean to hear the sound *without understanding* it, but with another construction may mean to hear and *understand*. The translators well knew this but refused to let the harmony appear that is in Luke's narrative, choosing rather to promote Disharmony. So they translate, in Acts 9:7, "hearing the voice" and in 22:9, "did not hear the voice." That is lack of good will or even respect for the Word of God. And it falsifies Luke's witness. Thayer gives the latter passage as meaning: "to perceive by the ear what is announced in one's presence." Paul's companions "heard the voice," in the sense of noting that there was a voice; but "they did not understand the voice." in the sense of "perceiving by the ear what the voice announced in their presence." The Greek of the two statements is not the same. The RSV translators translate it as if it were the same. It falsifies the witness, in hatred of Harmony, in love of Disharmony in the Bible. It is an insult to the memory of the great historian Luke, a disservice to truth and a manifestly haughty attitude of contempt for the Bible. All these men are authors of books. What would they think if some one translated *their* books into a foreign language in any such hostile fashion? That they know better is clearly seen by their translating this same verb "heed" (John 10:8); "listen" (Mark 9:7); and "understand" (I Cor. 14:2). Yet the passage in Acts 22:9 is more favorable to a friendly and fair translation than in these cases.

Our Lord is Made to Ride Two Asses, Like a Circus Clown

Luke says (19:35) this: "and throwing their garments on the colt they set Jesus upon it." Could Matthew be translated in harmony? Yes, and normally so. Matthew 21:7 can easily mean: "they brought the ass and the colt, and put their garments on them, and he sat thereon." The Greek has "put their garments on them, and he sat on them." Any sensible reader would know the second *them* means the garments. But the RSV translators have made that natural interpretation impossible. They quote an Old Testament prophecy in this crazy manner: "Behold, your king is coming to you, humble, and mounted on an ass, and on a colt, the foal of an ass." Clown stunt, on two asses. Now the thing that would be amusing, were it not so serious, is that when the Old Testament RV translators came to translate this same prophecy they rendered it thus: "humble and riding on an ass, on a colt the foal of an ass." Not only do the translators in the two Testaments show this discord, but the Disharmony of the NT translators is unnecessary, unnatural, and contrary to their translating habits elsewhere. They could easily have rendered this Greek: "on an ass, even on a colt," one animal. They do that very thing in the very context of this incident, in John 12:13. "Blessed be he who comes in the name of the Lord, *even* the King of Israel." Those who wanted any real Harmony of the Gospels would have used *even* again, for the same Greek word, in the other citation. Once again, as they stand at the judgment bar of Christ, whom they present in this ridiculous position, they may hear his judgment: "But ye *would* not."

HAD MARY A HUSBAND OR NOT?

The facts are as clear as the sun at noon in a cloudless sky. The RSV translators permit her to say: "I have no husband" (Luke 1:34). That is simple, clear, categorical. Why, then, make Matthew 1:18-24 utterly contradictory, presenting Joseph as the *husband*, when he was only betrothed? These gentlemen know that the Greek had only one word here used for the two meanings, betrothed or husband. The *facts* should determine the translation. In either case, the Greek says that Joseph was her *man (male)*. The same *male*, according to the Greek, was husband or *promised husband*, bridegroom-to-be, after the marriage or before it. The translation obeys the known facts, just as the corresponding word is wife or woman, according to the context or known facts. The enthusiasts for Disharmony have the bent to translate it the way in which it looks the worst for Mary and Jesus. For them to tell the truth in the translation would not harmonize with the bastard classification they give Jesus in the marginal note on page 1 of their New Testament. And why be such sticklers for translating the word *virgin* here, and repudiate it elsewhere, on every possible occasion? And now look on beyond. In Luke 2:5, the translators make Mary only one "betrothed," in Bethlehem itself. Merciful heavens! The tense of the verb is perfect, which certainly can mean that the betrothal has been consummated. "Other ancient authorities" even have the word *wife*. But our ever conjecturing translators would not give that fact when it protects the character of the mother of our Lord. They will not help the Harmony they hate, but foster the Disharmony they love.

Nobody *had* to do this evil deed. The Berkeley Version reads: "The birth of Jesus Christ came about this way: When His mother Mary was engaged to Joseph, before they were married, she was found to be pregnant through the Holy Spirit. But as Joseph, her fiancé, was fairminded and did not want to disgrace her, he planned to break with her just between them." The angel tells him to "marry" her and "he married her." And in Luke 2:5 even Moffatt has the sense to translate the Greek simply: "Mary his wife." Fair-minded translators could have easily given the true translation in Matthew 1:20 (*take Mary as your wife*), as others do (or *marry Mary*, as above quoted). There is not a messier nor more incompetent piece of translation in human literature than the birth stories of the Gospels in the RSV. Only deep irreverence or cowardly fear of modernist colleagues could achieve such a strident Disharmony in what the translators still manage somehow to call the "Word of God."

An Impossible Eclipse

A note on page 100 gives the cause of the three hours of darkness while Christ was on the cross as an eclipse: "*Or the sun was eclipsed.*" When did these gentlemen ever see an eclipse that left the earth dark for three straight hours? And how many times have you been told from the pulpit that an eclipse of the sun at full moon is an impossibility? To get rid of this miracle darkness, the RSV invents an eclipse, for further Bible Disharmony.

Disharmony in Translating the Same Words

Careful and competent translators are always zealous about this. Yet we have the identical Greek translated thus: "Do you not know that a little leaven ferments the whole lump of dough?", in I Corinthians 5:6; but in Galatians 5:9 we read: "A little yeast leavens the whole lump."

Luke's Lord's Supper Almost Liquidated

The great historian has only this left of all his history of the Supper: "And he took bread, and when he had given thanks he broke it and gave it to them, saying: This is my body." Period. Only that and nothing more. Yet these gentlemen are not hurt by that. They have for their ornate worship the elaborate rituals of the traditions of men. But we who have only the Bible as our authority in religion hate to see it mutilated. And even there, in the marginal wastebasket where they have thrown so much Scripture, they have done away with the Lord's words about his blood being shed for them. They have taken these words away from their natural association and thrown them clean across the sentence with *cup*, rather than with *blood*. This is a verbal nicety of pernickety modernists. Yet even Moffatt translates a full *Lord's Supper* and renders this part: "the new *covenant* ratified *by* my *blood* shed for your sake." And so, after their fashion, do the Berkeley and the Basic and others. Could the material of the cup literally be poured? Was it not the contents? And if it was the contents of the cup that was poured out, would not the adjective be masculine to agree with wine? And is it not neuter? And so does not the meaning leap across mere grammatical niceties and refer to the cup as the symbol of the blood "poured out," or as Moffatt has it, "shed" for you? The RSV act of hurling the phrase clean across the sentence, so that it is the cup that is poured, not the blood that is shed, suits a sacramentalist. Thus the great thing becomes the sacramental performance, not the worth of Calvary's blood.

The Horrible Disharmony of the Citations of the Old Testament in the New

There are many whole books on this subject. It is not an easy problem for the translator. Here reverence and accuracy need to blend. We have already encountered the problem in various studies which preceeded, and we shall leave the major part of the cases for the discussion of how Jesus used a version. His manner of dealing with it, as in all else, is our supreme example. But just here we show how the spirit of Disharmony operates, waging a civil war between Old and New Testaments needlessly in the citations.

The revisers have nearly a page about this problem and much more, indirectly touching it. We quote: "The New Testament section of the Committee deferred for some time the translation of such quotations, hoping to follow as closely as possible the wording which would be adopted by the Old Testament section in the passages quoted." This they first found impossible to wait for, then unnecessary, as they determined "to translate the text as given in the New Testament," which is exactly what they often *do not do*. "It was, therefore, as unnecessary as it was inexpedient to wait for the Old Testament section to complete its work." On that, there might be two opinions. Certainly a vast amount of Disharmony has shown up. (Citations from Introduction pamphlet on NT, pp. 25,26.)

CASES WHERE THIS WAS NOT DONE

Psalm 24:1 has "The earth is the Lord's and the fulness thereof." Now, in I Corinthians 10:26, look at this literary bad taste and utter lack of fidelity in the translation: "the earth is the Lord's, and everything in it." Now that is not a translation of the Greek. The Greek has *fullness,* too, but it is one of the manias of the RSV not to translate that word, in some passages. So here we have an utter refusal to translate either Greek or Hebrew original.

Now another attitude. Here is a case where they jump from the Greek original back to the Hebrew it is supposed to translate. In Matthew 21:42, what the Greek says is this: "The stone which the builders disapproved, this one came into place as the cornerstone (or, this was made the head of the corner): this (cornerstone) came from the Lord, and is wonderful in our eyes." It is held that, in the Hebrew, what corresponds to the feminine pronoun *this* (Ps. 118:22-23), was the equivalent of the Greek neuter pronoun, translatable as *this* (fact). That doesn't matter. The criterion adopted is to translate the Greek, and that declares that Jesus, as Cornerstone, is wonderful and that he came from God in that capacity. Of course, that is not popular doctrine, for both Catholics and the advocates of the New Catholicism want either Peter or Peter's faith to be the cornerstone, the head, the foundation. So in this one case alone, in all the New Testament, so far as I have noted, the Greek before us is bypassed, and the translators go back and translate the Hebrew that is not before them. They don't dare do that in countless other cases. Just here, robbing the Lord Jesus of his due praise, they simply close their eyes to facts and lean back to the Hebrew. The only possible reference of the Greek word *this* is to the cornerstone. It is wonderful, whether the RSV thinks so or not, and Peter or Peter's confession cannot rob that foundation of his glory. "The Church's One Foundation is Jesus Christ her Lord." Sing it, RSV translators! Or don't you ever sing?

Now take a third type of citation from the Old Testament, Psalm 45:6-7, cited in Hebrews 1:8-9. The difference here is not a question of either Hebrew or Greek, but of irreverent RSV English. All believing Christianity, taking its cue from the New Testament itself, believes this Psalm is Messianic. The RSV New Testament so takes it. But the Old Testament promoters of Disharmony repudiate the Messianic meaning and so translate it: "Your divine throne endures for ever and ever. Your royal scepter is a scepter of equity . . ." The *you* of the RSV indicates that the reference is not to God, and their decisions as to the text obey that prejudice. But the RSV New Testament scholars *must* take this as a Messianic Psalm. Not to do so is stark stupidity in translating Hebrews 1:8 "Thy throne, O God . . ." I repeat, the Disharmony of the *you* (un-Messianic) or the *thou* is not in any divergence that appears between Hebrew and Greek, but is in the mind of the translators alone. The unbelieving Jew or nominal Christian translates *you* as of one not divine. The New Testament, the RSV translators here, and the believing Christian everywhere, affirm the *thou* of faith in Jesus as the fulfillment of that Messianic Psalm. This kind of disharmony is found all along the line of New Testament citations of the Old, where Messianic prophecy is involved. In this we contrast later the RSV and Jesus our Lord.

NEBUCHAD-WHAT?

It is disgusting to see the RSV seesaw up and down between Nebuchad*nezzar* in Jeremiah 27:6; 28:3, and other passages, and Nebuchad*rezzar* in Jeremiah 32:1, and other verses. Is there any doubt about its being the same person? Why, then, the two spellings? I have commented on the half-dozen spellings of Moses, in Greek texts. But are we going to copy every variation of scribes of a time long gone in matters of absolutely no importance for the readers? There is a lot of this Disharmony.

THE DISHARMONY THAT SLANTS TOWARD COMMUNISM

The blind following of the KJ Version of the supposed communism of early Jerusalem Christianity, in utter outrage of the Greek, has already been commented on. The RSV translation of Psalm 15:5 is: "who does not put out his money at interest." That, if left that way, outlaws all modern business life. Did these translators never lend? Did they never borrow and pay interest? If they have willingly been a part of, and a party to, the banking world of creditor or debtor, do they "sojourn in God's holy tent" or "dwell on his holy hill"? Are they moral, by such a standard? Are they competent to translate a Bible they disobey at every turn of the road?

Interest very easily fades into usury. What is usury in the United States is interest in Brazil. Could they not indicate that in either the translation or a note? Furthermore, they use a vast system of clarifying references on most of the pages. Yet there is not a line below to indicate that this was a family measure in Israel, and that interest was legitimate in the dealings of Jews to those outside the holy nation. That is clarified in all dictionaries of the Bible (the new one of Harper's, for example) and could have been put into the references. Why were they left out, giving this cudgel to communism in such a noble Scripture? This is supposed to be a Bible for public worship. Would you read that, as translated, to an audience tempted by the communist demon?

This is a return to the Dark Ages. The popes taught a partial communism, both in the communal life of the monastic orders and in the increasing monopoly of the patrimony of the Church, and in the definite doctrine that no Christian could lend money. That turned all lending over to Jews, made the popes the worst offenders against their own doctrine, and bankrupted them sometimes as victims of these very Jews, whom they then sought to annihilate by persecution. Do we have here the alternatives of communism or contempt for our Bibles?

Similarly, we have Jesus translated as saying: "Lend, expecting nothing in return." In this high hyperbolical language, is it necessary to leap to the maximum reach of the hyperbole? Goodspeed, Williams, the Basic, and others translate: *not despairing, never giving up hope,* and so on. A Weymouth Version note says: "the only known meaning of the compound Greek verb *ap-elpizo is* . . . 'to lose hope,' 'despair' "; so RV . . . and most commentaries." One Nelson Bible delights in being in Disharmony with the other Nelson Bible. Now Jesus is purposely expanding the reach of the Law, in the Sermon on the Mount, to drive the Jewish world to himself, to a greater righteousness than that of the scribes and Pharisees. This was Jewish law, as to lending to Jews, unquestionably. It was meant to drive the hearers to Christ himself, as that greater righteousness, greater in kind, not in mere degree of Mosaic legalism.

Our Lord's general teaching is shown by his parable: *"my own with interest"* (Matt. 25:27 and Luke 19:23). "Why then did you not put my money into the bank, and at my coming I should have collected it with interest?" Why were not such Scriptures put in the references to these so easily misunderstood passages that Communists twist for their purposes in exploiting the ignorant? I do not suppose there was a single Communist among the RSV translators. But they certainly gave communism every possible aid in their version.

ARE VIRGINS HARLOT MOTHERS?

So we are told now. I never saw an effort against any Bible doctrine that did not attempt to find some rare use of a word that would seem to make uncertain its usual and accepted sense. This custom is now being followed as to the word virgin. Note the trend.

First, a distinguished Jew is put on the Committee of RSV translators and defenders of the RSV, though conservative seminaries are left unrepresented. Professor Harry M. Orlinsky, of the Jewish Institute of Religion, in New York, writes Chapter IV of the Introduction pamphlet. In it he says this of the Aquila retranslation of the Old Testament into Greek in the second century A.D. "Aquila, a convert to Judaism, made an independent and unique Greek translation of the Hebrew Bible. He incorporated the kind of Jewish interpretation which was current in his day, and he avoided the

Christological elements which had been introduced in the Septuagint text. Thus Aquila rendered the Hebrew word *ha-almah* in Isaiah 7:14 literally 'the young woman' in place of the word 'virgin' which the Christians had substituted for it." Now where is the proof that "Christological elements" had been introduced into the Septuagint text? Had that been true, would not the intense memory-capacity of the ancient Jewish mind have protested at once? Just because Aquila's idea of *independence* was to incorporate current Jewish interpretations, do we have to impute that idea to Christ? and his apostles? Then isn't it rather strange that Professor Orlinsky should worry over the translation *virgin?* Why not inform himself that the word *virgin* means prostitute, harem woman, unwed mother of a brood, and what have you? Strange the learned Jew didn't know that, if the defenders of the RSV know it so well.

Second, these RSV translators evidently didn't know or believe it. For it so happens that the word *virgin* is used of men, too. And how do the RSV translators translate *virgin men? CHASTE.* That's how. Now if *virgin* means *CHASTE* (Rev. 14:4), would it not seem that this is the accepted meaning of the term, in general?

Third, these exceptional meanings of words do not nullify the usual meaning. I know a city where men honk horns. A red light turns green. An impatient motorist leans on his horn. He complains about having to wait an "eternity" in this slow traffic. Now how long is an "eternity" to him? Just one minute. Did the word *eternity* come to mean only one minute? No. That is the very point of his hyperbole. He *wants* it to mean forever. He loves to exaggerate.

Now, just as truly, men could use the word *virgin* in sarcasm or cynicism or slang, or in a Kinsey-minded skepticism as to female virtue in general. I seem to recall that in *Quo Vadis?,* in Nero's Bacchanalian parties, some of the revelers dressed up as vestal virgins. That double meaning of chastity was not changed by the hellish farce that cynically adopted the term. They simply assumed a role. What would appeal to a prostitute and her admirers more than to attach to her role the title *virgin?* That would be good for many a smile of delicate irony. The marginal usage of a term by the lunatic or underworld fringes of humanity creates no confusion about the normal meaning of the word. The RSV revisers themselves being witnesses, this word means *chaste,* normally. Have we been reduced to the level of seeking the meaning of a Bible word in Egyptian brothels? Is the virgin mother of our Lord to be brought to the bar of *those* circles?

Last, may I return to the motive with which I began, which is the Roman Catholic world to which for nearly four decades I have been a missionary. My first thought as to Bible-burning was the anti-missionary influence of it in all continents. And I feel the same way about trifling with this word *virgin.* I utterly condemn mariolatry. But, by these tokens, I retain reverence. Virgin-besmirching tactics deserve no more respect than Bible-burning. At once, the whole priesthood of Rome screams: "See. I told you so. False Bibles. Don't buy them. If you bought one, burn it." And so the tide of flame that is fed by burning Bibles turns again home. And, honored virgin-besmircher, you have fed those flames. You are a grave antimissionary influence.

CHAPTER FIFTEEN

MISTRANSLATION BY WRECKING THE SENTENCE STRUCTURE OF THE ORIGINAL

RESTRICTING THE SPIRIT'S WITNESS: ROMANS 8:15, 16

WE USED TO READ: "YE RECEIVED THE SPIRIT OF ADOPTION, whereby we cry: Abba, Father. The Spirit himself beareth witness with our spirit that we are the sons of God." So the ASV. Now we read: " . . . you have received the spirit of sonship. When we cry 'Abba! Father!' it is the Spirit himself bearing witness with our spirit that we are children of God." That separates what belongs together, joining what the Greek text separates. It takes away from women their doctrine of adoption, open to either gender, and offers them "sonship." Yet *sonship* only makes men children, not sons. Far more serious, however, is the restriction of the witness of the Spirit. Paul wrote this complete sentence: "The Spirit himself bears witness with our spirit that we are the sons of God." The sentence structure is broken down, however, and from the fragments a new sentence structure is created. This limits the Spirit's witness to our spirit to the occasions when we cry "Abba! Father!" I don't ever remember praying that in my life, so according to the RSV I never had the fulfillment of this promise. Millions of believers, however, stand ready to testify that they are wrong in their self-imposed limitation of the Spirit. He does not restrict his witness to times when we happen to use an Aramaic word in praying. This mutilation of a key Scripture severely diminished the evangelical note in the Bible. Why falsify the Bible on this vital doctrine, thus falsifying its teaching on the vast areas of Christian experience? Is that a sacramentalist maneuver?

WRONG PREPOSITIONS IMPOSED: ROMANS 1:17

Already we have commented on the wrenching of the Greek grammar whereby an adverbial prepositional phrase is taken from the verb and joined to a noun, as if it were an adjective. So they get "The just by faith shall live" and wreck that modified doctrine by a note that says they live not by faith but by their faithfulness, the devil's old doctrine of salvation by works. Here, however, we note the wrecking of another prepositional phrase. "From faith to faith" becomes now, by some magician's art, "is revealed through faith for faith." The Greek says neither that nor anything like it. Our modernists like to exalt their subjectivism to the standing of revelation. The canon, for them, has never been closed. And they receive revelations that they follow rather than the Bible. Even though they contradict the Bible, and each contradicts the other, yet that is just the rolling of the ship of relativity, and all are headed for the same goal. If you have a spurt of faith, that is revelation *through* faith, and if you take it as such it is revelation *for* your faith, even if not for anyone else. Such is the wrong and tendential translation: "through faith for faith." The Greek stresses progressive sanctification through progressive faith in Christ and belief of the truth. God's righteousness in our life rises from faith, and it goes on to more faith and greater faith, and so we grow in living by our faith. The just shall live by faith. The once-for-all reach of faith obtains the once-for-all benefits of redemption, justification, regeneration, adoption, initial sanctification (in the Hebrews sense); and the growing, perennial aspects of faith reach the unfolding of eternal life through all our pilgrimage. Why throw a primary Scripture into unpardonable confusion by incompetent and tendential translation? Moffatt had the happy idea in Hebrews 10:38 of translating: "The righteous shall live on by his faith."

COURTESIES TURNED BACKWARD: ACTS 25:13

Here we have an official visit. Festus is the host, Agrippa, the guest. But the RSV reverses the amenities of the occasion and says: "Agrippa the king and Bernice arrived at Caesarea to welcome Festus." But they were the guests, Festus, the host; they, of royal rank, Festus, a subordinate. So the amenities are reversed and the guests "welcome" the inferior host. Maybe some papyri give that meaning to the word, but certainly not exclusively. So we have the translations: "to pay official respects" (Williams); "came on a state visit"

(Goodspeed); "pay a complimentary visit" (Weymouth); "pay their respects" (Moffatt), and so on.

EYES CLOSED TO GREEK GRAMMAR: TITUS 3:5, 6

Having commented the general unfaithfulness in translating Titus, I wish here merely to stress the pronoun *which,* about the Holy Spirit. The reference can be to no other than the Spirit. The Greek has a grammatical construction called the "assimilation of the relative to the case of the antecedent," and by it *which* here is changed to the case of the antecedent, and its construction. Paul thus said: "According to his mercy he saved us through the washing of regeneration and the renewing *of what Holy Spirit he poured out upon us richly . . ."* (or, that Holy Spirit whom he poured out upon us). My Nestle's Greek Testament gives in the margin one sole reference, to Joel 2:28, the same Scripture quoted in Acts 2:17. There can be no possible doubt that *Spirit* is the antecedent of the relative pronoun. It means *whom. Which* is irreverent, breaks the reference to prophecy and tends to sacramentalism. *Which* would naturally, in the misleading English, go back to *washing.* The case forbids the relative pronoun to agree with *washing;* the gender forbids it to agree with the two nouns *regeneration* and *renewing.* It is directly assimilated to agree with *Spirit.* The translation is *whom.* See now the snare of Moffatt's sacramentalism, headed out to prove affusion as baptism: "he saved us . . . by the water that means regeneration and renewal under the holy Spirit which he poured upon us richly . . ." The Greek does not have *water* and it does not have *means.* There never was a day when water meant regeneration. There is no preposition *under* in the original. By inserting *water* and *pouring* here Moffatt got an insinuation of affusion as baptism and by inserting *means* he got in Calvin's wobbly, hesitant semisacramentalism. Maybe Moffatt was dead before the RSV Committee reached Titus. But in this translation he seems to be yet speaking. No. The Holy Spirit is poured on the believer in his regeneration and renewal, not in some "second blessing" or in a second story of the house of Christian experience. Having been poured out fully on Pentecost for all the gospel age on that first missionary

church, he comes now in regeneration and refreshing power
on every saved person. This is no place for a sacramentalist
which, confusing utterly a great doctrine.

THE WRECKAGE OF ROMANS 4:11

More sacramentalism falsifies the gospel of grace. Paul
wrote: "And he received the sign of circumcision, a seal of the
righteousness of the faith which he had yet being uncircumcized." This the RSV changed into "He received circumcision
as a sign or seal . . ." That is something entirely different from
what Paul said. This is another case where the evil genius
of Moffatt prevailed. There is no either/or doctrine here.
Circumcision was both. Now Baptists believe in signs, pedobaptists in seals. This seems to give you your choice. Either/or.
It equalizes them. That is not the true picture. Abraham had
in circumcision both. The ceremony signified spiritual cleans-
ing, regeneration, the circumcision of mind and heart. But,
in the national Abrahamic covenant circumcision was the
seal, and of so grave importance that the uncircumcized was
cut off from his people, alien to the covenant. When you say
"circumcision" to the pedobaptist, he sees infant baptism.
And he wants it to be the seal of the covenant of grace, making the family the unit in Christianity, safe within the covenanted mercies, sealed to that unit by its unanimous baptism.
But the seal in Christianity is far different from Israel's carnal
regime. "In whom (Christ) also ye, having heard the word
of the truth, the gospel of your salvation, and in whom having believed, ye were sealed by the Spirit of the promise, the
Holy One, who is the earnest of our inheritance . . ." So Paul
wrote in Ephesians 1:13, 14. Of the perversion of this passage
we have already written. Here, in Ephesians 4:30, and in
other passages we note that in the gospel of our salvation the
Spirit seals, not infant baptism. That is` pagan materialism.
Neither infant baptism nor any other sign, seal, or sacrament,
nor all of them put together, ever sealed the possession of the
grace of God within any human soul. This RSV translation is
willfully false, utterly inexcusable, evidently tendential, to any
first-year Greek student. Did these gentlemen think that nobody in America knew Greek outside the Chicago-Manhattan-
Boston axis of infidelity? Did they think to do this to the

gospel, in the service of infant baptism, with impunity? These systems are not on an either/or basis, not alternatives, not equal. One is the gospel of grace; the other, the gospel of sacraments, papal, pagan.

TESTIFYING AND TESTIMONY — HOW DIFFERENT!

Testifying is the act of being a witness; testimony is the truth you bear witness to. In II Timothy 1:8, the RSV makes that radical a change, falsifying the translation. They can't take such liberties and get away with it. Paul said: "Therefore (because ours is a spirit of power, love, and sound judgment) be not thou ashamed of the testimony of our Lord, nor of me his prisoner." Now that has been wrecked after this fashion: "Do not be ashamed then of testifying to our Lord . . ." The act of testifying is very, very different from the testimony borne. You find a lot of enthusiastic witnesses of Jesus among pagans, the Teacher of all teachers, the Ideal of mankind, the Mahatma of the mahatmas, the supreme Philosopher of life, all the superlatives on the human level. Eager to be testifying for Jesus, but the testimony leaves him on the Socrates, Buddha, Confucius, Gandhi, Lincoln level. It is utterly unchristian. Paul wrote something very different. Do not be ashamed of *the testimony* of our Lord; objective genitive, in Greek, the testimony about him, the witness borne to him in all his infinite meaning and worth. Nor is it correct to translate: "take your share of suffering for the gospel in the power of God." A man might say: "Well, there are 700,000,000 Christians of us. My share would be one seven hundred millionth of it all." No, friend. Paul said: "suffer evil with the gospel," identify yourself with its standing and treatment in your community, make wrongs done to it a personal offense to you. Here, too, there is a standard set up: "according to the power of God." Not as if you were linked with a forlorn hope, but as acting in full assurance of the unseen realities in this universe. Oh, how terribly the subjectivism of the RSV, hating a positive, objective, revealed, once-for-all faith, which forever constitutes our changeless testimony—how terribly the RSV has wrecked Paul's great counsel to a young preacher.

THE BROKEN LINK OF DIVINE JUSTICE AND FORGIVENESS

"Just and the justifier of him that is of faith in Jesus" (Rom. 3:26) and "faithful and just to forgive us our sins" (I John 1:9) are twin Scriptures. Our justification and all the subsequent forgiveness that ensues from it, day by day, are both matters of simple justice. Justice to Jesus and the transaction of Calvary and its covenant of grace; just to the believer in the light of the promises he accepted and knows God will fulfill. As a boy, I often wondered why it did not say: "merciful to forgive our sins." Then I came to know. When God justifies the believer, he metes out justice to Jesus, keeps his covenant with him, gives full value to his blood. It would not be right to collect our sin debt from Jesus and then collect it again from us. That he forgives our sins, in the light of Calvary, is simple justice. But the RSV wrecked the truth, divorced the justice and the forgiveness, out of sheer perversity: "If we confess our sins he is faithful and just, and will forgive our sins." They banished Christ's propitiation from the Bible, and the remission of sins. Now they simply falsify the translation so that the readers of the RSV cannot see that God's justice herein set forth has the purpose of remitting, forgiving our sins. This is a moral outrage.

WRECKING PARAGRAPH STRUCTURE AS WELL AS SENTENCE STRUCTURE

In Matthew 9:9 we have the call of Matthew to the public ministry, to leave his business for Christ's sake and witness. Logically, the banquet in Matthew's home follows, if there is no effort at Disharmony of the Gospels. But there is. Then there is a riot of confusions as to *He* in various connections. Elsewhere, the RSV puts in the noun to which a pronoun refers, to clarify. Here the break of paragraph comes as if to separate verse 9 from verse 10. And the sense is wrecked by translating two very different verbs *sat*. There is an addition, *at table,* to the Greek to try to clarify the oriental custom of reclining for the meal. The Greek is clear and expressive. Matthew sat, at the seat of custom (v.9). He did not lie down there, of course. But he reclined (stated in note)—the Greek says he *lay up,* where we might say *lay down,* but it was in a half-reclining position. Then the Greek says that they *with (him)-lay-up,* with Jesus and his disciples. The utter confusion of the RSV here is either ill will or incompetence. And Mark 2:13-15 and Luke 5:27-29 show the same confusion except that the isolation is not of just one verse into a separate paragraph, as in Matthew. The Berkeley Version is perfectly clear and coherent, in all three Gospels. Why did not these gentlemen learn from the Berkeley? It could teach them a vast lot.

MATTHEW 28:17

Does any believer think that only eleven people heard the Great Commission of our Lord? So often, in the Gospels, we know by one narrative of the incident of the presence of persons whom the other historian does not mention as being there. There were certainly at least five hundred and eleven people there with their Lord. The superlatively concise narrative of Matthew says: "When they (the eleven disciples) saw him they worshiped him; but there were those who doubted." They certainly were not of the Eleven, after doubting Thomas had exclaimed, "My Lord! and My God!" I would be that fair to the several parts of the book if I were even translating an almanac. Yet some "scholars" have worked themselves up to a point of cowardice where they feel that any courtesy shown toward the authors of the Bible is a liability against their reputation as scholars. Poor dupes! You can understand the doubts of some of the five hundred who saw him for the first time. But doubts at this stage by the Eleven were psychologically impossible.

PETER'S OATHS AND CRYING: MATTHEW 26:74, 75

Abbott-Smith gives just one meaning to the verb here used in the better text: *to curse vehemently.* Certainly that deserves at least a place in the margin, and seems to me far preferable, as translation, to "began to invoke a curse upon himself." The Greek is very strong: "And he went clean out and away (*out -went out*) and cried out loud bitterly." The verb means audible weeping, not silent tears. There is no excuse for suppressing the translation to less than the minimum of its meaning, as we have shown so often that the RSV does.

MATTHEW 16:23

Jesus simply did not say: "You are not on the side of God, but of men." That simply is not true. He was on God's side. He was for the moment the mouthpiece of the tempter, but he was on God's side and on Christ's side. His thinking was never infallible except when God gave him revelations that were not of the flesh-and-blood line of thought. Just now Peter was reflecting human thought patterns alone. And Jesus used here the simple verb *think,* as the RSV translates it in Romans 12:3. He did not deny the fundamental choice of his salvation. Is this another stagger at apostasy? Mark 8:33 is the parallel passage.

MATTHEW 20:17, 18; MARK 10:33; LUKE 18:32

It is not correct to translate Matthew as saying: "as Jesus was going up to Jerusalem." The Greek says: "As Jesus was about to go up to Jerusalem." The parralel passages indicate that it was as they came to this turning point in their pilgrimage, his own to the cross. Because it came at that turning point, when he made the start on that lap of the journey, they followed him, afraid. There is no reason why this should not be translated correctly. American Christianity has enough Greek scholarship in its ranks to call a halt to this arbitrary carelessness or incompetence. Furthermore, it is gross undertranslation in many passages of the Gospels to speak of Jesus as being "delivered" to the chief priests, as if he were an express package. That verb, in that connection, means *betray.* Why talk about delivering him before the contract for betrayal has made any pledge to deliver him, or such a thing has come on the horizon? The KJ Version translates this very *betray* thirty-seven times in the Gospels. It ought to be translated so about John the Baptist, in Matthew 4:12 and Mark 1:14, "When he heard that John had been" *betrayed* (not *arrested*—that is overtranslation or mistranslation). The RSV makes the same mistake in other passages. The construction of the Lukan parallel is further wrecked, as to prophecy. "All things that stand written *through the prophets*" is what Jesus said. Where the prophets are seen, in the original, only as the medium through whom the Word of God came, they are by the RSV made the authors of prophecy. We are not to translate Scripture, and what Robert E. Speer called "the Bible's doctrine of itself," as if the human authorship were the only thing, the main thing, or the predominant factor. The Word came *through* prophets, and there is no excuse for hiding or falsifying that clear witness. It is a moral outrage that the RSV modernists should have added their whole theory of inspiration to the Bible by repeatedly forging the doctrine that the *men* were *inspired,* and adding that doctrine to the real Scripture. Raising checks is no more reprehensible morally than that forgery of Scripture. That they should feel so keenly the necessity of forging this Scripture, to help out their doctrine of inspiration, shows how utterly absent it is from the Bible as truly translated. Alas! So many who also want a doctrine of the inspiration of men, and not the God-breathed Word, will rally to this forgery as the very thing they want before their eyes and in their pulpits. It is a time for those who are true to declare themselves.

MATTHEW 20:21, 26-27

The Greek seems to me to mean clearly: "These my two sons," her only sons, and the context makes that clear. But the RSV translation, "these two sons of mine," would be correct if she had a dozen sons. Then the great principle laid down is: "Ye know that the rulers of the Gentiles lord it over them, and their great men impose their authority (the exercise, in its sphere, of legitimate authority is not condemned by Jesus). But it is not so among you. (The regime Jesus gave in that pilgrim church that walked with him is the norm of the ages. *They* did not exercise authority except as Jesus commanded, nor did they lord it over God's heritage. The "shall-not-be" translation, in verse 26, is wrong.) But whoever may wish to become great among you, shall be your servant; and whoever may wish to be first among you, shall be your slave." Look now at the RSV: (1) *Exercise authority* is put down as something wrong. It is not. Every official in any church has full authority to do what the work he was elected to do involves. Christ is not against authority. The Greek word is a compound verb, beginning with the preposition *down*. If you exercise authority *looking down* on your brethren, or *against* their rights or welfare, then authority becomes tyranny, imposed. (2) Then twice the RSV wrecks the future of moral obligation and substitutes that of necessity, *must*. That falsifies the record. This is a generation that has toyed with totalitarian authority and has, in that element of the population, lost all idea of authority except the human whim, which from the cradle to the grave must do as it pleases and have no inhibitions. Yet this very people are always hollering *must;* "The Church *must* do this or that." It is the *must*-y generation, insolent and futile. Nobody pays any attention and it has no Absolute, feels no authority, from juvenile ages on. Why should this itch to say *must* prove irresistible to these professors of the university axis of infidelity? It is a habit, gone to seed. Banish the "bourgeois morals" of the moral law and what you have left is a lot of futile little men running around and saying *"must . . . must . . . must . . .* The Church *must* . . .,"* till you remember Shakespeare's query; "upon what meat doth this our Caesar feed, that he is grown so great?"

WRECKING DOCTRINE, TOO: MATTHEW 21:32

The New Testament uniformly puts repentance before faith. That is vital truth. The semievangelicals and near-Catholics, for whom faith consists in the belief of dogmas, repudiate the Bible and always invert God's revealed order of truth, saying faith and repentance. That is as false and fatal a doctrine as can be found. Belief is not faith. Belief is related to facts, truths, doctrines; faith is related to Jesus as Savior, and by Spirit-born trust unites the soul to him in eternal life. And when you wreck that Gospel you have none left, so far as the revealed conditions of salvation in the human experience are concerned. This wreckage you see in the RSV: "You did not afterwards repent and believe him." That is willfully falsified by this RSV Committee, so short on ethics, so eager to say *must* to all the world. The Greek says: "But ye, when ye saw it, did not even repent (change your attitude, to sorrow) that ye might afterwards believe him."

Even if you take the *not even* and *afterward* with the first verb, you still have the grammar wrecked; not "sorrow in order to believe," but simply "sorrow *and* . . .," a translation utterly different from the Greek.

It may be objected that we do not have here either the usual verb *repent* or the usual sense *believe on Christ,* but merely *believe him* (John the Baptist). That is true. But in each case you have the introductory experience stated: godly sorrow, which "worketh repentance," followed by that inward belief of gospel truth, "spiritually discerned," which is the Spirit's preparation for saving faith in the Savior John preached, "the Lamb of God who taketh away the sin of the world." These heady Jews felt not the sorrow that causes repentance, nor did they inwardly accept John's gospel, which would have led to faith in their true Messiah. They did not so sorrow that they might later so believe John in presenting his gospel of grace. Whatever the two verbs mean, to change the relations of the second to the first and make them co-ordinate is a falsification of the record, in a very vital doctrine.

THROWING AWAY DIVINE EMPHASIS: MATTHEW 12:50

Christian lukewarmness and doubt does not like emphasis. That is one of the great and frequent losses in the RSV. In this passage, Jesus has this emphatic word which the RSV despises and omits: "Whoever does the will of my Father (who is) in heaven, is *the very one* (or, *he himself*) who is my brother . . . sister . . . mother." In the face of Mariolatry, now so current, that emphasis, cast out of the *new Bible,* is a great loss.

MATTHEW 13:41.

The Greek and the RSV, respectively, have: "all stumbling blocks and all those who practise lawlessness" and "all causes of sin and all evildoers." Neither the original construction nor the original meaning is preserved.

JOHN 3:31; 5:16; 5:35, 45; 8:25, 56, 59

Other verbal wreckage is: "does what is true" instead of "lives the truth" or "practices the truth," a deeply spiritual concept. And "did this," the wreckage of a plural, "these things"—it was the habit, the accumulation of offenses against their sabbath traditions, which infuriated priests and Pharisees (John 5:16). The Greek says: "That man was *the* burning and shining lamp," shining in the dim dawn of Forerunner times. The RSV will not permit it, reduces it to *a lamp*. Name any others whose rays broke that darkness, when John lit up. He was *the* lamp, for a while. But the RSV won't tolerate our Lord's saying what he really did say. The RSV worsened the ASV, in John 5:45, from "on whom ye have set your hope" to "on whom you set your hope." This is a very frequent offense, for the RSV shows little respect for the sense of the Greek perfect tense, one of its favorite offenses against the original. By their choice of words here you do not even know whether the tense is past or present. The perfect is both, in Greek, past action with present, abiding results. The translation of John 8:25 is simply impossible, the margin coming nearer, though harsher. Jesus could be harsh. The translation of John 8:56 seems to make Abraham merely *foresee* Christ's day, far distant, in the days of his flesh. That is not the idea. Jesus was the contemporary of Abraham, visited him in his tent. Abraham saw that day, that heavenly Visitor, and was glad. Again, the supernatural is discarded for a natural trick: "Jesus hid himself" (John 8:59). How could he, with the scribal bloodhounds right on him with hot breath? He "was hidden" from their view, says the Greek.

Matthew 26:31

Jesus, the cause of apostasy? So it would seem from the RSV in Matthew 26:31; "You will all fall away because of me." The Greek has "stumble (or be made to stumble) over me" (or at me). But Jesus was in no sense the cause of their stumbling.

Another Must-y Translation: Titus 1:9

The RSV, following Moffatt, has inserted *must* in these verses several times. They yearn to say *must*. Moffatt, however, has *doctrine* twice. The Greek structure of the sentence sets up a standard: "according to the doctrine (or teaching)"

Paul said: "holding firmly (they say: *holding firm to*. Is that the way they talk in the axis of infidel universities?) to the faithful word (the RSV says *sure word*, which is by no means the same) according to the standard of the doctrine (they say merely, *as taught*). . . ." Could the sentence structure be wrecked more?

I TIMOTHY 3:14-16; 4:4

Adding articles to the Scripture has changed doctrine in verse 14. In parentheses are the RSV additions to the Greek: " . . . how one ought to behave in a house of God (addition: *the* house), which is a church (addition: *the* church) of the living God (definite by meaning, the only one), a pillar and bulwark (addition: *the* pillar—as if only one pillar could hold up a superstructure) of the truth (the only time the Greek has, or has needed, the article)". This makes the passage pass to the number of those that treat of the Church General. That is not Paul's idea. He is writing about pastoral problems. They are inherently congregational. A church, any true church, every such church is a pillar, a bulwark of the truth. Truth is upheld and propagated locally. The RSV is serving its New Catholicism, owners of the new Bible. To them, a bishop is a "lord in lawn," as Carey's colleague Fuller wrote about the Episcopal pseudobishops of his day, a big boss in the Big Church. If the Greek doesn't have the articles, never mind. The RSV is the "authorized" version. It can insert desired articles where the Greek neither has them nor wants them. Each church had one or more bishops, in those days. They were, as E. Y. Mullins has said, local officers. The Scriptures are in accord. They are told how to behave in local churches and amid their problems. This the RSV liquidates as undesirable in the setup of the New Catholicism. Now they make bishops officers of *the* church, *the* house of God, *the* one and only pillar on which is balanced a superstructure called the truth. No wonder truth is so wobbly and sure to fall, in any Catholic system. A superstructure on one column is like an Indian juggler's trick. This is a stab at the very doctrine Paul is here teaching, a stab of Catholic hatred and bias. The apostolic witness is falsified.

Paul, at the mention of the mystery, which is *the truth revealed,* and only known by revelation, goes off into ecstacy over the great elements of that mystery: the incarnation (manifested in the flesh), his sinless character (justified—not vindicated—that is, declared righteous in his spirit, sinless to the depths of his being), seen of angels (supernatural witnesses), believed on in the world (faith stands never alone), the ascension (by some superficial thinkers not an element of doctrine, but to Paul the climax of the Redeemer's life among men). This is the Mystery of the faith, the truth in its essence, and churches are the bulwarks and columns of that apostolic truth in an apostolic Christianity. But this congregational truth and responsibility is liquidated and a Catholic Church, *the* only one on the horizon, is forged to usurp the functions that belong to the churches and their ministry. That way, truth perished, as truth has always perished at the appearance of every new Catholic apostasy. Truth dies today and liberty tomorrow. Enter the Inquisition. The Catholic apostasies are described, fittingly, in this connection (celibacy and Lent, called doctrines of devils). All God's creatures are to be received with thanksgiving by "those who believe and know." That is a good psychology, to be recommended to such RSV translators as are still alive. The Greek, though, has "the faithful who also know the truth." There is a letter fidelity, a formal and surface faithfulness that knows little and cares less for the truth, eternal and unchangeable. And that is a characteristic of all Catholicisms. Beware of it. Keep *faithfulness* joined with *truth,* known and lived. Finally, *consecrated* is substituted for *sanctified,* a doubtful wreckage of a word and doctrine. All told, the wreckers did a big business in this region of the Word.

I PETER 1:8, 9

Here, as so often is the case, the sentence structure is broken to pieces. Read this out loud: "Without having seen him, you love him; though you do not see him . . ." Isn't that a queer tautology? How precious was the classic tribute: "Whom having not seen ye love; in whom, though now ye see him not, yet believing ye rejoice with joy unspeakable and full of glory, receiving the end of your faith, even the salvation of your souls." That is here and now. But the RSV breaks it all up into separate sentences and seems to put salvation off till another life, a precious error to those whose most beloved doctrine seems to be the idea of apostasy, lugged in at every possible place for such mistranslations. But if we keep the sentence structure, we keep the references to the experience of grace through faith, in this life. In saying that we receive as "the end of our faith the salvation of our souls" there is a double connotation of *end*. Besides the *purpose* of saving faith, the *proximity* of faith to salvation is preserved. Salvation is the end of faith, as marriage is the end of the wedding. It is both purpose and immediate possession. The faith continues; the marriage is a reality. And so it is in salvation, for faith is union with Christ.

I PETER 2:7, 8

Both "authorized" versions throw away the real Greek declaration: "The preciousness (of verse 1, about Christ) is for you who believe." Then follows a gratuitous insult to the Savior: "a stone that will make men stumble, a rock that will make them fall . . . as they were predestined to do." I repudiate that as going far beyond the Greek, taking away human responsibility, and throwing on Jesus the blame of human depravity. It simply amazes me that any Christian could write such stuff and pretend he was translating. I fully recognize that there is a responsible unity in the universe. I recognize that both Old and New Testaments, in affirming that unity of all life, must attribute evil to the will of God, always permissively, often in the positive sense that evil itself comes as a punishment of previous evil. I would not diminish any true meaning of any true Scripture that teaches that. But "a stone of stumbling and a rock of offense" is exactly what the Greek says. Jesus is both of those things, by the will of man or by the sinner's blind stubbornness. But it is utterly false to mistranslate all this so as to throw all the blame on Jesus. How could any human being translate in such a fashion and so falsely? This is not far from the exact offense that the Gospels call the sin against the Holy Spirit. That attributes the work of Christ to the devil; this attributes the work of the devil to Christ.

II PETER 1:5-9

Peter's great classic is torn apart and reconstructed in utter ugliness. "Add to your faith virtue" is truer to the Greek than "supplement your faith with virtue." The verb means to *supply, minister*. The Greek says: "And, as to this very matter, bringing in alongside every eager diligence, also supply (add to) your faith with virtue (or, in your faith introduce virtue) . . . " No one is going to give an exact equivalent of the Greek, for it hardly exists in one English verb. But we could have been spared the loss of the beautiful and the classic, taken away from us to put in its place a verb just as far removed from the original as the old one it replaces. Then we have the anticlimax, "blind and shortsighted." The Greek adds the word meaning *being nearsighted* as explaining the sense in which he was blind. Then we have the Episcopal idea of confirmation inserted, changing the structure from adjective to verb. Peter said: "Give diligence to make your calling and election sure (or certain, firm)." Then the assurance is given that such diligence will assure one of never being capable of even stumbling. That has been changed to *fall,* as if once more sighting eagerly the pet doctrine of apostasy on the horizon. *The* entrance is reduced to *an* entrance. And so, line upon line, the sentence structure is changed, on purpose, to change the meaning of the original Scripture.

II PETER 1:4

The previous verse shows the arbitrariness of the RSV. Peter said: "that by these (the promises of the Word of God) ye might be made partakers (fellows in) of the divine nature, having escaped (better, fled away from) the corruption that is in the world through lust." The RSV sets forward the final clause, advances it from a subordinate clause to a co-ordinate verb, and obscures the great doctrine that by means of the Scripture promises we are now made partakers of the divine nature. Then, inverting the order and wrecking the structure, the Scripture promises are made the means of escaping the corruption of "passion"—not all "passion" is corrupt, unless we are to be delivered over, body and baggage, to celibacy.

I JOHN 2:20

The mania of putting a verb in place of a noun, or *vice versa,* shows its evil head in this Scripture. John wrote: "Furthermore, ye (emphatic) have an unction from the Holy One, and ye all know it." That was to give them discernment as to the ones who left their fellowship because they were never really of it. The unspiritual don't want to know that; they are set on calling it always a case of apostasy. Now the wreckage crew of the RSV comes and substitutes this: "But you have been anointed by the Holy One." How infinitely different. That might have been a momentary impulse of the Spirit, such as came on Saul for prophesying, on Balaam's ass, or on Judas for his feats of apostolate along with the rest. Having once been anointed, in some way and at some time, and having now and ever the unction of the Spirit, teaching us, are as different as daylight from dark. This is not even translation; it is trifling with sacred things.

I JOHN 3:3

If you have a hope, you have it. The basis, for the believer, is objective. But when you change this noun *hope* to a verb, and the pronoun *this* to an abverb, *thus,* you have changed the objective to subjectivism. That is the RSV idol. And they bowed down to it here and worshipped it. You are purified if you *thus hope,* leaving it a subjective, verbal attitude. And that is qualified adverbially, by the degree, manner or spirit in which you *thus* hope. This is false witness as to what John said.

I JOHN 5:1

"Whosoever believeth that Jesus is the Christ is begotten of God (*has been begotten of God*—the present faith proves the previous divine begetting which causes the new birth): and whosoever loveth him that begat loveth him also that is begot-

ten of him." Oh! Horrors! All that use of the word *beget!*
That will never do. Let the RSV at it. They can wreck all that
speedily. And so they did. What comes out of the magician's
hat is: "Every one who believes that Jesus is the Christ is a
child of God, and every one who loves the parent loves the
child." That, as a general proverb, which is what it becomes
now, is not necessarily true. Many a man is lovable and his
child destestable. The affirmation by John was not a general-
ization about all fathers, but about the love of God causing
fraternal communion of the born again. This went down the
drain, in the wrecking of sentence structure.

III John 2

What a blessed truth and how deeply spiritual the discernment of this passage, translated with veracity: "I pray that
in all things thou mayest prosper and be in health, even as
thy soul prospereth." That did not please the RSV. They
wrecked it, leaving us only: "I pray that all may go well with
you and that you may be in health: I know that it is well with
your soul." Unspeakable!

Revelation 1:5

John wrote: "the ruler of the kings of the earth." Two
of the three articles go into the RSV discard and we have left
only: "the ruler of kings on earth." Why?

There are scores of other such mistranslations that cry
out for Christian repudiation.

CHAPTER SIXTEEN

THE LOSS OF THE CONNOTATION OF BIBLE WORDS

RUY BARBOSA, THE GREAT BRAZILIAN SCHOLAR AND STATES-
man, once said: "Words have color and smell." So they have.
And sometimes it is not easy to carry over the aroma from
one language to another. It is true also that the translation
can give a color to the narrative or teaching that the original
did not have. We can, in this matter, only keep to our ideals
and seek for translations that approximate them the best we
can. One of the saddest defects of the new Bible is that it
seems utterly indifferent to the aroma and shades of meaning
attached to words, sometimes rightly and for centuries. This
is all brushed rudely aside with an odorless literalness. Take
cases.

PUBLICANS AND SINNERS

What a wretched translation we have of that classic
phrase, as classic in the English language as it was in the
Gospels and the Aramaic speech of our Lord's day. See what
is left of the phrase: *tax collectors and sinners*. Now there is
no odium to being a tax collector. That is, unless we are preparing a version just to circulate among bootleggers, moonshin-
ers, and gangsters who are avoiding the Treasury's investigation of their extortion money. Now centuries of use of the
King James Version have made *publicans* as evil a word to
us as it was to Jews of A.D. 30. What meaning can there be to
the parables of Luke 15, when the issue is eating with tax
collectors? What's wrong with a carpenter and some fisher-
men eating with a tax collector? This substitution is a cheer-
less lack of imagination. These men were not just tax collectors. They were more like ward bosses, gangsters, and
hoodlums, rolled all in one, plus the odium of being in the
service of a hated foreign government. *Tax collector* does
not translate the meaning, which includes the connotation.

THE "ARGUING" PAUL

Who likes an individual that is always arguing? Yet that
is the way the RSV presents Paul, in Acts 17:2, 17; 18:4, 19;

19:8, 9; 24:25. The KJ translates this verb into *speaketh,* once; *preached,* twice; *reasoned,* once, and *disputed* six times. The picture given by the RSV of Paul is pugnacious, unfavorable, repugnant; whereas that of Luke is persuasive, winsome, irresistible. Evidently the RSV is biased against Paul and is determined to use a verb about it him that popularly smells bad. Why should they pretend that the man did nothing but argue?

UNENDING TENT TALK ALL THROUGH THE BIBLE

The Tabernacle of Hebrew worship is associated with the Shekinah glory of God revealed. Majestic temples came and went, but the great interpretations of ancient Law, historic prophecy, and the Apology of Christ the Messiah, to the Hebrews began and ended with the Tabernacle as the divine pattern of Jewish worship and symbolic types, given from heaven in the mount of revelation to Moses. The RSV cheapens the whole Bible revelation shamefully by its plebeian language about this majestic center of historic revelation and worship. The connotation of *tent* is the circus tent, the scout's tent of roughing it in the woods, the pup tent with army paraphernalia, refugee life, and similar common usage. It is not worshipful. The KJ has *tabernacle* in Matthew 17:4; Mark 9:5; Luke 9:33; Acts 7:43, 44; 15:16; Hebrews 8:2, 5; 9:1, 2, 3, 6, 8, 11, 21; 11:9; 13:10; Revelation 13:6; 15:5; 21:3. It might have used *tents* in Hebrews 11:9. But the RSV uses *tabernacle* hardly a single time and most of the time says *tent.* This includes the most sublime references to things in heaven and on earth. Even the heavenly Temple is in a "tent" up there, though twice the language is so repugnant that the word *dwelling* is substituted arbitrarily. In the Old Testament, *tabernacle* is used some, Exodus 25-27, and other verses. But in the poetry of the Psalms the prosaic "tent" talk shocks the sensibilities of the reader, in the midst of the majestic and worshipful language.

There seems to be an impression in the minds of the RSV translators that because the New Testament was written in *koiné* Greek, therefore our English Scriptures should lose all their majesty, much of their meaning (the connotation), and the fitting atmosphere of the supreme literary revelation of all time. *Koiné* means common—not common in the sense of being cheap, crude, uncouth, but common to the whole Greek world of conquering Alexander. That language became common to all speech and writing, all over the Roman Empire, the Greek empire of thought and clarity and elegance. That this should be thought of as nothing above the level of street chatter is false and ridiculous. Such an idea unfits men to be translators.

Our religion came by revelation, of a higher order than mere tent talk. Yet see how the beauty and glory of our immortal hope has been irreverently and ruthlessly cheapened, in the new translation of II Corinthians 1:5. The KJ says: "For we know that if our earthly house of this tabernacle were dissolved, we have a building of God, an house not made with hands, eternal in the heavens." That is almost Paul's sense. Leave out *this* and change the verb to *destroyed* and you would have Paul's thought. Now see the wreckage left: "For we know that if the tent we live in is destroyed, we have a building from God, a house not made with hands, eternal in the heavens." The Greek speaks of "the earthly house of the (*this* perhaps oversteps the occasional demonstrative force of the article, but seems natural here) tabernacle." *The tabernacle* elevates our body to the position of the shrine of our inner worship, the Holy of Holies where God meets us. Now you can't say "the house of this tent." No. But don't let a little thing like a word in the original stand in your "authorized" way. Off with its head. Then you have what you want: "the earthly tent we live in." That cheapens it, falsifies it, flattens it as much as could be desired by the Bible's worst enemy. If what is in the Greek doesn't suit you, change it and don't even make a note in the margin, this time. It will dawn on the Nelsons, when the people make it dawn on them, that they have cheapened sacred and cherished expressions of our hope.

You cannot suppose that the author of the Epistle to the Hebrews used tabernacle terminology because the temple in its majesty had disappeared. It was about to disappear (8:13). He uses the original Pentateuch terminology of the tabernacle. For Israel, both Jew and Christian, would still have their Bible when the temple was gone, and its analogies would be clear, as to Christ and Calvary. But the RSV readers get none of the glory. They are left *"tenting* on the old campground."

MEN OF FAITH: GALATIANS 3:7,9

To millions, this phrase means men of exceptional faith, like Hudson Taylor, Mueller, Spurgeon, Judson. When the RSV uses the phrase in this Scripture they give an utterly wrong connotation to their words. There is no *men* in the Greek. *They who are of faith,* men, women, and children, all believers, are heirs with Abraham of justification by faith. This is bad blundering, lack of attention to the connotation of words and phrases that often mean something different from the sum of the meanings of each word in the phrase

FIRMAMENT

One of the first things my Hebrew teacher taught me was that the translation *firmament* in Genesis 1 and similar Scriptures was wrong. He insisted on *expanse* as the idea of the word, which accords with the majesty of the universe that awakens the praise of psalmists and prophets. But there is a mania that forbids this translation, though even Moffatt is not so crude as the RSV, but uses *vault*. That mania is thus expressed in the new million-dollar commentary, which describes the "firmament" as "a solid substance . . . flat earth, mountains around its rim, dome of the firmament resting on them as pillars (If the Church could rest on just one pillar, why not the universe, too?), windows in it . . . water came through them as rain." There is room for countless conjectures, but not room for even a note in the margin to inform the misled reader of the RSV that the Hebrew word means just what our telescopes show of the marvels of the heavens— *expanse*.

GODLY GRIEF

Men who have banished *conversion* from the Gospels have made a new beginning of the doctrine of repentance.

Now we are told that it is "godly grief" that produces "a repentance that leads to salvation" (II Cor. 7:10). Grief suggests bereavement. Does there have to be a death in the family before one may repent? There is a connotation of personal loss in the word, which disqualifies it to enter into the doctrine of repentance. The RSV permits Luke to report the rejoicing that God "granted repentance unto life." Why do they have to add a verb to the Scripture in II Corinthians 7:10—godly sorrow works repentance "that *leads* to salvation"? No. It works repentance unto salvation, just as repentance unto life. This mistranslation is an offense against the gospel of grace.

Given, Not Merely "Shown": II Corinthians 8:1

Grace and *given* are words that go together, not *shown*, which is not the meaning of the original nor has it affinity for the subject in hand. Grace was "bestowed on the churches of Macedonia," given in their liberal life.

I Corinthians 3:14,15

The way words have different color and smell, for these translators, from what they had for Paul, is seen in the mistranslation of this Scripture. It treats of the way men build life into churches and the rewards they get, after God's own fiery testings. Taking the words as they come, the Greek says: "If anyone's work abides which he built on, a reward he will receive." Rarely do you find a Greek sentence that runs even that close to the English sense, in the same order of the words. And he adds: "If anyone's work burns down, he himself will nevertheless be saved, but so as through fire," that is, coming through the fires of testing. Now *abide* is one of the words the RSV usually seeks to banish. The RSV tendentially substitutes *survives,* as if the person himself, not his work, were being discussed. The idea of a person about to perish, but "surviving," while utterly false translation and doctrine, is dear to the hearts of the apostasy-loving translators of this version. But it is alien to Paul's context or thought. Now, to aid the idea of apostasy (in the unbiblical sense of loss of salvation), and even maybe the doctrine of Purgatory, growing among bewildered Protestants, the word *only* is added to the Scripture here: "*only* as through fire." Thus a connotation of apostasy-loving doctrinaires is introduced here which is utterly alien to the grace-loving apostle of Christ's once-for-all redemption.

MATTHEW 19:28

Only twice do we have the word *regeneration* in the Bible, and once the RSV banishes it and substitutes this fanciful notion: "the new world." Let it stand as Matthew wrote it. It invites study. It was meant to. All creation is also to have a new birth. Why not retain the doctrine? Well, the reason, of course, is that this regeneration is otherworldly and not a one world, this world, affair, of bringing in the kingdom of God through socialism and its totalitarian "social gospel." This regeneration, like the personal one, can come only through Christ, so is not to be the result of economic planning and a vast bureaucracy, under pressure from clerical "prophets" who will shame or force some totalitarian Gestapo or dictator to do right and maintain the economic millennium. Do you notice a red coloring here that Matthew's Gospel did not have? Does it smell different?

GOOD TIDINGS OR GOSPEL—WHICH?

It is an interesting psychological and literary study to see just where the RSV permits the use of the word *gospel* and where the word is denied the New Testament authors and merely *good tidings* is put in the place of the banished *gospel*. To my mind, a tragic and sinister case is in the great Messianic program of Christ (Matt. 11:5; Luke 4:18; 7:22). We have shown the denial of the word *gospel* to John the Baptist, to Christ himself and his apostles, repeatedly. Here my purpose is to show the maneuver evident in this banishment of the gospel from the very definition of our Lord's purpose and ministry. Professor Latourette of Yale, speaking to the Southern Baptist Convention, as guest president and spokesman for the American Baptist Convention, in Miami, said that the fundamental doctrine and characteristic of the Baptists is that through them "the poor have the gospel preached to them." That is certainly the definition of Christ's program and the defense he made of it to the representatives of John the Baptist. Of course *gospel,* in these Scriptures, is taboo to the men who are, or were, running around the country saying or secretly abetting the propaganda that "Jesus was the first communist" and this is a communist manifesto. The good news to the poor, of course, is meant to promote *a be-all, do-all, control-all* government that will redistribute what wealth it does not waste and thus guarantee "social security." Many men have emptied this Messianic program of anything Christian and made it a wholly totalitarian materialism. Of course, they say that they mean for Christ to be the head of this totalitarianism, but there is not one single syllable of a program from Jesus as to how the economic problems of life are to be politically solved. The "planners" will set up their program and will give it the supposed blessing of our Lord, as the boss-to-be of this world economic millennium.

Jesus took over for his kingdom the figurative use of the Jews' Year of Jubilee not for the ends of a bald literalism, such as is here proposed, but in the great spiritual counterpart, in his redemption, of what Jubilee meant in Israel. Redemption itself was physical there and then, but Jesus gave to captivity in sin, slavery in depravity, ransom, redemption, and freedom their soul values in salvation and changed relations to God. To prostitute all this to a politico-economic program, exploited everyday and all the way by communists, to mislead the unwary, is the blindest folly any American of our day has been guilty of. The RSV lends itself here to this revolutionary snare, forgetful that revolution always means blood, militarism, politics, disillusionment, and false promises, except in the rare, once-in-a-century revolution made by the people themselves, not by professional planners and Bible mistranslators. We Baptists have been robbed of what Professor Latourette calls our primary mission in life and history. We shall have to give it up or give up this false and tendential translation, meant to serve the revolutionary planners—not to say plotters. What have you got against *the Gospel,* gentlemen? Why banish it from the place where it most of all belongs?

I Corinthians 3:8,9

Wages is introduced into this passage. It is not the subject. We have that treated of in Chapter IX. Here it is *rewards*. Paul, who is in the center of this stage, got no wages. But he counted mightily on his reward. The translators correctly retain that meaning, in verse 14. I dislike the double omission of the Greek emphasis, *his own*. If Paul wanted to stress that, why deny him the privilege? The apostle simply did not say we are "fellow-workmen *for* God." As the note says, the Greek has "God's fellow-workers." The very word *with* is the first half of the compound word: "workmen-with God." True, *God* is in the possessive genitive; he owns those who *with-work*, with him and with each other. The mistranslation here lacks the deepened tint of emphasis and the aroma of divine ownership and human stewardship in common endeavor. The original, however, is redolent with it all.

Sentenced to Hell: Matthew 23:23

I have pleaded for that translation in John 8:11: "Neither do I pass sentence upon you." But here it seems far truer to the original tones of the picture to say: "the condemnation of hell."

Went Out . . . Where? Revelation 6:2

"He went out conquering . . ." You want at once to look around and see from where and to where. Out of what? *Went forth* has something of the knight-errant tone.

Mismated? II Corinthians 6:14

That has a completely wrong connotation. It suggests matrimony, which is not the subject here. Business or guild associates who might drag one to the idolatrous festivals in temple banqueting halls are in the picture here. Any relation so tight as to suggest a yoke that pulls one along with an alien spirit is the forbidden thing in this Scripture. For example, the RSV Committee has a distinguished Jew on it. In no way would I diminish his liberties, his civil rights to reject and repudiate his Messiah, in any way that might seem good to him. But I do not think he has a right in a Christian Bible to share in the decisions, or to insinuate in the Introduction Pamphlet about the Old Testament that the Messianic element in the Septuagint was put in it by Christians. For example: "Thus Aquila rendered the Hebrew word *ha-almah* in Isaiah 7.14 literally, 'the young woman,' in place of the word 'virgin' which Christians have substituted for it." He doesn't seem to know the RSV defense that "virgin" can mean anything, so counts the LXX word *virgin* an interpolation, forged by Christians. Anyone yoked tightly with this unbelieving Jew, taking advantage of his position to attack our Messiah indirectly as not virgin-born, is in open disobedience to this Scripture. "What partnership between a believer and an unbeliever?" (Berkeley Version). Why, friend, they are partners in translating the Bible. That's what.

The principal men on this RSV Committee are also contributors to Ferm's *Encyclopedia of Religion.* Every sect of paganism and the Roman Catholic sect are allowed to paint their faith in the rosiest colors, while modernists reduce our Bible to ruins and are cynical about Baptists and Protestants. One of the men in that setup is Professor Morton Enslin. Early this year I read an article of his in a Jewish theological quarterly that poured contempt on the resurrection stories of the Gospels. He cites, with approval, one of his teachers who remarked that he had fished in those waters and had never even gotten a nibble. Think of a man pretending to be a Christian and being guilty of that. Yet the most eminent of the RSV translators are yoked with this unbeliever and other pagans in that ambitious literary enterprise. Maybe the fact that they did not want to condemn themselves is why this passages was shunted off to treat of mismated marriages, when that is not the subject at all.

Works Are More Than Deeds

The biblical connotation of the word *works* is far more than that of *deeds,* and in the doctrine of salvation by works the word is a part of the doctrine. Writers in *The Christian Century* have complained that the translation of the RSV is very unequal in value. To me, the book of Acts is the worst translation in the version's New Testament, and Revelation the best. Take these two words. In Romans, where the KJ had *deeds,* the RSV put *works* every time but one. But in Titus, the reverse was the order of the day. *Works* becomes one of the banished words, and we have *deeds* put in the place of KJ *works* seven times out of eight. The exception is Titus 3:1, where people are exhorted to be "ready for any honest work." The Greek says *good work,* and the idea is vastly different. We have shown already how the doctrine against salvation by works has been wrecked. A substitution like this, affecting vital gospel truth, is not something to settle by whims of hostile translators, to whom said truth is unpalatable.

COMMERCIALIZED RELIGION: MATTHEW 16:28

Here is the *quid pro quo* connotation of the judgment that the RSV attaches to the Scripture: "he will *repay* every man *for* what he has done." The Berkeley version says: "reward each according to his behavior." The translation of this preposition *for* is unpardonable. It is the one already studied, which means a standard set up. The idea of fixed truth or set standards doesn't appeal to these relativity-obsessed minds, so they jettison standards wherever they possibly can. The verb can mean either *repay* or *reward,* but the RSV itself translates it *reward* in Matthew 6:4, and other verses. If you think the judgment day is a bargain counter where Jesus is going to pay for what he got, then the RSV is your Bible. If you believe in salvation by grace, and rewards offered as incentives to fidelity and superior living given also by grace, like premiums to good students (disciples), then you had better stick to the King James and supplement it with the Berkeley. Even Moffatt here loves the grace of God enough to say *reward.* It is your own spiritual taste and smell which will decide whether you like the commercialized odor and flavor of this wretched RSV translation. With all the lovers of false gospels, this flavor of self-salvation is bound to be as popular as garlic in China.

POTPOURRI

Strike out "acted immorally"—weak translations act as a cloak of strong vices and sin—and leave in "giving themselves over (or utterly) to fornication." Strike out "saved" (because of its evangelical connotation), as to carnal Israel's political deliverance, and use, with the Berkeley, "rescuing" or "delivered," thus denying to the arch promoters of the doctrine of apostasy a proof text to their liking. Strike out "keep you from falling" and use "guard you free from stumbling" (sure-footed—Abbott-Smith). Say "Jude, slave of Jesus . . . to the called, who are stedfastly loved (perfect tense) in God the Father and guarded by Jesus Christ." Saying this at the very beginning of Jude, you won't be led off into the doctrine of apostasy by some tricky translation. Compare "before all time" (before every age, in Greek), Jude 25 with Revelation 10:6, translated by the RSV: "there should be no more delay." John wrote: "chronos (time) shall be no more." If the RSV posits, in Jude, an eternal regime "before all time," maybe we might allow John to posit that eternal regime after all time. Certainly the very existence of time is a very acute problem to theologians of our day. "No more delay" reminds you of a dish of gelatin whose flavor existed only on the printed label of the package. The odor of the Greek has all evaporated. Listen, all ye self-righteous and be comforted. The new Bible says: "He who does right is righteous." But halt before you settle in complacency. The translation is false. John wrote: "He who continually puts in practice the righteousness (God demands and gives) is righteous, even as he (the Giver) is righteous." You know the root by the fruit, a very different doctrine from the self-righteous pat on the back, in this superficial translation. Strike out "has the testimony in himself"; put back "has the witness in himself" (I John 5:10). This is classic truth, not to be trifled with. Even the RSV did not dare change, just above, "The Spirit is the witness." Here is where connotation enters in. While the *witness* here is an abstract word, it has the aroma of the Spirit's bearing witness to our spirits that we are the sons of God. What joy do you have in destroying a flower's beauty and smell? Now smell the Romanism in this notion: "those whose sin is mortal." I can smell "venial" in the air, right away. Is it possible that serious Protestants would put out a Bible with that kind of stench? "Not unto death" treats of this life; "mortal sin" sends you hopelessly to hell, after death; venial sin, to Purgatory. Why do the translators want to paddle in those waters? They are incompetent. Don't believe that John merely found that lady's "children following the truth." Strike out that false translation, agreeable to men with no Absolute, no truth, all relativity, for the Greek says those children were "habitually walking around inside the truth." They were not like Peter, following afar off nor like lost swamp dwellers, following an *ignis fatuus* of sacramental, sacerdotal delusion. John found them *walking* in the truth. Go thou and do likewise. If you walk in what you know, you will know more, "for if any man's will is to do his will, he shall know (concerning the doctrine, whether it is from God) whether the teaching is from God or whether I am speaking on my own authority" (or whether I am speaking merely from my own self). There is a bit of wrecking of the sentence structure, an avoidance of the aroma of "doctrine," and one or two other minor ills in the translation, but it still stands that the will to do brings greater capacity to know the divine revelation Christ gave. John saw that truth in action, in a lady's children. How about your children?

A FADED AND ODORLESS ROSE

Professor Charles A. Dinsmore is cited in one of the introductory pamphlets, released with the new Bible, as saying: "Words not only denote thoughts and things, they release feelings. They convince the mind, they also stir the heart." Many such words are the greatest losses of this version *propitiation, remission, gospel* (in key passages), *conversion* (in all but one passage), *regeneration* (fifty-fifty), *adoption* (largely), *bishop* (where embarrassing to false bishops), *presbytery* (the only case), the preposition *in* with the verb *baptize* (total loss), *Calvary, impute* (except where they apparently forgot), *abide* (all too often), *graces, confess* (several times), *rewards* (often), *hades* (in a key passage), *earnest* (in the doctrine of the Spirit), *wine* (as to ministerial ethics), *virgin* (prejudiced always, too scared to act where counsels of Mr. Facing Both Ways prevailed), *only begotten* (as *begot*—always), *truth* (I Cor. 13, etc.), *seed* (unless vegetable), *fornication* (off and on), *faithful* (as just seen), *inherit, collection* (Brethrenism), *members* (sometimes changed to organs), *slaves* (occasionally right), *flesh, carnal* (ill-smelling vocabulary to esthetic university professors of theological faculties), *Jehovah* (the banished Name), *words, the word* (whenever possible), *doctrine* (banished 34 times in the New Testament), *according to* (the preposition of *standards,* wherever they dared to—and they were outrageously daring—out of its 177 such uses in the New Testament), and many another word whose loss impoverished the Christianity of all those who are delivered over to the RSV for their public worship and private devotions. Such people are, of necessity, blind to whole blocks of New Testament truth, revealed in New Testament words, banished or butchered in the translating. Think, too, of the many, many additions to the Bible, plus their connotation: *inspired, rules,* and so on. The overtranslations and undertranslations vary the connotation from its real Bible influence; and in squeezing translation to the minimum we shall often see what is done to the Bible connotation lost. Then there is the horrible cheapening of the Word by a whole "tent" language of worship and ceremonial symbolism.

CONNOTATION MAY EQUALIZE SYNONYMS

It is well that the RSV did not follow Weymouth, and even the Berkeley, off into distinguishing the Greek verbs *to love* in John 21. That is a wild-goose chase. Perhaps a commentary may discern an almost intangible difference in the verb of Christ's questions and that of Peter's reply, but the connotation brings both over into the same area of thought. So with the two words for *other,* generally. The RSV forgets this, in translating the two words for *son,* at times. It makes Paul call Timothy: "my beloved and faithful child." Timothy was no child. He was not speaking affectionately to Timothy, but writing to a critical and faction-ridden church. This same word is translated "my son" in Matthew 9:2, and so on. Why could not the RSV show the same judgment about the same word in I Corinthians 4:16 and in Philippians 2:22? But Timothy is a "child" in I Timothy 1:2 and II Timothy 1:2, but, with the same Greek word, becomes "son" in I Timothy

1:18 and II Timothy 2:1. The distinction between possible synonyms, of varying senses, ceases to appear when the connotation in both cases is that of sonship. There is much nicety of translation of synonyms in the RSV that fails to translate the contribution of either context or connotation, which may equalize slightly differing synonyms.

ANOTHER CASE: I CORINTHIANS 8:13

Here you have two words for food, *yet they refer to exactly the same food,* and that identity of reference is the point. "Therefore, if food is a cause of my brother's falling, I will never eat meat, lest I cause my brother to fall." It is not *fall* (a RSV apostasy mania) but *stumble* or *be offended.* Now, the translators are exact, and exacting, in translating with a severe literalism the two words *food* and *meat,* or flesh. But a translation of the facts, the context, and the connotation, in the heathen temple environment and issues, makes the reference in both cases clear: meat offered to idols. Yet the RSV shows no sympathy at all for the strong negatives of Paul's utterance, so vivid in the Greek. The apostle virtually said: "If meat (food—the food in question) causes my brother to stumble, I will absolutely never eat meat forever (*while the world standeth* was Paul's effort to enter into strong negation) in order that I may not cause my brother to stumble." Moffatt makes the effort: "Sooner than injure him, I will never eat flesh as long as I live, never." That preserves the vivid color and the piquant flavor of Paul's Greek.

DEAN WEIGLE

The illustrious translator says: "We are on safe ground if we maintain that no word should be kept in the English version of the New Testament that has acquired a connotation that is misleading." (*The English New Testament,* p. 120). Amen.

CHAPTER SEVENTEEN

DICTION AND STYLE

THE EXCELLENCIES OF DICTION AND STYLE OF THE NEW version were commented on, to begin with. Nothing said here is meant to diminish that praise, deserved in thousands of cases. Here we enter the liabilities, on the debit side of the bookkeeping.

A SAMPLE

Here it is: "Law came in, to increase the trespass; but where sin increased, grace abounded all the more, so that, as sin reigned in death, grace also might reign through righteousness to eternal life through Jesus Christ our Lord." Now what could that mean to the university illiterates to whom our translators are accustomed to lecture? It is a version of Puritanic word-for-word translation, which is the worst kind of translating possible. Now listen to the Berkeley: "But law came stealing in to make the trespass more serious; yet, where sin fills up, grace overflows the more, so that as sin reigned in death, so grace might reign through Jesus Christ our Lord with righteousness that issues in eternal life." Some accuracy has been sacrificed there for beauty. But at least the thought movement is in clear English. That is what translation is for.

"BY GOD"

Isaiah heralds the Messiah thus: "Surely he hath borne our griefs . . . we did esteem him . . . smitten of God." That is gentle, clear. But the RSV changes it to "smitten *by* God." Compare also Revelation 12:6: "a place prepared of God" and "by God." How often is your university cynic going to read that phrase as cuss words? The RSV is very sensitive to young critics of *begat* and the word *fornication*. But can you imagine the glee with which a multitude of such phrases will be read with a pause before—"by God"?

MONOTONY OF DICTION

Note the sameness in Matthew 2:6: "least among the rulers of Judah, from you shall come a ruler." A variety of diction is an element of beauty and style. The original has it. The KJ has: "not least among the princes of Judah; for out of thee shall come a Governor, that shall rule my people Israel." The RSV chose to be poetic in form (broken lines) but lost nearly all the poetic beauty of the King James words.

"PERISHABLE": KEEP IN COOL PLACE

The double sense of so much English seems not to be on the horizon of our translators. We read in I Corinthians 15:52-54 about "the perishable" putting on "the imperishable." Where is there a young reader who will not immediately see the mark on express or freight: PERISHABLE?

DUMB

And when the youngster who reads only the "funnies" sees the statement that Zechariah "remained dumb," he will be sure that he knows a lot of fellows of whom that is true still. How much better the King James "remained speechless." Wasn't that a rather "dumb" bit of translation?

HOW COULD A SEED FALL "UPON" A THORN?

That is a literalism of translating a Greek preposition. But is there to be no respect to change of idiom? We used to read of how many angels could stand on a needle. But how many seeds could fall upon a thorn (Matt. 13:7)?

BRUTAL BLUNTNESS

Where would you find anything more so than the ending of Isaiah 6—blessed chapter? "The holy seed is its stump." And what sense is there in the statement: "whose stump remains standing when it is felled"? Contrast the poetic beauty and sense of the King James there.

A HEAVY SCHEDULE OF PRAYING

"Cornelius said: . . . I was keeping the ninth hour of prayer in my house" (Acts 10:30). Some fellow is going to think: The ninth. That is a whole lot of praying—nine hours!

And at home too. How different from the KJ: "at the ninth hour I prayed in my house." The Berkeley modernizes it: "Four days ago about this time I was home for my three o'clock worship."

"APPEARED TO TAKE AWAY SIN:"—AND DID OR DIDN'T?

The double sense of words, about which the RSV is so careless at times, leaves I John 3:5 open to the meaning: "He appeared (seemed) to take away sins," but maybe didn't. The KJ has "he was manifested," and so does the Greek, but the RSV has that mania of translating a passive verb by the active voice, and *vice versa*.

CAPITAL LETTERS EXPRESS DOCTRINES

What would you think of a version that would be writing about the patriarch Job but would spell it *job?* And what must we think of a version that writes of Jesus and spells it *son of God?* And why do we read *Creator,* in Romans 1:25, but not in I Peter 4:19? Yet right on the opposite page we read *the Majestic Glory.*

PREFERRING LONG, LATIN-BORN WORDS

The very same Greek word is translated: "are in debt to them," in Romans 15:27; but in Romans 1:14 it lost the terse affirmation "I am debtor" for the long, drawn out "I am under obligation to . . ." That is sophomoric. Nor is this the only case.

TOO FEW QUOTATION MARKS

The RSV introduces quotation marks into the Bible. That is fine. But it has used them with timidity in very important passages. Note the quotation marks in I Corinthians 6:12,13. There ought to be single quotes in II Corinthians 11 and other chapters where we have echoes of the criticism of Paul to which he replies. This is modern speech. David Smith is far more accurate in this than the RSV, which, after introducing quotation marks, uses them less than they should.

THE LOST CHORD: PSALM 68:26

"Bless God in the great congregation, the Lord, O you who are of Israel's fountain." How much clearer the KJ: "even the Lord."

ACTS 18:14

We have to choose between "wicked lewdness" (KJ) and "vicious crime" (RSV). Was there ever a crime that was not vicious? The Greek seems to come somewhere between.

SHALL OR WILL

Recognizing that our own language is in transition, and confessing the difficulty in any coherence, I still think that the RSV is heavily overweighted with *shall*. Why, in Luke 19:43, do we have: "For the days shall come . . . enemies will cast . . . will not leave." Moffatt has "Christ will," the RSV, "Christ shall give you light" (Eph. 5:14). The *shall* and *will* of I Thessalonians 4:14-17 obey the distinction between first and third persons. But in Matthew 16:19;18:18, Moffatt has *will* all four times where the RSV has *shall*. Which knew English? Neither translated the Greek, which says: "shall have been bound . . . shall have been loosed." It is the future perfect of command: "Let your binding and loosing follow what heaven has first revealed." Moffatt and the popes tell Peter to bind and loose and expect God to obey him. If there is arch folly in a translation, that is it. Now the RSV is not clear. Does it mean: "What you bind on earth *shall* be bound (already bound) in heaven"? Nobody knows. Why could not they have translated the Greek, fully and faithfully? Comparing Moffatt and the RSV in eleven verses in Matthew 16, Moffatt uses *will* twelve times, to the nine in the RSV, and uses *shall* twice to five in the RSV. The RSV has *shall* five times in Luke 3:5,6; Moffatt once for all. In Luke 10:15, the RSV has *will* . . . *shall;* Moffatt will. In John 16, we have *will* twenty-five times consecutively before a single *shall* interrupts. Moffatt interjects one more *shall*. There is much confusion.

Why Confuse Zechariah and Zachariah?

For three hundred years the KJ has distinguished between the Old Testament prophet and the priest of Luke 1. The spelling of English names is settled, unless for the very obscure ones. The Basic has both.

Hangover from the King James

After all the banishing of *publican,* lo: the "Pharisee and the Publican" as the title of page 91. And on page 152, we read of the "Apostolic Decrees," though below there, on the same page, they seem to have been "assembly"-born.

Leave the Bible's Ambiguity Alone

In the style of the Bible, ambiguity is often a characteristic. Such a case is James 3:1. "My brethren, be not many masters (*teachers,* mg.) knowing that we shall receive the greater condemnation." So said King James. We might better say: "Stop becoming (so) many of you teachers, for you know that we shall receive heavier judgment. For we all offend in many ways." The RSV translation, "Let not many of you become teachers . . . for you know that we who teach shall be judged with greater strictness," has these defects. It limits the judgment to the teachers. "We who teach" is an addition to the Word. It might mean that, but it might mean that the churches would come under judgment for these incompetent and self-seeking demagogues. Better leave it indefinite, for the responsibility is indefinite and wider than the teaching group. I often speak of the "blessed ambiguity" of some Scriptures. Let it be.

Confusion—Is It Deliberate?

A Bible's style should be clear, where the Bible itself is clear. In I Corinthians 11:19, Paul said clearly: "It is essential that there be divisions among you in order that the approved may become evident." It is not clear in either the KJ or the RSV. Both say: "there must be . . ." as we say that where there is so much smoke there "must be" fire. Let it be stated clearly. There *ought to be divisions* wherever that is essential to a witness against error and wrong. The timid translations here dodge Paul's insistence on division. He teaches division for the love of truth and right, just as he condemns it for personal issues.

"WENT AND DONE IT"

In its efforts at "common" (koiné) talk, the RSV almost equals the "went and done it" line of colloquialism: "went and put" (Matt. 18:30); "he departed; and he went and hanged himself" (27:5). The Greek has "went away," in both cases, which would break the similarity with the uncouth phrase. "Took and ate" would be more like the Greek: taking . . . ate (Luke 6:4).

BOOKISH

It seems bookish to me to say: "You traverse sea and land" (Matt. 23:15). Rooted in our classic phrases is: "Ye compass sea and land," and the first meaning of *compass,* in my dictionary, is "go around," and that is what the Greek says, not *go across.*

HARDLY THE HOUR FOR SARCASM

The diction of Matthew 26:40 seems to me a misreading of our Lord's emotions in Gethsemane. He was not impatient, exclaiming sarcastically: "So." He mildly says to Peter, as a gentle reminder: "So ye were not strong enough to watch with me through one single hour?" And I like to think that compassionately he said, finally: "Sleep right on the rest of the time and rest some more (continue to rest)." And the now calm and resolute Savior lets them sleep, watches over them till peril draws near; then, after this pause, stirs them with the command: "Lo, the hour has come near and the Son of man is betrayed." The angel-strengthened Jesus showed not a sarcastic impatience but the same calm care for his own by which he later delivered his mother to John. The RSV has changed the punctuation to create an impatient, sarcastic Savior. It is poor literary discernment.

Punctuation

Contrast the following. As it is: "The gospel for which I am suffering and wearing fetters, like a criminal" (II Tim. 2:8). Paul thus seems to be "suffering fetters," a queer phrase. Why not punctuate differently? Write:" The gospel, for which I am suffering, and wearing fetters like a criminal." Better still, retranslate the whole somewhat mutilated sentence: "Keep in memory Jesus Christ, raised from the dead, of the seed of David, according to my gospel; in him I bear up under wrongs, even to the extent of fetters, as if I were a criminal. But the Word of God is not fettered" (II Tim. 2:8).

Turning Back to Victorian Age Diction

Don't you smile when you read about a Pope "Pius"? Can any other word bring back so quickly a Victorian-age vocabulary, and the student reaction against it, as the word *piety?* Aside, then, from being a gravely erroneous translation of the great gospel word *righteousness,* it turns the clock back to the era of college sneers at everything Victorian. It is hardly for these translators to take that backward step. Jewish righteousness was largely a matter of saying prayers, ostentation of alms, highly self-advertised fasting. The theme of the Sermon on the Mount is the better kind of righteousness Jesus taught. The RSV abandoned the theme, just at the point of their Master's empasis on it, in the translation of Matthew 6:1; "Beware of practicing your *piety* before men." *Righteousness,* inward righteousness, with no religous ostentation, is the subject here.

A Belittling Vocabulary, Deflating the Gospels

Modernism shrinks all the panorama of the Gospels. It gives us a few months' tragedy of a peasant agitator in a backward civilization. In this enlightened day, that is criminal ignorance and incompetence. Palestine was a land of cities, not a rural scene. It was the fullness of times, even from the ages-old standpoint of the Creator of time. There was no illiteracy. Every child had the training of home and synagogue—a school, worship, and social center. The Jews were at the crossroads of the world, under the full blessings of the *Pax Romana,* bilingual, with the ends of the earth coming from the Dispersion every great feast day. They had superlative artistic beauty, sculpture, architecture, a wonder of the world in their temple. Herod had been a patron of all the arts, even of the Olympian games; wholly Greek cities abounded, even to having a federation, Decapolis. The whole New Testament thought-level presupposes the highest grade of culture and thought-life and thinking capacity the world has ever known. The RSV cannot even reach that level in its translating. To call Jesus a "peasant" is stark stupidity.

Now don't shrink all that, as Peruvian Indians did their captives' heads. The RSV tried it. Its "Gospel Parallels" shrinks the literature, excluding John largely, to shrink the time limits. It shrinks the geography: "Jesus went up into the hills" is the false translation of John 6:3. The word is *mountain,* and it is definite and in the singular number. Why the false rendering? Furthermore, the cities of Palestine were cities. There a big population of the land dwelt, behind walls, in wartime. The word *city* is not limited to the Chicago-New York-Boston axis, where the RSV translators dwell. Palestine was full of cities. The Harper *Dictionary* mentions several by the name of Ephraim, but the RSV reduces one of these to a "town" (John 11:54), also Senator Joseph's Arimathea (Luke 23:50), and so on. Better let the geography alone. Maybe they weren't cities to a Chicago eye, but by their own standards they were *cities.* And Palestine was a city population. You can't shrink the head and features of the Gospels to tennis-ball size, for you don't know the Peruvian formula for that shrinkage.

The shrinkage of the facts by a shrunken meaning given to clear words is part of this effort. John is our witness to the effect that "Judas, who was in the act of betraying him, also knew the place, because often Jesus was brought there along with his disciples. Therefore, Judas, when he had taken the cohort and some officers from the chief priests and from the Pharisees, comes on there with lanterns . . ." (John 18: 2, 3). The language, "Jesus often met there," is queer, even with the addition, "with his disciples." The fact is, he was brought there with others. A British commentator thinks that garden was the property of Mark's father, and that is how Mark happened to be there at that hour with only a sheet around him. He came to act as host, for his family, to the beloved Master and his circle, and, aroused unexpectedly, he ran to see what was what. Now General Judas cuts quite a figure here, with the Roman Cohort and the "colonel" (Berkeley, v. 12) and the temple officers and the whole priesthood and their drummed up mob, all under the momentary command of scout Judas. Why rob him of his fleeting and only glory? These are a few of many shrinkages.

CURRENT TALK

In Revelation 16:14, "demonic spirits" sounds like *The Christian Century* and Reinhold Niebuhr. Does the Bible have to take on that load? Why not translate the Greek that is there?

MORE PRISSINESS

The phrase is Dorothy Thompson's. This act of "lying close to the breast of Jesus" (John 13:23; 21:20) seems like more of it. Dear me. Picture the scene, but don't anybody get closer than "close" to anybody else. And yet these standoffish translators probably called each other Jim, Edgar, Luther, and Bill, in their intimate gatherings. Why the squeamishness? Yet these same men, who won't let a masculine head get close to a masculine bosom, will ruin Psalm 2 by translating: "with trembling kiss his feet."

BRINGING A GOOD WORD INTO BAD REPUTE

That is done in Luke 23:41, where crucifixion is called the due *"reward* of our deeds." That is cynicism, and the converted thief did not say it. The man said: "We are getting back things (sufferings) worthy of the (deeds) which we practiced." Crucifixion was too good for their crime record.

SCANDALOUS TALK

"It pleased God through the folly of what we preach to save those who believe" (I Cor. 1:21). That may be Paul's

idea and still give a superlatively different idea from what
Paul wrote. There is, in the first place, the RSV mania for
change of sentence structure. Paul did not write: "the folly
of what we preach." He wrote: "the foolishness of the preaching." Let it stand. There ought normally to be two Greek
words, one indicating the *act* of preaching, the other the
thing preached. But we only have one of the two in our Greek
New Testament. So it inevitably accumulates something of
the two meanings. At least the connotation is the act of preaching. There is no other way to write *act of preaching*. This is a
case of blessed ambiguity of the original. And even if determined to have only the content of the sermon as the meaning, the RSV does not show Paul's evident sarcasm as his
Greek did to his Greek readers. Moffatt translates with single
quotes: 'sheer folly' of the Christian message. Phillips has:
"simple-mindedness" of the gospel message, and "foolishness" and "weakness" below. These relieve the heavy tones of
the picture. The RSV cited is overtranslation, with a cynical
flavor. In Paul, the cynicism is in the Corinthian philosophical
smog, not in the clear air of Paul's love of preaching.

SEESAW, MARGERY DAW

This same word is found in II Timothy 4:17 and is translated: "the word." Paul has just told of opposition to his
"words" and the RSV refused to translate him. They have
a complex against the *words* as being *the Word*. So they
change *words* to *message*. Then they have a complex also
against *preaching,* so, lo and behold! they change *preaching*
to *the word*. Funny minds. And this is called translation.

CHEAPENED TRAGEDY

Language worthy of the hour is priceless. We had that:
"Behold the man: . . . Behold your King" (John 19:6,14).
Now what we have left by men who do not understand majes-
tic language is: "Here is the man: . . . Here is your King."

THEY FORGOT THEMSELVES

That was in Psalm 42:3,10, where they did not allow

the dignity of a *Thou* to the human personality the first time,
but did the second time. "Where is your God . . . thy God?"

BREAKING PARAGRAPHS AS WELL AS SENTENCE STRUCTURE

This is in Philippians 1:18,19, where Nestle (Father)
has no paragraph. They make one, and right in the middle of
a sentence: "in that I rejoice: and I *will* rejoice." This they
break into two paragraphs, and translate "I shall rejoice," as
if *shall* with the first person were the way to stress future
emphasis.

THE SAVIOR'S HOUSE UNROOFED?

In Mark 2:4, it is interesting to note that it seems to
have been our Lord's own home that was invaded from the
roof. But the RSV is more ruthless than the invaders. They
"removed the roof *where he was*"—that is all. But with its
mania for changing sentence structure, the RSV made that
more serious: "they removed the roof from above him." That
normally means all the roof. The facts show vividly in the
original: ". . . when they had dug up (Abbott-Smith) . . ."

INFERIOR DICTION

Here is a collection: "dumb" again (Mark 9:17; Luke
11:14); "go to hell" (Mark 9:43); "rob by . . . accusation"
(Luke 3:14); "shatters him" (Luke 9:39), (who picked up
the pieces?); "a man who had demons" (like having smallpox
or polio or seven-year itch?), (Luke 8:27); "a severe beating
. . . a light beating" makes revolting what, on Jesus' lips, was
not revolting (Luke 12:47,48)—translate it, man, instead
of beating around the bush. Compare the dignity of KJ and
RSV: ". . . will appoint him his portion with the unbelievers"
versus ". . . and put him with the unfaithful" (Luke 12:46).
"The last copper" (Luke 12:59) is rather an anticlimax as
the ending of a great discourse. "Can blind lead blind" (the
Greek) seems to me far better without adding *man* twice:
"Can a blind man lead a blind man?" There is dignity in
"Can the blind lead the blind?" "Such godless chatter" has
to leap over "the word of truth" to find a remote antecedent,

poor style indeed (II Tim. 2:16). "Both to the people and to the Gentiles" (Acts 26:23) is utter confusion. Who would dream that "the people" means Israel? Moffatt has "People." In Acts 27:9, "the fast" is meaningless. Horrors: Here is *begat* surviving in Deuteronomy 32:18. I confess that "bless themselves by" another is utterly meaningless to me, so I think it must be to other readers (Gen. 12:3; 18:18; 22:19, and other verses). "Fallen for me" sounds queer (Ps. 16:6). This was to be the Bible that all could understand. What does *mallow* mean (Job 30:4)? "Anything else in all creation" (Rom. 8:39) is a wordy mistranslation that spoils the simplicity and beauty of a great climax in revelation.

PROFESSOR GOODSPEED'S JUSTIFICATION OF THIS STYLE

Speaking, of course, in general and not of particular items, Professor Goodspeed advocates this "plain informal style" for a translation, on this basis. "This discovery (the Greek *koiné*) has put the New Testament translation in a new perspective. For if it is written in plain informal style, it should be translated in such a style."

And again: "The New Testament . . . owes almost nothing to literary artistry, and everything to the ideas it had to convey. To convey them with the utmost directness, simplicity and vigor was the chief concern of its writers. And if this was the aim of its writers, it should be also that of its translators." Precisely so. And that has been the primary charge of this discussion of the RSV weaknesses. It has not translated. It has not been direct. It has not given the simple meaning but followed all sorts of crooked paths of prejudice and bias. It has not the vigor of what it translates. It has banished a lot of words it hated and found no others to transmit the ideas of the original. It has adopted poetry in form and shown no poetry in spirit, in many cases.

Now "directness, simplicity and vigor" are themselves majestic elements of style. They made Lincoln. They portray the deep thought of great souls. They give the reverent mind's own innate "artistry" to the products of the pens of Paul, Luke, and John. Rough-hew the translation as you will, there is no literature comparable to the parables of Jesus.

The more truly and simply you translate *their idea*—and not mere verbal literalism of a technical nature—the greater the literary achievement.

The *ideas*, that's the point. The *ideas*, ah! There's the rub. The RSV deficiencies are primarily in its lack of perception, or in its determination not to transmit to the reader, the *ideas* of the Bible. No true translation can hide the majestic style of *ideas*, the thought style. It is well to remember that Luke wrote more of the New Testament than any other. He is antiquity's greatest historian, said Ramsay. The simplicity itself of Luke's majestic contents of gospel history far surpass the artificialities of a Thucydides style. It is precisely the *simplicity, directness and vigor* of Luke and all the rest that we want, and don't get, in the RSV. The Acts, I repeat, is its worst specimen. The solemnity of a document depends on the nature of its *ideas*. Luke gives us the one inspired history of the most important half century in this planet's history. The Epistle to the Hebrews is an elaborate apology for Christianity, in its formal break with its Jewish environment. There is a vast amount of figures of speech in the New Testament, a great element of style in any literature. The Epistles are not mere letters, no matter who says they are. Who ever adjured the recipients to have a mere *letter* read to all, far and near, by the very name of deity? Put back the word *Epistle* in its place. Professor Goodspeed never wrote an Epistle. He can't even translate one and retain its dignity and worth.

In spite of this brave pretense, the RSV has not even tried to follow this "directness, simplicity and vigor" that it has thus exalted. It breaks up sentence structure with little concern about worsened sound and connections. It suppresses the most innocent and pure sex references with what Dorothy Thompson calls prissiness. It uses big words for little ones, as "under obligation" for *debtor*. It selects a monotonous phrase, "stedfast love," in one Testament, and leaves *mercy* in the other, raising what Dorothy Thompson calls an "umbrella" over the love of God, whether it is raining or not. It brutally changes gospel language to a shorter form no mind can fathom, in order to follow its mania for banishing certain prepositions, as in the case of "repentance to God" (Acts

20:20), for example. What in the world can "repentance to God" mean? What does "through faith, for faith" mean?

The dignity of a style really comes from the majesty of the ideas. Debunking the content of the New Testament thought begot the low literary level of the language used. The Christian revelation has an inalienable majesty, whether it be partially preserved in Basic English or in the baseball jargon of a Billy Sunday, or the Negro dialect of slave John Jasper, or in the humble but Bible-soaked public prayers of an illiterate convert on the mission field. How much more should that be true in the greatest writing ever published in our mother tongue? If that tongue is still capable of the eloquence of a MacArthur, the tender pathos of a Madame Chiang Kai-shek, or the rolling thunder of a Churchill, equally powerful to stir a generation to war or peace, or to awaken the calculating admiration of foreign Nobel Prize judges, then certainly our new Bible should not sink to the level of university illiterates who read only the funny pages or to any subservience to their sex-soaked prejudices. We have repeatedly affirmed and specified the gratitude the readers owe the RSV for its betterment of diction, style, and clarity, in thousands of cases. We as sincerely hold both Committee and publishers responsible for these horrors of diction and style.

CHAPTER EIGHTEEN

BIBLE SQUEEZERS

WHAT IS A LEMON SQUEEZER? IT COMES TO THE HANDS OF someone who has first broken up the structure of the lemon into halves, slices, or other fractions and is used to take out all the juice and leave only the pulp and skin. And what are Bible squeezers? They are translators or interpreters who likewise destroy the unity of the Bible and squeeze out of its divided parts all the juices of the supernatural, the revealed, the absolute in morals, the doctrinal, the inspired. This distressing phenomenon we see many a time in the new Bible.

As stated before, I have used some forty versions, including the RSV New Testament, in my translating, in writing commentaries, and in preparing a Greek grammar and dictionary for students in Brazil and Portugal. One of those is Dr. Edgar Goodspeed's version. Another is Moffatt's. The latter is unparalleled in audacity. The former has the quality herein described. I always expect to find all the supernatural squeezed out of Professor Goodspeed's translation, as far as that is possible. Both men have, at other times, a veritable genius for translation. But their influence on the RSV has been utterly baneful. What a pity it was so largely made in the image of these two men's minds.

REPETITION, WHERE IT IS RIGHT, AND GOOD PEDAGOGY

The first case I give of the RSV squeeze is Matthew 5:37. Jesus said: "Let your word (conversation or speech) be Yes, yes, No, no; and whatever is in excess of these is from the evil one." Now the RSV, for good or ill, has squeezed out half of what Jesus commanded, and added a conjunction Jesus did not say, giving us: "Let what you say be 'Yes' or 'No'; anything more than this comes from evil." See the changes: *word* to "what you say"; half of the words recommended is suppressed; the plural is reduced to singular, to conform to the squeeze; *or* is added. If that was what Jesus meant, why did he not say so? If he had in mind to cut out every superfluous word, why did he not do as he said? The answer is that Jesus was here urging *repetition* as the one legitimate way of emphasis, rather than swearing and exaggeration. Repeat it.

Don't just say yes. Say it over again. Repetition is the divine pedagogy: "line upon line, line upon line", like the chorus in a song, the oft repeated words of a mother in the home. But the RSV not only did not catch the meaning, it showed its obtuseness by eliminating our Lord's own repetition, which he gave as a terse model.

REPETITION AN UTTER SIN AND FUTILITY, IN PRAYER AND RITUAL

Our Lord commanded: "When ye pray, use not vain repetitions" (Matt. 6:7). So the KJ, the ASV, Williams ("whenever you pray, you must not keep on repeating set phrases"), Moffatt ("pray by idle rote"), Basic ("in your prayer do not make use of the same words again and again"), Goodspeed ("Do not repeat empty phrases"—at least he did not squeeze out the repetition), Weymouth ("needless repetitions"), Berkeley ("Do not repeat and repeat, as the pagans do), Thayer, and Abbott-Smith. The Berkeley adds this note: "Which applies to the words of this prayer. Too often they are not prayed but repeated. Leaders even say: Let us repeat the Lord's prayer." It is the same idea as the horrible repetitions of the Ave Maria vespers over the radio, as the prayer wheels of the orient, as the written prayer-banners left waving in the wind that every flutter of the fabric may be a prayer. The essence of all paganism is repetition of prayers for merit and success and relief. Jesus forbids it utterly. This New Catholicism is just about as much given to ritual and rote, repetition of "The Apostles' (the name is a falsehood on the lips of all who say it) Creed," the Lord's Prayer and all other repetitions from prayer books. Now what is the use of the New Catholicism's owning the new Bible and allowing it to make this utter repudiation of all the Orthodox, Episcopal, and Methodist disobediences of our Lord's command? By a simple bit of surgery, the RSV removed the great command, one of the supreme principles of the new era and the New Testament. Look, now, at the substitution: "In praying, do not heap up empty phrases." Of course, the beautiful prayer language of prayer books is not "empty phrases." So disobey Jesus to your heart's content, repeat, repeat, repeat. The RSV has revoked our Lord's command. The only question is that the Greek does not mean what they say it does. They simply repudiate the authority of their Lord, and the New Catholicism leads multitudes to do just exactly what Jesus forbids—for he still forbids it, the RSV to the contrary not withstanding. And this disobedience to Jesus is put as the number-one thing to preach, in the program put out in *The Speaker's Handbook for the Bible Observance,* used in the 3,000 communities in this country and Canada, page 37. In this treachery to Christ they most glory.

CLERICAL LORDSHIP OVER THE LAITY

There is no more unchristian translation in the whole RSV than Hebrews 13:17, "Obey your leaders." You don't do that to leaders; you follow leaders, if they lead in the right way, to the right destination. The hands are turned back to medievalism, which is what the New Catholicism will be sure to come to. Consider the wickedness of this evil rendering.

The verb translated *obey* is the regular verb *persuade.* Its connotation would certainly be that of persuasion. But the translators, of course, know this fact for the verb is found five times in this Epistle. In 6:9 ("we are persuaded better things"), 11:13 (KJ text, "were persuaded"), and in 2:13 and 13:18 it means to persuade oneself, and so trust. How then could our translators, in all candor, allow themselves to put in any Bible this brutal murder of the rights of the laity and the lesser clergy of unbiblically episcopal regimes? The Catholic versions in Brazil translate *prelates* where the RSV has *leaders. Obey* at one end of the sentence demands— and eventually will get—*prelates* at the other end of the sentence.

Look at the parallel uses of the verb. KJ translates the verb *persuade* twenty-one times, *trust* ten times, *believe, yield,* or *have confidence* thirteen times, and *obey* only six times. Let us examine these six times. In Acts 5:36, 37, but the RSV corrects the KJ and translates the verb *followed* in both verses. Why could they not consent, then, for Christians to *follow* their leaders, instead of this tyrannical autocracy? In Romans 2:8 and Galatians 5:7 the obedience is inner, abstract, voluntary, the persuasion we accept and hold to. In James 3:3, "If we put bits in the mouths of the horses, that they may obey us, we guide their whole bodies." There is not a single case left in the New Testament of one person obeying another except this medieval anachronism. The only analogy is the tamed steed. The clergymen seem to think now that, with the aid of the RSV, they can bridle, saddle, ride, and spur us to their heart's content. If you want to help on this evil apostasy, use the RSV and maybe you can lasso the people. But there will be millions like myself who loathe the false translation, the utter blindness to all sympathy with the connotation of the verb, and the treachery to democracy in Christianity, which this translation makes manifest, and these all will say: "Let the slaves of the clergy use the Bible they have invented after their own heart's desire."

"Obey your leaders". That is a contradiction of terms. I have been a church member since 1904 and have had a score or two of pastors, to whom I gave utter love and loyalty. Never one of them ever yet gave me a single command. I have been a minister of the Word since 1906, presbyter, bishop, pastor, in the Bible meaning of those Bible words. Never once did I give a command to any Christian, and I would not do so if I lived five hundred years. Nor is this anarchy. It is democracy. Baptists have given to *leaders* like Truett, Mullins, Sampey, Gambrell, and Rushbrooke, in their leadership, a loyalty that no pope could ever *command*. Leaders don't command. They lead. The RSV Christianized the tail end of this sentence: *leaders*. Now let them Christianize the head of it, banish this *obey* as they did so much of Bible vocabulary and truth and in its place put *hear, follow*, or some verb that is Christian and goes with leaders and their persuasive ministry.

THE STABILITY OF MORAL ATTITUDES

When men make a definite commitment of their souls to right or wrong, there is a permanence of attitude that finds expression in the end of our Bibles: "He that is unjust, let him be unjust still; and he that is filthy, let him be filthy still; and he that is righteous, let him be righteous still; and he that is holy, let him be holy still." That individualizes such commitments. The RSV slurs it over so you can't tell whether it is singular or plural in any but the first reference. *Practice righteousness* is watered down to *do right*. The real meaning of the verbs, as aorists, is: commit himself to injustice, commit himself to a filthy career, give himself over to the practice of righteousness, and be sanctified utterly. The KJ majesty is lost, the KJ errors and weaknesses are, in the main, perpetuated. And the even greater reach of the Greek is dismissed as not worth striving to get into the translation, as so often is seen in similar cases. How much possible clarity and force was squeezed out of the RSV by this decision!

An Unhygienic Mistranslation

The story of the baskets of surplus food, after the feeding of the thousands (Matt. 14:20; 15:37; Mark 6:43; 8:18, 19; Luke 9:17; John 6:12, 13), has an unedifying mistranslation in the RSV. They make it appear that the twelve apostles ran around and picked up off the ground the leftovers of bread that the crowds threw away and trampled on in the grass. That is an impossible idea and impossible of execution and repulsive and unhygenic in the extreme. Nor does the Greek mean that. The verb *can* mean took up, or took away, or just *took*. It can mean bore or carried, with or without *away* added. The affirmation is made about the *surplus* of the broken pieces. A stream can hardly rise higher than its source. So, as Goodspeed translates the verb "Pick up the pieces that are left," the RSV echoes this repulsive notion. But the Greek out of which Goodspeed squeezed this mistranslation really says: "Gather together the surplus broken portions," as they had come, clean, from the hands of the Savior and been left over. Of such clean peaces there were twelve baskets (one word) after the first miracle and seven baskets (different word) full of the surplus provisions our Lord's bounty supplied. There is no excuse for this revolting imagination. The Basic Bible says: "They took up twelve baskets full of broken bits which were not used."

Salvation-bringing Grace

So Paul wrote, Titus 2:11. As a quality of grace it was squeezed out of the RSV and, when the sentence structure was broken up, the noun *salvation* was loosely thrown in the sentence. Pity 'tis.

THE LECTOR OF THE SCRIPTURES

We have praised I Timothy 4:15 for preserving the witness to the public reading of the Scriptures. Why did the RSV not preserve that main idea also in Matthew 24:15, and other verses? Matthew expected his Gospel to be read in the churches and that the public reader would explain the apocalyptic figures. But that doesn't fit in with the idea of the Gospels which prevails in the Chicago-Manhattan-Boston axis of infidelity, which overshadows this version.

THE SQUEAMISHNESS OF PRISSINESS

Matthew 24:8 means: "the early pains of birth-pangs," as the Berkeley translated. But that would make the RSV saints of Victorian modesty blush. So there must be no mention of any consequence of sex. Let begetting and birth never be spoken of, and so our world will grow moral, and acquire the airs of gentlewomen of the long ago.

"THEREFORE CAME I FORTH"

That (Mark 1:38) is the incarnation. Harnack called such declarations of Jesus "programmatic." See now how the whole of it is squeezed out of the RSV rendering : "that is why I came out," as if it merely treated of leaving town. The difference between the translations is as vast as infinity.

THE EARTHQUAKE IN THE SOLDIERS' SOUL

The KJ says: "for fear of him (the revealed angel of the resurrection) the keepers did shake," language of earthquake phenomena. Literally, "the earth did quake . . . the keepers did shake," same kind of unearthly terror (Matt. 27:51; 28:4) In the RSV, "the earth shook . . . the guards trembled" are left after the squeeze.

UNSQUEEZING THE SQUEEZED

Luke wrote: "when the tens of thousands of the throng had assembled, he began by saying, primarily to his disciples: Guard yourselves against the leaven, which is hypocrisy, of the Pharisees." Change the order of Christ, if you like, but don't divide the number by ten. That is ninety per cent wrong. (Luke 12:1). Can you uncheapen this cheapness, "You give them something to eat," when we had "Give ye them to eat" (Luke 9:13)? And see this squeeze: "he said this plainly" (Mark 8:32), when Mark tells us: "He kept speaking the word boldly," the Word of the Cross. Then in Mark 1:45 and 5:14, notice how Mark said: "was away out, in deserted places," and "in the fields," but the RSV translates both as "in the country." Mark knew that the fields were full, and the country is not a desert or uninhabited. He had to search out lonely spots where neither the city population, the country folks, nor the traveling population could gather easily about him. Whether the translators see it or not, Mark knew more about that situation than they do, and they botch things up when they stop translating and go to putting in their own notions. In Luke 8:33 and 8:42, we have kindred verbs: the demon-driven swine fell down the steep incline in a ball together into the lake and were "suffocated" (choked, says KJ) and Jesus was all but "suffocated" (Berkeley) by the throng. Our translators seem weak in imagination. The vivid touches of the Gospels about such scenes, they miss or don't appreciate. A hog can swim. This herd did not just drown. They were literally "balled up" and asphyxiated, not merely drowned. So Mark 5:3. Note the vividness of Christ's real command, "Stand in the center" (Berkeley, Mark 3:3), and not the mere laconical, "Come here," of the RSV.

THE RSV DISMEMBERS SCRIPTURES

The point in I Corinthians 7:40, as I elsewhere comment, is the *also*: "And I think that I *also* have the Spirit of God"— he is no monopoly of you tongue-speakers. But the RSV left out the point. In I Corinthians 4:17, Paul said: "For this very reason (to remind you of my ways in Christ) I sent to you Timothy." The RSV squeezed that emphasis into a merely introductory *therefore*. The passive of the verb to see is so vivid in the resurrection narratives: "He was *seen* . . . he was *seen* . . . he was *seen*." That also is the declaration as to the

visit of Moses and Elijah, at the Transfiguration. But the RSV
prefers the less vivid *appeared* (Matt. 17:3) and parallels,
(I Corinthians 15:5, 6, 7). Even Moffatt retains "he was
seen," and the Basic has it and the Berkeley in part. There is
reality in the word of eyewitnesses. Why should it degenerate
into protocol stuff? And how great an opportunity they missed
to put in a note on Luke 9:31, giving another *Exodus,* a
greater redemption of a greater Israel of God, as the theme
of the heavenly visitors with the Savior. Do those who have no
Greek have no right to know the noteworthy things the Greek
says so emphatically?

IMPOVERISHING RICH PASSAGES

Paul's long sentence, Ephesians 1:3-14, has been cut into
two paragraphs and six sentences. The order has been inverted
from "in the heavenlies in Christ" to "in Christ . . . in the
heavenly place." That rather obscures the present reference
of the phrase. The *fore* out of the Greek verb meaning *foreordained* or *predestined* is simply thrown into the ash can
twice, both in verse 5 and verse 11, though translated *predestined* in Romans 8:29, 30 and Acts 4:28. Too much *predestination, fore*ordination, and eternal purpose, and *pro*vidence
here to suit the RSV. Adoption is banished. "To be his sons"
is not a proper substitute, for it might be in either the first
birth or the second birth that we were held by the RSV to be
sons of God, and the adoption is a forensic aspect of redemption, displeasing to them. That this election was "for himself"
(ASV) has been thrown out the window. Remission is again
banished from the Bible and forgiveness put in its stead in
this great doctrinal deliverance: two doctrines gone, adoption
and remission and part of the *fore*ordination or *pre*destination.
The *glory of his grace* is changed to *glorious* grace: but the
riches of his grace is left just so, not changed to *rich grace.*
Wasn't that partiality? The verb of verse 11 is thrown forward
to verse 12, thus making the accompanying phrases seem to
refer backwards and thus divorcing in effect the (pre)destina-
tion and the purpose that carries it into effect. But who cares
about predestination? Just Jesus and Paul and some who
love them and the truth they revealed. *Accomplishes* (the

achievement won being brought into view) is put in the place of *worketh* (which puts the process all in view, along the foreordained pathway of the divine working all the way to the successful end). There is no verb *live* in the Greek. It is the verb *to be*: our whole being, in Christ, is this great field of operations of divine purpose and grace. You can't make the glory inhere in our way of *living*. In the shakeup, two doctrines of the Holy Spirit are missing. *Earnest* is banished, as we have commented already. And the Spirit of the promise is made to be the promised Holy Spirit. He is more. He is the Agent of bringing to pass the rich Abrahamic covenant, as Paul had already written in Galatians 3:14, 18, and other verses. Finally, the word *redemption* is banished. If the enemy of souls were trying to mutilate Paul's great doctrinal masterpiece, in the New Bible, he must feel pretty well satisfied with himself.

In Ephesians 2:15, we have the repugnant doctrine that God abolished the moral law. The Greek says he abolished "the law of the commandments that were expressed in ordinances" (the ceremonial law). With their usual indifference to sentence structure, the RSV abolishes all commandments (the whole moral law) in spite of Paul's two restricting clauses. The RSV reads "abolishing . . . the law of commandments and ordinances." What keeps that from being antinomianism? Paul is so clear on that line. With this same mail he writes to the Colossians: "having blotted out the bond written in ordinances . . . he hath taken it out of the way, nailing it to his cross" (Col. 2:18—ASV). The whole ceremonial regime of Judaism, with its multiform sabbath system and dietary laws specified particularly, are canceled like a receipted bill that has been paid on Calvary and *taken clean out of Christianity*. But to remove the apostolic limitation, commandments "contained in ordinances" (ASV), is to abolish the moral law as well as the ceremonial. Romans 8 still makes that moral ideal a goal of the Christian life. It is the mania for breaking up the sentence structure that did this evil deed. The Colossian Scripture cited has been tampered with similarly.

The *before* is knocked out again in Ephesians 3:3.

The sense is approached in I Corinthians 4:6 when the

RSV reads: "that you may learn by us to live according to scripture." How much better here is Weymouth: "the maxim not to exceed what is written"; or Berkeley's "Nothing beyond what is written." But the RSV goes beyond what is written sometimes, stops short of what is written at other times, and goes off at a tangent frequently. To show where all this is done we should almost have to write a commentary on Paul's Epistles, not to mention other Scriptures.

We are the poorer when we lose something of value. That again is the point in II Corinthians 4:10, which the KJ has exactly: "always bearing about in the body the dying of the Lord Jesus" (the death-marks, Berkeley). Just *carrying* is the RSV. Something always left out. It is in carrying around always in evidence in us the dying of the Lord Jesus that his life in us is manifested.

And one would need another commentary to show the offenses against the Epistle to the Hebrews! Space considerations bid me desist.

CHAPTER NINETEEN

BIAS AND PREJUDICE, AND SOME IGNORANCE, SHOWN IN MARGINAL REFERENCES

WE HAVE SHOWN THIS FREQUENTLY ALREADY. THERE IS THE insult to the Savior on page 1 of the New Testament. We have also shown the foolish adoptionism of note *k,* page 67. Consider the further facts.

IGNORANCE OF HOW TO SPELL "HELL"

A dozen times we have the word *hell* in the New Testament, each time from the voice of Jesus except once, which came from his brother James. Every time, the RSV has the marginal note: "Greek *Gehenna.*" And every time they say it, it is not so. The Greek word is *geenna.* It has no capital letter to begin with. It has no *h.* Now why would the RSV scholars put this bit of ignorance or misinformation in the Bible a dozen times? Probably because it served their purposes. Going back to still a third language, by way of the Greek, there seems to be a reference to old Hinnom's son, of a dim distant past, to whom a valley outside Jerusalem is supposed to have belonged. So the doctrine of hell is supposed some way to take a beating by this remote etymology. There is a cheap vice of careless theologians that seek to define Bible words by their etymology, rather than by their use and meaning. Whatever this theory may give of satisfaction to unbelief, the statement that the Greek word for hell is *Gehenna* is simply false, inexcusably false.

"APOSTLES" OF THE CHURCHES? NO. MESSENGERS

In II Corinthians 8:23, note *j,* we find this bit of bias or careless thoughtlessness. Paul said: " . . . our brethren . . . are the messengers of the churches, the glory of Christ." That is Baptist talk, so the RSV sought to kill it in the margin by putting "Greek *apostles.*" That, too, is not true. The Greek is *apostoloi.* If they say: "But the Greek means *apostles,*" I deny it. It could mean *apostles,* if it were talking of Paul or the Twelve. But it isn't. And it simply does not mean *apostles.*

Period. The word *can* have several meanings, but it cannot have the meaning *apostles* when that is not what it refers to. The RSV Homer nodded till he almost fell out of his chair.

MEANINGLESS JARGON

It is a disgrace to any Bible to put in this note, which we find on page 71, about Luke 6:1; "Other ancient authorities read *On the second first sabbath* (or the second sabbath after the first)." Call the proverbial Philadelphia lawyer to see if any meaning can be read into that.

EXIT MARY THE BELIEVER

Only in the note 3, page 63 (Luke 1:45), do we still have the Bible fact that Mary was a believer: "Blessed is she who believed, for there will be a fulfillment . . ." Our Lord's mother was a believer. She was a lost sinner, as are all other mortals, till she was saved. Early her heart opened to God in faith and then she tells us she "rejoiced in God her Savior." It saddens my heart, as a missionary, when translators from whom we could expect better things make a present of these gospel facts to the Romanists. The New Catholicism does obeisance to the old. Nevertheless, she was and is a believer, saved by grace.

THE "DAWNING" OF A DAY BEGINNING AT SUNDOWN

On page 100 (Luke 23:54 notes) we read: "Greek, *was dawning.*" No. Again that isn't so. The papyri show abundantly that the word was used of the Hebrew evening-morning day or of the day that began as sunup. It meant either an A.M. dawning or a sunset beginning of the Jewish day. It is translated right in the text and there is no call for any note at all.

"THE BEST ANCIENT AUTHORITIES"

This is in note *n,* page 51. It tells how two verses are "omitted by the best ancient authorities." Bravo! Why could not the slavery to that meaningless phrase *other ancient authorities* be alleviated by a little emancipation elsewhere, too?

A Great Truth Beats a Retreat to the Margin

"The kingdom of God is in the midst of you." How? Where? Who? Wherefore? The truth is driven to the margin: "The kingdom of God is within you" (note z, Luke 17:21). Many authorities say there is never a single case in the Greek language where this preposition means *in the midst*. Dogmatic consideration led the translators to consult their logic, not their Greek, and force this false meaning on the text. The RSV translates it in Matthew 23:26 by *inside*. And that is what it means. This is not the evangelical way of translating. The principle of the inwardness of the kingdom is stated as a generic truth, whether a reality there to many or to few.

Christ's Sample Conversion Destroyed

On Calvary, Jesus gave a demonstration of salvation, offered a sample of his wares (Luke 23:42). He saved a great criminal, without merit, good works, character, priests (any priest but Jesus), sacraments, church, any altar but Calvary, any sacrifice but the blood of the Lamb. The man repented. The man believed. He was saved and went with Jesus that very day to the Father's house. "Today shalt thou be with me in Paradise." The man's declaration of faith— faith so brave when the strongest believers were doubting—is queered now till nobody has any idea what it means: "Jesus, remember me when you come in your kingly power." The translation is utterly false. The margin confesses it, saying: "Greek, *kingdom*." Very well then, why was it not translated kingdom? What trifling is this? There is no word for *kingly*, no word for *power*. The word that confessedly is there is not translated. Why? What explanation is to be given to Christian America?

Mothers Want Their Babies to be "Human Beings"

Well! "She no longer remembers the anguish, for joy that a child (note f; Greek, *a human being*) is born into the world" (John 16:21). No. That isn't true. What that Jewish mother wants is a *man* child. And that is exactly what Jesus, in his illustration, gave her. The word does *not* mean *child* and it does not mean *a human being*. It means *man,* in the general sense, which may include men, women, or children. When you are translating the Bible is no time for a feminist gesture.

"Magus" is Not Greek

The RSV says it is (note *l,* page 148, Acts 13:6). These gentlemen seem not to know the difference between Greek and Latin. The note says: "Greek, *magus* (as in Matthew 2:1)." Now that is a gratuitous insinuation. It seems to put the "Wise Men" on the level with Bar-Jesus. The note is incorrect. The Greek is *magos,* not *magus.* The word may mean *Wise Man,* such as came to worship the child Jesus, supernaturally led. Or it may mean a cheap cheat, a sort of fakir and fraud. But that does not mean the two possible meanings are equal and the reference to Matthew 2:1 is uncalled for, just another insult to Jesus. They were not a bevy of Bar-Jesuses who were led by a providential star to Bethlehem, nor was Jesus proven divine by any item of astrology. Just leave the two unrelated incidents alone and learn how to spell Greek words.

Learning Late

In note *n,* page 192 (I Cor. 9:5), the revisers show they have discovered that you can translate the Greek word *woman* to mean "as a wife." Right. Pity they did not know that when they translated Matthew 1:20, 24.

The Supper Mutilated Again

In Luke 22 we have a supper with only the bread. In I Corinthians 11, we have the broken body banished to the margin. The rituals of these gentlemen, of course, are not changed by the RSV. Just the Baptists and other non-ritualist denominations would have to put up with a mutilated ordinance; if we used this version.

Let us Have Peace with God: Romans 5:1 (mg.)

Goodspeed, Moffatt, Phillips, the Basic, Berkeley, Weymouth, C. B. Williams and many others accept the text: "Let us have peace." It is useless to argue it. The RSV seems to feel no responsibilities.

THE NOTE IN MATTHEW 16:18

The translation is: "I will build my church, and the powers of death shall not prevail against it." Note *u*; "Greek, *the gates of Hades.*" In so famous a passage, would it not have been better to translate, and leave to others the interpretation? There is no excuse for the capital *H* here or elsewhere. Hades is not a geographical proper name, like Havana or Houston. With a capital letter, the word is a proper name, the god of the underworld. But that it not the use of the word anywhere in the Bible. It means the world of the dead and is no more a proper noun than earth, heaven, or hell. Why should this old Greek god's name be put in our Bible, by the capital letter, in Revelation, "Death and Hades." Yet they call Jesus "a son of God," in reporting comment on Calvary.

"RABBI", NOTE *i*, PAGE 34, AND ELSEWHERE

Rabbi is not a Christian word. It was a Jewish title for men with a special culture, synagogue position, mission of teaching and preaching, and a technical education in the Torah and Jewish tradition. Two things made it an unfitting title for the apostles of our Lord and all his official ministry. The idea of the word itself is *great*. That does not fit Christian humility. Then, too, the rabbi was an unpaid volunteer. The ministry receives "wages," "gets its living by the gospel," receiving "double remuneration" for doubly hard achievement, involving toil in exposition of the Word. But it is important to preserve *Rabbi* in the Gospels. It shows that Israel recognized, popularly and on the synagogue level, the "Great Teacher" whom they knew in Jesus. Even to them he was of the class of Hillel, Gamaliel, and Paul. And Judas speaks his Jewish language when he addresses Jesus as Rabbi. John keeps this Jewish speech, long after the end of the Jewish War and Fall of Jerusalem. John and Mark even present the superlative form, Rabboni, *my very great teacher,* as the Harper *Bible Dictionary* stresses. The RSV is right ten out of the fifteen times the word occurs. Why not all the times?

"Natural" Does Not Mean "Unspiritual"

It indicates man, as is, in his depraved state. Not wanting to let that be apparent, the RSV translates *unspiritual* and puts the truth in the margin (note *e*, page 187, I Cor. 2:14). The close of verse 13 strikes me as utterly fanciful and wrong, not that the idea is bad but that it is an impossible idea to take from that Greek (note *d*).

Nor is "Spiritual" to be Rendered "Supernatural"

The idle tale that the Rock that gave water in the desert followed Israel around in the desert like a dog running after a farmer's wagon is nonsense. But Paul, in taking that fact for granted, says virtually: "That yarn has no historical basis." But Christ was indeed the spiritual Rock, of whom something comparable may be said. The contrast is between *literal* and *spiritual*, to justify spiritualizing the incident. There is no contrast or thought of natural and supernatural (note *o*, page 194, I Cor. 10:3-5). This fault appears three times. And it seems to be in the service of sacramentalism. Ronald Knox applies this boldly and openly to the sacraments, affirms first salvation by the supernatural food of the desert that corresponds, says he, to the Eucharist, after baptism *into* Moses, and then, finally, was followed by apostasy of Israel in the desert. Is the New Catholicism following the tutelage of the old?

Paul's Judgment on the One-Worldly

Throwing the word last, to give it great emphasis, Paul said: "If *only* in this life we have hoped in Christ, then of all men we are the most deserving of compassion." What meaning can there be to the RSV: "If in this life we who are in Christ have only hope . . . "? Moffatt seems to be the mentor here of the RSV: "Ah, if in this life we have nothing but a mere hope in Christ . . . " That certainly rates low the Christian hope. Such an idea forces its advocates to jump from verb to noun. So Weymouth jumps to the noun too: "If in this life we have nothing more than a hope in Christ . . . " I looked to see if these gentlemen believed that "we are saved by hope." No they repudiate that, too (Romans 8: 24), translating it: "In *this* hope were we *saved*," which Paul did *not* say. Here Goodspeed parted company with the crowd, translating: "If we have centered our hopes on Christ in this life, and that is all . . . ." So, more or less, Berkeley, Phillips, and Williams. The RSV has tendential translating, and utterly bad, banishing the truth to the margin.

EXHORTING US TO BE HUMAN BEINGS?

Note *a*, page 199 (I Cor. 15:49) exhorts us: "Let us bear the image of the man of heaven (as we have "the image of the man of dust"). Certainly there never was a man that consisted merely of *dust*. The Greek does not have *man*, these two times, and it does have the adjectives *earthy* or *earthly*. Our spirits, in the state of depraved humanity, are as earthly as our flesh.

ANOTHER ASSAULT ON RIGHTEOUSNESS

Marginal note *k*, page 207 (II Cor. 9:9), changes *righteousness* to *benevolence*. It seems to be a detested word in the RSV. First, it harks back to the Victorian age and becomes, of *all* things, *piety!* Then it gets a translation *right*. And now it is mere *benevolence*.

ANOTHER STANDARD RAZED

How often, when the Spirit of God raises a standard, by the Greek preposition *katá*, the RSV promptly razes it, by sheer audacity. It confesses this (note *b*, page 211 Gal. 1:11), saying: "Greek, *according to* (or *after*) *man*." The gospel is determined by the divine standard of revelation, not by human standards of philosophy or economics or sociology or ethics. This is repudiated by the RSV for the indefinite and meaningless phrase *man's gospel*.

RIGHTEOUSNESS TAMPERED WITH AGAIN

This is in note *e* (Gal. 2:21), where it is translated *justification*. But righteousness is the theme of the whole of Romans, and has many, many phases besides *justification*. The RSV translators are simply dissatisfied with the Bible.

"Anti-evangelical Bias" as to Messianic Prophecy

The Reverend J. Barton Payne, writing in *The Christian Observer* of October 21, 1953, analyzes the "anti-evangelical bias" of the RSV translation of the Old Testament, as to Messianic Prophecy. He shows that bias in cases of "choosing between possible translations," in "choosing improbable translations," "in rejecting the Hebrew Old Testament for secondary readings," and "in conjectural emendation." After analysis of these four classes of bias, this conclusion is given: ". . . were Jeremiah alive today he could well repeat, 'How do ye say, We are wise and the law of Jehovah is with us? But, behold, the false pen of the scribes hath wrought falsely."

Several of these passages we have already discussed. I cite his opinion, in part, only of the first (Gen. 12:3). "Genesis 12:3: 'In thee (Abraham) shall all the families of the earth be blessed,' a passive verb, indicating objective blessing from without. RSV: 'By you all the families of the earth shall bless themselves,' reflexive verb, indicating men subjectively blessing themselves using Abraham's name as a formula of blessing. The Hebrew *niph'al* stem may indicate either, but Gal. 3:8 shows that God intended the passive, the blessing from God being justification by faith. The Reformation stressed the principle of 'the analogy of Scripture': 'The infallible rule of interpretation of Scripture is the Scripture itself; and therefore, where there is a question about the true and full sense of any Scripture (which is not manifold, but one), it may be searched and known by other places that speak more clearly' (Westminster Confession, 1:9). Thus, for Christians, Gal. 3:8 settles which meaning to choose for Gen. 12:3. By disregarding the analogy of Scripture, the revisers of 1952 show serious bias." Of course, this is again the Hatred of Harmony, the Love of Disharmony in the Bible. We shall study this principle more in our investigation of how Jesus used a version. The marginal note *q* (Gen. 12:3) has the Messianic truth: "Or *in you all the families of the earth will be blessed.*" This is translated "*shall* be blessed" in notes at 18:18; 22:18; (note omitted at 26:4); 28:14; and Galatians 3:8; but, with its frequent inconsistency, the RSV calls Abraham *you in* Genesis and *thou* in Galatians. Funny, if it were not tragic.

THE PERENNIAL PREJUDICE AGAINST "WORDS"

This bias is shown in note *t* (Ex. 34:28), where the "ten words" as the name for the Decalogue is banished and commandments put in. How often *word* occurs for any revelation! The words, God-breathed, are the Word, be the reference to parts or the whole of Scripture. Same thing seen in Deuteronomy 4:13; 10;4.

THE ENDLESS CONJECTURES

A surprising thing about this interested me. You read through fourteen pages of the Old Testament without running on a note, "Cn," then on to page 27 for the second one, and only find the third one at page 74. But you find three on one page of the Psalms and two each on other pages. In each Testament the history, (except in Acts), is better translated than the doctrine.

THE MEAN AND CONTEMPTIBLE TRANSLATION

The Second Psalm has, to my mind, a mean and contemptible translation: "with trembling kiss his feet." The margin alleges uncertain Hebrew. This is a counsel to all the kings and rulers of the earth, so it has no reference to a tiny tenth-rate political entity which was, in its partial occupation of Palestine, a territory smaller than a Brazilian county. Most of the earth's surface did not then know that Israel existed and they hardly know it now. I know that kissing an emperor's feet is an oriental pusillanimity for they did it to the boots of the Shah of Iran the other day. And godly women did that to Jesus, too. But that is not our language. The Psalm has lost all appeal. It is repulsive in terminology. The reading of it leaves you with your face drawn and your nose turned up. Men who elegantly function on translating committees, with dilettante airs of verbal precision at the wrong places, are like a surgeon who would operate on your wife with graceful flourishes of the scalpel. Such men will never be able to understand how strongly Bible lovers feel about reverence for our Scriptures. The article just referred to tells the tricks whereby the RSV Committee got at this translation. I am not interested. One look tells me that it is wrong. The Old Testament had a very oriental way of saying *all men.* But they didn't translate that verbal literalism. They wouldn't translate *only begotten,* out of sheer prissiness, to get rid of *begot.* They wouldn't translate *gates of hades,* in a great Scripture, but gave the prosaic equivalent. They won't translate *fornication,* half the time. For that matter, they utterly banish great Bible words from the RSV, at will. Yet here they work their minds into a great devotion to a fancied literalism in language they well know believers apply and will continue to apply to Jesus, as an invitation to sinners to submit to his sovereign grace. It is all a pitiful perversity. Well does Dr. A. R. Crabtree, president of the South Brazil Baptist Theological Seminary, Rio de Janeiro, say, in the *Review and Expositor,* October, 1953: "The first ten verses seem to demand this exhortation to 'kiss the son' as an expression of loyalty and willingness to 'serve the Lord.' Various changes of the texts are found in the versions but none so radical as that of RSV." He holds that this Psalm has been "mutilated" and that other such mistranslations show "a case in which the bias of the RSV translators . . . made the psalmist say what they think he ought to have said, instead of letting him speak for himself." True. And with that outraged psalmist, apostles and prophets and their Lord could all stand together in protest, and proclaim: "So say we all." That bias was so great that in Psalm 110:1 they wrote: "The Lord said to my lord," though well knowing that their New Testament was thus repudiated when it said: "The Lord said to my Lord" (Matt. 22:44). Are not hatreds and complexes a matter for psychiatrists to look into? Modernism ought to give them a wide field.

A Complex on Sickness of the Messiah

The RSV has marginal notes from *s* to *y,* on the Twenty-Third Psalm. And it is nearly that bad on Isaiah 53. The more important the Scripture, the more they like to tamper with it. But the mania that is followed in the "Gospel According to Isaiah" is a sick Messiah, if any, rather than one who bore our sins. In place of "a man of sorrows" the margin gives us as our Messiah "a man of pains." Instead of "acquainted with grief" he is "acquainted with sickness." "He has borne our griefs" becomes "borne our sicknesses." "Carried our sorrows" becomes "carried our pains." "He has put him to grief" is changed to "he has made him sick." It is a sick Jesus. A noble converted nun, in Brazil, asked me, with a group, one day if Jesus was ever sick. I said: "The Bible doesn't say he was or wasn't, so far as I recall, and I hesitate to run ahead of the Scriptures. But I see no basis for any unauthorized judgment on our part, attributing sickness to a perfect Incarnation of God. Certainly he bore our sickness in the cures he wrought, and providentially still operates through remedies, hospitals, doctors, nurses, and so on. He bore them as a drain on his sympathy and supernatural strength, as when he felt the strain of healing the woman afflicted with an issue of blood, as when he was in a passion at the death of Lazarus (a fact of the Greek that our versions refuse to translate, by the way.) But that Jesus himself was sick seems to me improbable, to the point of being almost impossible. Sin itself is a sickness, morally considered, and that was the sphere of his substitutionary atonement." The RSV Isaiah certainly foresaw a very sick Messiah, if any. Yet we who believe think of him as the Perfect Man, radiating health and wholesomeness. As the Brazilians say: "He had health to sell" —without money and without price.

These are but samples of bias shown by marginal notes. If all were noted and clarified, a book would be needed for them alone.

CHAPTER TWENTY

MIXED FEELINGS AWAKENED

MIXED FEELINGS ARE THE NORMAL REACTION OF A BIBLE student who is also a reverent lover of the Word, as he reads the new Bible. One kind of feeling will be stirred by the text, the opposite by a note. When you begin to rejoice in a passage, you sorrow at the end because of error mixed with truth. When some delightful fidelity to the original is apparent, it is marred, often in the same sentence or context, by some indifference or contempt for another fidelity to the original that is just as urgent. This is not a theory. I give concrete examples.

FIFTY FAMOUS SCRIPTURES WELL TRANSLATED—EXCEPT ...

The RSV is like a museum of ancient art—rare vases slightly chipped, exquisite paintings torn or smudged, famous sculpture with broken parts missing. You must say of so much of its very best: "It is good *except* . . ."

John 3:16 is fine—*EXCEPT* half of the Savior's title *only begotten* is chipped off. The Greek does not have the simple word "only," but a compound word.

II Timothy 3:16 should be *Every Scripture,* not "all"; and *complete, fully equipped* has been nicked. Doubly *complete!*

Psalm 23 is almost perfect, but a note limits its horizon to this life, changing *forever* to "as long as I live."

John's Prologue is beautiful, better than before, but the Greek order of verse twelve, as in KJ, is far clearer and more impressive. And "only Son" twice is chipped truth.

The Great Commission is beautiful and the translation almost perfect. Why could it not be perfect, not changing to the singular our Lord's plural and very general demand: *all things whatsoever I have commanded,* or even Moffatt's "to obey all the commandments I have laid on you."? A wee bit chipped.

Isaiah 53 is rather faithful, but the margin paints a Sick Servant of Jehovah, rather than the *Suffering Sacrifice,* and he is "self-offered", instead of *God-offered.*

The margin almost began the Bible wrong and cheaply, with the loss of *In the beginning God.*

The Kingdom Parables (Matt. 13) are fairly accurate, but marred by the horror of mistranslating *tares* "weeds," and various petty manias, such as "fall away," "causes for sin," instead of *cause to stumble, stumbling blocks,* or such.

Isaiah 6, a favorite for beauty and power, ends in a "stump"!

I Corinthians 13 gloriously restores *love* to its primacy, rather than the cheap medievalism of Catholic "charity," but from stark prejudice banishes truth from *love's* loyalties, weakens the great verbs of *love's* manifold action to adjectives and lessens dignity of phrase.

Ezekiel's *Valley of Dry Bones* retains its fidelity and vividness, and the promise: "I will put my *Spirit* within you"; but turn back a page and you have as the New Covenant the mere promise: "And I will put my *spirit* within you." (Ezek. 37).

John 14 is mainly correct and blessed. It is a grave loss to make verse 2 a question, and deprive John's Book of Comfort of the assurance: *I would have told you.* Such a change makes one wonder about the mental judgment of the RSV. The cold, dead hand of Moffatt is at this Scripture's throat. And verse 30 is the loser, in disrespect to the Greek.

The fixed idea of invariably translating *Mercy* of the KJ as "Stedfast love" in the RSV wrecks a great promise of Isaiah 55:3, made to read: "my stedfast, sure love for David." How unutterably and unpardonably different from the *sure mercies of David,* or Moffatt's "favors promised faithfully to David," or the Basic's "an eternal agreement with you, even the certain mercies of David." Manias never help translators. But New Testament translators often correct manias of their Old Testament colleagues (Acts 13:34), at least partially. What a tragedy that there was neither unity nor harmony between the OT and the NT sections of the Committee.

Why should Moffatt be followed in reducing the third Person of the Trinity to the "holy Spirit", (Ps. 51:11; Isa. 63:11)? As a matter of fact, that is Moffatt's reduced name for the *Spirit* generally, but here he uses "sacred Spirit."

The classic on salvation by grace, Ephesians 2:8, improves much, but when the Word said: *and this not of yourselves,* it meant salvation by grace *through faith.* The RSV wrecked the structure and the resultant idea when it translated: "this is not your doing." Really, people don't *do* salvation or *do* grace or *do* the sum of it all. What is the objection to translating, rather than improvising? Neither the grace nor the Spirit-born impulse to faith nor the resultant salvation has its origin in us.

Ephesians is one of RSV's worst. We have commented on a score
of grave mistakes. The classic on Christian unity can make twenty-
one. It limits the divine fatherhood by adding "us"—"us all"—and
seems to postpone our hope as a destiny to which we were called
rather than a present element of the experience of salvation: *in one
hope of your calling,* common to all who share that hope. Eph. 4)

After Isaiah 40:13 has been cited in the New Testament twice
(Rom. 11:34; I Cor. 2:16) as "mind of the Lord," the OT Committee
comes out with the translation: "the Spirit of the Lord." The LXX
has *mind* and Moffatt, "the mind of the Eternal." At least the clarification of a note should be given the reader.

But now in Isaiah 2:1 we read, in a passage quoted as Messianic
in Matthew 12:18-21, about "my spirit" (RSV—OT) and "my Spirit"
(RSV—NT). These are senseless divergences. *There is one Spirit.*

Jude's counsel, never more needed, is: *contend earnestly for the
faith"* (KJ) "which was *once for all* delivered to the saints." Both
are right. Why may we not have both in one version? Some would
transliterate the Greek *epiagonize* for the faith, as we transliterate
baptize. While the meaning is not *agonize,* it certainly is an intense
struggle and striving. "Once for all delivered" (RSV) ought to go
with the *earnestly contending* (KJ). The Greek has both.

What sort of millenialism moves the RSV to say that the beheaded
martyrs "came to life" (Rev. 20:4)? It *could* be so translated. But
that is not the normal translation. Goodspeed and Moffatt put this
in John's mouth, but is it not tendential, to portray the contemporary
Christians as expecting an impending earthy kingdom? Is this a present
to premillenialism or a sop to Schweitzer's apocalyptism?

You have to join the RSV translation and the marginal note to get
the real Scripture about marriage, "one flesh," in Matthew 19:6.
Squeamishness?

Does the kingdom *belong* to "such" (as believing children)? No. They
belong to the kingdom, and to the King. The RSV (Matt. 19:14)
just got the meaning turned completely around.

I like "My house shall be called a house of prayer for all the nations." But when I turn from Mark 11:17 to Isaiah 56:7, it is "for
all peoples." How sad they couldn't get together.

How we hunger for a John the Baptist revival that will bring a triple
conversion: *convert* many . . . to the Lord their God, *convert* the
hearts of the fathers to the children and the hearts of children to their
fathers, and of the disobedient to the wisdom of the just (Luke 1:16,

17; Mal. 4:5). Till then, look for juvenile crime to mount. And by banishing *conversion* from prophecy and gospel, the RSV aids all crime.

Isn't it nice for the RSV to slip up sometimes and call Jesus "Thou" (Mark 1:11; Luke 3:22)? I'm so glad they forgot.

What a terrible disappointment to read: "My kingship is not of this world" (John 18:37). Is that so twisted so that the kingdom of God may be identified with socialism?

What a terrible impoverishment Christianity has suffered in that the pattern of the results of the Spirit's power have dwindled now to the "mere fruits" metioned in Acts 2:42.

"There is salvation in no one else" starts you off thinking there *is* salvation, then checks you like a dog pulled back by a leash. How much poorer than *Neither is there salvation in any other; for there is none other name under heaven given among men, whereby we must be saved* (Acts 4:12). That passage's stock went down, in the RSV market, about seventy-five per cent. And it is one of the very great Scriptures.

Philip *preached unto him Jesus* (from Isaiah 53). What a pity that had to shrink up to "told him the good news of Jesus" (Acts 8:35, RSV). It ought rather to expand; "preached to him Jesus as the gospel." This very verb, by the very RSV, is translated on the very same page (verse 40) "he *preached* the gospel."

Acts 10:47 is careless in the RSV, saying: "who have received the Holy Spirit just as we have." That isn't true. The phenomena of Pentecost were quite different. All the Greek says: *have received the Holy Spirit as well as we* (KJ). Carelessness is never a virtue in translators.

If you want to see a fair-minded translation of the shortened critical text of Acts 20:24, read the Berkeley: *However, I am not concerned about anything; neither is my life dear to myself except . . .* Contrast this rash translation: "I do not account my life as of any value . . ." Can you imagine Paul's saying irresponsible things like that?

There has to be an ear for good music in a translator—the music of words. How sweet and vigorous the KJ (Rom. 5:5): *Hope maketh not ashamed, because the love of God is shed abroad in our hearts by . . .* Contrast the RSV: "hope does not disappoint us, because God's love has been poured into our hearts through the Holy Spirit *which . . .*" That sounds as if the Holy Spirit might be some sort of sieve. Note the irreverent *which*. They promised to eliminate that fault.

"I delight in the law of God, in my inmost self" (Rom. 7:22), just before Paul says: "Wretched man that I am." Yet it sounds as if it was in the heart of Romans 8. Much more sensible and restrained is KJ: *For I delight in the law of God after* (*katá*, the preposition of standards) *the inner man*, simply means the keen legalistic fervor of Paul by the standards of an Old-Testament-enlightened conscience.

"Let him who boasts, boast in the Lord" (RSV, I Cor. 1:31). The connotation is wretched—sounds bad, smells bad. Do any of these gentlemen sing: "In the cross of Christ I boast?"

The RSV of I Corinthians 12:13 is a wrong translation, meant to boost a false doctrine. "By one Spirit were we all baptized into one body." Paul did not say that. He wrote: *In one Spirit* (*In the communion of one Spirit* is the translation of Conybeare and Howson) *were we all baptized into one body*. That means the doctrine of regeneration before baptism and church membership. Whenever the Bible talks about baptism in the Holy Spirit, *Jesus is the baptizer*, the Spirit the element into which one is baptized. By translating this falsely, everything the Gospels and Acts say about the baptism in the Holy Spirit is falsified, and wicked sentimentalists use this false Scripture to lead the unwary astray, saying: "See. There is just one baptism, and that the Holy Spirit gives. There is just one body (Church) and this Holy Spirit baptism puts you into it." Thus all the New Testament says about baptism and churches is canceled and this one false translation carries on a little civil war against the rest of the New Testament. False translation springs from false interpretation and leads further on down the same road.

Fine translation, "the majority"; poor translation, "punishment" (II Cor. 2:6). Better: *censure*.

Christ does *not* "always lead us in triumph." Silly notion. *He leads us in his triumphal train*" (figure of a Roman triumph). So Goodspeed. All the figures of a Roman general's pageant of triumph, Paul a prisoner of Christ, are here. Pity the RSV could not see that and give it expression (II Cor. 2:14-16).

The love of Christ "controls" (RSV)? Or *constrains*? The latter is more. *Control* is authority. *Constrain* is motive power, greater than resides within our own self-will. (II Cor. 5:14).

"I robbed?" says Paul (II Cor. 11:8, RSV). Here is where quotes would come in. "So I 'robbed other churches' . . . did I?"

"Have this mind in you" (Phil. 2:5, RSV)—good translation. "Which you have in Christ Jesus"—impossible translation.

Philippians 3:2 is better than either text or margin of the RSV: *We are the* (true) *circumcision* (the real Israel of God), *who worship God in the Spirit and glory in Christ Jesus and have placed no trust in flesh.* Wonderful trinity.

The name *Christian* was a name of popular contempt, in New Testament times. But we are told to live *"under* that name" (I Pet. 4:16). It is an impossible translation.

The tender ministry of Paul is compared to a "nursemaid taking care of *her own* children" (I Thess. 2:7). The RSV did not see it, or squeezed it out of the Scripture. Our loss.

I wonder if I Thessalonians 4:14 does not mean what the Greek seems to want to say: "So also will God bring those who have fallen asleep by means of Jesus, with him (in his second coming)." For *he giveth his beloved sleep,* though now no Psalm says so (Psalms 127:2).

To my way of thinking, the RSV I Timothy 3:16 and James 1:27 are mutually unaware. Better not introduce "religion" into the Timothy passage when it is not there in Greek.

The translation "the sow is washed only to wallow in the mire" is a bit hard even on the sow. (II Pet. 2:22.)

I miss the truth that *the whole world lieth in the evil one* (I John 5:19, ASV), lies there asleep, like a baby in its berth. The RSV evasion of the meaning impoverishes us.

Denunciation loses its judgment value, as a divine sentence spoken by Jesus, when *Ye fools and blind* sinks to the street level of "You blind fools!" (Matt. 23:17). Irreverence!

The concrete is more vivid than the abstract or the generic. Christ compared his care to a *hen gathering her chicks under her wings.* The RSV has made it "brood." But a hen isn't a brooder! (Matt. 23:37).

You be the judge of this diction: "The scribes sit on Moses seat." I prefer *sit in* (Matt. 23:2). The name of this kind of diction changes is legion.

These fifty passages of Scripture are like chipped vases,

marred sculpture, paintings slightly damaged. They leave
you with mixed feelings.

THE USE OF CAPITAL LETTERS

Certainly we cannot complain that it is scanty. The RSV
has "Death and Hades" in Revelation, has "the Lamb" (14:1),
but also "the Devil" (12:9), "Day," "Night," "Heaven,"
"Earth" (Gen. 1), "the Day" (II Tim. 1:12), of course "the
Word," "Sheol," and "the Pit" (Ps. 16:10, and others), and so
on. Yet Jesus is reduced to "a son of God," to "my lord" in an
Old Testament passage that is quoted as "my Lord" in the
New, and the *Holy Spirit* assumes lower-case levels in half the
Old Testament passages about the *Spirit of God.* The *Sun of
righteousness* who had *healing in his wings* has come
down, in the RSV (Mal. 4:2), to where he does not rate a
capital letter: "the sun of righteousness . . . its wings." In
Genesis 49:10, the Messianic hope is translated out of the
Bible, except a marginal reference to the disappeared
"Shiloh"; "until Shiloh come," and even that is put merely
as an alternative to "until he comes to Shiloh." No more do
Star and Scepter come out of Jacob—just a "star" and a
"scepter"—(Num. 24:17). In Psalm 45, *Thy throne, O God*
has dwindled to "Your divine throne" and a note in which the
Messianic is still given second place as the lesser of two other
possible translations. I should think that *Dispersion,* as the
proper name of the non-Palestinian Jews, merits a capital
letter in James 1:1 and I Peter 1:1 just as truly as it does in
John 7:35. Is it because the Rome-Peter line of propaganda
wants to take away these Epistles from the Jews and give
them to the dispersed Christians, under a figure of speech?
Translation, with modernists, obeys all sorts of controlling
theories, and especially in the use of capital letters. Peter is
in the Orient, writing to the Oriental Dispersion. Let him tell
the truth about himself in his own letters, which, of course,
modernism denies him.

Tell me why is God the "Creator" in Romans 1:25 and
merely "creator" in I Peter 4:19? Why is Jesus the "Shepherd"
in I Peter 2:25 and merely "the great shepherd" in the most
beautiful doxology of all literature, Hebrews 13:20? Why

should Jesus be merely the "pioneer (?) of salvation" in Hebrews 2:10, when the very same Greek word becomes "the Author of life" in Acts 3:15, "pioneer and perfecter of our faith" in Hebrews 12:2, and again "Leader and Savior" in Acts 5:31—four different translations in as many Scriptures? Is that a Bible-wide carelessness or Love of Disharmony again? Why do we have Jesus called "the Holy and Righteous One" (Acts 3:14) but less reverence shown in countless passages? Why do we not have *Son of man* in Revelation 1:13. No mere "son of man" ever had any slightest resemblance to that divine Figure. You never can tell what the RSV is going to do, in the way of reverence or irreverence. One time you have a Savior of the lower-case level and another time of Capital Majesty and Magnitude. But I remind you of the nose of the camel in the tent.

PUNCTUATION THAT "POSITIONIZES" TRANSLATORS

Translators can blot out the Nicene Creed by a period, within the limits of a given Scripture. I was reading just now a condescending interpretation that coolly affirmed that Christ is never called God in the Bible. Do such men follow Jehovah's Witnesses, in their version, and say that the Word "was god"? Probably not. They simply throw out of court all the witnesses, such as Thomas and John who affirm the contrary, and then break up sentences by the artifices of anti-Nicene punctuation and so discard a Savior who is God. Yet they will shine in Evanston in the Council of the New Catholicism, which is supposed to have no adherent who does not worship Christ as God and Savior. Can you beat that for hypocrisy?

In the whole matter of punctuation, it would help the RSV to order a truckload of commas, to separate things that are separate in thought. We have shown the carelessness of Acts 13:39 elsewhere. Take James 5:10. Nestle (Father) has a comma after "prophets." Thus the prophets who are put before us as examples are all classified as men who "spoke in the name of the Lord." But the RSV merely says: "take the prophets who spoke in the name of the Lord," as if a lot of prophets were exemplary who *did not* speak in the name of the Lord. The double offense of translating by a singular a plural noun and disregarding punctuation makes Paul say, in II Corinthians 7:5, "our bodies (mistranslation of *flesh*) had no rest but we were afflicted at every turn—fighting without . . ." That looks as if Paul were a street brawler. The grammar is: *We were afflicted . . . fighting.* See the RSV, in contrast: "afflicted on every side; without were fightings . . ."

PARAGRAPHS DISRUPT DOCTRINE

A case in Romans 10:4. There is no break in the thought here. The apostle says: "Christ is the end of the law (as death is the end of life) *so far as righteousness is concerned* (not in any antinomianism: all moral law is re-enacted and expanded by Jesus) to every one who believes. For Moses writes that the man who practices the righteousness which comes from the law will live thereby." The RSV changes that to suit its own whims. *Righteousness* disappears from the former sentence and in its place is put a dislocated clause with the verb "justify" added, also the phrase "who has faith." Then the word *for,* linking closely the two sentences in Paul's logic, is coolly thrown away and a new paragraph is made, thus disrupting the logic, so unwelcome to sacramentalists. The reason that the law ends in Christ is because it never offered the slightest hope to any but the perfect, for it called for condemnation of everyone who fails to live it continuously, which is exactly everybody. By breaking the continuity of the thought with a new paragraph, a great, clear doctrine is left in confusion, after it had already been wrecked in its wording.

THE ORDER OF WORDS MAY BE VERY EXPRESSIVE

Look, in I John 2:19, how clear the truth is now: "*they all* are not of us." If they don't *continue* in Christ's Word, they never were his disciples. A different order, *not all,* (I John 2:19, KJ) might mean: "Not all of them were ever Christians, but maybe some were." The RSV has clarified doctrine here. But in the total testimony, with the new Bible's love of the doctrine of apostasy, we have mixed feelings.

A TRANSLATION THAT HAS NEARLY ALL THE FAULTS: HEBREWS 3:14

It keeps the KJ wrong punctuation. Nestle put a period at the end of the verse. The word *beginning* is banished. The changes in the sense are wrong and wrongheaded. It is a cunning sectarian doctrine of apostasy. There is a lot of under-translation. It is of the program of Disharmony, denying eternal life to the believer. It wrecks the sentence structure. It suffers from Bible squeezers. Here is what the Greek really said: "For we have been made partakers of Christ if indeed we hold fast the beginning of our confidence firm to the end. While it is said *today,* do not harden your hearts, if you hear his voice as at the provocation (at Meribah)." The future judges the present; the performance, the possession; the fruits, the roots; the life, seen as a whole, the reality of the original salvation. That is the coherent doctrine of the Bible, deliberately wrecked here by all sorts of translation trickery. And that, too, awakens in us mixed feelings.

CHAPTER TWENTY-ONE

THE KNOWN AFFINITIES OF THE TRANSLATORS

IT IS WICKED TO DISAGREE WITH JESUS. I DID NOT SAY THAT IT is criminal, immoral, bourgeois, unrealistic, unpopular, or out of style. Wicked it is, the supreme religious fault, contrary to the entire genius and spirit of revealed Christianity. If you disagree with Jesus, he ceases at that point to be your Teacher and you withdraw from his discipleship. You put another teacher, or self, above Jesus. Your decision of loyalty or disloyalty to Christ, in your intellectual life, is self-revealing. Our affinities betray us.

This is the generation that has been noisiest in its pretense of honoring Jesus as Teacher. If you come to Jesus as Teacher you must enroll in the courses he teaches. You would not go to a teacher of Chinese to learn Hebrew, or to a school of medicine to study law. And it is arrant folly and stark hypocrisy to pretend to be a disciple of Jesus when neither his one Textbook nor the courses he taught from it have any interest to your soul.

The course Jesus came to teach is truth. "To this end was I born, and for this cause came I into the world, that I should bear witness unto the truth. *Every one that is of the truth heareth my voice.*" The yielding soul follows its natural affinities, on the natural plane, the cultural level, in the educational environment. On the supernatural plane, the course is reversed and righted, the level is the progressive and self-corrected revelation of the Bible, and the environment is the illuminating Spirit, in whom we live and learn. So the Christian life is the soul's adjustment to these two sets of affinities, which the New Testament calls the mind of the flesh and the mind of Christ.

This programmatic *word,* spoken on trial, on the Day of the Cross, was nothing more than Jesus had been saying all his life through. To the Jews he said: "Ye cannot hear my word. Ye are of your father the devil . . . he is a liar, and the father of it. And because I tell you the truth, ye believe me not. Which of you convinceth me of sin? And if I say the truth, why do ye not believe me? He that is of God heareth God's words (Notice the plural, modernist, even if it gags you): ye, therefore, hear them not, because ye are not of God." He had given those Jews a revealing test: "Then said Jesus to those Jews which had believed on him, If ye continue in my word, then are ye my disciples indeed (the future per-formance demonstrates the present state, we have found so often taught); and ye shall know the truth and the truth shall make you free." The power of natural and supernatural af-finities stands out in these Scriptures like Jordan and the Dead Sea on the topography of Palestine.

"The Word" came "full of grace and truth," for those two are inherent affinities. How can a graceless soul, or even a self-sufficient, culture-proud, popularity-seeking, back-slidden mind of a real but misled Christian have any affinity for truth apart from saving, sanctifying, illuminating, and in-structing (Tit. 2:12) grace? For spiritual things are spiritually discerned. Affinities reveal.

The method of Christ's school is revelation. He is the truth, is the Word; so he pulls the curtain aside and the truths he reveals are the words he spoke. Yes, he does more. He is the truth he reveals. His Person is revelation, his life, his re-deeming work, his character, his mission, his atoning sacri-fice, his resurrection, his ascension, his appearances both before and after his ascension. But the permanent transmission of all these truths, that come from the Truth, come through his words. "The words that I speak unto you, they are spirit and they are life." You can no more receive the truth from Jesus apart from his words than you can receive light from the sun apart from its rays. A man's affinities, that make his yielding, cowardly soul unresponsive to the Bible, reveal his fundamental attitudes to Jesus as Teacher.

Truth is often defined as reality. I have no objection. That is why I deny the idea of sacramentalism. When all the warring Catholic sects of Occident and Orient lift their raucous voices in unison and affirm that a baby they wet with holy water is born again, made a child of God, incorporated into the body of Christ, and has original sin's effects washed away, I say: "Halt. Stop right where you are. There is no reality in that. The millions of "early wet" Catholics show the facts in their lives, morally impotent, spiritually unreceptive, artificially one (?), ecclesiastically and intellectually enslaved. There is no *reality,* so no *truth,* in the pretenses of the dogma of infant baptism." The same goes for sacerdotal grace of orders, papal infallibility, external Church unity, in the role of Caesar's concubine, and all the rest of that unholy brood of untruths and unreality. No falsehood, no matter how deeply enshrined in dogma, or by what ornate prelates proclaimed, has any relation to the truth but that of the antichrists who promote that falsehood.

All revealed truth is so related to Jesus Christ, as Creator, God and Savior, Lord of life, Revealer, Teacher, Sacrifice, Priest, Friend, Reformer of Old Testament regime and its revelations of a preparatory and partial nature, Way, Life, Judge, and every other title he wears—

> *Crown him with many crowns,*
> *The Lamb upon the throne—*

that it is neither known nor assimilated in conscience and life except by our faith in Jesus Christ as Word, Revealer by his words, Truth.

When a soul yields to truth's supernatural appeal, its affinities are such that the man not only believes the truth but *"does the truth,"* lives fundamentally in harmony with the great realities of the universe, known in Christ by the Christian experience. So Jesus prayed: "They have kept thy word . . . For I have given unto them the words (always the context makes clear that the Word is the words whereby it is revealed) which thou gavest me . . . Sanctify them through thy truth: thy Word is truth." My point here is that men whose affinities are not in tune with revelation are unfit to be translators of the words of revelation. They are out of harmony with the truth they are under obligation to transmit with all fidelity. "It is the set of the sails, and not the gales, that determines how we go."

Let us turn now to examine the affinities of the translators. Is there within their minds, as revealed in *their* writings, this affinity with truth, revealed in the Word of God, as we have seen Christ's affirmations in John 8:44-46, 32;1:14,17;18:37;14:6;17:8,14,17? I am not here speaking of truthfulness. I have full faith that no one of these men would swear falsely or bear false witness against his neighbor, nor be lacking in the other things, commandments of the moral law. But in this investigation we come on places where the translation given is a question of the veracity of God, the Author of the Bible, or of the translator, the interpreter of the original Word of God and the chosen channel for its meaning to pass into the English of our day, for the new Bible. In such cases, we face a grave ethical problem. Whose veracity is lacking, that of the Revealer or that of the translator? There are not two answers to that question. When a translator gives, through bias and prejudice, a palpably false translation, such as we see in many of the cases above studied, affinities for error and unfaith have led him ethically astray. The outcome is sheer falsehood, whatever be the mental processes of the translator. And no true witness for Christ can be a party to that falsehood merely because he fears that if he exposes it and proclaims the truth denied, some one will accuse him of a "personal attack."

The bias we call modernism is a slow growth. It starts in a classroom. An infallible professor is believed when he makes the Bible appear unbelievable; he ridicules, then rapes the Word of the Savior himself to force that student to give up his faith in Scripture, under the pretext that he will, in that surrender, "know the truth" of the falseness of the Bible. That "truth will make him free" from Christ. "Free" he then is for a materialistic philosophy, "scientism," socialism, and the rest of unbelief, as far as he may let himself go, unless curbed by that same teacher because he is fearful of revealing himself, if the students go too far. By the time a man has sat in many classes, every one a Waterloo for his faith, in some matter, *his affinities for* these unbeliefs disqualify him to translate the Bible. He must twist it to fit the dogmas of unbelieving professors, or else his "truth" has not "made him free." He is a man in modernism's livery, must do his assigned job. The result is the vast literature of unfaith, published by the authors of the new Bible before being chosen translators. On that record, overwhelming in amount and cataclysmic in its false witness against eternal verities, these translators have been chosen to do their job. And they have done it well. The Bible is due to pass out of American life as the major moral factor, if this new version prevails. This deed is done with an eye back on those professors of college and university theological department classrooms. It shuts its eyes to all consequences, for the sake of conformity to the *"assured results"* of the scholarship that hates and destroys all respect for the Bible.

WHO ARE THE TRANSLATORS?

On the flap of the paper cover of this Bible, twenty-two names are listed as the translators. Of these, thirteen are university professors and five are Union Theological Seminary professors, who live and move and do their thinking under the pall of Columbia University. There are three Yale professors, two from Harvard, two from the University of Chicago, two from Oberlin, one from Vanderbilt, one from Johns Hopkins, one from the University of the South, and one from the University of Michigan. There were six ex-officio members, two from Chicago, one from New York. These controlling minds come from the great American centers of what that noble Baptist minister, Dr. Rufus W. Weaver, has called "The Revolt Against God," which he especially classified as "The Revolt of Culture Against God."

Some names on a committee are merely honorary, so far as actual work done is concerned. Professor Weigle says (p.13 of NT Introductory Pamphlet) that there were nine members of the New Testament section who worked upon it. Of the nine, seven are from this Chicago-Manhattan-Boston axis of unbelief. These universities are in a pitifully small area of the United States, to hold such a monopoly of power. Under their pall of rationalism, their part of the United States has almost lost its Christianity. Unitarianism, vastly beyond the narrow confines of the mere Unitarian sect, rationalism, Judaism of many sects and Catholicism of many brands have almost swallowed up this RSV axis of committee membership. These men are the cultural representatives of Christianity's greatest mass failure, this side of Germany, which they have all too blindly followed in its revolt against God. Men of that type are not fit to translate the Bible. Their affinity for German rationalism is shown by the fact that three of them, according to *Who's Who,* studied in nine German universities.

FREE CHURCHES—FREE FROM THIS RATIONALISM

In Britain men speak of "the Free Churches." The rather meaningless phrase refers to certain denominations that are, or were, nonconformists in regards to that great misnomer, "the Church of England." We need (and, bless God! we have), by the thousands, really free churches in America. They have never been enslaved to the intellectual leaders of this revolt of much university culture against God, in Chicago, New York, and Boston, the RSV axis. These free churches, and millions of free and believing men and women in Christ, will never accept a version handed down from the foes of revealed Christianity, and who lead a stark failure of their brand of Christianity, by the judgment of the masses of their fellow citizens who live near them and are influenced most by them.

QUOTATIONS FROM THE TRANSLATORS OF THE RSV

It would be easy to quote a library of volumes of extracts from the writings of the men who are the principal translators of this Bible and are the foremost representatives of this university axis of modernistic unbelief. Thoughtful people ought to know that record; scholarly students of theology do. I am not able financially to print such a library, or even one volume of it. I shall have to be both fair and far more brief. These men are known in their printed works. But they are also known in general works just as accurately. That picture I give here with fairness. It so happens that Vergilius Ferm has printed recently (1945) *An Encyclopedia of Religion.* In that summary of all religions I note seven articles by C. C. Craig, of Oberlin; twenty-five by Professor Edgar J. Goodspeed, of Chicago; eight by Professor J. Philip Hyatt, of Vanderbilt, once a Baylor University Baptist, now a Vanderbilt "Disciple," according to *Who's Who.* Seven are by Dean Luther Weigle, of Yale, mainly historical and containing some fine studies of early colonial preaching on the moral principles of our American Constitution and the Declaration of Independence. Six are by Professor Frederick C. Grant, priest of the Episcopal Church, of Union Theological Seminary. Assuredly no one of these is responsible for the statements of the other. But their association in a book like this, "unequally yoked together," as I have shown, with unbelievers like Professor Morton Enslin, and with a lot of pagans, and the like, as well as their personal utterances, carries a certain weight in the minds of thinking men. Consider a number of citations.

PROFESSOR GOODSPEED

This principal author of the book's New Testament studies speaks of "the descent of the spirit," page 3, dates Luke and Acts "far after Paul's time." He places the "beginning of its scripture" (that cherished by Jewish piety) as "the finding of Deuteronomy in the temple . . . in B.C. 621." It "became the nucleus of the Jewish Law, Gen.-Deut." "The prophets, Former and Latter, came to be recognized as authoritative between 250 B.C. and 175." "Christianity began as a religion not of the letter but of the spirit, and inherited a rich religious literature; moreover its keen apocalyptic expectations were unfavorable to literary composition," page 117. (We have discussed the repudiation, even in the RSV, of this translation of the favorite modernist Scripture, à la King James, about letter and spirit). The Epistle of James is held to be written in the second century, page 385. Jude is called "pseudonymous," page 407. It is dogmatically stated that the Gospel of Mark was written in Rome, probably by Mark. "It remained the pattern gospel all through the long gospel-making movement, which saw the writing of a score of gospels," page 469. An anonymous Matthew is held to have "cast Jesus' teaching into six sermons" and to have been a Jew of the Dispersion, writing not for Jews but for Greeks, page 476. On page 627 it is declared dogmatically that the letters of Paul were "not meant for publication" and that they were "for a generation left unpublished." Dogmatically also, I Peter is said to be meant for publication, and to be "an encyclical from the Roman church to the Christians of Asia Minor . . . aiming to correct some attitudes taken in the Revelation." Nothing but Disharmony in these theories. Why the general address of I Peter is proof of its being meant for publication and the general address of some of Paul's letters is proof that they were not meant for publication is not clear. The Revelation, of course, is described as "strongly influenced by the recently published collection of Paul's letters" and is held to be "strongly colored by the vocabulary and imagery of Jewish apocalyptic . . . by Greek drama, dawning Christian history, and the collected Pauline letters," page 691. The crux of the Thessalonian correspondence is analyzed as the "idleness of some who thought that the Day of the Lord had come," page 784.

THE LATE PROFESSOR C. T. CRAIG

This Oberlin professor wrote that heaven "is the biblical term for the expanse which seemed to the ancients to cover earth as a dome vault in which the heavenly bodies seemed to be placed . . . In later Christian theology heaven was looked upon as the celestial abode of the redeemed dead. That is really not witnessed to in the New Testament (Think of that! Can you beat that for infidelity? W.C.T.); in Revelation the martyrs are temporarily in heaven but they are soon to reign with Christ on the earth (Rev. 7:9ff; 20:4). But it is inhabited by various angels, some of them hostile to God (Rev. 12:7ff.). Hence heaven had to be redeemed in the eschatalogical constitution," page 327. Professor Craig died a bit ago. I hope he is where he thought he wouldn't be. I wonder what was the hope of a man like that. Why, of all men on earth, would "such a one" want to translate the Bible, unless to do it harm? On page 415, in explaining the *kenosis,* this interpretation is given of Philippians 2:7: "The heavenly Christ gave up what he possessed . . ." Could anyone make a more irresponsible statement on any subject? Dr. Craig says: "Wellhausen showed that the original tradition (about lives of Jesus) consisted of small pericopes (1911). These were classified according to form by Dibelius (1919) and Bultmann (1921) and others. The result is that New Testament scholarship now generally realizes that it is impossible to write a life of Jesus. No chronological framework for it exists, and the individual traditions inevitably bear the mark of the interests of the apostolic church," page 447. That reduces the New Testament to shreds and writes an interrogation point on each shred. On page 451, Professor Craig says: "The final form of the gospel tradition placed the resurrection of Jesus on the third day (Sunday) rather than 'after three days.' Though the seven day week corresponds to the Jewish practice, they did not name their sabbath for their God. In Egypt, months and days were named for gods." There is much more of like implications.

PROFESSOR J. PHILIP HYATT

Of Genesis, he writes: "Moses is considered to be the author by Jewish, Christian and Islamic tradition, but the book is the product of a long process of writing and editing by J., E. and P, reaching its final form about 400 B.C. . . . The first eleven chapters contain profound religious myths which resemble those of other civilizations of the ancient Near East . . . The remainder of Genesis consists of legends . . .," page 296. Let these gentlemen get them out a mythology to their liking and as many books of legends as they can entertain the childish with. But let them keep unholy and irreverent hands off our Bible. It has a right to be translated by men who give it their faith.

Yet Professor Hyatt is a party to the solemn declaration of the new Bible that Genesis is "The First Book of Moses." Here he places what he considers a flat falsehood on the very first page of what he translates and sends that falsehood out to millions, over his signature. That is a grave moral problem in his life. And some day he will face all the readers of the new Bible before the judgment bar of God and give account of its seducing effects, to which he is a party. On page 400 he denies the trustworthiness of Joshua. I and II Kings are held to be of Deuteronomic origin, and from that source is supposed to have come "the doctrine of centralization of all sacrificial worship in the Jewish temple, and of divine retribution for human deeds," page 419. The book of Ruth is thus described: "The book has usually been interpreted by modern scholars a work of the Persian period designed to protest against the strict views of this age (e.g., of Ezra and Nehemiah) regarding inter-marriage with foreigners. This date has recently been doubted; the language of the book and its socio-legal background (if real rather than purely fictional) suggests a late pre-exilic, date." Professor Philip Hyatt makes one mistake in words. He says his is the interpretation of "modern scholars." Of course, he means *modernist* scholars and pseudo-scholars.

USING SOUTHERN BAPTIST SCHOLARS AS A BLIND

Much is being made of illustrious Southern Baptist names as a blind, to hide the nature of this version from unsophisticated readers. I refer to A. T. Robertson and John R. Sampey. (By a strange blindness toward scholarly and moral values, the Fern *Encyclopedia,* which mentions hundreds of names, many that the general reader never heard of before, including even Father Divine, does not have either Robertson or Sampey on its horizon. For these men, there have been only three scholars among Southern Baptists: John A. Broadus, three and a half lines; E. Y. Mullins, four and a quarter lines; and W. H. Whitsitt, seven lines. Father Divine has thirty-eight lines. The Baptists who write in the *Encyclopedia* never heard of A. H. Newman, Robertson, Sampey, W. O. Carver, or George Truett. Yet they give forty-four lines to Benjamin Warfield and fifty-four to John Gresham Machen. While members of the RSV Committee are co-authors of that book, "unequally yoked together" in its authorship, they do not share its contempt for Baptists just now. Rather are they using Southern Baptist scholars as a blind, in the propaganda in the South, indeed in general. Kindest reference are made to Dr. Sampey (Introductory OT pamphlet p. 18) and "his official position as chairman of the Old Testament section." However, that was terminated before the translating work was done. Dr. A. T. Robertson died in 1934 and had absolutely nothing to do with the translation, so far as is indicated. The conservative translations of these men are on record. and their interpretation that demands such a faithful translation. There is no excuse for trying to throw any blame for this present version on these two revered names, or for implying any approval on their part to perversions of the Scripture they utterly detested. I have cited Dr. Sampey on the traditional ending of Mark's Gospel. He certainly did not detach it from the Gospel and put it in the basement of a footnote.

The OT Introduction Booklet says, page 4: "Dr. Yates, after eight years of active service, accepted the pastorate of the Second Baptist Church, Houston, Texas, and has since then shared in the committee's work only by correspondence and the criticism of proofs." I had a conversation, in Louisville, Kentucky, with Dr. Yates about this version, on my furlough of 1945-46. I could not, and would not, of course, reproduce the conversation, which was private. I should say, however, in view of these facts, that this detachment of Dr. Yates, and his books, with their known biblical loyalties, seem to me to leave Dr. Yates free from any responsibility for wrong translations or attitudes herein criticized, except as he may put himself on record as favorable to them. That I regard as impossible.

The whole use of Southern Baptist conservative scholars as a blind for the radicalism of much of the wrong spirit and results of the version seems to me a base injustice both to the men involved and to our people as a whole. Our Sunday School Board continues to use the Uniform Lessons and is associated with this general organization in that one respect. They have given public assurance that they do not expect to use the RSV in their publications. They are in no sense co-sponsors of this new Bible. The best reply to this misrepresentation of the facts will come from our churches themselves and the attitude they take toward this version in public worship and private devotion. I have taken part in worship and gatherings of all kinds this past year in ten states. The place the RSV occupied in those gatherings was virtually nil, except perhaps in one per cent of the number, and that was in every case purely individual. Time will make the reply of our autonomous churches more and more clear and vocal. There is a longing of our Greekless laity and Christian women to know the facts. That is my reason for writing.

THE CONSTANT "FLUX" OF THE COMMITTEE

Professor Irwin thus described the working of the Old Testament Committee: "The alignment of the committee was in constant flux." By this he meant the grouping of members on the issues that followed one after the other, always changing. But that is true also of its makeup. "The initial draft of the revision of each of the books of the New Testament was prepared by one or two members of the Section, to whom it was assigned." After discussion, "a new draft, prepared by Dr. Moffatt, in the light of the decisions then reached was . . . distributed for further study, "pages 13-14. "The first meeting of the reconstituted committee began at 9 A.M., Dec. 3, 1937, in the Directors' Room of the Union Theological Seminary, New York. It was to prove the only meeting of the full committee," page 16, OT Introductory Booklet. Five more Old Testament scholars were added to the committee in 1945. A second edition of the Old Testament revision was worked out. Professor G. R. Driver, of Oxford University, on invitation, "read and commented upon the drafts of many of the Old Testament books" (idem., p. 92). Famous name! You see that it is virtually a different committee at the end of all this flux.

Dean Weigle says: "Translation is an art . . . Of all the characteristics of a sound translation the reproduction of the spirit of the original text is the most difficult to attain. It is as rare and as elusive as is the best in any art. It may be hindered by the temperament, character, and spirit of the translator . . . or by the temperament, character, and experience of the people for whom the translation is made and the spirit of the age in which they live" (p. 12 of the English New Testament, by Dean Weigle). Affinities, then, are of the essence of this problem, affinities with Jesus as Teacher and the truth which he teaches by his words, or affinities with rationalism, unbelief, modernism, and subjectivism. What affinity for a true and spiritual translation would such university professors have, in the atmosphere of unbelief in which their whole academic life is lived? The affinities of the makers of the RSV are in an artificial world, unrelated to the currents of American Christianity that flow in the homes, the churches, and the hearts of the "common people", to whom Jesus made his special appeal.

TRANSLATOR FREDERICK C. GRANT, ON THE GOSPELS

The translator whom Mr. Ferm seems especially to have chosen to write on the Gospels is Professor Frederick C. Grant, of Union Seminary, of course. His is the article on

"Form Criticism," the style of theological unbelief that became all the rage with American modernists about the time our nation conquered Germany in the Second World War. We conquered their cities; they our university theological departments, such as created the RSV. His analysis of the Gospels (p. 285) as defined by the *Formgeschichte* movement, so victorious over our timid doctrinal soldiers, is this: "The Old Stories (including the Passion Narrative), Parables, Sayings, the Great Miracle Tales, Legends. It is of course recognized that later editorial settings (or "frames," *Rahmen*), interpretations, revisions, and constructions must be removed." Professor Grant does not affirm these theories, merely presents them in the name of Dibelius and others—presents them, without dissent, with no defense of the Gospels, though such theories reduce the Gospels to fragments, with a tiny minimum that is believable.

Professor Grant does commit himself to one thing: "Perhaps the chief value of form criticism is its emphasis upon the fact that the gospel tradition was handed down within the group, the church." Of course, that is false. There was no such limitation. Luke wrote to an individual, and one, judging by the use of the honorific title, who was not yet a church member. There is not the slightest mention of the word *church* in three of the Gospels. And the one that mentions the subject is the Gospel especially to outsiders, the Jews, and very naturally quotes the Savior where he reveals his purpose first, as to "*my* church," versus the old Congregation of the Lord that he so often attended in its temple gatherings; and, second, as to church discipline, as Christians were to practice it, versus the local synagogue discipline to which the Jews were accustomed. The word *church* does not mean community. This is just one more nexus between the new Bible and the New Catholicism. The old Catholicism of the popes maintained that the Church was before the Bible and guarded it and formed its canon. The New Catholicism goes the popes one better and holds that the Church created the Gospels out of its own "Old Stories, Miracle Tales, Legends," rehandled anonymously in endless turnovers of modifications. The RSV translators out-Herod Herod, give more to this Catholic myth than the medieval Catholicism does. Contrary, therefore, to all the facts,

Professor Grant speaks of the "impersonality and anonymity" of the Gospels (p.308). Why did the RSV, then, fool the public, speaking of "the Gospel of Luke" and "the Gospel of John"? Professor Grant uses both those phrases, verbatim, on page 39 and page 40 of the RSV NT Introductory Pamphlet. That is a moral problem. That he could in one book give those Gospels authors, as if speaking sincerely, and in another book allege their "impersonality and anonymity," is an ethical issue no modernist will ever escape till he stands before God's judgment bar and takes it all back with shame, before men and angels. Did I not read the other day of the illustrious gentleman's death? Ah! how much better he knows now that he is away from Union Seminary. Could he only come back from the dead and tell us better than he wrote. Yet I hear one say down the centuries: "If they hear not Moses and the Prophets, neither will they be persuaded, though one rose from the dead."

Professor Grant writes at great length on the many sources of the Gospels and adds: "This multiple Source Hypothesis fits the requirements of the Form Criticism: the earliest sources are fragmentary crystallizations of the oral tradition." (p. 757.)

PROFESSOR GRANT ALSO ON JESUS CHRIST

To Professor Grant is given the high honor of writing the chief article of the book: "Jesus Christ" (pp.392-394). Here are excerpts, which I quote without comment: "Every item in the evangelic tradition has to be examined and accepted or rejected upon its own merits." "The oldest tradition represents Jesus as a native of Nazareth. The later legend of his birth in Bethlehem was doubtless inspired by the dogmatic interpretation of the Old Testament." "He must indeed have been baptized (or baptized himself, as the custom was) at the bidding of John." "It is not at all improbable that Jesus' ministry included Judea as well as Galilee, but this must remain a probability rather than a certainty." "The journeys of Jesus can no longer be traced on a map." "Jesus taught that God is the Father of all men and that they are brothers in the one great human family. Passages in the gospels which seem to

point in the opposite direction are probably assignable, upon
other grounds, to a strain of tradition affected by ultra-Judais-
tic groups in Jerusalem in the 40s and 50s." "He did not proclaim himself as Messiah." "The story of the last days of
Jesus is of course told from the Christian point of view and
was never looked upon as a documentary account of the pro-
ceedings. It is a question whether or not any of the disciples
or other early Christians had personal recollection of what
transpired in the high priests' court. What we are told in the
Marcan Passion Narrative is probably either hearsay or in-
ference." "For the primitive church it was not the historical
Jesus but the spiritual Christ, the Lord of his community, the
church, which was all important." At the very beginning of
this article, Professor Grant had simply dismissed as "Catholic" the "approach" to the interpretation of Jesus which would
"begin with the idea of the Incarnation . . . took our flesh upon him . . . His life, therefore, was a sucession of divine manifestations and his teaching had the oracular quality of the
final proclamation of eternal truth."

Dr. Grant dismisses John's Gospel as containing only a
"substratum of historical reminiscences . . . largely overlaid
by later theological and mystical exposition." "Even in Mark"
there is declared to exist this "theological element." You
would think theology was leprosy, yet this gentleman spent
a life in living off the propagation of that leprosy. Professor
Grant is—or was—a priest (something utterly alien to revealed Christianity) in an unscriptural Episcopacy. Priest
Grant succeeded in reducing Christianity to ruins and rubble,
right where, in the same book, brilliant Roman Catholic and
pagan spokesmen for their religions glorify their founders,
"saints," and systems of thought. And the foremost members of
the RSV Committee, including the chairman, are unequally
yoked with the unholy deed; and some of them contribute
the most unchristian and antichristian thought I have read in
a half century of Christian ministry. This is the spirit of the
New Catholicism and its new Bible. You can understand now
why the RSV murders Messianic prophecy. They don't believe, in so far as they accompany Professor Grant, that Jesus
"proclaimed himself to be the Messiah." Why, then, leave
Messianic prophecy in the Bible?

THE HURRAH AND THE BALLYHOO

Haste makes waste. The unseemly rush to get this new Bible on the market, just to take one instance of its evil results, made the translations of the Old Testament Scriptures cited in the New outrageously contradictory or divergent from the language the Old Testament Committee *later* adopted. If they could only have waited and gotten together! The effort was made to get titanic approval and commitment, before the people and their ministry had time to examine the new Bible. Many thus committed themselves irresponsibly. About 3,400 rallies were held. A lot of morally low-down, but politically high-up, politicians, whom the people quickly repudiated in disgust, were roped in to give the sanction of Church and State, which is of course a thing the New Catholicism is very eager for. Look how it is related to the State in Europe. Of course, not only the crapshooters in Washington, but many fine men in all the capitals, from office, classroom, and pulpit, came, saw, and were conquered, without having been allowed even a peep into that to which they were giving their total approval, for all the people. They are going into this New Catholicism just as carelessly, just as unsuspectingly, just as irresponsibly, with the same ballyhoo and hurrah, from Evanston on, next year and after. One and one half millions of people were present. The newspaper space and slick-magazine space sought and given was formidable. Now two million copies have been sold. A big profit goes to the Council of the New Catholicism.

WILL IT WIN?

Wait and see. You can't fool all the people all the time. Is this the victory? The publishing event has been pushed by skilled advertising as no other event in literary history, many say. Yet Harper's *Bible Dictionary* (p.165) says that within a year after the Revised New Testament was published in England, in 1881, three millions of copies were sold. Did it win? This very version is a tombstone to Nelson's other "authorized" Bible that also seemed sure to win. A great battle against these revisions was waged. The warriors who fought lost. But the people who were indifferent to them gave them the victory later. The English and the American Revisions are both dead. The King James, which they meant to supplant, lives on, more read, more loved, more preached than ever before.

DISAGREEMENT WITH CHRIST IS WICKED, I REPEAT

This is not an academic discussion. Jesus Christ has never been wrong. When men disbelieve, it is because of mental and moral defects in them, not in Jesus. When they use chicanery and cunning and the pressures and politics of ecclesiastical propaganda, they can teach even Tammany new tricks. The supreme difference between a conservative Bible faith and so-called "liberal" unfaith is a difference in ethics, common morals, and reverence for the Absolute. No man ever went off at a tangent from the Bible except because of a moral quirk in his character and in mental integrity. To that I attribute the root errors of attitude that have made the new Bible what it ought not to be. That can go along with a surface sincerity and stable character in things not affecting the Bible. The falseness and wickedness are in the fundamental attitudes that array the soul against God and Christ and the Bible. Men's affinities identify them morally. That holds for translators.

THE SENSITIVENESS TO UNIVERSITY ILLITERACY

It is perfectly natural that a group of modern university professors should be sensitive to what I have spoken of as "university illiterates." By the term I mean a generation whose education has been in materialistic subjects and whose faith has been wrecked in the classroom by sneers at the Bible. I could quote from the world's best and greatest as to this shameful fact, the lament of thoughtful people on every hand. I took a special course once with John Gresham Machen, in Princeton. Many university men took his courses. This one required a massive library investigation, personal consultations with the professor, classroom work, and a lot of writing. The classroom work was on what seemed to me a low level, though very exacting. Dr. Machen explained that to me one day privately: "We get students from all the universities and colleges. You have to teach them the elementary things about their own and any other language. They have no idea what a noun is, a verb, a pronoun, or an adjective. It has to be made simple and clear, as for children." That is seen in his book for beginners in Greek. Now it is to these university illiterates that our new Bible has been adapted. They have heard blatant mockery at the sex frankness of the Bible. So out the window it goes, even to the point where John 3: 16 is operated on to remove the latter half of "only begotten." These university illiterates have heard ten thousand sneers against "the old War Lord Jehovah." Out the window went the covenant Name. They will allow Dr. Kinsey to speak very plainly of sex, but not the Bible, so fornication is banished—not from life but from the moral vocabulary. Read *God and Man at Yale,* by William F. Buckley, Jr., if you want to see this problem of religion in the university from the inside.

HATRED AFFECTING AFFINITIES

A quotation has been given about Coe's *"virulent antipathy* toward traditional religion." Modernism hates conservative scholarship with an unholy hatred. To the person who has not kept track for decades with the intolerance felt toward conservatives, as shown in such episodes as the rape of Princeton and the hounding to their death of such scholars as John Gresham Machen and Robert Dick Wilson, it is impossible to know how deep the hatred of "liberals" is for "conservatives." Many of these are unutterably cowed. There is academic freedom for every voice that denies and insults the Savior and his Word, but none for conservative faith, in spheres where modernism is in control. It is tolerated only in institutions also about to be raped a little later on, but where a few conservatives serve now as a blind. Jesus said: "Everyone that is of the truth heareth my voice." Men's affinities are portraits of their very souls. Every disagreement with Jesus shows a moral defect in the culprit.

THE RSV REPRESENTS A HAS-BEEN PHILOSOPHY

The control of religion by the dominance of men cowed by the university illiterates is passing. A translation begotten of that fear speaks yesterday's idiom. Its translators are has-beens. The revolt against them is on. The "assured results" they put above the Bible have progressively made Germany, Britain, and America pagan at the top, but the renewing is coming from the ground up. A man said to me on my last furlough: "There is no future for foreign missions, all the world is going communist." The RSV translators seemed to think so, too. It isn't. This is "the end of an era," the era domineered by that type of mind. The new president of Yale repudiated the former president's religious outlook and announces a different one, far closer to revealed religion. Just as the RSV finally came out, *Theology Today* gave a whole issue to "Science and Religion in the Universities." It brings many voices in repudiation of the era and the affinities represented by the RSV. *The British Weekly* has had articles recently on the "cruelty of scientism." Men cry aloud publicly now in protest against John Dewey. Even Harvard stirs in revolt against Unitarianism. Communists in professors' chairs are squirming like worms, in the flames of public indignation. An educator in another university protests, virtually, that there is no academic freedom without equal academic responsibility. Just as the "affinities" of the RSV for a dead day triumph, in shame and violence to the Scripture and insult to the Lord Jesus in many ways, lo! their day is past. They are has-beens. They won't yield easily. But the people will write of this "Authorized Version"—"Mistaken Idea Unauthorized, by the Supreme Court of Public Christian Opinion."

CHAPTER TWENTY-TWO

WHEN OUR RELIGION LOSES ITS "THOU"

"THOU" APPEARS COUNTLESS TIMES IN THE RSV. THE HURRAH and the hullabaloo assured the country that "thou" had gone. But it has been retained, in a very jerky, inconsistent fashion. We have cited cases where it is used of Jesus in New Testament passages but not in the Old Testament passages translated in the New. The Old Testament and the New Testament Sections of the Committee were at civil war, on that issue, repeatedly.

The Bible that refuses, generally, when it thinks about it, the reverence of a "thou" to Jesus, gave that honor to old fallen Babylon: Of her we read: "Alas! alas! thou great city, thou mighty city, Babylon! In one hour has thy judgment come." And several other lines are peopled with "thou," denied to Jesus. Of course, we are told, there is something poetic about Babylon—not about Jesus. She must be honored with "thou" poetic reverence. But the Second Psalm may be spoken in the common speech of over-the-fence gossip.

This is a very arbitrary decision by the RSV. They take the place of God. When he himself says "thou," in both sides of a dialogue, they assume the mastery and say: "No! God, let's go fifty-fifty. To thee we shall say *thou*. But we will only permit thee to say *you* to the people." Time and again you feel the lopsidedness of that decision and its uneven style. One side of the dialogue says "thou"; the other side says "you." They seem to have made up God's mind for him, contrary to what he himself deliberated.

The RSV introduction coolly assures us that the people (the university illiterates, of course) never hear this language except in the Bible. Strange ignorance. Don't these gentlemen ever go to church? Have they never sung hymns? Let the next translators know hymnology. Every Sunday morning millions worship in "thou" hymnology. That is the most frequent use of poetry and verse in American life. It follows into family worship, weekday prayer meetings, mothers so croon to their babies, people so lighten the burden of work every day of life. "Thou" is all over the American scene, except for our university illiterates who were educated on sneers against

327

the "old War-Lord Jehovah." I suppose they would not sing: "Guide me, O thou great Jehovah!"

Our university illiterates—do they study Shakespeare? How are they going to understand the English language, above the level of the "funnies"? What will they do with history, American and English oratory that made history, Quaker talk and much else historic?

Consider the polyglot origin and makeup of our population. To begin in New England, New York, and Chicago, the RSV axis, there are vast areas of foreigners where the whole talk in the home is a "thou-thee" conversation. There are a half million Portuguese in the U.S.A. and they talk "thou" talk. Most of the other Latins of our countrymen, here by the millions, do, too. So do many other languages. Their worship in the multitudes of churches of their faith has grounded that in their thought and reverence for all religion. It is nowhere alien to *them*.

If our Bibles are not to have "thou," in fair and sensible translation, no matter who is spoken to, then they had better not have the word at all. The Basic Bible excludes it altogether. The mixture is horrible. When you hear a man praying "Lord, we thank you for the blessings, thou hast showered upon us in your wonderful love," doesn't that give you the creeps? Yet I have heard college and seminary professors and pastors of large churches of cultured people pray in just as mixed up a manner. Perhaps that is a transition to a non-thou age and manner of speech. If so, let our Bible say "you."

THE MORALS OF A "THOU" TYPE OF PERSONAL RESPONSIBILITY

Let's examine two Decalogues. You have the KJ and the RSV before you. Let's see the Basic (*you* talk) and the Moffatt (*you* talk, too).

BASIC	MOFFATT
You are to have no other gods but me.	You shall have no gods but me.
You are not to make any image or picture of anything in heaven	You shall not carve any idols for yourselves, the shape of any-

or on the earth or in the waters under the earth; you may not go down on your faces before them or give them worship: for I, the Lord your God, am a God who will not give his honor to another; and I will send punishment on the children for the wrongdoing of their fathers, to the third and fourth generation of my haters; and I will have mercy through a thousand generations on those who have love for me and keep my laws.

You are not to make use of the name of the Lord your God for an evil purpose; whoever takes the Lord's name on his lips for an evil purpose will be judged a sinner by the Lord.

Keep in memory the Sabbath and let it be a holy day.
On six days do all your work: But the seventh day is a Sabbath to the Lord your God; on that day you are to do no work, you or your son or your daughter, your man-servant or your woman-servant, your cattle or the man from a strange country who is living among you; for in six days the Lord made heaven and earth and the sea, and everything in them, and he took his rest on the seventh day and made it holy.

Give honor to your father and to your mother, so that your life may be long in the land which the Lord your God is giving you.

Do not put anyone to death without cause.

thing in heaven above or on the earth below or in the sea; you shall not bow down to them nor worship them, for I the Eternal, your God, am a jealous God, punishing children for the sins of their fathers, punishing those who hate me, down to the third and the fourth generation, but showing kindness to thousands of those who love me and obey my orders.

You shall not use the name of the Eternal, your God, profanely; for the Eternal will never acquit anyone who uses his name profanely.

Remember to hold the sabbath sacred. Six days you may labor and do all your business, but the seventh day is the sabbath in honour of the Eternal, your God, and on it you must do no business, neither you nor your son nor your daughter nor your slaves, male or female, nor your cattle, nor the alien who is among you; for in six days the Eternal made sky and earth and sea and all that they contain, and then he rested on the seventh day; therefore the Eternal blessed the sabbath, making it a sacred day.

Honor your father and your mother, that you may have a long life in the land which the Eternal, your God, is giving you.

You shall not murder.

Do not be false to the marital relation.	You shall not commit adultery.
Do not take the property of another.	You shall not steal.
Do not give false witness against your neighbor.	You shall not give false evidence against a fellow-countryman.
Let not your desire be turned to your neighbor's house, or his wife or his man-servant or his woman-servant or his ox or his ass or anything which is his.	You shall not covet a fellow-countryman's household; you shall not covet a fellow-countryman's wife, nor his slaves, male or female, nor his ox, nor his ass, nor anything that belongs to a fellow-countryman.

Now what is lacking in these You-type Decalogues? Certainly not a high moral standard. The question is manifold: (1) Do we well to say "you," when God says "thou"? Might not our judgment weigh less than God's, in his and our comparative knowledge of mankind? (2) Is there the moral directness, the spiritual pungency, the personal note of responsibility in "you" which there is in "thou"? The Committee itself in more than one place confesses that it debated this question for two years. Pressure of the moderns won, over reverence and power of moral appeal. (3) As a basis of national morals is "you" or "thou" better? There exists no conscience in the interstices between the *persons* who constitute the State and the citizenship. God spoke to the *nation* Israel, assembled in his presence, not personifying the people but laying all moral obligation directly on the personal conscience. The whole of a living organism functions though the health and life in every part. When we lose our "thou" morality, no bureaucracy will ever discover any substitute. Collectivism is essentially unmoral.

Worship is a primary consideration of thoughtful Christianity. *The Lutheran* (July 29, 1953) says: "Reasons why they prefer the King James translation, rather than the RSV, for liturgical reading at Sunday services came from the Committee on Liturgy which has prepared a new Service Book and Hymnal for Lutheran Churches . . . In numerous verses, say the commissioners: 'the RSV text uses words less current in

English today than the AV word it replaces, and in many cases a word whose meaning is less clear and more difficult to pronounce.' Another criticism is on the question of prose rhythm. In the King James translation there is 'the smooth-flowing meter of classical Latin, of which the 1611 translators were deeply conscious.' Commissioners said: 'it is hard to believe that the translators of the RSV even thought about it.' (Just as they seem never to have remembered at all that people sing. W.C.T.) There should be no objection to using in Scripture reading in church a language which differs from everyday English, the commissioners urge: 'We have military and naval English, educational and scientific English, sociological and medical English, legal and business English, officialese and gobbledygook.' The King James English is 'the specialized language of the English-speaking part of Christendom.'"

When our religion loses its "thou," it loses much of the spirit of its reverence, courtesy, social, and literary charm. *The Bible Translator* calls attention to the lack of courtesy in much modern translation, utterly alien to American courteous use of pronouns. Many ancient and modern languages demand the order of pronouns: "I and you and he," says Eric F. F. Bishop. That's not the way we show courtesy. Just the reverse order of pronouns is indispensable. Yet the RSV, with all its modernity and modernism, never seems even once to have thought how rude it is to have Paul say: "myself and Apollos" (I Cor. 4:6); "I or they" (I Cor. 15:11); "my spirit as well as yours" (I Cor. 16:18); "for me and for yourself" (Matt. 17:27); "I and the Father" (John 10:30); "my . . . your, my . . . your" (John 20:17). If it was going to be modernized, why put the first personal pronoun first so often? Every courteous reader would unquestionably say Apollos and I, my Father and I, and so on. The RSV liquidation of half the "thou" Scripture in our religion and retention of the other half, seems to me a further discourtesy, this time to God himself—to whom discourtesy is irreverence—added to this mania for putting self first in a letter-fidelity of the translation to an order of words in the original, precisely where the idioms differ utterly.

Again in *The Lutheran,* we find these words from Elson

Ruff (Sept. 2, 1953): "Much of our hour in church is not intended for our instruction. It is the offering of prayer and praise, which we make to God . . . But it is quite right for this language to be exalted and noble, tinged with mystery, because that is what worship is . . . Our hymns and prayers and chants are in the language of poetry and don't have to be kept up to date . . . The church is more than a schoolroom. It is the temple where humans encounter the tremendous mystery of the divine Lord. This is no ordinary transaction. Let it take place in the most sublime and beautiful language we can devise."

Besides the loss of moral directness, courtesy, reverence, and literary charm above discussed, simple clarity is horribly sacrificed at times. In Philemon 2:4 the RSV leaves the impression of a letter to "you," whereas Paul said "thou," Philemon alone. In Genesis 32:28, the RSV either does not admit the truth of the narrative, nor all our devotional language grown out of it, or else it inconsistently calls God "you." In Luke 22:32, the RSV has to add a note to clarify its adjacent pronouns "you," one singular, one plural. Luke 3:22 has the Father address Jesus, "thou," in utter inconsistency. On page 457, you again find necessity for explaining where "you" is plural. On page 625, there is an utter confusion of "thou" reference to God and an immediate and confusing "you." You utterly miss, in the RSV, the greatly significant fact that Jesus says "thou" to Nicodemus, but through him speaks to his whole body of Pharisees: "*Ye* must be born again . . . *Ye* do not receive our testimony" (John 3:7,11). The RSV made not the slightest effort to be clear. The KJ is clear, but the RSV is utter confusion, at the point of departure in Deuteronomy 5:32, where God leaves off talking to Moses with "thou" and begins talking to Israel with "ye." There is a King James hangover in Galatians 4:27, "thou" and even "who hath," which the Old Testament committee, in Isaiah 54:1, made to come back to taw. If consistent, Matthew 11:10 takes away from Jesus his Forerunner, making John the Forerunner of God. For sound, read this: "Lord, have mercy on us, Son of David" (Matt. 20:31). The heart cries out for the King James: "O Lord, thou Son of David." "Thy eyes" (Ps. 139:16,) and elsewhere makes my flesh crawl. Well does Walter Russell Bowie say (Introduction to NT Booklet, p.63): "We have lost something of beauty when we left behind us some of the more intimate personal pronouns, and the stately endings of our verbs. 'What are you doing' lacks the gentleness of 'Whåt doest thou?' 'Where did you come from?' sounds harsh beside 'Whence camest thou?' Reluctant recognition that a lovely word once instinctively used is no longer part of current speech, changes 'there were in the same country shepherds abiding in the field' to 'In that region there were shepherds out in the field'; but, so saying, it is as though for a moment a glory seems to fade." The plural call to repentance is strong in the message of both John and Jesus, Matthew 3:3; 4:17; and in Matthew 20:22, for lack of the distinct plural pronoun, you have to turn back and read again to see where Jesus leaves off speaking to the ambitious mother and addresses himself to the eager sons, for whom their mother was a front. Professor Goodspeed keeps the record straight, in Matthew 23:37, "O Jerusalem, Jerusalem, murdering the prophets and stoning those who are sent to *her*." That shows the pronouns of the second person must be singular. But the RSV, for a dead uniformity, changes "her" to "you" and no one can tell that the city is personified and addressed in the singular.

In God himself there is the spirit of *noblesse oblige*. We are made in his image. He addresses us as "thou" as naturally as we so address him in prayer. It is of the dignity of the human spirit. "All souls are mine." Their Maker honors them and magnifies their worth and value and responsibility with the divine "thou!" When we lose it in our religion we have despised a divine gift and calling.

CHAPTER TWENTY-THREE

HOW JESUS USED A VERSION

THE SEPTUAGINT VERSION OF THE OLD TESTAMENT WAS THE Bible of our Lord, his people, his apostles, the early churches, and the writers of the New Testament, which came alongside the original Scriptures as the literary revelation of the truth and will of God. How Jesus acted toward that version of the original Hebrew Scriptures must inevitably be of the greatest importance to reverent Bible students. We may feel certain that six elements enter into his use of the LXX.

They are these: (1) The Hebrew original was the sole literary authority. Books on the quotations from the Old Testament in the New show that our Lord and his apostles neither approved any opposition of the LXX to the Hebrew nor did they fail to revert to the original and correct the current Greek translation, when it misled the people. (2) The LXX was in the hands of the religious teachers of the people. Where the version in common use, memorized by all the faithful in many of its sayings, varied from the original, the variation and the original could both be true, as far as the sense was concerned. Jesus did not make public worship a class in textual criticism. He let the version stand, when its citation gave truth to the ears, even though that true wording was not identical with the Hebrew truth. (3) The LXX sometimes added truth, which the Hebrew did not contain. Our Lord sometimes used that truth, though not accurate translation, without a disconcerting lecture on textual criticism in the midst of the public worship. (4) He let minor inaccuracies pass, when not for the moment apposite to the matters in hand. There is a time for all things. Had he presided over a new translation for his people, he might well have modified the language, probably without doing violence to the continuity of the religious life and thought of his people. (5) He quoted freely. He summed up citations. And his own words were summed up. I have often shown that verbal accuracy and inspiration do not involve verbatim citation and inspiration. (6) The Author of the original Hebrew Scripture and the Greek citations of it by our Lord and his apostles, in forming Christian doctrine and recording it in new Scriptures, is the inerrant Spirit of God. Within the liberty of his purpose, and of the style, limitations, and message of the authors of the new Scriptures, the Spirit "moved" the Scripture writers to their God-breathed New Testament in utter harmony of Old and New. Never did the Holy Spirit err, nor did he let his Anointed One err, whose relation to that Spirit was measureless.

"THE BEAUTY OF HOLINESS"

Now take this King James phrase, *the beauty of holiness* for example. I love it. But it has disappeared from our RSV altogether. In its place we have merely "in holy array," in I Chronicles 16:29; II Chronicles 20:21; Psalms 29:2; 96:9; 110:3. Moffatt rules the RSV idea with his "in sacred vestments" or "festal attire." In other words, "the beauty of holiness" has degenerated into clerical vestments, which is about as low as a noble idea can sink. This butchery of a great thought, with no horizon for any spiritual sense to its possibly figurative meaning, seems to me superlatively stupid. Again, affinities reveal.

THE STANDARDLESS SPIRIT NOW

The Bible is a book of standards, of principles, of eternal truth, not of RSV "rules." Whatever the merits or demerits of the translation, literally, may be, I shall always regard as true the King James testimony of Isaiah 59:19; "When the enemy shall come in like a flood, the Spirit of the Lord shall lift up a standard against him." History is a witness to that recurring experience in life. That has been true and forever will be, however the words may rank as translation. All we have left is: "for he will come as a rushing stream, which the wind of the Lord drives." Or the RSV's dominant Moffatt: "for his vengeance pours out like a pent-up stream, driven by a blast of wind." Where did Moffatt lose "the Lord" out of that RSV wind? You see the ruins. *Wind* equals *Spirit; rushing stream* was *flood.* If there were not this itch to get rid of the Spirit of God in the Old Testament, who knows what standards of the Spirit might yet have been raised? If this great sentiment is not Bible, it is true as Bible, and it is a factor the RSV may well fear. I give these two samples of the type of translation Jesus left in his Old Testament and used as truth, even if less than accurate. The RSV is hard on any truth it may sacrifice by letter-fidelity to the original, but leaves stagnant error and adds new error to it by carelessness as to the Word. The Berkeley Version leaves in margin or note or parentheses such blessed words of the King James. Modernist inconoclasts would never be able to understand that, not even in Jesus.

A CASE OF LXX DIFFERENT FROM THE HEBREW

Our Lord uses his "authorized version," true, as truth, though inaccurate, as translation. Compare Malachi 3:1 with Matthew 11:10. The usual battle between Old and New Testament Sections of the RSV Committee caused the usual conflict: "thy face," "your face." Jesus did just as countless ministers do with the King James Version every week. The translation is approximate, and is itself truth, in harmony with all the truth that is translated. So you don't turn your sermon into a complex course in textual criticism or exegetical niceties. You go ahead and preach the truth translated, whether it is exactly the accurate translation of a slightly different truth or not. That is the way Jesus did with a version, when nothing more than that was involved.

PUTTING MORE IN A TEXT THAN HAD BEEN THERE BEFORE

That, too, Jesus did. It had not been there before because Jesus gave the revelation previously in "mystery" (as yet unrevealed truth, but due to be revealed in the fullness of time), but that comes into its hour of being understood like a diamond shining when in the dark room a light is suddenly turned on. "I am the God of Abraham . . ." is a case in point. "God is not the God of the dead, but of the living." God was saying: "Abraham lives." So Jesus interpreted Scripture. You do not say: "I am the owner of my great-grandfather's cow." She is nonexistent. You don't own her. Jehovah did not reveal himself merely as able to say: "I *was* the God of Abraham." I *am*. He is not the God of has-beens, but of living realities in continuing, immortal personality. So Jesus illumined the inherent sense of an ancient Word that had not had that known meaning, but that you see at once, once the light of our Lord shines upon it. Just so we see the inherent Messianic program, world missions, all prophecy's message, all progressive revelation in the Old Testament as *now illumined*. That is what Professor W. O. Carver calls "All the World in All the Word." It unifies all the Bible, in Jesus Christ. It identifies the Spirit who came in special mission on Pentecost with the Spirit operating all through Old Testament eras of revelation.

Now may I ask a question? Would you wreck Christ's Scripture and so deprive him of that great illumined truth? Would you perhaps translate the word Abraham and make that Scripture read "I am the God of a father of many nations" and maybe then change it a bit to "I am God, father of many nations"? The RSV, knowing the proper translation of our Christian Old Testament, for Christ illumined it, has wrecked that deliberately, in ways similar to what would be true if they had decomposed and recomposed the Scripture, "I am the God of Abraham." The Old Testament was our Lord's Bible. For Christians, it ought to be translated after a Christian, *Christ-ian,* fashion. It was our divine Teacher's Textbook and he was the subject matter and so interpreted the Word. The Spirit made the original so it will bear this illumination when the Light of the world shines upon it. If you disagree with Jesus about his Bible, you are not fit to translate it. Leave it to believers. Go join the Jews, if you are bent on reducing the Old Testament to a mere anthology of Jewish literature. Christians have a right to a Christian Old Testament that means to us what it meant to Jesus.

THE FIRST QUOTATION

This is the famous battlefield text, Isaiah 7:14, cited by Matthew 1:23. It is slightly different from the LXX text. The RSV won't translate the second word of it at all: "Behold, *the* virgin . . ."—*the* virgin par excellence, *the* virgin of all virgins, blessed among women, the mother of our Lord. This is not an anonymous unknown. It is *the* virgin. Let the RSV translate its Greek New Testament or give place to those who will translate it. Its translation here, at the dawn of our supreme literary revelation, is simply false, deliberately so. We

are translating what Matthew wrote, citing approximately
his Septuagint Bible. Translate it. Else the people will know
you for what you are.

A Seventh Parallel

There is a seventh parallel between our Lord's use of his
Greek version of the Bible and our use of versions. The Apocrypha had no place in Scripture he recognized, any more
than in ours. In the reference work before me there are cited
271 New Testament quotations from the Old, and as many
more references and quotation of phrases. And this does not
include the Revelation, which is pictured by Westcott and
Hort as almost made up of Old Testament language, conscious-
ly or unconsciously quoted by John. Professor Goodspeed
has published a so-called complete Bible, including the Apocrypha. Of course, the Bible plus the Apocrypha is not a
complete Bible any more than gold plus the dross that has
been separated from it is complete gold. Naturally, modernism,
having reduced all the Scriptures of both Testaments largely
to apocryphal writings, wants to put them together, so as
further to allege that they are all of a kind. As yet they do
not dare. When the New Catholicism gets more powerful, it
will undoubtedly go back to the Apocrypha and other medievalism. There will always be an election of grace, however,
that, like its Lord, will never quote an apocryphal writing
as Scripture. Jewish nationalism is the explanation of their
addition of the Maccabean type of Apocrypha to their older
translation of genuine Scripture, for use in their Gentile environment. But the synagogue, as older and of wider sway
than the Septuagint, always had as authority the Hebrew
scrolls as sole Scripture. That our Lord approved. But even
in the Introduction to the NT Booklet, page 31, Goodspeed is
allowed to say: "The familiar New Testament groups, scribes
and Pharisees, saints and sinners, demons and angels, are not
introduced to us in the Old Testament but in the Apocrypha."
Irresponsible chatter! Just open your Bible and read about
"scribes." Even the RSV, which to remove the evidence, translates the word *secretary* in II Kings 12:10;19:2, and other
verses, retains the word *scribes* in II Chronicles 34:13; and

Jeremiah 8:8, which still happen to be in our Old Testaments. No angels in the Old Testament? "How readest thou?" Genesis 16:7 shows one dealing with Hagar, and the ministry of angels goes right on from one end of the Old Testament to the other. And of what "hosts" is our God the Lord of? As for demons, we have both Satan and "devils" in the OT, though the RSV has introduced mythology in the Old Testament, with the word *satyr,* in their stead. The Old Testament is full of saints, as Hebrews 11 stresses in its great roll call of them, and all Scripture exalts them as "the excellent of all the earth," as the saintly Sampey used to translate a Psalm. Sinners? Even the RSV recognizes "great sinners" in the populace of Sodom, away back in Genesis. So about the only word Professor Goodspeed can really find a beginning for in the Apocrypha is the Pharisee. Are we to incorporate a lot of spurious Scripture in our true Bibles just to get the Pharisees a trifle earlier?

THE BAGGAGE THE RSV CARRIES ALONG WITH IT

This just shows what a vast amount of excess baggage, full of religious contraband, the RSV carries along with it. We have shown its hasty sponsorship, and payment, given to the "Gospel Parallels," a piece of as blatant infidelity as you would find anywhere. These "Introductions" carry a lot of alien thought against the Bible, such as has just been mentioned. *The Speaker's Handbook,* for the thousands of festivals celebrating the RSV appearance, to boost the ballyhoo, says, on the back inside cover: *"The Interpreter's Bible,* published by the Abingdon-Cokesbury Press, is the best modern commentary on the Scriptures in English . . . ." It is all a multi-million-dollar effort, in unison, to destroy the faith of a generation in the Bible as the God-breathed Word. Vergilius Ferm's anti-Christian *Encyclopedia of Religions* is, in many of its worst features, the product of RSV translators. The Sears, Roebuck new encyclopedia, successor to the *Encyclopedia Britannica,* which they sold to the University of Chicago, has its religious articles largely produced by the modernist RSV experts, and it is amazing how far they push the Scriptures away in the distance, chronologically, from their real authors. The leaders of the RSV were leaders of the New Catholicism in Amsterdam and have made its propaganda for "One Church" their theme, in varying degree. All these concomitants of the new Bible propaganda belong to a setup of interlocking directorates of the new Bible and the New Catholicism. And that is as far from our Lord's use of his original Bible and its Greek Version as the East is from the West.

ETERNAL VIGILANCE FOR TRUTH

The synagogue existed to bring, orally and up to the minute, translation and application of the Hebrew Word to mind, heart, and life. Jesus, the Twelve, and Paul, as well as a great fruit of the Forerunner like Apollos, mightily used the weekly worship of their people for such translation and correct preaching of the meaning of the original Scriptures. We shall need that forever. No matter what version we have or may yet acquire, its interpretation must always be brought up to the hour. Bible words must have Bible meaning. Jesus saw to that, in the use of his version for teaching and preaching, weekly and even daily. He went constantly back of the Greek version to the right original. That was a constant, up-to-the-minute correction of the version's faults. We shall see that exactly that has been done in pulpit, religious press, Sunday schools, Young People's organizations, and Training Unions for all. There is already a vast public correction of the King James Version, patent to the American Christian mind. No correction of the RSV is yet generally made. The King James errors are less a peril. Three centuries have forewarned Bible readers.

CHAPTER TWENTY-FOUR

THE MOTION IS THE PROPERTY OF THE HOUSE

MY TESTIMONY HAS BEEN BORNE. I LOVE, IN THE RSV, ITS every betterment of English and increased simplicity of style, the new devices in a Bible that help understanding, the poetry, the quotes, and the sparkling genius here and there of skilled translators. I love the removal of the Romanism that clutters up the King James, a medieval hangover. I love the body blows at modernism, if the translators are sincere. Especially do I appreciate their translating the sense rather than the mere verbiage, as to that big "all-day sucker"—our grand-mothers would have said "sugar titty"—of the modernist cynics: "The letter killeth, but the spirit giveth life," now really evangelical to the heart, "The written code kills, but the Spirit gives life." I love the better text followed, as in Romans 8:1 and many other places. I love most of the titles, wish there were more. I love the printing and the binding—why should a Bible be black? I love the reverent *Thou* to God the Father, and even to God the Son, where the RSV censors forgot themselves and let it slip through. I love *love,* successor to cold, sham, medieval *charity.* For all these countless bene-fits I give praise to the translators and thanks to God. May they every one permanently adorn the English Bible of to-morrow.

But alas! I am forced to give other witness, to be true. I weep over the folly of not removing a lot of other King James errors, as grave as those which were taken away. I repudiate the dictatorlike decree of banishment to many of the greatest words that channel to us the revelation of truth: *gospel, convert, adoption, regeneration, remission, propiti-ation, Calvary, impute, abide, graces, confess, rewards, hades, the earnest of the Spirit, virgin, only begotten, truth, seed, faithful, inherit, collection, members, Jehovah, doctrine, word, bishop* (in its Bible sense), and even the "relaxing" of stern revelation, given in evil words that define evils: *flesh, wine, fornication, Sanhedrin, carnal, slaves, and others.* I loathe the RSV salvation by the maternity ward. There were "priests" among those who did this and they allied themselves, for the enslavement of mothers, with that black-robed crowd of evil men whose collars are turned the wrong way. "Their collars are turned the wrong way because they are going the wrong way," said one who had escaped that tyrannical fraternity that heads back to the Dark Ages. That breed ought not to have control over any version of I Timothy 2:15. Let them banish, next time, this maternity-ward salvation and keep the great words of revealed truth. This banishment "ought ye to have done," and "not have left undone" the keeping of the Bible's great words of truth.

"If a man love me, he will keep my words" is a great text for translators of new Bibles. The RSV group say they did not change a doctrine in the Bible. How can they say that when they utterly or partially discarded the God-chosen, God-breathed words that are the incarnation of those doctrines? The simple fact is that they hardly left a single doctrine of the Word intact. Here is their own sentence from their own Version, pronounced by their own Judge and Savior: "He who *does not love me* does not keep my words." These great discarded words of revelation are tombstones of a dead and discarded love to the Savior, by his own judgment.

THEOLOGY IS THE MEANING OF THE BIBLE

Professor W. A. Irwin (Introduction to the OT Booklet, p. 14) insists that "there is no place for theology in Bible translation." But that is the same as saying there is no place, in Bible translation, for the meaning of the matter translated. For the *meaning* of the text in its context is precisely the theology of that Scripture. This grows, as the many meanings of many Scriptures become one, into biblical theology, the meaning of the Bible, and systematic theology, the harmonious relating of the component parts to the whole truth revealed. Certainly no Baptist would ever agree that there is any place in theology for anything but the meaning of the truth revealed in the Scriptures. You first know the meaning, then translate it.

It is interesting to note that Professor Irwin, in a rather ill-mannered (as when calling criticisms of the RSV in his zone "the ignorant nonsense that goes about here in the

Southwest") and bitingly sarcastic article in *The Review and Expositor* against Professor Clyde Francisco's discussion of Isaiah 7:14, has this to say: "The young woman, then, was a special woman, whom Isaiah singled out as a sort of sacred woman to become mother of the wonder child." This theory, which he copies from the Jews, in their unbelief and definite hatred of the Isaiah prophecy, Professor Irwin calls the "harem theory," saying: "Medieval Jewish commentators . . . regarded the *'almah* as one of the women of the harem, a view then developed into the belief that she was to become the mother of Hezekiah." So he conceives one more "conjecture" (his own word) "that the *'almah* was a definite young woman in the king's entourage on this fateful day, whom Isaiah addressed in person with the astonishing prediction that she was to be the mother of Immanuel."

The points made to justify Professor Irwin in making himself a disciple of medieval Judaism, to avoid believing in this prophecy of the virgin birth, which he accepts, are these. One of these is *the definite article,* which both Sections of the RSV Committee could not in any wise be brought to translate in either Testament. She was a harem "virgin" (?) and Isaiah means her, not the virgin of virgins, forever blessed among women. Now, friend, just look at that theory. He imagines an "entourage" that would include the harem. Did oriental kings parade *that* personnel? Were those slaves and slatterns to be seen in the royal court, in an audience granted the great prophet of God before the counselors of the realm? And did Isaiah catch the eye of one of these veiled *official* virgins, whether actually so or not, and give her the wink, saying that *she* is to become the mother of this "God-With-Us," this "wonder child"? Is this the pusillanimous lowness to which Bible interpretation, and the false translation based on it, has sunk, at the expense of Nelson & Sons? I have seen only one parallel to that. It was Professor Morton Enslin's breaking forth hilariously, in the *Jewish Theological Quarterly,* to pour ridicule on the Gospel narratives of the resurrection of Jesus, as a "pond" where neither he nor his erudite professor could even "get a nibble." Professor Irwin got a nibble in the medieval Jewish harem theory, by which he explains the *the* in Isaiah 7:14 and Matthew 1:23, but he cannot be induced to translate that *the* in either Scripture. By which fact, his whole horrible bias against the Word of God will stand condemned by every reverent and right-thinking student of the Word. He goes all the way back to prehistoric literature to get the language of these harem "virgins" and posits that calamitous euphemism in Isaiah's mind, without a smidgeon of evidence—just following the Messiah-rejecting Jews. But the *the,* right here in the Isaian text, and the closer-still New Testament citation of it, he refuses to see. I need hardly say to you that, to me, that is wicked.

My witness is borne to the additions to the Word of God, such as *inspiration* recklessly sown all through its pages, prizes distributed by the RSV sponsors for all and sundry, added to the Scripture, without one single syllable in the original to justify this tendential recklessness. We have seen the cunning sectarian bias against fundamental Baptist truth, much of it precious also to many other denominations. The Methodist doctrine of apostasy is the pet idea of the RSV, put into the English shamelessly when it was not in the original Word. I have never seen a more steady, repeated, and conscienceless forging of Scripture to favor a theory than right here. The word *stumble* is inevitably made to mean *fall.* And *commit apostasy* is falsely injected into Hebrews 6, to bolster a doctrine that utterly denies John 3:16. The overtranslations, the undertranslations, the squeezing of the meaning by translators' bias and prejudice, the Love of Disharmony and Hatred of Harmony, go even to the daring point of, by RSV sponsorship and payment, putting out a Disharmony of Gospel Parallels—"parallels" with human traditions for long centuries after the apostolic times. We have seen the ignorance and prejudice of countless marginal references and notes— unable even to tell the public how Greek words are spelled. We have seen how often a verse is good at one end, bad at the other, awaking mixed feelings. We have seen the wrecked sentence structure and the lost connotation of Bible words. We have seen that when this camel of modernism gets into the tent, you have no room for faith. When your Christ is, by a dubious note, declared to be a bastard child of the unwed, whose hot passions ran away with them during their courtship, what difference does the rest of the Scripture make that acclaims him "God only begotten," as William Temple translated John? This is the witness I bear.

THE MOTION IS THE PROPERTY OF THE HOUSE

It is as great a pity to lose the excellencies of the RSV as it is to harbor in American Christianity its vices. What shall we do? Use the good; shun the bad.

It is a well-known principle of parliamentary law that a motion, once presented before a deliberative body, cannot be withdrawn by the mover. *The motion is the property of the house.* Even if he repudiates his motion, the house can still consider it, amend it, approve of it, or reject it.

"Christ as a son over his own house (is faithful), whose house are we" (Heb. 3:6). The motion is the property of the house, the spiritual Israel. The World Council of Churches is outside that Israel, as far as its hordes of adepts of infant baptisms of Orthodox trine immersions of squalling Greeks, Russians, and Baltic-Balkan victims of that pagan rite are all the regeneration such "Churches" profess, plus the Reformed— but not too much "reformed," "retaining" countless traditions of men—the State Churches of Europe and its "ecumenical" colonies of this badly reformed Christianity. Only the believers in Christ—Christ in them the hope of glory—constitute that Israel. They do, whether they are in the orb of that worldly Council, or in the shadow of the Councils of Trent and the Vatican, or the score of other petty Catholic sects, or the evangelical denominations that believe in regeneration but do not unanimously possess it because of spurious evangelism or of adoption in the family unit in religion. People are not saved by denominations, or by the Church or churches, true or false. They are saved personally by the crucified and risen Savior, Priest, Sacrifice, and King in his kingdom. That kingdom has no citizens but the personally, experimentally redeemed. There are no children of the devil in the body of Christ through infant baptism. Christendom is not the Israel of God. It owns no Bible.

Our Bible belongs to our Christ. Thirty-nine of its books were his before they became ours and he interpreted them once and forever. His Spirit completed that literary revelation, in the New Testament. The whole belongs to Christ and those who are in Christ. They are *the house* and any motion concerning the Bible is the property of that house, if to our Bible that motion is any way related. The house of God's own Israel will decide by its mass decisions, each individually made, whether the motion prevails. A Committee of Bible Translators plus Nelson & Sons made them an authorized Bible a half century ago. The people did not dispute the copyright at all, but, in mass decision, left that Bible strictly alone, even though some owned it. I was one who owned it and used it. Then there came the 1911 Bible, with great advertising in the papers. I bought it and used it. I do not now know a single human being that owns a copy except myself. Even ministers to whom I mention it are nonplused, and that was only forty years ago. They, for the most part, never heard of it. I own and use, too, the 1881 Bible, of which 3,000,000 copies were soon sold. I never see in minister's libraries any copy of that but my own. It belongs to the few. It remains to be seen whether the RSV will march down to oblivion like these others. Never mind the ballyhoo. There was a Babel once, product of an ancient World Council and dream, that began with a great ballyhoo. But it missed its dream of reaching to heaven. And that is where these matters have their control, and the control shows up here below in the decisions of those who live "in the heavenlies" with Christ, not in the proud councils of a lot of robed ecclesiastics, whose collars are headed back the wrong way, to medievalism. The motion is the property of the house, "which house we (believers of every name, but genuine believers with a responsible personal trust in a personal Savior)—"which house," I say and so says the Book, "we are." We will every one of us cast our vote on this issue, in the sovereignty of a redeemed conscience, responsible directly to God.

The motion is the property of the house. There is nothing original in the RSV but some of its errors. Let them pass. Let Nelson & Sons be their funeral home. Anything of truth and merit that has enriched Christian readers of the RSV is not original. It came from *the* original. Every new Bible is the sum of all the versions that went before. It is the product of the theological education its translators were given, no matter how much some of them hate theology. The insights they have and use came to them, mainly, from books and guided study. So that to translators foremostly comes the Bible's query: "What hast thou that thou didst not receive?" Every new insight the RSV contributes to our knowledge of the Bible is the property of the Christian public, which pays its price, gets what it buys, and decides on whether it will throw away its present Bible before something better comes along. You can't run a monopoly on ideas, especially when they constitute a universal revelation that came from God. I am not thinking at all now in terms of the Nelsons' copyright. Let them have that, and let the worldly council and its publishers divide the spoils. If the RSV fails—and it has already failed morally and intellectually—all that is good in it will yet live in the minds of those to whom the Bible, which they translated so carelessly, belongs.

When it becomes apparent that the RSV has failed, in its achievement and in its fidelity, then the house, not just the House of Nelson, but the house of believers, can make a Christian, not a modernist, revision of the King James Version, or a new translation for public and private worship. Perhaps the Nelsons will gracefully retire and let someone else have a chance. They have tried twice and failed, a century-long failure maybe by the time the story of their second defeat is told. Maybe they will see it and cease to trouble Israel. The natural representatives of the Israel of God in our land, and in all lands, are the Bible societies. They furnish us our Bibles for missions in every land. They have succeeded in more than 1,100 languages. If given a chance, they might succeed in our American speech, as a branch of the English language. Both the Scots and the English are also making new versions now. Would it be too much to hope for a common version for the English-speaking lands? Perhaps so. The Church of England domineered over two versions: maybe they still would want to, and succeed. But viewpoints could at least be shared. It is to be assumed that a Committee of Translators of the American Bible Society would be representative of American Christianity. That might include a modernist scholar or two. But let them share the positions in proportion to their real strength in Bible-using and -worshipping American Christianity—a very tiny minority. We could be sure that the American Bible Society, after the RSV blunders, would not pick a committee from a narrow, tightly local, axis of American infidel universities, and head it all up in Union Seminary.

Part of the business of every Bible-loving Christian ought to be to help the Nelson Bible to fail in its plans of conquest, and help it to join the Sheol of dead versions, illustrious shades among which it will find itself much at home.

SLANDERING THE KING JAMES VERSION

Till the RSV fails and a better version can unhurriedly come into being—younger scholars had better be chosen than this so obsolescent RSV Committee—we are chained to the King James. With all its faults, that is not so bad as it seems to all who are aware of the out-of-date language of that classic and of its many errors in both text and translation. The next generation deserves something better. In a thousand other languages, the Bible societies have produced something better. So could our solid, spiritual scholarship, if given a chance, without going off at a tangent after infidel university manias of yesterday. Nevertheless, we have now the King James in pulpits and homes. Is that a hopeless situation? Re-read Dr. Buttrick's or Dean Weigle's appraisal of the King James and see. The RSV propaganda has been unfortunate and, to a certain extent, slanderous. They simply say, in the bluntest fashion, that the King James text had five or six thousand errors. That is true, and *the impression left is utterly and wickedly false.* They do not tell, in that context, that great authorities like Westcott and Hort affirm, with proofs, that the errors of text are mainly about trivial things, spelling, punctuation, clarifying notes of one scribe that a later scribe copied into the text. They do not tell those they misinform that Westcott and Hort affirmed that these errors leave in doubt less than a thousandth part of our Bible, as read in that version.

Are there no errors in the RSV text? Yes, probably more thousands than in the King James, at least in the text as they have handled it in the translating. They have broken up the sentence structure countless times, and lost a lot of the connection, slipped in their own erroneous ideas. They have added and subtracted, squeezed out and soaked in, discarded connotation and punctuation, capital letters and lower-case type, paragraphing and words and verses. The RSV has its own thousands of errors, and it follows a lot besides the text it is supposed to be translating. Then add the conjectures, of which there are really far more than those they had the grace to tell of. Tit for tat, is what the RSV must expect, on this charge.

WE KNOW THE KJ ERRORS: WE DON'T KNOW THE RSV ERRORS

Every year tens of millions of Americans study the King James Bible in their Sunday schools, read it in their homes, hear it preached from their pulpits and in the open air and over the radio, and have a vast teaching literature that tells them the King James errors. There are probably millions of American children today who could tell you that *let* means *hinder*, in certain KJ passages. *We know the main King James errors* all over the land. But the RSV errors are not known. Some of them are not known even to their translators. They were sincerely in error, a lot of times. Just now the big denominations are not calling attention to the RSV errors. The theological magazines seem cowed by the prestige of the RSV axis of university professors, and if a man breasts the storm he is anathematized by his colleagues. Modernist teachers in the Sunday schools that use the RSV are not going to show up modernist errors. Not before the end of this century could the American public be as well informed of the errors of the RSV as they now know those of the KJ version. We are far safer, in our use of the Bible, if we have in the hands of the people a version whose errors of speech, text, and translation they know by centuries of teaching, than if we find in homes, pulpits, and classrooms a version whose vast sum of errors no human being as yet has fathomed. I have myself notes on far more than twice as many as I have here mentioned. And when I have mentioned an error, it has been a typical one with all too many parallels, in a host of these matters studied.

OUR SELF-CORRECTING KING JAMES

Here is mine, a teacher's Bible with the usual helps. In its very margins, countless errors and inferior translations are right there corrected. If a verse is not in the best manuscripts, that is stated. But there is no surgery with the incisions left open. Nor is there to be found the leveling remark: "Other ancient authorities." That makes a dim twilight in which all cats are brown. It is not scholarly.

I do not remember hearing a Baptist quote the Great Commission in pulpit or classroom without giving it as it finally got into the RSV, with the exception of the word *close*. We have generally said *end* or *consummation*. Countless audiences, of many denominations, have been informed that Paul wrote: "There is therefore now no condemnation to those who are in Christ Jesus." Period. There is a vast, spiritual, informed Christian public in the United States and Canada and the British Isles and colonies that knows all the principal errors of the King James. Why not make a catalogue of those errors, and those of the RSV, and then resolve to have a Bible that is free from them all?

The RSV has been so presented by its promoters, translators, and advertisers, as to destroy faith in our Bible, as known. You can find better statements in the Introduction Booklets, but the people do not read them. The Bible they know has been slandered by the RSV ballyhoo. It must be defended, without any denial of the errors in translation that really exist. A man who is not just as insistent in rejecting the King James errors as he is the RSV errors is looking in his mirror at the face of a hypocrite. We long for the correction of all these errors, in a version yet to be.

Take just a few examples. Matthew 14:26 says: *It is a spirit*. The RSV changes that to "It is a ghost." Dear me. Would you have suspected the RSV of that? The mg. of the KJ says *apparition*, which is less definite and so more true to the situation. In Matthew 5:41, we read: *And whosoever shall compel you to go a mile, go with him twain.* The RSV substitutes "forces you . . . two." That does not help us to the sense of our Lord's command. The KJ margin says: "*Gk. commandeer.*" Ah! That's it exactly. The King James margin beat the university axis of modernism's professors completely. You will find this true in many, many cases. You will find that the KJ margins have anticipated the RSV emendations, right there in your Bible. You will find the imperative instruction: "Read," in many cases where the KJ tells you the right word to substitute for its wrong one. And I note just that in a lot of preachers I have heard on this furlough. They read or cite the KJ version and then the correct idea, saying: "Or better, *commandeers.*" Or they say: "Others translate, *commandeers.*" It hardly makes an interruption in the line of thought, but gives the truth clearly. And much of this truth is found right in the King James margins. And you are not just told that "other ancient authorities" doubt the wording of a text. You are told the facts, as to the degree of probability by which a change is due.

Till we get a Bible that has neither the KJ faults nor the RSV faults, if you change Bibles, here is what happens. You take on a lot of new errors that nobody can yet inform the public about. It will take a generation to do it. You lose the King James' rightness in many, many of the *great Scriptures*: you get the RSV rightness in many minor points and, too, its wrongness and sometimes wrongheadedness that mar its translation of many, many of the most vital Scriptures. The RSV as one in many study Bibles on your desk will be a help; but as a Bible for public worship it will prove a calamity and an apostasy from the Word of God.